Privacy Protection and Computer Forensics

Second Edition

For quite a long time, computer security was a rather narrow field of study that was populated mainly by theoretical computer scientists, electrical engineers, and applied mathematicians. With the proliferation of open systems in general, and of the Internet and the World Wide Web (WWW) in particular, this situation has changed fundamentally. Today, computer and network practitioners are equally interested in computer security, since they require technologies and solutions that can be used to secure applications related to electronic commerce. Against this background, the field of computer security has become very broad and includes many topics of interest. The aim of this series is to publish state-of-the-art, high standard technical books on topics related to computer security. Further information about the series can be found on the WWW at the following URL:

http://www.esecurity.ch/serieseditor.html

Also, if you'd like to contribute to the series by writing a book about a topic related to computer security, feel free to contact either the Commissioning Editor or the Series Editor at Artech House.

For a listing of recent titles in the *Artech House Computer Security Series*, turn to the back of this book.

Privacy Protection and Computer Forensics

Second Edition

Michael A. Caloyannides

Artech House
Boston • London
www.artechhouse.com

Library of Congress Cataloging-in-Publication Data
A catalog record for this book is available from the U.S. Library of Congress.

British Library Cataloguing in Publication Data
A catalog record for this book is available from the British Library.

Cover design by Yekaterina Ratner

© 2004 ARTECH HOUSE, INC.
685 Canton Street
Norwood, MA 02062

International Standard Book Number: 1-58053-830-4

10 9 8 7 6 5 4 3 2 1

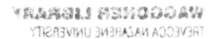

To my late parents, Akylas and Etta. Parents never die; they live through their children's thoughts and actions and through their children's children.

Contents

7   Basic Protection from Computer Data Theft Online   115

8   Practical Measures for Online Computer Activities   127

11   Practical Encryption 219

Introduction

If you give me six lines written by the most honest man, I will find something in them to hang him.

—*Cardinal Richelieu*

In any country's court of law, evidence is as compelling as—and often more compelling than—personal testimony by a credible eyewitness.

The well-known warning given to criminal suspects in American movies "anything you say can and will be used against you" applies to any country and is not limited to criminal proceedings, but applies to civil litigation as well where no such warning is given. Furthermore, what "can and will be used against you" is not only what you say, but also what evidence can be obtained against you.

Most every person knows only too well that evidence can—and has often been—planted, manufactured, or simply taken selectively out of context to paint an image that bears little resemblance to reality.

Up until about a decade ago, documentary evidence was mostly on paper. Even computer evidence amounted to reams of printed pages. This is no longer the case. The electronic version of a file that was created by and/or stored in a computer can be far more damaging to an individual or to an organization because it contains not only the documentary evidence itself but also "data about the data" (such as when it was created, when it was revised, how it was revised, using whose software).

There is nothing "personal" about a personal computer (PC) other than who paid the bill to buy it. Contrary to popular belief, it usually contains a lot of data—some of it potentially quite incriminating—that got in there without the owner's awareness or consent. One's PC is the most sought after piece of evidence to be used against one. A personal computer is not at all private in the eyes of the law; besides, most countries do not have laws protecting privacy. If a personal computer's data storage (hard drive, floppy disks, tape backups, CD-ROMs, USB "keys," etc.) is confiscated or subpoenaed—and this is done with increasing regularity nowadays—then anything in it "can and will be used against you"; even though a lot of it has been entered without your consent or awareness, you can be convicted none the less because most judges and juries are unaware of the many ways that illegal data can enter your computer behind your back.

Most individuals and companies have always been careful of what they commit to paper or say over the telephone; in litigious contemporary societies cognizant of assorted discrimination laws, individuals have also learned to be very reserved in what they say to each other, especially within a company or other organization. Yet those very same individuals treat electronic mail, or e-mail, like a private channel that enjoys some magic protection from unintended recipients; comments that one normally would never put on paper (gossip, off-color jokes, or worse) are routinely confided to personal computers and to others through e-mail. Yet e-mail and computer records are far more permanent than any piece of paper, and e-mail is far more likely to reach unintended recipients than a plain old message in a mailed envelope. Also, whereas there can only be a single "original" of a paper document (that can haunt a company or an individual in court), a copy of a computer record is as admissible a piece of evidence as the original record.

Society today favors more informality than in years past. This applies not only to personal communications between individuals but also to the corporate world that is trying to encourage creativity, esprit de corps among employees, and candor. Whereas in the past there was a fairly rigid hierarchy in most any organization, and one had to go through layers of management filtering to reach upper management, e-mail has effectively allowed anyone to bypass the hierarchy and protocol and contact anybody else directly; this is done, ostensibly "in confidence," when in fact the exact opposite is true because of the permanence and indestructibility of e-mail.

It is worse than that; individuals tend to entrust personal (and corporate) computers and e-mail with casual comments (such as gossip, innuendo, biases, and outright illegal plans) that, if shown to a judge or a jury, can evoke an emotional reaction resulting in unexpectedly harsh verdicts.

One often hears that statistical analyses can be presented to support just about any preconceived notion; this is so because of selective inclusion and exclusion of data made possible by the fact there is a lot of data to select from to make one's case. The same applies in spades to computer evidence: There is usually so much data in a confiscated or subpoenaed computer that, if judiciously selected, can present a judge or jury with what may appear on the surface be compelling evidence of anything that an unscrupulous prosecutor or litigant's unethical attorney wants.

One might tend to dismiss all of the foregoing as applying to others. As the next sections show, nothing could be further from the truth. *It applies to anyone using a computer (and that is practically everyone) for any purpose.* In addition, it is of direct interest to lawyers and future lawyers, to corporate officials, to employees with access to employers' computers, to sole proprietors and individual entrepreneurs, to law enforcement officials, to politicians, to medical doctors and other healthcare providers, to college students, to information technology specialists, to hackers and aspiring hackers, to mental health professionals, and so on.

And one more thing: Investigation of the contents of one's computer does not require physical access to that computer. In most cases it can also be done (and has been done by assorted hackers, by software companies, and others) while one is online (e.g., connected to the Internet or to any other network); in many cases it can even be done by anyone with a few hundred dollars to buy commercially available equipment while the targeted computer user is connected to nothing and is merely using his or her computer in the "privacy" of his or her own home. While evidence obtained with no physical access to a targeted computer may not hold up in court in some nations, it still provides the creative investigator with a wealth of information about the targeted person; armed with knowledge of what to look for and where to find it, that investigator can then home in on that same evidence with legal means, present it in court, and never mention that its existence became known through legally inadmissible means.

Interestingly, in the United States at least, what little privacy exists for data stored in computers within one's premises does not exist for data stored off-site with third parties, such as on the Internet. Legislation is premised on the assumption that even though information is increasingly stored in networks off-site, such information has no legal expectation of privacy.

Unlike, say, classical mechanics or advanced mathematics, information technology is evolving at an unprecedented rate. Even so, a concerted effort has been made to keep this book "current" for a few years; this is done by explaining the fundamentals (which do not change) and also by providing directly relevant sources of information that the interested reader may access to stay up to date on the latest.

There are plenty of books on what amounts to best practices in computer forensics; this is not yet one more. Indeed, given how needlessly unintuitive some of the most popular software suites for computer forensics are, the aspiring computer forensic investigator would do better to attend the pricey training classes offered by such software suites' vendors.

Computer forensics is quite powerful against all but the most technically savvy computer users. The fundamental problem that eludes most uninformed judges and juries is that computer forensics cannot show who put the data in the suspect's computer; there is a large set of ways whereby potentially incriminating data enters our personal computers without our knowledge, let alone acquiescence. Given the ease with which a responsible, law-abiding citizen can be convicted (or fined or lose custody of his or her children) on the basis of such computer evidence of wrongdoing that the accused had no part in, this book is intended for all computer users and their lawyers. In particular, it is intended

1.   For any professional or business person who has the legal and ethical obligation to protect proprietary business information or intellectual property stored in a computer entrusted to that person from being stolen by an unscrupulous competitor or by a thief;

2. For attorneys defending wrongly accused individuals when the evidence produced is in computer files, whether in criminal or civil legal proceedings;

3. For any responsible person who does not want to be unfairly persecuted on the basis of computer data that he or she had no part in creating;

4. For the government official in a sensitive capacity where it is absolutely essential that no data from his or her computer be retrieved by unauthorized third parties regardless of their resources;

5. For any individual whose laptop may be among the hundreds of thousands of laptops stolen every year and who does not want his or her personal, medical, and financial information, let alone his or her company's proprietary information, to become public.

No background in information technology, beyond a typical working familiarity with computers, is assumed; this book is intended to stand on its own two feet.

As with any tool, like a kitchen knife or a hunting rifle, or with a technique, such as the use of chlorine to wipe out bloodstains or biological agents, computer forensics and computer counterforensics can be used for both legal and illegal purposes. This book emphatically does not condone the illegal use of any of the techniques it presents.

Inevitably, some readers will ask whether law enforcers shouldn't have the right to monitor Internet usage and even individuals' computers in order to identify a crime and collect evidence to prosecute. Allow me to answer with a few questions in the tradition of the Socratic dialogue:

1. Should law enforcers be allowed to look into citizens' bedrooms and bathrooms to catch criminals (e.g., those growing drugs in their house, as happened recently in a case that went all the way to the U.S. Supreme Court)? Where do you draw the line as to which technical means law enforcers can use to peek into citizens' affairs?

    a. Do you draw the line to include the Internet but no more? Why?

    b. How about thermal imaging of the inside of a house?

    c. How about placing hidden microphones in houses for good measure?

    d. How about placing hidden video cameras in houses?

    e. How about requiring all residents to submit to monthly lie detector exams?

2. Should law enforcers be allowed to look in all citizens' houses as a matter of routine screening just in case some crime is being committed? (This is the equivalent of wholesale Internet interception looking for keywords or other indicators to identify the perpetrators).

3. If law enforcers are only allowed to look at some citizens' houses (those suspected of a crime), and if they find evidence of a totally different crime, should they discard this new evidence for which they did not have authority to look? If not, how does that differ from wholesale monitoring of everyone for good measure?

4. Who defines "crime" beyond the obvious (murder, arson, etc.)? In some countries it is a crime to criticize the government. In others it is a crime to say that its leader is ugly. Should law enforcers be allowed to monitor Internet traffic or to do forensics on computers for evidence that a citizen said that the leader is ugly?

5. Should the popes of years past have been allowed to monitor the Internet (which did not exist, but never mind that) to collect evidence that Galileo believed, horror of horrors, the earth was not the center of the universe (a horrible crime then, punishable by death)? In short, what social price are you willing to pay for security from crime as defined by the state? Are you willing to surrender all freedoms to be crime-free?

6. And assuming that some Internet connection shows evidence of a crime (I would be interested in your definition), how are law enforcers going to prove who did it, given that one's IP address can be hijacked by total strangers (e.g., by Wi-Fi war drivers).

This book deals with security from hostile computer forensics (mostly on one's computer, but also on one's digital camera, fax machine, and related computer-like electronics), as distinct from network forensics, which in this context is snooping into users' online activities. Computer forensics deals with anything and everything that can be found on one's computer. Network forensics, on the other hand, pertains to evidence like logs kept by Internet service providers (ISPs) and other remotely located networked computers. Network forensics is most relevant in the investigation of remote hackings, remote denial of service attacks, and the like. Even so, because most computers today are connected to the Internet at one time or another, this book also covers those aspects of network forensics that affect anyone connecting to the Internet.

All trademarks are hereby acknowledged as the property of their respective owners.

CHAPTER

1

Contents

Computer Forensics

1.1 What is computer forensics?

Rather than getting embroiled in definitions and semantics, let's say that computer forensics is the collection of techniques and tools used to find evidence on a computer that can be used to its user's disadvantage.

If the evidence is obtained by, or on behalf of, law enforcement officials, it can be used against one in a court of law—or, in the case of totalitarian regimes, it can seal one's fate without being presented in a court of law.

If the evidence is obtained by one's employer or other party with which one has a contractual association, it can be used against one in administrative proceedings.

If the evidence is obtained by a third party, it can also be used in the commission of a crime, such as blackmail, extortion, impersonation, and the like.

It is noteworthy that the computer in question does not even have to be owned by the user; it can be owned by an employer or by a totally unrelated party, such as an Internet cafe, school, or public library.

Computer forensics is customarily separated from network forensics. The former deals with data in a computer, whereas the latter deals with data that may be spread over numerous databases in one or more networks.

1.2 Why is computer forensics of vital interest to you?

1.2.1 As an employee

Recently a Northwest Airlines flight attendant hosted a message board on his personal Web site on the Internet. Among the messages posted on it by others were a few anonymous ones by other employees urging coworkers to participate in sickouts (which are illegal under U.S. federal labor laws) so as to force that airline to cancel profitable flights during the 1999 Christmas season. Indeed, over three hundred Northwest Airlines flights were cancelled during that time.

Interestingly, Northwest Airlines obtained permission from a federal judge in Minneapolis to search 22 flight attendants' computer hard drives located not only in union offices but in their homes as well so as to find the identities of those who had urged the sickouts.

Other companies, too, have sued in an effort to find the identities of posters of anonymous messages whose content was deemed disagreeable by these companies; they include Varian Medical Systems, Raytheon, and others.

The result of such lawsuits is that the suing companies get the courts to subpoena computer records and data-storage media; if what is subpoenaed belongs to a third party (such as an Internet bulletin board), that third party often complies right away without even bothering to notify the person who posted the contested message(s).[1]

The bottom line is that individuals who post electronic messages deemed disagreeable by anyone else can have their identities revealed—to the extent that this is technically possible—and their personal computers subpoenaed.

An employer can be (and often has been) held liable for the actions of his employees, whether those actions involve computers or not. E-mail sent by employees even within the same company can be used as evidence against an employer to show, for example, lax enforcement of antidiscrimination laws, patterns of biases, assorted conspiracies, and the like. In an effort to prevent such legal liability, employers can (and often do) legally monitor employee activities involving company computers, just as they can (and often do) monitor all employees' phone calls on company telephones. It is interesting to ponder how this would extend to the increasing number of employees allowed to work from home[2] using their own personal computers.

1.2.2 As an employer or corporate executive

Many have heard by now of the embarrassing, to Microsoft, e-mail found that made references to "cutting the air off" from the competing Netscape Internet browser.

Numerous other companies had electronic files subpoenaed during legal civil discovery processes that proved to be damaging to those companies; such companies include Autodesk, which received a $22.5 million judgment in a case where some e-mail appeared to support an allegation of theft of trade secrets from Vermont Microsystems.

1. AOL and Microsoft notify chat room posters 14 days in advance before they comply with a civil subpoena. Most others give no such notice.

2. This is not entirely altruistic on the part of employers, although it certainly benefits employees who need to stay at home for such valid reasons as risky pregnancies, illnesses, need to care for sick children, and the like. From an employer's perspective, there is less need for expensive office space and ancillary office equipment.

Sloppy deletion of evidence usually hurts more than it helps; in Autodesk's case, evidence of partially deleted evidence was found on an employee's work and home computers to support Vermont Microsystems' case.

Even effective deletion of such electronic evidence is not necessarily a viable way out either. Hughes Aircraft Company lost a wrongful termination case brought by Garreth Shaw, a former attorney of that company, largely because of some routinely deleted e-mail; in this case, Hughes allegedly had a policy of routinely deleting electronic messages older than three months, and Shaw's attorney argued that Hughes should not have done so after it knew that it was being sued. Sprint Communications settled a case of alleged patent infringement involving Applied Telematics after a court found that Sprint had destroyed pertinent electronic evidence.

Encryption of files by individual employees in a manner that the company cannot decrypt can also get an employer into legal trouble. According to John Jessen, chief executive officer (CEO) of Electronic Evidence Discovery of Seattle, Washington, if electronic evidence is subpoenaed and a company cannot decrypt it, that company could be charged with "purposeful destruction of evidence."

An employer has an obvious vested interest in ensuring that no employee steals a competitive edge that exists in the form of proprietary designs, marketing plans, customer lists, innovative processes, and the like.[3] Corporate espionage is a fact of life [1]. Theft of intellectual property, it is claimed, is costing U.S. businesses more than $250 billion every year according to the American Society of Industrial Security of Alexandria, Virginia, with most of this theft being perpetrated through electronic means.

1.2.3   As a law enforcement official

Computers can be used to commit crimes and to store evidence of a crime that has nothing to do with computers. The former category includes cyberfraud, illegally tampering with others' computers through networked connections, and the like. Tampering could pertain to any crime whatever, including murder.

Fake credit card generating software is openly available on the Internet, and so is software for fake AOL account generation. The amount of fraud perpetrated online is rivaled only by the amount of fraud perpetrated offline.

Criminal prosecutors can, therefore, often find evidence in a computer that can be presented in a court of law to support accusations of practically any crime such as fraud, murder, conspiracy, money laundering, embezzlement, theft, drug-related offenses, extortion, criminal copyright

---

3. One may recall the 1993 accusation by General Motors (GM) that one if its former senior employees and seven others had stolen thousands of proprietary documents before joining a competing foreign automaker. GM was awarded $100 million in damages.

infringement, hidden assets, disgruntled employee destruction of employer records, dummy invoicing, and so on.

Unless law enforcement individuals know enough about how to collect the required data and how to maintain the requisite chain of custody in a manner that will hold up to challenges by a presumably competent defense, chances are that, in many regimes at least, such evidence will be dismissed by the court.

1.2.4   As an individual

Anyone accessing the Internet—and that is a few hundred million individuals worldwide, and that number is rapidly growing—is vulnerable to ending up with files on his or her computer whose possession may be illegal under local law, and yet he or she may never have actively solicited them. This can happen as follows:

1. While browsing the Web, we have all come across Web sites that also flash assorted images of nubile females in scant clothing as part of ads that show up on the screen. These images can (and often do) get stored in one's hard disk automatically. If it turns out that the images depict females who are under age, or (in some countries) if the images are merely explicit, regardless of the age of the person in those images, they can be deemed to be evidence of having downloaded and possessed illegal material.

2. When we receive e-mail containing attachments, even unsolicited e-mail that gets deleted without even being read, depending on the e-mail program used and how it has been configured by the user, the attachments usually stay on one's computer despite the deletion of the e-mail message itself. One must take special steps to delete those attachments or to configure his or her e-mail software to delete attachments when the e-mail that brought them in is itself deleted.

3. It has been documented numerous times that, when one is online on the Internet or on any other internal network, it is usually possible for a savvy hacker at a remote site (which can be thousands of miles away) to gain free run of one's computer and to remove, modify, delete, or add any files to that computer. This obviously includes being able to add incriminating evidence.

In all of the above cases, it would take an Internet-savvy defense lawyer to convince a typical nontechnical judge or a jury of nontechnical "peers" that such illegal data files just happened to be on the accused individual's computer (which, in fact, may well have been the case). If the files are deleted by a "semisavvy," hapless user, this can make things even worse because those files can often be discovered through computer forensics; at that point, the accused person will also have to defend him or her self for not only having ostensibly downloaded and possessed them but also for having taken active steps to delete that evidence.

Innocent individuals who never connect their computer online to anything are not immune from hostile computer forensics either.

1.2.5   As a lawyer for the defense

Given that a rapidly increasing percentage of all legal cases (both criminal and civil) involve computer-based evidence, the legal training of yesteryear is not enough.

A lawyer must be extremely well versed in the ins and outs of computer forensics in order to defend a client with competence Anything less would be a disservice to the client.

The lawyer must be able to address competently such issues as the following, as well as numerous other case-specific issues:

1.   Could the computer data used against his or her client have been altered, damaged, corrupted, or in any way modified by the manner in which it was obtained and handled?

2.   Are all procedures used in the forensic examination "auditable" in the sense that a qualified expert can track and attest to their soundness?

3.   Is any of the information that may have been obtained by the prosecution during the forensic examination of the computer covered by the confidentiality protection of the attorney-client privilege?

4.   Can the prosecution demonstrate a chain of custody of the data that precludes any possibility that such data could have been contaminated in any way?

5.   Could a computer virus, Trojan, worm, or other such software have been activated after the data was copied and caused the data to be altered?

6.   Can the prosecution prove that the accused was the sole user of the computer in question?

7.   Could the data used as evidence in the client's computer have been placed there without that individual's knowledge?

Even if computer-based evidence is not brought to bear against a lawyer's particular client, a competent lawyer may well wish to subpoena the "other" party's computer-based records, if appropriate, in order to argue a case in his or her client's favor. Situations where this could be relevant might include, for example, cases of wrongful termination, discrimination, harassment, conspiracy, breach of contract, tort, libel or defamation, copyright infringement, violation of applicable regulations of the securities industry, and so forth.

1.2.6　As an insurance company

Insurance companies have an obvious interest in discovering evidence of fraudulent claims of any kind (e.g., auto insurance, medical insurance, workman's compensation), as well as evidence of crimes and conspiracies that may have resulted in subsequent claims (e.g., arson, willful destruction of property in order to obtain insurance compensation, professed loss of insured valuables). Evidence of such crimes is very likely to reside—however fragmented—in claimants' computers, which can be subpoenaed.

Automobile insurance companies in particular have been benefiting lately from having forensics done on the computers that control practically all cars sold today. These computers' primary purpose is to optimize gas mileage by sensing and responding to numerous input variables that affect an engine's performance. Such computers typically store at least the last few seconds' worth of data prior to an accident; such data includes the speed, amount of breaking, gas pedal position, whether or not the windshield wipers were switched on, and so forth.

1.2.7　As a user of others' computers

It is becoming increasingly common for those who travel to use Internet-connected computers available for a fee at such places as hotels, convention centers, Internet cafes, and the like. Some Internet-connected terminals are also available at no charge in schools and universities, booths by Internet service providers (ISPs) that want to sell ISP subscriptions, public libraries, and so forth.

One must remember that the user of others' computers must have absolutely no expectation of privacy. Every keystroke can be—and often is—captured, and this includes login passwords, encryption/decryption keys, plus the full content of messages and attachments.[4]

1.3　If you have done nothing illegal, you have nothing to fear: not true anywhere!

This statement has been parroted by numerous persons in positions of power over many generations. It is content-free because

1. One may genuinely believe that he or she is doing nothing wrong, but given the impossibility of knowing the myriad laws in the books and the fact that they change all the time, one cannot know for sure.

2. One may be doing nothing wrong now, but the law in many countries can change in x years retroactively with no statute of limitations.

---

4. See, for example, http://www.hotel-online.com/News/PR2004_1st/Feb04_RemoteInsecurity.html, http://www.landfield.com/isn/mail-archive/2001/Feb/0144.html, and others.

3.   One may have done nothing wrong, but at least some of the many people with arrest authority might—wrongly—think he or she has. To prove one's innocence may take financial resources that far exceed what a common mortal has and still not succeed; witness the number of individuals exonerated with DNA forensics, after they had been executed in the United States. The situation can reasonably be expected to be far worse in the many countries that have far fewer safeguards against the miscarriage of justice than the United States has.

4.   One may have been framed by law enforcement. Sadly, as was illustrated in a recent case in Los Angeles[5] when a handcuffed person was shot to death by police, who then framed him for a crime, such gross abuses of police authority can occur even in the most advanced countries, let alone in ones where policemen are emperors in effect.

Furthermore, privacy is not a "cover for crimes," as some law enforcers would assert, because

1.   There are some activities, such as having conjugal relations with their spouse, visiting the lavatory, and so forth, that civilized people want to keep private. The presumption that one would only want to keep some activities private out of fear of incrimination is therefore patently false.

2.   Given that different people hold different religious and other beliefs, it is often very dangerous for one to allow his or her locally unpopular beliefs to be known by others.

3.   Civilized countries require police to have warrants before any search or seizure; the same goes for interception of telephone conversations. This does not mean that one has something to hide; it means that society has decided that the right to privacy supersedes any police desire to monitor everybody's house, bedroom, bathroom, and office. Warrants are issued (in theory at least) by an impartial judge after police have made a compelling case for each. The idea that citizens should surrender privacy in order to prevent crime is why the U.S. Constitution has Fourth and Fifth Amendments. The framers of the U.S. Constitution recognized that government will find it easier to try to take citizens' rights away than to concentrate on specific law enforcement problems. As all totalitarian regimes demonstrate, it is easier to treat all people as criminals than it is to catch the criminals. And, in general, violating citizens' privacy does little or nothing to prevent crime.

5.   See www.wsws.org/articles/2000/mar2000/lapd-m13.shtml, http://projects.is.asu.edu/pipermail/hpn/2000-October/001706.html, and www.worldfreeinternet.net/news/nws185.htm, for example.

4. A pseudonymous Usenet posting in mid-December 2000 argued eloquently that the statement "If you are doing nothing wrong, you have nothing to worry about" implies an invalid presupposition. It is similar to the old joke "When did you stop beating your wife?" The (hopefully incorrect) presupposition there is that you were beating your wife. The incorrect presupposition with "If you are doing nothing wrong, you have nothing to worry about" is that privacy is about hiding something. Just as there is no way to answer the beating question without correctly resolving the incorrect presupposition, there is no way to answer the "nothing wrong" question without resolving the incorrect presupposition. Privacy is not about hiding something; it is about keeping things in their proper context. Why do we need to keep things in their proper context? For a host of reasons. One is that certain actions performed in the context of one's home are legal, but when performed in the context of a public place are (usually) illegal. Taking a bath or shower, or having sex for instance. The difference is the context. The action is the same. When one removes the context, things one does every day can suddenly become illegal.

1.4   Computer forensics

Computers have replaced a lot of paper. It is no surprise, therefore, that instead of subpoenaing or confiscating paper records, one subpoenas and confiscates computer records these days.

Additionally, e-mail has replaced a lot of paper correspondence, telephone calls, and even idle gossip by the water fountain. To a litigiously minded person, e-mail is therefore a treasure trove of information because it contains not only the information that used to be on paper in years past, but also contains

1. Information that never made it to paper (such as gossip and telephone conversations);

2. Information about the information (such as when something was said or written, when it was modified, who else it was sent to, and when it was ostensibly deleted, all of which is referred to as "metadata").

Ultimately, computer forensics is done because it can be done cheaply and also because it usually pays off.

1.4.1   User rights to privacy?

User rights to privacy are highly country-specific.

In the United States, for example, employer-owned computing resources in the workplace can be examined at all times by the employer. The concept of "reasonable expectation of privacy" applies where an employee can show that he or she had a reasonable expectation of privacy. This expectation evaporates into thin air, however, when the employee has had to sign a pre-employment document advising each employee that the employer's computers can be monitored at will by the employer or when the employee is faced with a splash screen warning at every login attempt to the effect that usage of the employer's computers or employer's network usage constitutes consent to monitoring.

In the United Kingdom and most European countries, stricter guidelines apply even to employer-owned computers and networks.

1.4.2 The forensics investigator must know up front

If evidence gathered in a forensics investigation is to be used in legal, or even administrative, proceedings against someone, then the forensic investigator must know this up front so that the collection and handling of the data is done in strict adherence to legally sanctioned rules about collection and the chain of custody.

These rules amount to procedures that must be followed to ensure the following:

1. The data claimed to be in the suspect's computer is provably coming from the subject's computer and was in no way altered by the process of extracting it. If the suspect's computer was booted (turned on), for example, then a forensics examiner can no longer claim that no alteration was made to the suspect's computer because the process of booting Windows from someone's hard disk writes data to that hard disk (e.g., to the swap file, the desktop.ini file).

2. The data collected from the suspect's hard disk (or any other media) has been handled in a manner that could not possibly have allowed that data to be contaminated or otherwise changed between the time it was collected and the times that it was analyzed and presented to a court or administrative body.

If the forensics examination is held for information gathering purposes, then the above strict legal requirements need not be followed. Other requirements may need to be followed, depending on the specifics of the situation. For example, it may be essential not to alert the subject of a forensics investigation that such an investigation is being done.

1.4.3 Forensics is deceptively simple but requires vast expertise

Contrary to popular belief, there is no mystery to computer forensics. This is why a huge cottage industry of self-appointed computer forensics "experts" has come into existence during the last few years. Sadly, while there are numerous experienced and competent computer forensics experts, it is getting increasingly difficult to identify them in this sea of mediocrity.

Even though the basics of computer forensics are very easy, computer forensics requires experience and competence. The reason for this apparent contradiction is that whereas anybody can use a forensic software package to browse through a target disk, experience and competence are required to determine the following:

1. *What to look for:* Computer forensic software merely opens the door and does not point the investigator towards anything. Like an experienced detective, the investigator must, based on experience and knowledge, know what to look for in a nearly limitless sea of data.

2. *Where to look for what is sought:* Going through the few hundred billion bytes of a typical modern hard disk is pointless unless one knows where to look. Again, there is no substitute for knowledge and experience. As an example, computer forensic software will not tell the inexperienced investigator that netscape.hst, which is not readable with a text editor, contains the history of a user's activities with the popular Web browser Natscape Navigator/Communicator. The experienced investigator has to be familiar with the peculiarities of a large number of computer software packages to know where each stores what and for how long.

3. *What indicators to look for that suggest what is hidden and where:* Often, what is of interest is not a word or a fragment of an image but something far more elusive, such as the following:

    a. Indication that a file or a disk has been overwritten. Why was it overwritten, when, and with which software?

    b. Indication that the disk being investigated contains (or contained) software whose use suggests a sophistication beyond that of the disk's owner. Is that owner benefiting from the technical support of others? Who? Why?

    c. Indications of incongruity. The disk's owner is a shoe salesman who hates computers, yet his computer has large, digitized sound files. Why? Are they a cover for steganography?

The worst-case scenario, which plays itself out on a regular basis in courtrooms around the world, is when an inexperienced computer forensics person testifies in the court of a technology-challenged judge and jury, who believe every word that this presumed expert says. Judges and juries (and, sadly, most defense attorneys who went to law school before computers became a staple of daily life) believe incorrectly that:

1. Just because some data was found in a suspect's computer, the suspect put it there; this is patently false.

2. The data about every file in a computer (e.g., date/time stamp of a file, when it was moved from which folder to which folder, when it was renamed or deleted) is sacrosanct, believable, and unchangeable by another person; this, too, is patently false as Section 1.4.6 discusses.

1.4.4 Computer forensics top-level procedure

If a computer to be investigated is on, the first decision to be made is whether to turn it off. Generally, one should turn it off unceremoniously, not through an orderly shutdown process, which may involve steps to over-write files. If the computer is networked and the process of turning it off would alert an accomplice, then one has to assess the pros and cons of turn-ing it off.

The next step should be to photograph the screen (if it was on), all con-nections to the computer, and the insides of the cabinet.

Because the process of booting the Windows-based computer will most likely write onto any connected hard disk, the investigator must never boot that computer. Instead, all magnetic media (hard disks, floppy disks, super-floppies, Zip and Jaz disks, and so forth) must be disconnected from the computer and copied individually onto the forensic investigator's hard disk; this must be done after a digital digest (hash value), using either the MD5 or, preferably, the SHA-1 hashing algorithm, is applied so that the investiga-tor's copy can be certified to be an exact copy of the original.

Copying one hard disk onto another is fraught with danger unless special care is taken, especially if the source and the target disks (i.e., the suspect's and the investigator's disks) are the same size; this is so because it is easy to make the mistake of copying the investigator's hard disk onto the suspects, rather than the other way around. Ideally, the investigator should have a box dedicated to performing this task without the possibility of error.

Once the suspect's hard disk is copied onto the investigator's disk in a manner that can be shown to result in an identical copy of a suspect's media,[6] the actual forensics analysis begins. No special forensic software suite is needed; a judicious collection of numerous freeware tools would be adequate for someone who knows what to do, why, and how. All-inclusive forensic software suites make the forensics analysis easy and efficient and also provide a track record of acceptability by many courts.

The analysis consists of the following logical sequence of steps:

1. Eliminate from analysis all files known to be of no forensics interest, such as the executable portions of popular software. To ensure that what is eliminated is truly, for example, word.exe and not some

---

6. This used to be done with software, such as Safeback v3 (http://www.forensics-intl.com/thetools.html), whose sole function was to make such identical copies. This function is included in today's forensic software suites like Encase from Guidance Software.

other file that has been intentionally renamed with that name, the identification of "known" files is done on the basis of whether or the digital digest of each such file matches exactly the correct digital digest of that file known from some dependable source.

2. Using digital digests of notable files that have been already encountered before in other investigators (e.g., for bomb_recipe.txt), the investigator looks for all files known to be of interest.

3. What is left now is everything else that must be analyzed. The investigator must now analyze the entire remaining hard disk, notably including all unknown files, unallocated disk space, and the slack (space between end-of-file and end-of-cluster marks) for whatever is being sought. It is here that the investigator's competence and experience comes in. The forensic software has no idea what the investigator is looking for; it is up to the investigator to define the search in an effective manner. It may be for keywords (a simple task), images (also a simple task), or patterns of computer usage (a much harder task).

4. If nothing is found, the investigator may elect to look for evidence of any steganographically hidden data, especially if the computer contains telltale indicators that steganography software has been installed or used. Most forensic investigators are quite uninformed or misinformed about steganography (see Section 11.5). In a nutshell:

    a. Amateurish steganography such as what is openly available over the Internet[7] can be readily detected.

    b. Professionally designed steganography that is used extremely sparingly and where the ratio of hidden files to overt files is very small cannot be detected.

5. If still nothing is found, then one usually quits unless the case is one of extreme significance (e.g., a case of national significance) that warrants the ultimate forensic investigation technique intended to find files that have actually been overwritten. This involves forensics microscopy, where the magnetic surface is examined with a high-power microscope that can actually look at individual magnetic particles to infer the minute perturbations indicative of what the magnetization may have been before a "zero" or a "one" was overwritten.

6. The last step is documenting the findings and presenting them.

---

7. See Steganos, JSteg, Hide and Seek, Steg Tools, and numerous others, all of which can be found at http://www.stegoarchive.com and elsewhere.

1.4.5   Forensics specifics

As already stated, one does not need all-inclusive forensic software except for the convenience and the acceptability of their analysis in some nontechnical circles. A good complement of freeware can do the requisite individual tasks. For example, searching an entire hard disk for keywords is easily done with SectorSpyXP, which is available online from numerous sources. This is depicted in Figure 1.1, where the software was asked to find the keyword "Windows."

One must be cautioned that often a keyword (e.g., "bomb") does not appear intact in any single sector; part of it (e.g., "b") may be in one sector and part of it (e.g., "omb") may be in a distant sector. This is so because Windows write files on whichever sectors it finds available at the time, and it may very well break a single file into numerous noncontiguous sectors.

Keyword searching for "BOULAMITE" will take one to the sector that has the Windows registered owner's name and affiliation.

All-inclusive forensic software suits like Encase from Guidance Software can also handle numerous personal digital assistants (PDAs), Redundnt Array of Inexpensive Disks (RAID) disks, Flash media (e.g., the popular Universal Serial Bus (USB) key-like plug-ins that seem to be replacing floppy disks as temporary storage media, are formatted like a hard disk with a file allocation table (FAT), and have their own slack and unallocated space, like a disk.

It is noteworthy that renaming a file to something less alerting (e.g., bomb.jpg to holy.txt) actually works against you. Each file type (such as .jpg files) has a unique header that is not changed when the file's name is changed. In the case of .jpg files, that header is "xFF\xD8\xFF\xFE"; changing the file's name to holy.txt will only cause that file to be flagged to the

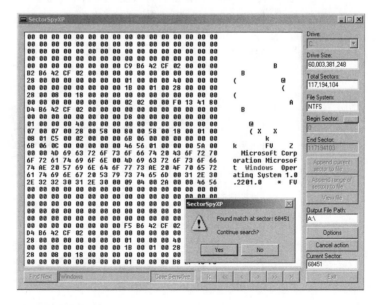

Figure 1.1   Keyword search with SectorSpy XP.

forensic investigator as an intentionally misnamed file, as shown below, thereby subjecting it to even more scrutiny. In Figure 1.2, an example from Encase software, "!Bad signature" means that the file suffixes (.wpg and .xls) in these files' names do not match the headers at the beginnings of these files.

Amusingly, the practice of misnaming files to confuse others appears to have also been practiced by Microsoft in the case of the logos.sys and logow.sys files; both of these files have a .sys suffix, suggesting that they are system files whose removal will prevent the computer from booting; in fact, they are bitmaps of splash screens (i.e., ads for Microsoft).

Searching for the link files (.lnk) in the following locations will show which shortcut was created, when, and to which file:

 • Windows\Desktop;
 • Windows\Recent;
 • Windows\Start;
 • Windows\Send.

Such files could be use to contest defense claims that a suspect had no idea what a file was or how it got there.

The investigator can also search in print spooler files, because files sent to a printer are usually spooled in a file on the hard disk before being printed. The spool file is not intentionally overwritten by Windows. There are two kinds of printer spool files:

1. Shadow (.shd) files show the file's owner, printer name, file name, and printing method ["raw" or enhanced metafile format (emf)].

2. The .spl file, which also contains the file to be printed, is created even if one prints from a floppy disk.

The existence of a file in the printer spool can again contest defense claims that a suspect had no idea what a file was or how it got there, unless

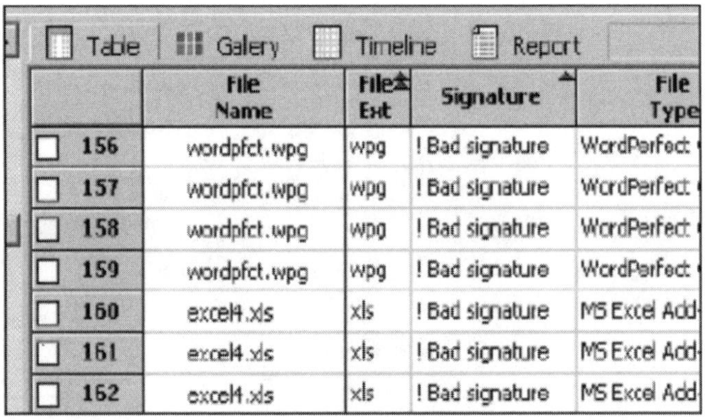

		File Name	File Ext	Signature	File Type
	156	wordpfct.wpg	wpg	! Bad signature	WordPerfect
	157	wordpfct.wpg	wpg	! Bad signature	WordPerfect
	158	wordpfct.wpg	wpg	! Bad signature	WordPerfect
	159	wordpfct.wpg	wpg	! Bad signature	WordPerfect
	160	excel4.xls	xls	! Bad signature	MS Excel Add
	161	excel4.xls	xls	! Bad signature	MS Excel Add
	162	excel4.xls	xls	! Bad signature	MS Excel Add

Figure 1.2 Easy Identification of modified file suffixes.

the printing action is claimed to have been intended to answer that question.

Deleted folders and their contents' names can often be recovered as well, as long as the data has not been overwritten. Encase and similar software programs make this process easy, as shown in Figure 1.3.

Files sent to the Recycle Bin (a British-sounding term, as opposed to the American term *trash can*, reportedly conjured up by Microsoft to avoid a legal battle with Apple Computer about its "Trash" icon) can be recovered even if they have been deleted as long as they have not been overwritten. Even if they have been overwritten, their names can often be recovered from the INFO file that is created whenever a file is added to the Recycle Bin, as shown in Figure 1.4.

Figure 1.3 Recovering deleted folders with Encase.

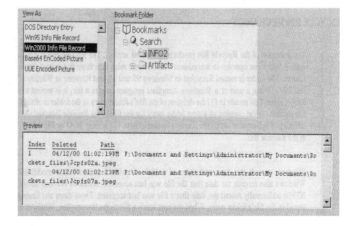

Figure 1.4 Recovering deleted files even from the Recycle Bin.

New Technology File System (NTFS) security permissions are irrelevant and offer no protection from a forensic investigator because the investigator is not operating within a Windows environment in the first place.

The forensic software can also search for the metadata about files (e.g., date of creation) unless the file was created with DOS prior to version 7.

Depending on the software package, operating system, and language support added, computer forensics is obviously not limited to the Latin alphabet, but can handle foreign languages as well, as shown in Figure 1.5.

An investigator who is comfortable with a particular foreign language can do a keyword search in that language just as well as he or she can in English. Indeed, today's national security organizations must have the in-house competence to handle computer forensics in numerous foreign languages, including languages written right to left.

Equally important, a competent forensics investigation should also include search on metadata, such as when a file appears to have been created, renamed, moved, deleted, overwritten, and so forth. A computer forensics investigation should also be able to reconstruct, to the extent possible, even deleted "compound files" [i.e., files whose data is shared among more than one individual files, as is the case with Registry, Microsoft Outlook, and Outlook Express files (.dbx and .pst files), among others]. An example of an Outlook e-mail file reconstructed with Encase is shown in Figure 1.6.

1.4.6 Digital evidence is often evidence of nothing

Courts, judges, and juries are increasingly faced with computer forensic evidence rather than physical evidence. Because judges and juries are, on the average, quite uninformed about the admissibility and believability of what is presented as evidence, "experts" are usually summoned to testify and inform the court about these issues; the problem is that most (but not all) of these computer forensics "experts" have a vested interest in their stock in

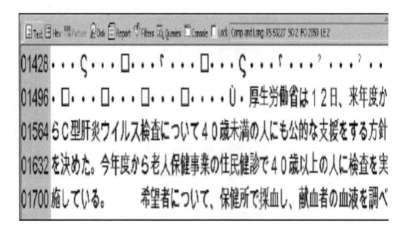

Figure 1.5 Foreign-language forensics.

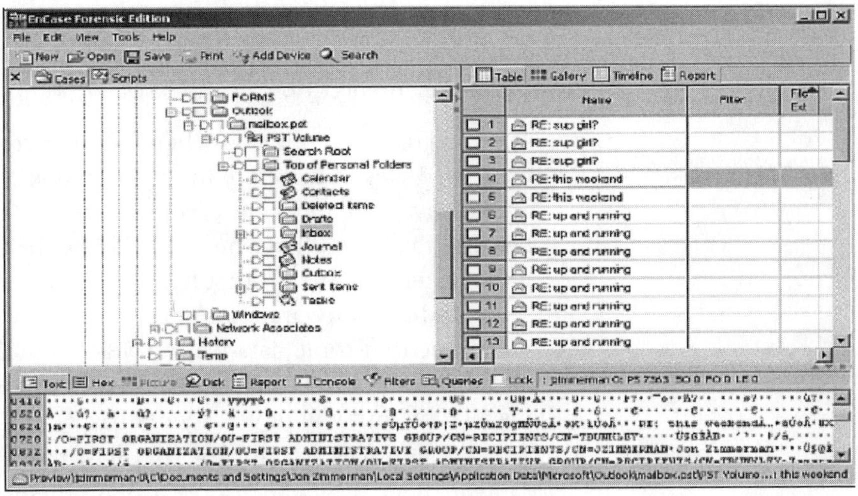

Figure 1.6 Forensics on Outlook and Outlook Express.

trade, which can be reasonably expected to slant their views in support of the professed infallibility of computer forensics.

Unlike conventional analog data, such as the shade of gray or the subjective recollection of a witness, digital data, which takes one of two very unambiguous values (zero or one), is misperceived by the average person as endowed with intrinsic and unassailable truth.

In fact, quite the opposite is true. Unlike conventional analog data and evidence, for which experts with the right equipment can often detect tampering, digital data can be manipulated at will, and depending on the sophistication of the manipulator, the alteration can be undetectable, regardless of a digital forensics expert's competence and equipment.

The potential for a miscarriage of justice is vast, given that many defense lawyers, judges, and juries are unaware of the esoteric details of computer science. This "dirty little secret" about digital evidence is conveniently soft-pedaled by the computer forensics industry and by the prosecution, both of which focus on those other aspects of the process of collecting, preserving, and presenting digital data evidence that are indeed unassailable, such as the chain-of-custody portion of handling digital evidence.

Lets take a common example of computer evidence. A suspect's hard disk is confiscated and subjected to forensics analysis, and a report generated for the court states that the hard disk contained this or that file, that these files dates' were this and that, and that these files were renamed or printed on this and that date, thereby negating the suspect's claim that he did not know of the existence of these files, and so forth.

A typical judge or jury will accept these facts at face value, but should not for the following reasons:

1. The data found on someone's hard disk (or other mass-storage media) could indeed have entered that hard disk through any of the

following ways without the suspect's knowledge, let alone complicity. All of these paths for surreptitious data entry are very commonplace and occur on a daily basis.

a. The hard disk was not new when the suspect purchased it and contained files from before the suspect took custody of it. This applies even in the case of purchases of "new" computers because they could have been resold after being returned by a previous buyer. Even if that hard disk had been wiped by the seller and the software reinstalled, there is no physical way to guarantee that some data was not left behind; this is why the classified community will never allow a disk to leave a secure installation, but will physically destroy it.

b. A large number of software packages today (referred to as "adware" and "spyware") take it upon themselves to secretly install unadvertised files and a capability for the software maker to snoop on the individual's computer through the Internet or other network. If this "snooping" capability should be exploited by a third-party hacker who routinely scans computers for this "backdoor entry," then files can be inserted on the suspect's computer at will.

c. Obtaining full control of anyone's computer through the Internet does not even require that such adware or spyware be installed. Microsoft has been admitting to numerous existing security flaws in its operating systems and applications, especially its Internet Explorer, that allow anyone to gain full control of anyone else's Internet-connected computer and insert files into it without the victimized computer owner knowing anything about it. Discoveries of new online backdoor entries to anyone's computer have been appearing at an average rate of at least one per month for the last several years.

d. When any of us browses the Internet, we often mistype and end up inadvertently and unintentionally on a Web site that is often an adult site. Even without mistyping at all, however, one can still end up at an incriminating site for the following reason: Hackers have often doctored up entries in the domain name servers (DNS),[8] which amounts to doctoring up the directory that is accessed every time we type the name of a Web site we want to see.

e. Even in the absence of any of the foregoing, it is a fact of life that the Internet is largely free to the user; because nothing in life is

---

8. The Internet does not "understand" names such as www.cnn.com and only understands addresses in number form, such as 209.146.168.2; the translation from a name to a number is done each and every time we type a URL name (such as www.cnn.com) by the DNS, a network of computer servers around the world that does just that for a living.

really free, the revenue source for many "free" Web sites we visit on the Internet comes from advertising in the form of pop-up ads, scrolling text, images, and the like. Often these advertising images are not for facial crèmes and vacation packages, but show unclad underage persons. Although one can rapidly go to a different Web site, the fact is, unless one has gone to the trouble to change the Web browser's default settings (of storing Web pages on the disk) to not storing anything, these offensive images get stored ("cached") on one's hard disk drives. Over a period of time, enough to them collect in any of our computers and an overzealous prosecutor can claim that there is an "obvious pattern or proclivity that stretches over a few years." A hapless defendant will have a very difficult time convincing a technology-challenged judge or jury that he or she knows nothing about how those images got there.

f.   Unless one lives by oneself and never admits anyone into his or her house, chances are that one's children, spouse, or a friend or relative will use his or her computer during a computer's typical lifetime of a few years. In that case, it is not inconceivable at all that such other persons could have visited Web sites that you or I would not have patronized.

g.   Unsolicited e-mail is as common as the air we breathe. Many of them peddle get-rich-quick schemes, pyramid schemes, sex, and just about everything else. Most people ignore them; many delete them. But here is the problem: Aside from the fact that deleting does not delete anything (it merely tells the computer that the space on the disk occupied by that file or e-mail, which is in fact not erased at all, can be used in the future if the computer feels like it), hardly any of us goes to the trouble to delete the *attachments* that often come with such unsolicited e-mail. And, even if we did, the attachment would still remain on our hard disks for the same reasons. Perhaps nobody, other than computer experts, will go to the trouble of overwriting the offensive attachment because Windows does not include any provision to overwrite anything; one has to buy special software for this, and most people don't. And even if one did go to the heroic step of overwriting a file with specially purchased software, to the delight of the forensic investigator who has a vested interest in finding something incriminating, the name of the file, which could be quite incriminating in and of itself and which is stored in a different location on the hard disk than the file itself, would not be overwritten. Again, the hapless defendant will have a very hard time convincing a nontechnical jury that such offensive files were not solicited (or even tolerated). Even if one went through the heroic steps of overwriting unsolicited e-mail attachments and

their separately stored names (nobody does that), fragments of
these incriminating files may still be found by forensic investigators in the swap file.

h.   Wireless access in the United States is increasing at an explosive
      rate. It can be found at McDonald's, Starbucks, in many airports
      and hotels, and most important to this discussion, in our homes
      where we may like to access our high-speed Internet connec-
      tion from anywhere in the house without running wires all
      over the place. The literature is full of the technical details of
      how insecure this Wi-Fi standard is. Out of the box, Wi-Fi is
      configured to require no password, no encryption, and no secu-
      rity at all, and most users do not tinker with those default
      settings. Now, radio travels over far larger distances than what
      these boxes claim, and it is not uncommon for a home Wi-Fi to
      be accessed a full 5 miles away if one builds a directional
      antenna and drives around town looking for other people's
      home Wi-Fi's to connect to, a practice known as "war driving."
      Once connected, which is a trivial matter because there is no
      security, the war driver has full access to the victim's computer
      and Internet connection. This means that files can be placed on
      or removed from the victim's computer, and it also means that
      the war driver can leave a long trace of illegal Internet activity in
      the victim's ISP's records. Now imagine the very common situa-
      tion where the victim is at home, is the only person at home,
      and the war driver uses the victim's computer to engage in any
      one or more of the multitude of illegal activities that can be con-
      ducted over the Internet. The finger will be pointed at the victim
      as being the "obvious" perpetrator; good luck convincing an
      uninformed court that the victim was a victim and not the
      perpetrator.

i.   Computers crash sooner rather than later. The typical course of
      action is to take the computer to some professional to access
      one's prized personal and business data. Computer repairper-
      sons use special diagnostic software, test the computer's
      Internet functionality, and have every opportunity, although
      hardly any motivation, to place data on the repaired computer.
      A few years later, the owner of the computer is likely to have
      forgotten about the repair altogether and never to bring it up in
      his or her defense.

2.   Computer forensics examiners like to substantiate their findings
      by pointing out the time/date stamp associated with different
      computer files as if those time/date stamps were kept in a vault inac-
      cessible to mere mortals. This is patently false. The date/time stamp,
      as well as every single bit of data in a computer's magnetic media,
      can be altered undetectably so that the evidence found by the
      forensic investigator will substantiate what the alterer wants it to. All

it takes is a disk editor, which is openly available (e.g., in Norton Utilities), to change any metadata (data about data, such as who did what and when) in a computer, be it the date/time or anything else.

3.   Unlike conventional film-based photography where a competent investigator can usually determine if an image has been doctored, digital images (such as those taken by any surveillance camera) can be altered in a manner that no expert can detect if the alteration was done professionally enough. Noise and blur can be digitally added to the end result to further hide from an expert any digital tinkering that might have been detectable at the individual pixel level. "Pictures don't lie" is a now a lie.

4.   As with digital photography, so with digitized sounds. Unlike the analog sounds of yesteryear (e.g., the infamous gap in the tape recordings of Nixon's office, where a careful study of the background noise can detect alterations in analog recordings), digitized files of sounds can be altered at will. If the alteration is done professionally enough, it will be undetectable even during a forensics examination of the digital file.

In summary, we are witnessing a new phenomenon in today's courtrooms. All of us store on our computers more and more information about our lives and activities. This has resulted in an explosion in computer forensics on confiscated or subpoenaed computers based on the incorrect assumption that the computer contains only what we put in it. An entire cottage industry of computer forensic investigators, some more qualified and competent than others, has sprung up to service the insatiable appetite for such services by all.

The legal and social problem with this phenomenon is that most individuals in the legal and law enforcement professions are unaware of at least some of the many ways whereby the data they present as evidence is really not evidence of anything because it is routinely placed on computers without the knowledge or complicity of their owners.

Similarly, evidence based on one's ISP's records is evidence of nothing because Internet accounts can be (and routinely are) accessed by third parties without the account holder's awareness or complicity, even if he or she was the only person at home when the alleged Internet access occurred.

In summary, defense lawyers and judges should get urgently needed remedial education in the shortcomings of digital forensics. Digital evidence should be viewed with extreme suspicion, regardless of the competence or qualifications of the computer forensics expert witness. While the chain-of-custody portion of how the evidence was handled may have been impeccable, the raw digital data on which a forensics analysis was done can be easily and undetectably tampered with by anyone with the right background. Digital evidence is often evidence of nothing.

One can review numerous trend-setting legal cases involving computer forensics.[9] A reader should avoid forensic vendors' Web sites as they present an understandably biased view of the serious issues behind the use and abuse of computer forensics.

Selected bibliography

The field is evolving at an unprecedented pace, both because the laws themselves are changing rapidly in an attempt to keep up with today's reality and because the technologies themselves are changing rapidly. The days of the floppy disk and of the hard disk having only a few hundred megabytes of storage capacity have been replaced by USB keys, hard disks with hundreds of gigabytes of storage, increasing use of encryption, and privacy-enhancing user practices that negate forensics. Additionally, computer forensics is increasingly being applied to such popular consumer devices as fax machines, cell phones, digital cameras and camcorders, MP3 music players, and even car computers.

These textbooks only scratch the surface. To stay current, the interested reader will have to follow developments online on a weekly basis, if not more often.

Mohay, G., (ed.), *Computer and Intrusion Forensics,* Norwood, MA: Artech House, 2003.

Casey, E., *Handbook of Computer Crime Investigation: Forensic Tools & Technology,* New York: Academic Press, 2001.

Marcella, A. J., and R. S. Greenfield, (eds.), *Cyber Forensics: A Field Manual for Collecting, Examining, and Preserving Evidence of Computer Crimes,* Boca Raton, FL: Auerbach Publisher, 2002.

Vacca, J. R., and M. Erbschloe, *Computer Forensics: Computer Crime Scene Investigation,* Boston, MA: Charles River Media, 2002.

Winkler, I., *Corporate Espionage,* Rocklin, CA: Prima Publishing Co., 1997.

Prosise, C., et al., *Incident Response and Computer Forensics,* 2nd ed., New York: McGraw-Hill, 2003.

9. See http://www.krollontrack.com/CaselawNewsletter/CurrentNewsletter, http://californiadiscovery.findlaw.com/el_ disco_websites.htm, and www.blkbox.com/%7Eguillory/electron.html.

Locating Your Sensitive Data in Your Computer

As with most any methodical process of achieving a goal, removing data from computers to prevent such data from being seen by unauthorized eyes involves sequences of specific steps. This chapter, as well as some that follow, are therefore less narrative and present lists of steps that the security-conscious reader is encouraged to take.

This chapter discusses effective ways for users to permanently remove (wipe) from their computers data that should not fall into the wrong hands. As with removing weeds from a flowerbed, the reader must be very careful not to inadvertently remove files that are needed or to remove other data needed by the computer to operate at all.

2.1 Deleting does not delete—what does?

2.1.1 General

Our computers' hard disks contain a mirror of our lives these days. E-mail, love letters, tax returns, and privileged communications with our lawyer are all saved on our computers for our benefit and, unless we take measures to protect our privacy, for the benefit of anyone who steals our computer and also for that of any computer forensic investigator hired by anyone who feels like suing us.

In a business setting, proprietary information, marketing plans, and lists of clients and of prospective clients constitute every business's lifeblood. If these fall into competitors' hands, the commercial entity will likely go bankrupt; if it is a publicly held company, its stockholders will claim negligence and will rightly sue. Similarly, in a medical setting, health-care professionals are legally required in many countries to safeguard the confidentiality of patient data. The penalty is jail time in many cases.

Government users of computers are similarly required to ensure that the data entrusted to them cannot fall into unauthorized hands.

Despite all of the foregoing, the reality of life is that laptops do get forgotten in taxicabs and airplanes, and most all computers are eventually sold, donated, recycled, or thrown in the trash. At a minimum, computers regularly get sent to the repair shop, almost invariably with their hard disks in place.

What about the sensitive data they contain?

As an experiment, MIT's Simon Garfinkle purchased 158 used hard disks from Ebay and was easily able to recover a large number of files whose originators would have been extremely embarrassed if they had known that such files had been left behind (see http://www.computer.org/security/garfinkel.pdf).

Law enforcement has been quite successful in promulgating the self-serving fiction that only criminals with something to hide would have an interest in ensuring that sensitive data in their computers needs to be rendered inaccessible by all others. In fact, quite the opposite is true: As discussed above, individuals and organizations can be held legally liable for failing to ensure that sensitive data cannot be accessed by third parties. It is technically impossible to hide data from "all except law enforcers"; as such, one must either hide it from everybody or from nobody. Given the legal obligation of businesses, individuals, and professionals to prevent unauthorized disclosure of sensitive data, one must hide sensitive data from all.

Achieving this is very difficult.

To begin with, even if one undertook the heroic measures needed to make a sensitive file truly disappear from magnetic media, there is a high likelihood that copies and earlier versions of that file exist on numerous other places in the same magnetic media. These copies can have unrecognizable names or their names may be invisible in the normal default directory lists. To make things worse, chances are that there will be fragments of such earlier copies of such sensitive files scattered all over one's magnetic media. Furthermore, even though our screen and printer shows the latest version of a Microsoft Word document, the electronic version of it in the computer will most likely contain the full history of how it evolved from the very first draft onward, and this history can be seen by anyone with the know-how.

If one is using Windows rather than DOS, one pays a high security price for the convenience of using a graphical user interface (GUI). Unbeknownst to the user, most Windows-based applications create temporary files on the hard disk at unadvertised locations using unrecognizable names so that, should the computer crash for any reason, such as a power failure, the user will not have lost the file he or she has so laboriously typed. Because Windows and its application software are not clairvoyant and cannot tell if a computer will crash or not, they usually create and save such temporary files for good measure; if the computer does not crash, as is usually the case, these temporary files remain in one's computer.

As a minimum, a security-conscious user should take the following preliminary precautions in Windows-based platforms that offer minimal protection; a more comprehensive list is recommended in Chapter 6:

1. Find (by experimenting) the actual location (folder name) where your particular software saves temporary files. If the application software you are using allows you the option, change it to another folder in a RAM disk (see Section 6.2.2 on enhancing the security of Windows installations through the use of RAM disks). This way, the temporary file will not be written on the hard disk. This is not enough though; one must still worry about the swap file, discussed in detail in Section 2.3.

2. Disable "Allow background saves" and "Save auto-recovery info" if possible. In Microsoft Word it is under Tools/Options/Save. Also, disable "Track changes," and enable "Accept all changes." This will prevent the electronic version of a document from including its history of evolution. Better yet, convert the document into an Adobe .pdf file before sending it as an electronic document to anyone.

3. Do not delete a file using the normal DOS or Windows command because that makes it very hard to find its remnants so as to really remove it securely in the manner described later in this section.

4. Use "Save as" rather than "Save." If the latest version of a file by any one name is shorter than the previous version, then the "extra" data from the previous version will stay in the last "cluster" used by that file when it is saved (between the "end of file" and "end of cluster." If you use "Save as" with a different name each time (such as "File1," "File2"), then that problem won't come up, and you can securely delete all of these individual files later on.

5. Make sure that the names you give to files you save are not very descriptive of the contents. It is much more difficult to remove the names of files (which are stored in a different place and are handled differently) than it is to remove the files themselves.

The point is that secure deletion of any one file and its name is not a simple proposition; it must be viewed only as part of the secure cleanup of an entire disk and never as a secure removal of (the latest copy) of a single file.

But lets assume that, somehow, one feels confident that the only file that needs to be deleted has been identified and that the issue is how to make it disappear. Disappear from whose sight? The nosy maid's? The computer hacker's? The computer forensics firm's? The eyes of someone even more sophisticated?

For starters, not just the file itself, but all of the following information *about* that file, must disappear: the file's name (which was hopefully chosen with some care to be nondescript and not incriminating itself), the date it was created, the date it was last accessed, the date it was renamed, the folder it was moved from and to, and so forth. All of these bits of information are stored separately on a computer disk.

Using the delete command achieves absolutely nothing. It merely changes a single character in the disk's file allocation table to indicate to the computer that the spaces taken by that file may be overwritten in the future if necessary. The file remains on the disk in its full glory. (If delete really worked, then the many available versions of undelete would not, would they?).

Using format does not remove sensitive files either, contrary to popular belief. All that formatting does is write over the file allocation table, which contains the 64,000-plus pointers to the exact locations of the clusters on the disk where the various files were. It merely "zero-izes" these pointers. Even if one uses the "full," or long, version of format, the computer only tries to read each cluster to find if it should be marked in the file allocation table as "bad"; the files themselves are not overwritten at all.[1]

It follows that to remove a sensitive file and its separately stored name and date stamp, one must overwrite them. Overwriting a known file is easy, assuming that there are no temporary or other copies of it and no evidence of it in the swap file (see Section 2.3). Removing the file name and its attributes is not.

2.1.2 Disk wiping

In view of the foregoing, disk wiping (the process of overwriting all sensitive data on a hard disk so that such data cannot be retrieved by others) is a very complex business. Interestingly, Windows does not offer a single means for users to overwrite their sensitive files; rather, Windows makes it extremely difficult to remove sensitive files because of the many ways that it leaks sensitive information into assorted obscure places on one's storage media.

As a result, numerous software packages have evolved (some for pay and some for free) that have varying degrees of success in truly eliminating sensitive data from one's computers.

The problem is that even the best of them cannot work as well as one would have wished for the following technical reasons:

---

1. So-called low-level formatting of a hard disk does, in fact, "zero-ize" all contents of all sectors. Most integrated desktop environment (IDE) hard disk manufacturers do not provide a utility for doing this, however; only some Small Computer System Interface (SCSI) hard disk manufacturers do. Low-level formatting of a hard disk will defeat software-based means of recovering data from such a disk, but may or may not defeat microscopic examination of the magnetic particles of a disk.

1. Windows and Windows-based application software products create and use files that cannot be removed from within Windows (e.g., the swap file discussed in Section 2.3) while Windows is running. One has to exit Windows, reboot with a different operating system (e.g., DOS), wipe the sensitive files that Windows won't let one touch, and then reboot. Most disk-wiping software does not do that. In fact this is one of many tests one should use in assessing if the disk-wiping software of one's choice is acceptable or not: If it purports to do everything from within Windows, it is unsatisfactory.

2. Disk-wiping software has no way of knowing which legitimate-looking files created by assorted application software should be eliminated. For example, Netscape Navigator/Communicator's netscape.hst has no socially redeeming reason to exist other than to compromise users' security; it stores information about all that one has ever done with Netscape Navigator/Communicator since it was installed. This file needs to be overwritten manually every time one wants to clean up one's disk.

3. Disk-wiping software usually does not touch the Registry files. Yet this is precisely where Microsoft's Internet Explorer stores one's Web-browsing activity. This way Microsoft could claim (when it tried to defend itself against the U.S. Department of Justice's famous antitrust litigation) that its Web browser is an "integral part of the Windows operating system." It is, but it doesn't have to be as the Netscape and Opera Web browsers demonstrate.

4. Windows stores the names of files and data about those files in a different place than the files themselves and treats those names differently. Even if a file has been deleted, Windows keeps its name forever and does not mark the space taken by that name as being available to be overwritten by newer data as it does with the space take by the deleted files themselves.

5. Even if one somehow manages to take care of all of the foregoing "gotcha" threats, an even more insidious one is next to impossible to get rid of: The typical high-capacity hard disks of today come with a number of sectors held in reserve. When a data-containing sector in the disk is deemed by the hard drive's own "smart" firmware to be marginal (e.g., when there are occasional errors in reading the data from it), the hard disk's own firmware does the following behind the user's back without informing the user:

   a. Copies the data from the marginal sector to one of the sectors held in reserve;

   b. Assigns the logical address of the marginal sector to the new sector that the data was copied to;

   c. Mothballs the marginal sector without overwriting the data in it after that data was copied to the new sector.

No disk-wiping software in the world can touch the now mothballed sector because it no longer has an address; hence it does not exist as far as any software is concerned. On the other hand, a forensic investigator with access to the disk drive manufacturer's firmware can readily access those sectors and all data in them!

One can now readily appreciate why disk wiping is a very complicated task and why all software products that purport to do it fail quite miserably. Largely because of item (5) above, the reader is advised not to depend on any such software for wiping hard disks clean and to destroy physically the storage media before selling, donating, or disposing of magnetic storage media. The only secure fix is to physically destroy the magnetic media.

2.1.3   File- and disk-wiping software

In view of the foregoing, the user who wants to keep his or her hard disks, but wants to clean ("sanitize") them up enough to prevent unauthorized viewing of data in them, is advised to follow the following procedure:

1. Use full disk encryption. These are software products that encrypt the entire disk track for track and sector for sector, with the exception of the boot sector, which contains no sensitive information. Make sure that you use a password that is very hard to guess. The recommended software packages are shown in detail in Section 6.4.1. Ideally, this should be done on a brand new disk before one installs any operating system or application software so that no data can end up in the mothballed sectors described under (5) above. If it is done after a disk has been used, protection will be offered from all threats except these mothballed sectors.

   Also, keep in mind that full disk encryption protects one only when the computer is turned off; when the computer is turned on, it is vulnerable to hardware keystroke interceptors, to hidden overhead cameras, to the interception of the radio-frequency emanations that every computer radiates to varying degrees (see Section 4.7), and to any hacker online. Protection from these threats requires different countermeasures described in the corresponding sections in this book.

2. If full disk encryption is not taken advantage of as recommended and one wants merely to get rid of a single file, then supershredder.exe is recommended; see www.cotse.net/users/bluejay/supershred.html for detailed step-by-step advice on its use. Keep in mind that this will only eliminate the single file in question; it will not touch temporary files, history files, or the swap file. TIF-Clean is an excellent small utility to clean up the litter left behind by Internet Explorer; it runs in the background every time Windows is started. See http://www.staff.uiuc.edu/%7Eehowes/resource3.htm, where it can be downloaded.

3. If one does not want to use full disk encryption to sanitize one's hard disks, then the first step is to use software products that try to clean up the electronic litter left behind by assorted applications software and by the operating system. This must be done before any disk wiping. The best of these software packages are the following:

    a. SecureClean by White Canyon Company (http://www.white-canyone.com). This one shows a before and after view of what it finds in the hard disk. It does not remove files used by Windows.

    b. Window Washer by Webroot Software (http://www.webroot.com). This, too, does not remove files in use by Windows.

    c. Eraser by East Tec Software (http://www.east-tec.com). This causes the file length to be set to zero, renames the file with random symbols, and places a .tmp extension on every file it removes.

    d. BC Wipe by Jetico (http://www.jetico.com). Although BC Wipe is free, the full Best Crypt package from the same source is highly recommended in that it offers the option to encrypt your swap file as a default from that point on so that you no longer need to worry about data leakage from the swap file. Like East Tec's Eraser, it eliminates the names of the files being wiped, whereas most of the other software packages do not do that.

    e. Track Eraser Pro by AcesSoft Company (http://www.acesoft.com).

4. Use two or, preferably, more different disk-wiping software packages in sequence. Do not trust any one of them alone. Make sure you have enabled the option to overwrite the files you want removed. Some packages use odd terms for overwriting (e.g., "bleach" in the Window Washer software).

5. Defragment the disk. Defragmenting is emphatically not a substitute for, but an adjunct to, disk wiping.

6. Now use a disk-wiping software package to overwrite the free space and the slack (space between the end of file and end of cluster) in your disk. This can take a long time (hours), so it is not the sort of thing you want to do in a hurry when the chips are down. The best software for this is Eraser by www.tolvanen.com. The option to have multiple overwrites is not as appealing as it may seem because many hard disks look at the request to write different things sequentially to a given sector and shortcut the process by only writing the last sequence. You are better off overwriting once, then returning when this is done and overwriting everything again from scratch.

    Ensure that you specify the overwriting of the swap file; this can only be done outside Windows from DOS using ERASERD, which comes with that software.

7. Use some forensic software to see if you can still find what you tried
    to remove. A set of simple and free software packages is Directory
    Snoop and File Recover. The best of them all is EnCase from Guid-
    ance Software (http://www.guidancesoftware.com) (which is used
    by roughly 90% of the police departments in the United States and
    the United Kingdom) to double check if a file that is supposed to have
    been removed has in fact been removed, along with all references to
    it. A full check of a typical 100-GB hard disk can take hours. Do not
    use Encase from within the same computer you are interested in
    checking for the absence of sensitive data; otherwise, you risk creat-
    ing temporary and other files containing precisely the keywords you
    don't want to find.

Keep in mind that if the computer you are trying to clean is a networked
corporate one, the network administrator can readily detect what you are
installing (or have installed).

Numerous other software packages for overwriting data are reasonably
good, but each has its own peculiarities and shortcomings. See www.cotse.
net/users/bluejay for an objective comparison. Specifically:

1. The file-wiping function of many versions of Pretty Good Privacy
    (PGP) freeware has been found to be flawed. If one wants to use it
    anyway, see http://www.cotse.net/usersbluejaypgpwipe.html for a
    thorough hand holding on how to do it properly.

2. The disingenuously named Evidence Eliminator has a lot of contro-
    versy associated with it because of its makers' scare tactics in
    advertising it.

A more complete list from www.fortunecity.com/skyscraper/true/882/
Comparison_Shredders.htm includes information about shredders' other
qualities (or lack thereof), such as availability and pricing.

Other additional software products are available for disk wiping that
have not been specifically evaluated. They include, but are not limited to,
the following:

▸ Shredder 2.0 by Strafor Systems;

▸ Cover Your Tracks 3.0 by FatFree Software (http://www.ffsoft-
  ware.com);

▸ Shiva, Destroyer of Files by Isis Software (http://isis-software.com);

▸ Nuker by Genio.

Because disk cleaning can take many hours, it is self-evident that a
security-conscious user cannot use it against an imminent threat. If one is in
such an environment (e.g., a totalitarian regime), one must disk clean on a
very regular basis on the assumption that the door could be broken down by
an intruder at any time.

2.1.4   Magnetic microscopy forensic examination of disks

Albert Bell Isle of Cerberus Systems identifies three classes of computer forensic threats to files. Class 1 attacks use forensic software only. They can be defeated by disk overwriting of

1. All copies of a file (including fragments of it);
2. The entire file allocation table and names files and their attributes;
3. The swap file.

Class 2 attacks use special amplifiers and signal processing and can recover, with variable degrees of success, some overwritten files. The degree of success depends on specifics, such as how many times a file has been overwritten and with what data patterns, the physics of the magnetic media in question, the disk size and manufacturer, and so forth.

Class 3 attacks use magnetic force microscopy (MFM), which is derived from scanning probe microscopy. Techniques based on MFM are very expensive and can potentially get around most any kind of software-controlled overwriting. According to Peter Gutman [1],

> [E]ven for a relatively inexperienced user the time to start getting images of the data on a drive platter is about 5 minutes. To start getting useful images of a particular track requires more than a passing knowledge of disk formats, but these are well-documented, and once the correct location on the platter is found a single image would take [a few minutes] depending on the skill of the operator and the resolution required. With one of the more expensive MFMs it is possible to automate a collection sequence and theoretically possible to collect an image of the entire disk by changing the MFM controller software.

The latest variant of MFM uses magnetic force scanning tunneling microscopy (STM).

The basic principle of STM is based on the tunneling current between a metallic tip, which is sharpened to a single atom point, and a conducting material as shown in Figure 2.1. (For a tutorial, see www.chembio. uoguelph.ca/educmat/chm729/STMpage/stmdet.htm).

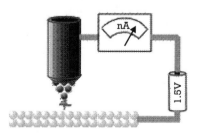

Figure 2.1   Scanning tunneling microscopy (simplified diagram). [Courtesy of Tit-Wah Hui (thui@uoguelph.ca).]

STM is more sensitive and may damage the surface of the disk being investigated. According to Gutman, "There [were—as of 1996], from manufacturers sales figures, several thousand SPM's in use in the field, some of which have special features for analyzing disk drive platters, such as the vacuum chucks for standard disk drive platters along with specialized modes of operation for magnetic media analysis. These SPM's can be used with sophisticated programmable controllers and analysis software to allow automation of the data recovery process. If commercially-available SPMs are considered too expensive, it is possible to build a reasonably capable SPM for about US$1,400, using a PC as a controller." There is also a new patent on Magnetic Disk Erasers in Japan (see http://www.research.ibm.com/journal/rd/445/patents.html)."

From the attacker's perspective, an assessment is likely to be made as to the possibility of using any less expensive, alternate ways of obtaining the same data, such as those discussed in Sections 4.1 through 4.9.

The best reference on advanced attacks against magnetic media is a somewhat dated paper (1996) (www.cs.auckland.ac.nz/~pgut001/secure_del.html) by Peter Gutmann of the Department of Computer Science of the University of Auckland (pgut001@cs.auckland.ac.nz), titled "Secure Deletion of Data from Magnetic and Solid State Memory."

An excellent collection of stunning photographs of microscopic remnants of "erased" magnetic recordings can be found at Digital Instruments's Web site http://www.veeco.com.

In general, the forensic analysis of magnetic media using conventional microscopy is becoming increasingly difficult because of the ever-increasing density of magnetic storage in off-the-shelf commercial media used by practically all computers nowadays. Today's densities approach 1 GB per square inch, which means that the intrinsic size of magnetic features is smaller than the wavelength of even blue light. That is why a new technique, MFM, which uses the power of SPM, is needed to do forensic analysis on such media. This technique allows one to "see" features as small as 50 nm (1 nm = 0.000000001m).

2.2   Where is the sensitive data hiding?

Unfortunately for the privacy-conscious professional, sensitive data is hiding in far too many places, all of which have to be considered.

To understand where and why, some minimal technical background needs to be presented first.

2.2.1   Cluster tips or slack

Whereas the LP music records of yesteryear stored music in a long spaghetti-like single groove, computer disks are divided into a large number of totally separate bins that store information. At the risk of oversimplifying the issue, each such bin is called a "cluster" (because it consists of a bunch of smaller bins called "sectors," but that is irrelevant to this discussion).

The size of each bin (that is, how much data can fit in each cluster) depends on the total capacity of the disk, on the operating system being used (that is, whether it is DOS, Windows 95, Windows 98, or Windows NT), and on what each user has selected in cases where there is a choice. The size of each such cluster can vary from 256 bytes (one byte is essentially one alphabetical symbol or number) all the way up to more than 65,536 bytes (always a power of 2; i.e., 2 multiplied by itself a number of times).

DOS and all versions of Windows share one rule: They will not allow any one such cluster to have data from more than a single file (a file can be a piece of software, a user-created document, an image, and so forth). Of course, a file may well require numerous clusters. For example, lets assume that the cluster size is 512 bytes and that a file takes 768 bytes; this will take about one and a half clusters. It is important to understand what happens to the remaining half cluster.

Windows will never write less than one cluster-full of data onto a cluster; if it only needs to write half of the cluster, it will mark where the file ends (a.k.a. the end-of-file mark). If the cluster is relatively small, the computer will usually fill out the rest of the cluster with whatever data happens to be floating about in portions of the computer's electronic memory [a.k.a. random access memory (RAM)]. The security nightmare that results is obvious: Passwords that were manually typed and went to RAM, never intended to be immortalized for posterity one one's disk, may well end up in this "dead space" between the end-of-file and end-of-cluster marks and stay there for the benefit of whoever can retrieve that information.

If the space between the end of file and the end of the cluster is substantial, the computer will usually not bother to write anything in that space, allowing whatever had been written there before to survive—again to the delight of the forensic investigator.

This space between end of file and end of cluster is known as a "cluster tip" or slack in the computer forensics trade. It is one of the most productive areas of a computer forensics investigation of one's computer.

Indeed, there is very little, if anything, that a computer user can do to prevent sensitive data from getting placed on the hard disk in the slack. About all one can do is to use special software (some available freely worldwide; some available commercially) to erase any and all data placed by a computer on one's disk behind one's back.

2.2.2   Free space

When a computer file is deleted using the normal delete command in DOS or by placing it in the Recycle Bin in Windows, the file is not deleted at all. (If it were, then the many undelete commands would not work.)

The portion of the disk that records which file is where merely makes a note of the fact that this particular file is no longer desired and that the space it occupies on the disk can be used in the future by other files if necessary.

In the course of using a disk, be it a hard disk, a humble floppy disk, or most any other magnetic storage media, one ends up having a disk with a lot of ostensibly deleted information that is very much present for the benefit of a computer forensic investigator. This so-called free space is a goldmine of information for the forensic investigator and a major headache for the computer user. About the only way to get rid of those files is to do the electronic equivalent of erasing them by overwriting those clusters with assorted patterns of nonsense data.

But even that is not enough. The name of the thusly erased file is stored in a different location of the disk; if the name is incriminating (say, freedom.doc in a totalitarian regime), the user can end up in trouble if the disk is analyzed by a forensic investigator.

Changing the name of the file (from freedom.doc to long_live_the_leader.doc) is not enough either. Computers are a forensic investigator's dream because in addition to the files themselves, they also contain data about each file. Such data could include when the file was created, when it was modified, what software was used, and so forth. The security-conscious user must see that it that this data about the data is also erased.

2.2.3 The swap file

This is an important topic in itself and is treated in Section 2.3. By way of a summary, this is the portion of a hard disk that Windows uses for temporary storage of data that would normally have belonged in the volatile RAM but doesn't fit there. As such, this file can include just about anything, specifically passwords that were never intended to end up on a hard disk, drafts that were never saved to disk, and so forth. The more RAM one has, the less one needs a swap file, Microsoft admonitions to the contrary notwithstanding. If one has enough RAM, one does not need a swap file at all; fortunately, one can easily set the swap file size to zero in such a case.

Removing the swap file is not much different from removing any file. One should find it and wipe it (i.e., overwrite it a number of times). Its location can be anywhere one wants it to be, and it is called win386.swp in Windows 95/98 for historical reasons.

Overwriting it cannot be done from within Windows. One can boot, for example, from DOS, find it, and use a good overwriting utility to wipe it.

2.2.4 Spool and temporary files

As files are sent by a user to the printer, they are usually spooled to a queue (a file created for the occasion on one's hard disk). As soon as they are printed, they are "deleted" from this queue, which means that they remain on the hard disk in the spool files for a forensic investigator to find until and unless that disk space is overwritten intentionally or in the normal course of storing other files on the hard disk.

2.2.5 Forensics on nonmagnetic disks

Whereas magnetic media used to be about the only media used for recording personal computer data in the past, today one can avail oneself of
other media as well, such as the popular USB key devices (see Figure 2.1),
which use the same technology used in digital cameras and MP3 music
players.

Such solid-state media (no moving parts) are every bit as vulnerable to
the same computer forensic techniques as conventional digital media. They
use clusters just like magnetic media and usually adhere to the FAT32 standards used in practically all non-NTFS magnetic disks. As with magnetic
disks, ostensibly deleted data stays very much alive until it happens to be
overwritten; similarly, data in the slack (the space between the end-of-file
and end-of-cluster marks) can survive for many years, long after the user
has forgotten about it.

2.2.6 History files

Many software applications have the habit of creating a history file of what a
user has done with that application. A typical example is the still-popular
Netscape Web browser Navigator/Communicator that creates a file called
netscape.hst; interestingly, this file

1. Is not needed by anything and can be safely deleted (at which point
    Navigator/Communicator will create a new one from that point on
    unless active measures are taken by the user to prevent that—see
    Chapters 10 through 14);

2. Records everything a user has done with Netscape Navigator/Com-
    municator online or offline since the software was installed;

3. Is not readable with conventional Windows text editors, so the aver-
    age user is kept in the blind as to its function (it actually uses
    Berkeley DB 1.85 hash table format).

Microsoft system software and applications have comparable tendencies
to create assorted history files. Unless the user knows their names and locations, chances are they are not deleted or modified.

Even some security-related application software, such as some firewalls,
create a history file showing the dates and times for every instance of a
user's going online.

2.2.7 Data in the registry files

This is an important topic in itself and is treated in Section 2.4. Many users
are rightly reluctant to tinker with the Registry because some mistakes
could render the computer unbootable; yet, this is precisely where a lot of
information of interest to forensic investigators resides.

2.2.8 Data from sloppy use of personal encryption software

The installation ritual of most application software involves numerous in-between steps, such as decompression, creation of temporary files, and so forth, all of which are stored in a temporary folder that is often specific to each such application software. Once installed, these files are sometimes deleted (meaning, they are left behind, but are invisible in the directory); often they are not. In all cases, they are left behind for the benefit of the forensic investigator unless the user takes active steps to overwrite all such files. In fact, the ones left undeleted are the worse offenders in that most users assume that what is left behind is still needed by the newly installed application, and such users will not remove them securely or otherwise.

2.2.9 Nonvolatile memory

When a computer is first turned on, it has no idea what to do with itself; it does not know if it has any magnetic media or anything about them, it does not know the date/time, it does not know how much memory (RAM) it has, it does not know whether to try to go to a hard disk first or to a floppy or to other media (such as CD-ROMs), and so forth.

All this information has to be stored somewhere other than a disk (which the computer initially does not even know whether it has or where it is), or the user would have to enter it manually every time. Nonvolatile memory almost always uses Complementary Metal Oxide Semiconductor (CMOS) technology; the name is a reference to the technology being used, which is an electronic memory that consumes very little power so that it can survive for many years with just a small external battery even if the computer is unplugged.

That same nonvolatile memory also stores any bootup passwords that some users enable. In theory, unless an aspiring user knows the magic password selected by the authorized user, he or she will not be able to get past this step. In practice, one can remove the battery keeping the information in the CMOS chip alive, whereupon, when the computer is turned on, the unauthorized user will be asked to enter his or her own choice of a new password (in addition to manually having to enter the system-related data, which can be done within a few minutes).

Additionally, many computer manufacturers who have tired of users' forgetting their CMOS passwords and asking for technical support have provided for backdoor-entry passwords that users can use to gain access to the respective manufacturers' computers. Needless to say, these backdoor keys have been posted on the Internet for anyone who wants them (see Section 4.11.1).

2.3 The swap file as a source of forensic data

2.3.1 General

The swap file (a.k.a. "paging file" or "virtual memory") is a major source of forensic information for a computer investigator. To an individual interested in maintaining the privacy of his or her computer files (e.g., an attorney with clients' privileged files, a physician with patients' confidential medical data, a businessman on a trip with a laptop containing his company's proprietary designs), this is a relatively easy threat to remove, although most normal users are only vaguely aware of it.

Basically, the swap file is a large space on one's hard disk. It typically takes up a few hundred megabytes', that is, a few hundred million alphabetical letters', worth of space. Windows places anything here data that currently resides in RAM memory (the electronic memory that "evaporates" when the power is turned off, as opposed to disk memory which stays) that Windows does not need at a particular instant to make room in memory for other data that is needed at that instant. An instant later, different data may be needed in memory, and Windows will juggle what is in RAM and in the swap disk file so that it has in RAM memory what it needs at any one instant in time. This way, a user with limited RAM can run more with less such memory.

From the perspective of the security-conscious reader, this file is an unmitigated disaster because it can end up including just about anything, such as passwords typed on a keyboard and never intended to be stored on disk, copies of sensitive files, and so forth. Even if a user securely deletes all evidence of a sensitive file (see Section 2.3.2), the swap file, if not specifically wiped, may well contain a copy of that same file or portions of it.

The amount of space allocated to the swap file on a disk is determined by Windows itself (in the default situation), but can be altered by the individual user. One would reasonably think that the more physical RAM memory one has, the less swap file size is needed; amusingly, Windows feels otherwise and assigns more swap file space when one has more RAM.

One can specify exactly how large a swap file one wishes to have (if any). Go to Start/Settings/Control Panel/System/Performance/Virtual Memory and specify what amount you desire (if any). One can ignore admonitions by Windows about not allowing Windows to decide this. In general, one would be well advised to have as much RAM memory as possible (at least 256 MB for Win95/98/NT/2000), and to disable any virtual memory completely. Doing so still leaves the hard disk with the last version of the swap file (called win386.swp in Windows 95/98/Me or pagefile.sys in Windows TN/2000/XP). This must be securely removed. If one has elected to allow numerous programs to run in the background (e.g., virus checkers, software firewalls), then one's RAM requirements can exceed the minimums suggested above. A good way to find just how much RAM one is actually using under normal circumstances is to run a small utility called SWAPMON by Gary Calpo of Flip Tech International, which is widely available at http://www.pinoyware.com/swapmon/index.shtml.

Even if one elects to have some disk space allocated to the swap file (not a good idea from a security perspective, as per above), it is strongly recommended that this amount be fixed by the user and not by Windows (which is the default setting), despite admonitions to the contrary by Windows. It is far easier for security utilities that wipe clean the swap file to do this on a fixed-size swap file than on one whose size changes all the time. The reason for this is obvious: If the size of the swap file is fixed, then wiping it (i.e., overwriting it) is straightforward. If its size changes all the time, then it is quite possible that its last size is smaller than the size of the previous time that the computer was used; wiping the smaller swap file will leave the evidence contained in the disk space that accommodates the difference between the smaller last swap file and the bigger previous one untouched and available to any forensic investigator.

The procedure for setting a fixed swap file is similar to that shown below for setting no swap file: The user simply selects the same value for minimum and maximum size of the swap file.

2.3.2   Securely wiping the swap file

This can only be done from DOS and never from within Windows. When starting, Windows opens up the swap file with exclusive access and doesn't allow any other application to access it to prevent the system from crashing.

Do not trust any wiping software that runs under Windows and claims to wipe the swap file. Many such programs try to do this by allocating very large amounts of memory and hoping that the operating system will write it to the disk, thereby—hopefully—overwriting the swap file; this is unacceptably insecure.

Some well-written disk-wiping files, however, wipe the swap file well because they "drop down" to DOS before wiping the swap file. Examples include Access Data Corporation's Secure Clean and others.

Because no one wiping program can be entirely trusted, a security-conscious user is well advised to use two different such programs in tandem, preferably one of them from within DOS.

Possibilities for wiping the swap file from DOS include the following:

1.   Using a DOS version of PGP, type pgp—w win386.swp.

2.   Using RealDelete (available from http://www.bonaventura.free-online.co.uk/realdelete), type realdel [win386.swp] /per /garb. The brackets are needed to wipe a file as a foreground task and the additional switches select personal security level—just one overwrite in this case—and a random data overwrite.

3.   Using Scribble, type SCRIBBLE /A/K c:\windows\win386.swp. The /K switch allows the file to remain as an entity after it is wiped clean.

Because a swap file is typically a few hundred megabytes long, this wiping will take a few minutes to complete.

Windows NT allows one to delete and overwrite with zeros the swap file as an automatic part of a shutdown. According to Microsoft's own Resource Kit, one must edit the Registry[2] (type regedit at the Run dialog) and go to

```
HKEY_LOCAL_MACHINE\System

\CurrentControlSet

\Control

\Session Manager

\Memory Management

ClearPageFileAtShutdown REG_DWORD

Range 0 or 1

Default 0

Set it to 1
```

Note that Windows NT will not overwrite the entire swap file because some of it is being used by NT. To overwrite the entire file, one must do so outside Windows (NT or any other platform). This can be done manually or using any commercially or freely disk-wipe software (see Chapters 9 through 12).

Do not change the size of the swap file by editing the Registry. To create a new paging file or to change its size, go to Control Panel/System/Performance/Virtual Memory/Change.

2.4   The Registry as a source of forensic data

2.4.1   Why is the Registry a major source of forensic evidence?

Most any user of Windows wants the computer to remember such things as which little icons he or she wants on the screen and where, what resolution monitor the computer is using, whether a a modem is connected to the computer and on which port, and so on. It would be very annoying and time-consuming to have the enter such information every time one turned the computer on.

In the Windows 3.1x days (Windows 3.1, 3.11 and Windows for Workgroups), all this information was stored in two easily accessible and readable files: win.ini and system.ini. These files were (and are) readily readable and editable with any text editor. If one uses a word processor for that function,

---

2. Caution: Back up the Registry first before doing any editing. How to do so depends on which version of Windows one is using. In Windows 95/98, for example, one can do so with Start/Run SCANREGW. In Windows NT, one can do so by creating an emergency backup disk with Start/Run RDISK /S.

on should make sure that the edited end results are saved as text-only and not as a formatted document.

With Windows 95/98/NT, these two files were replaced by the Registry, a seemingly bottomless pit full of data that is hard to read and much harder to edit. There is no file called the Registry per se. Instead, the Registry is the collective name for two very unique files called user.dat and system.dat, with the former being the biggest threat. They are unique in the following ways:

1. To even view them, one needs a special software (graciously provided by Microsoft) called REGEDIT or, in the case if Windows NT (which also accepts REGEDIT) REGEDT32; the latter does not recognize all the data types that REGEDIT does.

2. What you see is not what is there! Entries that have been removed with the above two software pieces are, in fact, nor removed at all! Appearances notwithstanding, they are very much there, but have been merely marked as "no longer current." A forensic investigator will find them extremely easily. Entries that have been edited out by REGEDIT do not get removed.[3]

3. Even if one does, in fact, truly remove offending entries in the Registry (using techniques presented in Sections 2.4.3 and 2.4.4), the slate still has not been wiped clean. A forensic investigator can easily find those entries because Windows stores backup copies of the Registry just in case it is corrupted and needs to be restored from a known working version (such as the backup copy). Removing the backup copies is doable but not recommended because Windows does, in fact, crash for many reasons, and a working copy of the Registry is a godsend; otherwise, one will most likely have to reinstall everything on the affected hard disk from scratch, including Windows and all applications software. For this reason it is extremely important always to have a (nonincriminating) fully functioning copy of the Registry around.

4. Windows and many applications software take it upon themselves to store far, far more in the Registry than any privacy-minded person would ever want. This includes, but is not limited to, the following:

    a. One's name, address, company affiliation, phone number, and so forth (entered by an unsuspecting individual when installing Windows and/or many application software);

---

3. Not until the Registry becomes as large as 500 KB, which will include a vast amount of ostensibly removed sensitive information, or until one types REGEDIT/OPT from within DOS. This is controlled through the line Optimize=1 in the scanreg.ini file in one's \Windows subdirectory.

Regedit does not really remove and compress the Registry (even though it pretends that it does) because the Registry is too long, and it would take some time for Windows to compress it to fill the hole every time an entry in it was removed.

b.   If Microsoft's Internet Explorer is used as a Web browser, what was browsed on the Internet recently, regardless who used that computer to do the browsing;

c.   Who uses the computer and what each user's preferences are;

d.   Every software product that was ever installed and what one did with each (most software that one uninstalls does not bother to remove its installation paper trail);

e.   Serial numbers and passwords in many cases of applications software;

f.   Messages downloaded from the Usenet newsgroups that leave traces to varying degrees in the Registry (if one lived in a totalitarian regime and patronized newsgroups dealing with freedom and equal rights, one may not want evidence of that to remain on the computer);

g.   Plaintext passwords in files that were supposed to be encrypted (look in content.ie5 and history.ie5).

Any and all of this information can be retrieved not only by a forensics examiner of one's computer, but also by any half-decent hacker while a user is on the Internet or any other network (unless special precautions have been taken as discussed in detail in Chapters 7 through 9). This is clearly unacceptable.

2.4.2   Where is all this private information hiding in the Registry?

The Registry consists of two key files: user.dat and system.dat. user.dat contains all sorts of personal information, which can be easily verified, usually to one's shock, by opening it with Notepad or Wordpad. One can then do a wildcard search (meaning a search for anything which includes any desired sequence of letters) for whatever one would wish were not in there, such as personal letters, proprietary business topics, and so forth. Do not edit this file with either Notepad or Wordpad.

Do not attempt to edit or clean up the Registry unless you first do the following:

1.   Back it up.

2.   Know how to restore it from such a backup if you inadvertently mess it up.

Section 2.4.3 spells out how to back up and restore the Registry.

In Windows 95/98, it is a good idea to run Registry Checker from the Startup/Programs/Accessories/System Tools menu before shutting down to be alerted to any Registry problems before shutting down.

2.4.3 Backing up the Registry and restoring a corrupted one

Windows NT

Start/Run rdisk/s. This will ask for a floppy disk to be inserted into the A: drive, onto which the computer will save the entire Windows NT Registry.

Restoring the Registry from this disk is done by following the standard Windows NT restore process (see Windows NT documentation), which amounts to starting a reinstallation, but opting for a Registry restoration when the option is offered.

2.4.4 Cleaning up sensitive data in the Registry

First of all, keep the following in mind:

1. Windows keeps multiple copies of the Registry so that if the most recent gets corrupted, Windows can use the precious copy and still function. As such, cleaning up the last copy is not enough. On the other hand, overwriting all of the previous versions is very risky in case the latest version has become nonfunctional as a result of careless editing. Remove the previous versions only after you have made sure that the latest version is stable.

2. Editing the Registry with REGEDIT gives the illusion that offending lines are removed; they are not. They are only marked as being offline. If you want to really remove them after editing REGEDIT, use RegClean.exe available free from Microsoft.

Do not try to edit the Registry file "as is" with any text editor or even a hex editor because of the high likelihood of corrupting it. Instead, do the following:

Method 1

1. Start/Run regedit.

2. Search for and remove any and all references to whatever you consider sensitive, making sure not to remove default settings that Windows needs to run. For instance, the "secret file" that Media Player uses to store a list of recently played items is in HKEY_CURRENT_USERS\Software\Microsoft\MediaPlayer\Player\ Recent\URLList. Delete all values except "Default."

    A related concern is information in the file index.dat. It, too, can be examined using any text editor (e.g., Notepad or Wordpad).

    The biggest concern may well be with the most recently used (MRU) list kept in the Registry, which essentially records one's latest batch of activities with the computer. This has no socially redeeming value other and could potentially entrap the user.

    One should delete all values except those showing a "Default" as a value in each and every one of the following keys:

- HKEY_CURRENT_USER\Software\Microsoft\Windows\Current-Version\Explorer\Doc Find Spec MRU;

- HKEY_CURRENT_USER\Software\Microsoft\Windows\Current-Version\Explorer\FindComputerMRU;

- HKEY_CURRENT_USER\Software\Microsoft\Windows\Current-Version\Explorer\PrnPortsMRU;

- HKEY_CURRENT_USER\Software\Microsoft\Windows\Current-Version\Explorer\RunMRU;

- HKEY_CURRENT_USER\Software\Microsoft\Windows\Current-Version\Explorer\StreamMRU.

    Not all of the above keys may exist in every computer. Again, do not delete the "Default" value. Also, do not remove any files that list all of the folders in your disk drive; if you do, you won't really lose anything, but your settings and preferences will revert back to default settings.

3.   Boot into DOS.

4.   Type regedit /e registry.txt (the "/e registry.txt" suffix exports the Registry into a text file called "registry" as a single text file that one can use to see what is in the suspect Registry and also to restore the Registry if it is inadvertently corrupted).

5.   Look at the text file called "registry" with Wordpad or Notepad to ensure that nothing inappropriate is still there.

6.   Now type regedit /c registry.txt. Restoring a Registry file this way without editing it should remove references to files that were edited out (but not truly removed) with REGEDIT.

Method 2

To compact the Registry in order to really remove entries that have been edited out with REGEDIT, go to DOS first (by clicking on the "Command Prompt" icon in the Start/Programs list, or, better yet, by turning the computer off and booting into DOS) and type Scanreg/opt. Scanreg/fix from within DOS should also clean up fragments in user.dat.

    Caution: As stated above, Windows maintains backup copies of the Registry as user.da0, system.da0, user.da1, system.da1, and so forth. Cleaning up the primary Registry does not clean up these backups.

    It is not a good idea to delete these backups, just in case one has damaged the Registry inadvertently, and it has to be restored from a working backup.

    After one has ascertained that the newly cleaned-up Registry works, then one can force backups of it as shown above.

    This still does not wipe the forensic slate clean because deletion and overwriting do not usually remove what was there before. One must then go through the process of wiping the disk clean as discussed in detail in

Section 2.1, which includes overwriting the slack (a.k.a. cluster tips), the free space, and the file names.

This is all very tedious and, as a result, unlikely to be followed by most individuals on any regular basis. A convenient alternative is for one to use software available either commercially (such as the disingenuously named Evidence Eliminator from http://www.evidenceeliminator.com in the United Kingdom), Secure Clean from http://www.whitecanyon.com, Window Washer from www.webroot.com, or other such software.

Evidence Eliminator seems to have done a thorough job of covering many of the bases (but not to the extent claimed by its advertising), but there is a cloud of suspicion about it in connection with the allegation that in the case of "blacklisted registration numbers" (the number that one enters to convert it from the one-month free-trial version to the paid version), it may pretend to eliminate sensitive data, but in fact may not. Also, while it may be a very good program of this genre, numerous Usenet postings allegedly written by that company have done a disservice to its reputation.

Reference

[1]   Gutman, P., "Secure Deletion of Data from Magnetic and Solid State Memory" hhttp://www.cs.auckland.ac.nz/npgut001/pubs/secure_del.html

Specialized Forensics Applications

3.1 Digital watermarking

Clearly, today's society cannot function without the legal protection of intellectual property on a global scale. The creators of practically every technology in use today (e.g., MRI medical imaging machines, lasers, video recordings), of pharmaceuticals, and of every piece of art, rightfully need to be protected from those who would profit or otherwise benefit at no cost from these creators' work.

Anything, copyrighted or not, can be digitized, stored, and sent out to the world nowadays: music, text, photographs, images, speech, and so forth. And copyrighted or not, digitized information can be copied and distributed worldwide on a massive scale, whether via the Internet or physical means, with astonishing ease. Justifiably, the owners of the intellectual property or the copyright holders take great offense to losing revenue and credit for their work. What is the solution?

Laws criminalizing copyright infringement, in and of themselves, are no more effective than laws banning bad weather.[1] This is well known to any patent holder because patent applications are intentionally circumspect so as not to allow someone else to figure out exactly how the patented implementation works by reading the patent. Certainly the process of

---

1. Although the Napster and Gnutella of a few years ago have gone legal, the practice of illegal trading of music pieces from CD music albums has become more sophisticated through the use of peer-to-peer networks. The well-publicized series of lawsuits against a few hundred individual teenagers and their parents by the Recording Industry Association of America (RIAA) has backfired through the very negative public relations atmosphere that ensued.

appending a "©" after some published work does not physically prevent anyone from violating the copyright.

One must actively protect the copyrighted material. This is far more complex than it seems for the following reasons:

1. From a business perspective, any technical means to protect the copyrighted content must not interfere with legitimate purchasers' use of it. Recent deployments of copyrighted technology on music CDs that prevent users from playing those disks on some CD players and on computer CD players have backfired as buyers have stopped buying such CDs altogether.

2. Many music artists feel that they can get more exposure (and more sales downstream) by making their own early work available online, thereby short-circuiting the CD distribution channels.

3. From a legal perspective, any such laws or technical means also must not interfere with legitimate users' other legal rights, such as the fair use right (in the United States) to make an archival copy. Currently, the U.S. Digital Millennium Copyright Act (DMCA) of 1998 (see Section 16.4.1) is in direct conflict with this legal right, as are the various copy-protection schemes used by DVD vendors.

4. A determination must be made that a copy is truly unauthorized. Under the fair use doctrine, it is perfectly legal (and quite wise) for George to have an archival copy of a DVD that he purchased. It is not legal for Mary to have a copy of George's DVD, however.

5. Identifying a truly unauthorized copy of copyrighted work is not particularly useful for law enforcement, which wants to know who made it.

Unless some means can be found to demonstrate that a copy of a copyrighted item is illegal and which original it came from, effective prosecution is unlikely. Furthermore, the high legal cost and intensely negative public relations impact of prosecuting an underage person for making an

---

Independently, the DeCSS software allows one to break the (weak) encryption used by the Hollywood studios in DVD disks. As many may know by now, the U.S. courts ruled in favor of the Motion Picture Association of America (MPAA), which represented the Hollywood studios and made it illegal for U.S. Web sites even to post the URL of the many places where the DeCSS code could be found; this led to the humorous result of individuals sporting the DeCSS code on their T-shirts as an act protected by the First Amendment to the Constitution, which protects free speech. However, in a major setback to the MPAA that underscores the futility of expecting different sovereign nations' laws to become uniform, in December 2003 the Norwegian appellate court affirmed the decision of a lower Norwegian court, which found the young creator of DeCSS innocent of all charges.

unauthorized copy of an item that would have cost about $15 to buy are disproportionate to the cost of the alleged offense[2].

Quite clearly, there is a growing need for "digital watermarking" technology that can:

1. Show the origin of the work copied.

2. Show that it is copyrighted or someone else's intellectual property to preempt the "I didn't know" defense.

3. Show, if possible, the exact pathway that the unauthorized copy took from the original authorized owner to the present unauthorized one, so that the correct individual(s) can be chastised for the breach of trust.

4. Show whether the digital image has been altered.

Figure 3.1 shows the use of digital watermarking in highlighting the specific areas where a watermarked image has been altered.

A digital watermark has to be robust, meaning that it should survive efforts to remove it. For example, if the work being protected is an image, the digital watermark should not be "washable" with the extensive image-enhancement operations that any user of an image-processing software, like Adobe Photoshop, can perform (e.g., cropping, resampling, filtering, color and contrast changes).

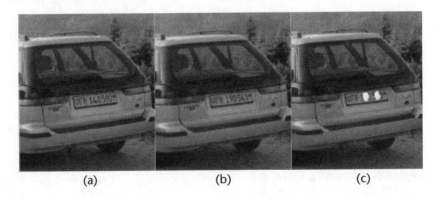

     (a)   (b)   (c)

Figure 3.1 (a–c) Digital watermarks for verifying integrity. Digits 4 and 9 were swapped in image (b). Watermarking causes the changes to be highlighted.

2. This writer intentionally avoids the term *piracy*; it is a term that evokes images of drunken savages roaming the high seas, attacking peace-loving vessels, torching, raping, and killing. Use of this evocative term to characterize a teenager's possession of a nonpurchased copy of a computer game was an ingenious act of self-serving posturing by software, CD, and DVD makers who wanted to capitalize on the evocative connotations of the term. *Unauthorized copy* is a far more accurate term.

Technically, this is a tall order: Some image-saving formats (such as JPEG) are intentionally "lossy" in that they remove a lot of information from an image, thereby massively reducing the size of the digital file; to their credit, they do so with an impressively low reduction in the visual appeal of the image. A similar situation exists with music files: MP3 reduces the amount of digital storage required without a perceptible difference in the quality. Thus, it is a lot to ask the following of a digital watermark:

1. That it be preserved despite such drastic reductions in the digital storage requirements (hence, the information content) of a digital file;

2. That it be imperceptible to our ears and eyes so that the sound file or image appeals to our senses.

The technology behind digital watermarking is no different from the steganography used to hide the mere existence of messages (see Section 11.5).

The two classes of techniques used amount to:

1. Modifying part of the file (e.g., changing the least significant bit of some pixels (picture elements) or sound files)

2. Modifying the entire file by spreading the digital watermark (or steganographically hidden message) over the entire file.

Some of the most sophisticated digital watermarks involve two watermarks: one that is simple to spot and remove, whose purpose is to mislead a transgressor into thinking that the watermark has been removed, and a second that is much harder to identify and that is intended to catch the transgressor.

Commercial digital watermarking products can be found at the following URLs, among others:

▸ Aliroo, http://www.aliroo.com;

▸ ICE Company, http://www.digital-watermark.com;

▸ Digimarc, http://www.digimarc.com;

▸ Fraunhofer Institute for Computer Graphics, http://syscop.igd.fhg.de.

Numerous new companies are entering this potentially lucrative field. Indeed, the Hollywood-based entertainment industry has been proceeding very aggressively towards the establishment of numerous digital-watermarking schemes. The Galaxy Group of consumer electronics companies (IBM, NEC, Hitachi, Pioneer, and Sony) have already agreed on a new digital-watermarking standard. Numerous venture capital firms, such as a new Korean firm TrusTech, are doing likewise.

Not to be outdone, watermarking-negation schemes have also been proliferating, and several software packages, such as the following, exist that can negate a digital watermark in many cases:

1. 2Mosaic_0.1, at http://www.cl.cam.ac.uk/~fapp2/watermarking/ image_watermarking/2mosaic, can take a JPG image that has been watermarked, divide it into many smaller images, none big enough to contain enough information to prove the existence of the original watermark, send them across the Internet, and then reconstruct them at the other end.

2. UnZine, available for Win9x, removes the digital signature from a digitally copyrighted image.

3. StirMark removes most of the watermarks available commercially. It is available from http://www.cl.cam.ac.uk/~fapp2/watermarking/ image_watermarking/stirmark/index.html.

3.2   The British RIP Act and the US Carnivore (DCS1000)

The effectiveness of any measure is not measured with a yes/no verdict, but is a question of degree and ultimately of cost-effectiveness.

The Regulation of Investigatory Powers (RIP) Act of 2000 is a new British law that authorizes a number of British authorities to intercept Internet communications and to seize decryption keys used either to protect the confidentiality of such communications or to protect the confidentiality of data stored in individual computers. RIP dictates that every electronic communication has to be sent to the Government Technical Assistance Center (GTAC), which is being established at the London headquarters of the British security service, MI5 (analogous to the U.S. FBI). The official text of this law can be found at www.legislation.hmso.gov.uk/acts/acts2000/ 20000023.htm. See also www.idg.net/ic_238302_2340_1-1483.html.

"Carnivore" was the disingenuously chosen name for a computer-based tool used by U.S. federal law enforcement authorities; it has now been renamed DCS1000 as of early 2001. It is intended to be attached to an ISP's circuits—with ISP permission—where it scoops up a large amount of traffic. Subsequently, law enforcement personnel identify and read the portion of that collected traffic that pertains to a targeted individual for whom a duly executed court warrant has been obtained. See www.robertgraham.com/pubs/carnivore-faq.html and www.cdt.org/security/carnivore.

Other countries are likely to have equivalent laws and devices that have not received any publicity, notably including the use of force without the authority of any law.

All of these laws and devices will be largely ineffective in their intended purposes for the following technical reasons:

1. Internet communications can defeat interception simply by establishing end-to-end encryption between one's computer and the host computer to which one is connected.

a. This is already routine in the case of Secure Socket Layer (SSL) connections to Web sites that handle most individuals' online purchases using credit cards. It is simple to extend SSL connections to the entire connection.

b. The forthcoming new Internet protocol IPv6 will allow any two computers to negotiate and use session-specific encryption for each session and to destroy those keys automatically immediately thereafter, thereby rendering them inaccessible to law enforcement.

c. Freely available software products (see Section 10.2.5) allow any two individuals to establish fully encrypted two-way voice communications; the encryption keys vanish the moment their respective computers are turned off.

2. Any individual in the world can establish an Internet account with an out-of-country ISP. Such ISPs are not bound by the provisions of any one country's laws to provide local authorities with data, such as a targeted subscriber's e-mail. Of course, in a totalitarian regime that has the technical means to monitor all telephone communications leaving the country (including satellite and cellular ones), a call to an out-of-country ISP would be alerting.

3. It is routine nowadays for individuals to have numerous ISPs and to change some or all of them at a moment's notice and very frequently, especially as many are free today. With the proliferation of ISPs, it is not cost-effective for law enforcement to target each and every one (either with an RIP-authorized hardwired connection or with a Carnivore device).

4. The use of publicly accessible terminals (e.g., Internet cafes, public libraries, terminals at airports and in hotel lobbies, Wi-Fi "hot spots"; see Section 13.2), in conjunction with recently created, free Internet accounts at out-of-country servers, will make it impossible for law enforcement to identify who is communicating with whom. If encryption is added to the brew, then the content will also be inaccessible.

5. Strong and properly used steganography (see Section 11.5) makes it very hard for law enforcement to identify the mere existence of encrypted traffic. If the messages are brief and have a prearranged meaning (e.g., a Usenet message that states, "For Sale: One dining room table and four chairs," could have the prearranged meaning, "Let's meet at location number one at 4 P.M."), then detection will be impossible.

6. One-time-pad encryption, openly known about for a very long time (see Section 10.2.1), can easily be used so that the key to be surrendered to law enforcement yields an innocuous decrypted message while another key, whose existence will not be acknowledged, would be needed to yield the real message.

7.   Outgoing PGP-encrypted e-mail (see Section 11.3), if properly con-
     figured, cannot be decrypted by the sender but only by the recipient,
     who may be in another country. The in-country person could only
     decrypt incoming PGP-encrypted e-mail, over which he or she has
     no control and for which he or she is therefore not likely to be held
     legally accountable.

In conclusion, the following is evident from the foregoing:

1.   Laws and devices will catch the unsophisticated target of computer
     forensics but not the technically sophisticated one, who presumably
     is (or should be) of most interest to law enforcement. Mundane petty
     crime does not justify the use of national-level massive resources and
     expenditures when it is clear from the above that the real threats
     (terrorists, narcotraffickers, and so forth.) will be able to defeat any
     such broad-scope surveillance systems.

2.   As time goes on and technical sophistication trickles downwards,
     more and more targets of computer forensics will be out of the reach
     of law enforcement.

3.   From an economic perspective, the costs of implementing technical
     means for the wholesale interception of Internet traffic will rapidly
     reach the point of diminishing returns because of the combined
     effect of encryption, steganography, increasingly vast amounts of
     traffic, practically achievable anonymity, and the global nature of
     the Internet.

In view of the foregoing, the logical inference is that the deployment of
massively expensive surveillance techniques like the United Kingdom's RIP
Act, the United States's DCS1000, and other countries' equivalents, are
either

1.   Not well thought out;

2.   Intended for large-scale control of a country's own citizens, not for
     the professed reason of catching terrorists and narcotraffickers.

Finally, one must consider the fact that both RIP and DCS1000 (and
related tools) have far more technical capability than that allowed by applicable laws in their respective countries. Responsible professionals are
expected to abide by such laws and not to exceed their authority, and by
and large, most do.

Selected bibliography

There is a vast amount of background and reference material on digital
watermarking. More than 60 pages of references can be found in an anno-
tated bibliography on information hiding by R. J. Anderson and F. Peticolas

of the University of Cambridge's Computer Laboratory. Some of the most relevant of these references are the following:

[1]   Anderson, J., (ed.), "Information Hiding: First International Workshop," *Lecture Notes in Computer Science, Isaac Newton Institute, Cambridge, England,* Vol. 1174, Berlin: Springer-Verlag, May 1996.

[2]   Bender, W., et al., "Techniques for Data Hiding," *IBM Systems Journal,* Vol. 35, Nos. 3/4, 1996, pp. 313–336.
       This provides a good survey of techniques used in data hiding.

[3]   Hsu, C., et al., "Hidden Digital Watermarks in Images," *IEEE Transactions on Image Processing,* Vol. 8, No. 1, January 1999, pp. 58–68.
       This document discusses JPEG image watermarkings that survive cropping, enhancement, and lossy JPEG compression.

[4]   Minitzer, F., et al., "If One Watermark Is Good, Are More Better?" *International Conference on Acoustics, Speech and Signal Processing,* Vol. 80, pp. 2067–2070.
       The document shows why the order in which watermarks are applied is important.

[5]   Paskin, N., "Towards Unique Identifiers," *Proc. IEEE,* Vol. 87, No. 7, July 1999, pp. 1197–1207.
       This is a good tutorial on the overall subject, including definitions and requirements.

[6]   Schneider, B., et al., "Subliminal Channels in the Digital Signature Algorithm," *Computer Security Journal,* Vol. 9, No. 2, 1993, pp. 57–63.
       Discusses covert communications channels that a user of a digital signature algorithm can use.

[7]   Solachidis, V., et al., "Circularly Symmetric Watermark Embedding in 2-D DFT Domain," *International Conference on Acosutics, Speech and Signal Processing,* Vol. 80, pp. 1653–1656.
       This document shows a watermarking means that is robust to rotation and scaling.

For some technical papers on digital watermarks, the interested reader is referred to the following documents, which can be obtained from the Internet:

Brassil, J., et al., "Electronic Marking and Identification Techniqes to Discourage Document Copying," *AT&T Bell Labs,* Murray Hill, NJ, http://www.jjtc.com/ Steganography/bib/3000031.htm.

Low, S. H., et al., "Document Marking and Identification Techniques," University of Melbourne, http://tsi.enst.fr/~maitre/ tatouage/icip97/maxemchuk-97.pdf.

CHAPTER

4

Contents

How Can Sensitive Data Be Stolen From One's Computer?

4.1 Physical possession of one's computer

The fact that physical possession of one's computer by a third party allows that third party to search for all data on it is self-evident and needs no further elaboration. It is the basic premise behind computer forensics. If there is any unencrypted information left behind on one's confiscated, stolen, or borrowed data-storage media, and if the forensics investigation is competent enough, that information will be found. Physical possession does not have to be clandestine; when computers are taken to be serviced, service technicians and, by extension, anyone else they give your media to have full access to them.

4.2 Temporary physical access to one's computer

Temporary physical access to a targeted computer is just as good as full possession of it if such physical access lasts long enough to allow one to make a full copy of the disk(s) in the targeted computer. For legal reasons related to having to show in court that the disk(s) copied could not have been contaminated by the copying process, the disks have to be disconnected from the targeted computer and connected to another one that will copy them. Safeback is one of the standard pieces of software used to make a track-by-track and sector-by-sector copy of a targeted disk onto another disk of equal or greater capacity. Encase, a full suite of forensic software, includes this copying function as well.

If the purpose of the forensic investigation is to collect data without having to show it in court, then disks can be copied without being removed from a computer as long as the

53

investigator has taken steps to ensure that there is no booby-trapped soft-ware running that will delete or modify the disk(s) being copied by a stranger.

There is a darker side to temporary access to one's computer. An entire industry, as well as a major subculture, has evolved and matured whose purpose is to exploit large numbers of compromised always-on personal computers for profit or just for fun. Spammers (senders of unsolicited e-mail), threatened by the increasing amounts of legislation against such unsolicited e-mail, have turned to staging their mass mailings from unsus-pecting users' computers; similarly, perpetrators of distributed denial-of-access attacks use large numbers of unsuspecting users' computers (called "zombies") as staging platforms for attacks against the target selected. Last but not least, war drivers (see Section 13.2.2) use unsuspecting users' Wi-Fi wireless access points to access the Internet to perpetrate any illegal act they feel like.

4.3   Commercial hardware keystroke loggers

Keystroke recorders have been around for years. One such example is a commercial device that is openly available worldwide from a New Zealand firm that goes by the name of Keyghost Company (http://www.keyg-host.com), which looks like a small adaptor on the cable connecting one's keyboard to the computer. This device requires no external power (and hence lasts indefinitely) and no software installation (and hence cannot be detected by any software).

Numerous versions are available to anyone; these are shown in Figure 4.1.

Figures 4.2 and 4.3 below depict the keystroke-capturing device itself, with and without adaptors for different computers.

The device comes with the requisite adapters and manual out of the box for installation by nonspecialists, as shown in Figure 4.4.

When installed, the commercial keystroke-capturing device looks as shown in the Figures 4.5 and 4.6.

The high-end models, which sell for less than $250, can store upwards of 500,000 keystrokes; this is about 80,000 words, or about a 160-page

Model	Capacity	Ghost Playback	Encryption	Fast Download Adapter	Casing
Keyghost II Professional SE	2,000,000 Keystrokes	Yes	128 bit	Yes	EMC Balun
Keyghost II Professional	500,000 Keystrokes	Yes	128 bit	Yes	EMC Balun
Keyghost II Standard	97,000 Keystrokes	Yes	None	No	EMC Balun
Keyghost Mini Covert	120,000 Keystrokes	No	N/A	Yes	PS-2 Plug
Keyghost II Security Keyboard (Pro)	500,000 Keystrokes	Yes	128 bit	Yes	Keyboard
Keyghost II Security Keyboard (Std)	97,000 Keystrokes	Yes	None	No	Keyboard

Figure 4.1   Various versions of keystroke capturing by Keyghost device.

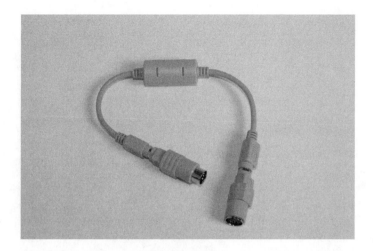

Figure 4.2 Keyghost keystroke-capturing device with some adaptors.

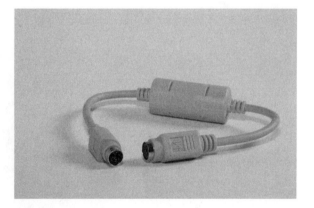

Figure 4.3 Keyghost keystroke-capturing device without adaptors.

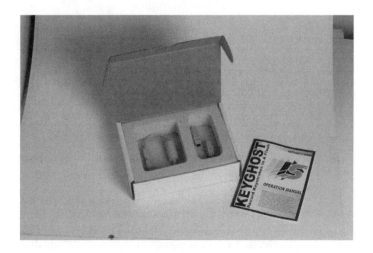

Figure 4.4 Keyghost keystroke-capturing device is easily installed by anyone.

Figure 4.5 Unmodified keyboard cable.

Figure 4.6 Modified keyboard cable.

paperback book. Special versions can be ordered from that company that can capture and store one to four million keystrokes.

A *keyghost mini* looks like a normal keyboard extension cable.

One can also buy a standard or Microsoft Natural keyboard with the keystroke-capturing device built in, making it totally invisible shown in Figure 4.7.

The captured keystrokes are stored in the device in 128-bit encrypted form (i.e., unbreakable for all practical purposes). Unlike the software-

Figure 4.7 Invisibly modified keyboard to capture keystrokes.

based, commercial and freeware keystroke-capture products discussed in Sections 4.3 and 4.4, hardware-based keystroke capture works even if one boots a computer from a floppy disk or CD-ROM and is independent of the operating system used. It can be placed on password-protected computers without having to defeat such passwords. In fact, a device such as this can also capture the initial BIOS password optionally used by any computer—for what little that is worth as a BIOS password is easily defeated anyway.

If the entire data-storage area of the device is filled up unretrieved, the device will proceed to overwrite the oldest stored data.

The information captured by the device can be retrieved by anyone who can get physical access to the computer by entering the appropriate installer-selected password; this can be up to 12 characters long so that it will be highly unlikely that such characters could ever be typed accidentally. Alternately, the device itself (cable or keyboard) can be swapped with a normal one that looks the same and taken to another computer where its contents can be retrieved at leisure.

4.4 Commercial software keystroke loggers

Numerous software products are openly available on the Internet, some for a fee and many for free, that record all keystrokes. There is a vast collection of them, and most can be accessed by doing a keyword search for "keyloggers."

A particularly odious category of software keystroke recorders comes in the form of an electronic romantic greeting e-mailed to one's beloved spouse or significant other. Upon clicking on the professed romantic attachment, the victim ends up with a keylogger that surreptitiously e-mails the victim's keystrokes to the sender of this romantic greeting or a regular basis.

In addition to keystroke capturing, many products, like Keykey from
http://www.keykey.com/index1.html, also record snapshots of the victim's
screen so that the attacker also knows what the victim is looking at (see
Figure 4.8).

Notice that the options include capturing screens at preset intervals or
when the mouse or keyboard is used in a mode defined by the surreptitious
installer.

4.5   Going online

Unless a user has taken drastic and current measures to prevent access to his
or her computer by others on a network or the Internet, there is a vast rep-
ertoire of ways whereby a knowledgeable person can extract data from a
user's computer while that user is online. The extent of what can be
remotely extracted in this manner ranges from literally everything on one's
hard disk to nothing, depending on what protective measures have been
taken (see Chapters 7 through 9).

4.5.1   By one's ISP or by anyone having compromised the ISP's security

The primary security threat to a computer connected to the Internet is not
so much the malicious remote Web site or the malicious remote
hacker—although both of these threats are very real—but one's own ISP.
The ISP is always in a position to know everything that one does online,
who one connects to, the content of e-mail sent or received, who one communicates with and when, and so forth. While ISPs do not have a financial
interest in monitoring subscribers' online habits, they do have to comply
with local court orders and often with mere requests by local law enforcers

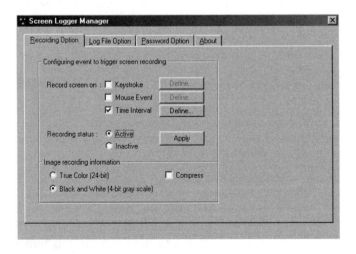

Figure 4.8 Keykey screen-capturing options.

even without a court order.[1] The workarounds available to the user in this case include the following:

1.   Connecting to remote Web sites with SSL encryption (see Section 9.7.1), which provides end-to-end encryption between the user and such sites. The ISP is incapable of knowing what data is moving back and forth, but can see which remote Web site one has connected to unless that site is a proxy (see Section 9.6).

2.   Using a virtual private network (VPN) connection to the remote site, as per Chapter 12. Similar comments to (1) above apply.

3.   Using encryption to hide the contents of e-mail and attachments. This still does not hide the from whom and to whom information unless the user has also elected to use multiple concatenated remailers (see Section 8.5.2) in which case the ISP may knows that a remailer is being used.

While the simple methods above do provide the protection shown, they also raise the user's profile in the eyes of the suspicious ISP or local investigator as someone who is hiding something.

If one wants to communicate in privacy without alerting anyone, not even the ISP, then more advanced techniques are called for, such as those discussed in Sections 8.5.2 and 9.5 through 9.15.

4.5.2   By a legal or an illegal telephone tap

Anything that an ISP can see can also be seen through a tap on the communications medium used to connect to the Internet, be that a telephone line, a cable modem, an xDSL line, or a wireless link. Most any wireless link (e.g., cellular phone, Wi-Fi connection) eventually becomes a wired connection where is it is more practical for someone to intercept.

4.5.3   By remote Web sites that one accesses

The litany of ways whereby remote Web sites can extract information from one's computer online is almost endless. (See Chapters 7 through 9 for protective measures. Rather than enumerating the vast number of such threats, Chapters 7 through 9 approach the topic from the perspective of wholesale negation of them.)

The use of cookies has been correctly blamed for allowing Web sites that one accesses to track one's Web browsing habits. (A *cookie* is simply a small amount of data sent by the Web site one has visited to one's computer

---

1. Additionally, ISPs may have a financial interest in a user's online activities: A company called Predictive Networks was promoting a scheme that would pay ISPs to track users' every move on the Internet so as to sell detailed profiles to numerous buyers who wanted to target their advertising (see http://home.mpinet. net/pilobilus/CS01.html, http://www.vortex.com/privacy/priv.09.13, and www.predictivenetworks.com).

and stored on one's computer; such data is supposed to be readable only by the site that sent it but can in fact be read by any Web site that elects to do so.)

In fact, a Web site does not need to store anything at all on one's computer to track one's browsing habits. As one accesses any Web page, that site has to know the user's IP address in order to send the information asked for. If that site elects to record the IP address for posterity, then it can easily tell if one has visited that site before. This is particularly true for users with a fixed IP address (such as most users with xDSL or cable modem access, who have not deployed protective measures), but is not true for dial-up users because such users get a different IP address every time they dial up their ISP to connect to the Internet.

4.6   Spyware in your computer

There is a very large amount of such software. A small sampling is provided below:

1.   Mom (http://www.avsweb.com/mom) tracks a targeted individual's online activities.

2.   WinWhatWhere's Investigator (http://winwhatwhere.com) offers a broad range of capabilities including keystroke monitoring, Internet tracking, and so forth.

3.   Raytheon's (Lexington, Massachusetts) SilentRunner is intended for Network monitoring. The program uses algorithms to analyze communications patterns and turns its analysis into three-dimensional pictures.

4.   Silent Guard from Adavi Company is advertised to be the "premier surveillance software that allows a single user to monitor keystrokes and Internet traffic for later review." This software can monitor up to 49 computers in real time from a single screen and even provide alarms to the person doing the monitoring "when users reach objectionable Web sites or inappropriate text content based on a dictionary of the user's choice."

4.6.1   By commercial spyware and adware

Most individuals are unaware of the monetary value of their names and buying habits. Supermarkets in the United States have long been offering substantial discounts to shoppers who agree to fill out a form with their name, address, phone number, and e-mail address. Similarly, the many "free" ISPs are not free at all: Instead of getting paid in cash by users, they get paid by selling the users' names and Web-browsing habits; this information is, in turn, converted into cash by the commercial advertisers that it is sold to both upon new subscriber signup and subsequently after subscribers' online habits have accumulated.

A lot of free software (and some commercial for-purchase software) makers have also learned the commercial value of software users' names and choices (measured in terms of what other software exists on a user's computer as well as his or her online habits). The moment such a "free" software is installed on an unsuspecting user's computer, it starts collecting and relaying such data; this often continues even if that program is never used and even if it is uninstalled, hence the epithet "spyware."

A current list of software reputed to do this can be found at sites such as the following:

- http://home.att.net/~willowbrookemill/spylist.pdf;
- http://www.grc.com;
- http://www.alphalink.com.au/~johnf/dspypdf.html;
- http://www.infoforce.qc.ca/spyware.

The interested reader is encouraged to check the Usenet forum ALT.PRIVACY.SPYWARE for the latest information on the topic.

Fixes against adware/spyware

1. A fairly effective piece of software against adware is against adware is called Ad-aware is available freely from www.lavasoftusa.de.

2. Spybot Search and Destroy from www.safer-networking.org is amore effective against spyware.

3. A user should determine if a new piece of software in his or her computer has any reason to access the Internet; a good firewall (see Section 9.18) will alert the user most of the time, but not all of the time,[2] if a program is trying to access the Internet, at which time a user can permit or not permit that to happen.

4. If one has nothing better to do, one can do the job of the Ad-aware software manually and search one's computer for such telltale file names as ad.dll, advert.dll, and so forth. If in doubt, rename them; if everything still works (hard to check if one has a typical complement of a few hundred pieces of software installed), delete them. In particular, look for and remove any of the following:

- Dssagent.exe
- Adimage.dll

2. If a piece of software has installed the capability on one's computer to access the Internet thorough valid ports and through other valid software (e.g., using port 80 of one's Web browser while that browser is being used by the user anyway), then depending on the firewall and how it is configured, the user may be oblivious to this. About the only way to catch such an unauthorized hijacking of one's computer and software is through the use of a packet sniffer that actually looks at and displays all data entering and leaving one's computer. One such sniffer is WinDump, which can be obtained, for example, from http://netgroup-serv.polito.it/windump.

> • Amcis.dll
>
> • Amcis2.dll
>
> • Anadsc.ocx
>
> • Anadscb.ocx
>
> • Htmdeng.exe
>
> • Ipcclient.dll
>
> • Msipcsv.exe
>
> • Tfde.dll
>
> • Tsad.dll
>
> • Vcpdll.dll
>
> • FlexActv.dll

5. Look in the Startup folder for any inexplicable entries and remove
    them. Sometimes adware and spyware will reinstall entries in the
    Startup Folder; in this case, assuming that one knows what sequence
    of letters to be looking for, one can look in the Registry for that
    sequence and delete those references.

    Caution: Do not edit the Registry unless you know what you are
    doing (see Section 2.4).

Other unauthorized backdoor santas

1. *Netscape Navigator/Communicator:* Do not use Netscape's Smart
    Update. It has been shown to report to Netscape. Go into Edit/Prefer-
    ences/Advanced/SmartUpdate and uncheck it.

    Unless you are particularly fond of AOL Instant Messenger in
    Netscape Navigator/Communicator, remove it as follows:

    a. Go to C:/Program Files/Netscape/Users and remove the short-
        cut for AOL Instant Messenger (launch.aim) for each and every
        profile you have. Do not run Netscape until you complete the
        additional steps below because the program will reinsert the
        shortcuts just deleted.

    b. Go to Search/Find/Folders and enter "AOL" and, separately,
        "AIM." Delete any folder identified with either name.

    c. Run REGEDIT and search for the string "AOL" and, separately,
        "AIM." Delete every entry identified that is clearly referring to
        the AOL Instant Messenger.

        Caution: Ensure that the entry being deleted is indeed referring
        to AOL's Instant Messenger before deleting it. See Sections 2.3
        and 2.4 about caution that must be exercised when editing the
        Registry.

    d. Reboot.

    e. Double-click on the Netscape icon and make sure everything
        works fine.

2. *Any registration wizard:* Don't use them. Time and again, companies, including very reputable ones, have been caught using the online registration process to send to the software maker a lot more than the registration information, such as a digest of what is in one's hard disk.

3. *Eudora and other software:* Most new software packages, notably including Adobe Photoshop, a number of video-processing software products, and even the e-mail client Eudora have an unfortunate habit whereby the software regularly "calls home" without notifying the user. The makers of Eudora (and other software makers) assert that this is done solely to check if a newer version of the software has been released; the fact remains, however, that their respective home servers are notified on a regular basis whenever a user uses his or her copy of the software, and this happens without the user's knowledge. This unfortunate feature can be and should be disabled as shown in Section 8.3.3 in the case of Eudora. An easier fix is to enable one's software firewall to seek permission before any software can access the Internet and to deny such permission on a permanent basis.

4. *Microsoft's WebCheck:* This manages subscriptions and user profiles for Internet Explorer v4 and v5 (if you don't use subscriptions, and online privacy dictates that you shouldn't, you don't need it) and is a "parasite" run by the Registry using the entry HKEY_LOCAL_MACHINE\SOFTWARE\Microsoft\Windows\CurrentVersion\Run BrowserWebCheck="loadwc.exe."

   Caution: Removing this line can cause endless subsequent errors.

5. *PKWARE:* This also installs a parasite that allows advertisements to be carried inside zip files. It is launched by the Registry with the entry

   HKEY_LOCAL_MACHINE\SOFTWARE\Microsoft\Windows\CurrentVersion\RunTimeSinkAdClient="C:\ProgramFiles\TimeSink\AdGateway\TSADBOT.EXE"

6. *HP registration:* This often installs a registration parasite if one does not register the product. It takes up 6–20 MB and runs remind32.dll, which nags one to register. Remind32.dll is executed from Start/Programs/Startup.

7. *Borland C++ 5.0 (DOS):* This also installs a registration parasite that takes up 1 MB of disk space and is invoked by the following line in the win.ini file:

   [windows]load C:\BC5\PIPELINE\remind.exe

   Clearly one can remove both the above line and the remind.exe file itself.

8. *Microsoft's Office 2000 Script Editor:* This allows one the option of installing the Machine Debug Manager (mdm.exe) through

the Registry entry HKEY_LOCAL_MACHINE\SOFTWARE\Micro-soft\ Windows\CurrentVersion\RunServices.

The problem is that it creates temporary files every time one boots the computer and never deletes them, thereby posing a security threat.

Some of the spyware programs that also install the spyware portions will refuse to run if one removes that spyware functionality; "Go!Zilla" is one such example. Some will keep reinstalling the spyware function. To get rid of it one must remove the software that keeps installing it.

4.7 van Eck radiation using commercially available systems

All information in this section is based entirely and exclusively on the openly available sources identified in this section.

4.7.1 General

Back in 1985, Wim van Eck published a paper called "Electromagnetic Radiation from Video Display Units: An Eavesdropping Risk?" [1]. Electro-magnetic radiation as a computer-security risk was mentioned in the open literature as early as 1986 [2]. Since then numerous articles on the subject have appeared on the Internet, such as those shown in the general references at the end of this chapter and numerous others available for down-loading from the Internet. Additionally there are numerous openly available scientific documents on the subject, such as those shown in the general references at the end of this chapter.

This should come as no surprise; in the United Kingdom, where TV fees have to be paid on a regular basis, vans are routinely deployed equipped to detect the oscillators of TV sets and to compare them against the list of those who have paid for operating a TV. In fact, according to University of Cambridge's Ross Anderson, unpaid TV fees are a main reason why women in the United Kingdom end up in prison if they cannot pay the £1,000 fine if caught.

In "Data Security by Design" (http://jya.com/datasec.htm), George R. Wilson asserts that such emissions can be picked up "as far away as half a mile" using "a broad band radio scanner, a good antenna and a TV set—all available at electronic stores such as Radio Shack for a few hundred dollars."

Markus Kuhn and Ross Anderson write in "Soft Tempest: Hidden Data Transmission Using Electromagnetic Emanations" (University of Cambridge, Computer Laboratory, United Kingdom, at http://www.cl.cam.ac.uk/~mgk 25/ih98-tempest.pdf):

1.   "Power and ground connections can also leak high frequency information" (page 126, paragraph 3).

2. "Yet another risk comes from 'active attacks' . . . . [A]n attacker who knows the resonant frequency of (say) a PC's keyboard cable can irradiate it with this frequency and then detect keypress codes in the retransmitted signal" (page 126, paragraph 3).

3. "A reader of an early version of this paper reported that he was able to get data signals out of a U.S. Tempest-certified equipment by directing a 10GHz microwave beam at it" (page 126, paragraph 3).

4. "Smulders showed that even shielded RS-232 cables can often be eavesdropped at a distance" (page 126, paragraph 1).

That same paper by Kuhn and Anderson depicts a piece of test equipment alleged to be capable of performing such an interception, the DataSafe/ESL Model 400 by DataSafe Ltd. of Cheltenham, United Kingdom (see Figure 4.9).

The tests performed by the same researchers, Kuhn and Anderson, proved the feasibility of such interception. Figures 4.10 and 4.11 depict the original screen of the computer being intercepted and the display at the eavesdropping site. Both images are reprinted with the Kuhn and Anderson's permission. It is noteworthy that the targeted computer is a laptop, which had long been considered safe from VanEck radiation in comparison to desktop computers!

In the conclusion, Kuhn and Anderson state, "Things will be made much worse by the arrival of cheap software radios . . . [which] will allow low-budget attackers to implement sophisticated Tempest attacks which were previously only possible with very expensive dedicated equipment."

An image of the equipment used is provided in Figure 4.12.

4.7.2   Protective measures

Protective measures are based on basic physics, which any college student is well aware of. One simply has to squelch all sources of radiation by

Figure 4.9 DataSafe/ESL Model 400 laboratory equipment.

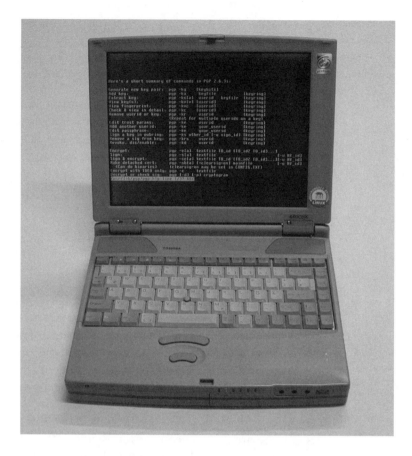

Figure 4.10 Screen display of encryption key setup on targeted computer.
(Courtesy of Markus Kuhn and Ross Anderson.)

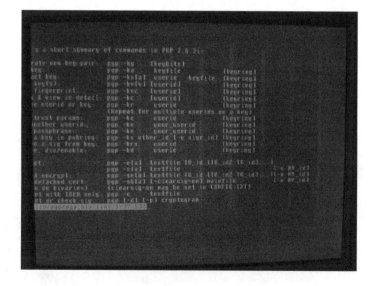

Figure 4.11 Intercepted image of encryption keys using van Eck radiation.
(Courtesy of Markus Kuhn and Ross Anderson.)

Figure 4.12 Standard laboratory equipment used for van Eck interception by Kuhn and Anderson. (Courtesy of Markus Kuhn and Ross Anderson.)

shielding the entire enclosure and by preventing the signals from reaching the cables that leave these enclosures (such as cables for power, monitor, peripherals, mouse, keyboard). This is quite tedious in the case of desktop computers and nearly impossible in the case of laptop computers.

A U.S. patent (US5297201) offers "A system for preventing remote detection of computer data from tempest signal emanations" (http://patent.womplex.ibm.com/details?patent_number=5297201).

According George Wilson in "Data Security by Design" (http://jya.com/datasec.htm), shielding from electromagnetic emanations is the protective measure one can deploy to thwart this threat to privacy. To this effect, there are numerous companies (such as TeckNit, at www.tecknit.com) that offer assorted Electromagnetic Interference (EMI) shielding products.

An interesting protective scheme is, in fact, built into some openly available versions of the popular encryption software PGP: It offers one the option of using a fuzzy font that is claimed to be difficult to intercept through emanations.

Similarly, SCRAMDISK (see Section 6.4.2) offers a red-screen mode for one to enter a password in a manner that is claimed to defeat a Tempest attack; this only works for U.S. QWERTY keyboards and not for European and Asian nonstandard keyboards (unless one uses only figures and numbers for the password).

Similarly, one can download zero-emission-pad freeware from DEMCOM, which makes the Steganos Security Suite software, at http://www. steganos.com/english/steganos/zep.htm.

Figure 4.13 shows the example provided on that company's Web site of how it modifies the fonts that get displayed on the screen.

An excellent reference for fonts that ostensibly defeat the interception of unintended emanations is at http://www.infowar.com/resource/99/resource_040599b_j.shtml. Downloadable fonts are available at www.cl.cam.ac.uk/ ~mgk25/st-fonts.zip, which contains Soft Tempest filtered and antialiased versions of the Courier font produced using the public-domain X11 pixel font—adobe-courier-*-r-normal 40-386-75-75-m-0-iso8859-1. The two available fixed-glyph cell sizes are 13 × 24 pixels and 8 × 13 pixels in both medium (m) and bold (b) weight.

According to www.infowar.com/resource/99/resource_040599b_j.shtml,

> Since filtered fonts require successful eavesdroppers to come much closer to the target machine, they reduce the probability of a successful interception of confidential text considerably. They are therefore a valuable additional precaution that can be applied easily to maintain a reasonable level of communication and computer security. Tempest protection by filtered fonts and related techniques are in the process of being patented internationally.

The reader interested in preventing compromises of privacy through this technology should read the patent description by Kuhn and Anderson titled "Low Cost Countermeasures against Compromising Computer Emanations" (U.K. patent application no. 9801745.2, January 28, 1998).

Figure 4.13   Freeware fonts for some protection from emanation interception.

4.7.3   Optical emanations and their interception

What used to be considered esoteric technology in years past is now commercially available to anyone. The know-how is openly available on the Internet worldwide, and the hardware and software are just as openly available. It was not too long ago, for example, that global positioning system (GPS) receivers and miniature cameras were considered esoteric devices; yet today they are built in most cellular phones sold worldwide.

A conventional phosphor-tube computer screen or TV [known as a cathode ray tube (CRT) as distinct from a flat panel display] is, in fact, painted by a single beam, which paints the screen sequentially (but rapidly) left to right and top to bottom. Although the eye cannot perceive this and only sees the end result of the entire screen, the fact remains that the instantaneous light intensity coming out of a CRT screen over time is made up of the instantaneous brightness of each dot on the screen as it is being painted by that beam. Granted, the persistence of the fluorescence by the pixel is such that the eye cannot see the flicker if the refresh rate is fast enough, but the flicker is there nonetheless and would be readily sensed by any sensor faster than the eye. This is the essence of interceptable optical emanations and is amply documented in the professional literature, especially in some excellent work from Cambridge University in the United Kingdom.

In simple terms, the security threat amounts to this: If a sensor can look at anything illuminated by a conventional computer CRT screen, such as the user's white shirt, the image of the CRT screen seen by the user can also be reconstructed in many cases by the persons operating that sensor. The reader is referred to the two excellent technical references on this listed at the end of this chapter.

4.8   Being on a network, cable modem, or xDSL modem

Equally serious is the security threat that results from merely being online. Unless one has taken drastic steps to defend against a wide assortment of hacking attacks (see Chapters 7 through 9), one is highly likely to become the target of trolling hackers who delight in identifying and exploiting the security weaknesses of anyone who stays online long enough. Such attacks can be minimized by doing the following:

1.   Using a good firewall (see Section 9.18).

2.   Not staying online for long. Hacking attacks probe one's weaknesses based on one's dynamically assigned (meaning: changing every time one goes online) Internet Protocol (IP) address. An IP address is the unique identifying address of anyone connected to the Internet; it is the equivalent of one's telephone number. Because there are more Internet users than there are IP addresses, an ISP has a pool of such IP addresses from which it selects one at random to assign to each user

when that user goes online. The ISP then reuses that address for someone else when the first user goes offline and someone else needs an IP address. The longer one stays online with a single IP address, the longer a hacker has to probe for weaknesses. Users of high-speed connections (cable modems and xDSL lines) would be well advised to disconnect their computers from the network when not actually using them.

3. Using virus/Trojan/worm protection software and keeping it current. This means checking for updates once a day or, if one uses a computer sparingly, prior to each new use.

4.9 Other means

The commercially available techniques and equipment discussed for van Eck radiation interception are basically passive. Yet, the commercial sector is full of devices that transmit information fed into them. As such, an interceptor who has somehow obtained physical access to someone else's premises (or just to that someone else's computer, such as when it was taken for repair) could combine data interception with a small radio transmitter and transmit the intercepted data out to wherever the receiver is.

The only limits on how to send out data collected from a targeted computer are imposed by one's imagination, nerve, and pocketbook.

4.10 Insertion of incriminating data in your computer by others

It is almost as easy for a remote entity to retrieve information from one's computer online as it is to place files on it. Given that mere possession of some kinds of material by individuals is strictly illegal in some regimes (e.g., subversive files, bomb-making files, files marked as classified, and even erotic imagery), one should be particularly careful about the possibility that incriminating evidence may find its way in one's computer. Similarly, defense attorneys must also be aware of this possibility. This incriminating evidence can be intentionally inserted by a remote party; it can also be unknowingly received, in the following ways, by an innocent user who never solicited it:

1. One is accessing an Internet Web site and either mistypes the URL or the correct URL takes one to the wrong site (say, a pornographic one) as a result of DNS[3] problems or DNS hijacking.

3. DNS servers are the telephone directories of the Internet. When one types www.somename.com, a DNS server is queried to produce the IP address (e.g., 123.456.789.012) that corresponds to that name. Time and again, hackers have managed to poison select DNS servers to deny access to numerous Web sites.

2.   One is accessing a legitimate Internet site on the Web, which is also supported by advertising revenue (as most are today) obtained by flashing unsolicited images and windows on the user's screen. Those images end up getting saved on the user's computer despite no active clicking or other act by the user.

3.   One receives unsolicited e-mail (spam) with attachments. While most of us will delete the e-mail (which really does not delete it at all), hardly anyone deletes, let alone overwrites, the attachments to unsolicited e-mail.

4.   Most everyone who has installed a Wi-Fi (802.11b,a,g) access point at home, or even just a Wi-Fi card in his or her laptop, is vulnerable to having total strangers insert/remove/alter files on their computers unless specific preventive steps have been taken (see Section 13.2).

5.   Most anyone allows others to use his or her computer at one time or another or installs software with a function that is hidden from the user.

In these cases, one is very vulnerable to incriminating files finding their way onto the computer without the user's knowledge, let approval or solicitation.

4.11 Security protection steps that don't work well enough

4.11.1 The fallacy of CMOS password protection

Any computer user has the option to enable a CMOS password, ostensibly to prevent the computer from booting at all. In reality it is totally useless as a protective measure, except against a nontechnical person who has only momentary (and I mean momentary, as in less than a minute) access to a computer. It can be readily defeated by momentarily removing the CMOS battery from a computer, which erases the CMOS password along with all other CMOS data. Even more quickly, the CMOS password can be defeated in many computer models by entering a default password among a list that is openly available on the Internet. BIOS manufacturers grew tired of users' calls asking for help when they forgot their BIOS passwords, so they enabled backup passwords.

4.11.2 The fallacy of password protection offered by popular commercial software

Password protection of files (e.g., those created by Microsoft Word, Excel, Worperfect) also does not provide any substantive protection against anyone other than a totally nontechnical, casual snoop. One can purchase software built by, for example, Access Data Corporation in Utah (www.accessdata.com) for only about $150, which breaks this password protection in very short order.

4.11.3 The fallacy of protection by hiding files from view

One can hide file names in Windows or DOS. In the case of Windows, one simply right-clicks on a file, selects "properties," and checks the "hidden" attribute. In the case of DOS, one simply types attrib [file name] +h. These schemes are not intended to hide anything from a snoop, but merely to reduce the clutter of file names (and icons, in the case of Windows). All a snoop has to do is undo this hiding process, which does not even have to be done for each file. In Windows one can set the properties of the Windows Explorer to display all files whether hidden or not.

4.11.4 The fallacy of protection by hiding data in the slack

Placing a file intentionally in the slack (i.e., in the space between the end-of-file and end-of-cluster; see Section 2.2.1) or deleting it (but not overwriting it) so that it can be retrieved by one later does not provide protection. Any forensic examination routinely examines all data in the slack and the free space.

4.11.5 The fallacy of protection by placing data in normally unused locations of a disk

Placing data in tracks and sectors of a disk that are normally unused by an operating system is an old trick that goes back to the days of the Apple II computer. It was used by software games ostensibly to prevent users from copying the disks. These disks used their own disk operating systems to read those normally unused tracks; it did not take long before users did, too, in order to copy those disks anyway. Most any determined forensic examination of a disk will access the data hidden this way, too.

4.11.6 The fallacy of protecting data by repartitioning a disk for a smaller capacity than the disk really has

This scheme involves more work, and it might even fool some people but not all of them. The idea is to take a disk of, say, 200 GB, and to place the sensitive data in the sectors which correspond to the last, say, 80 GB of physical space. One can then repartition the hard disk (through the FDISK command, which, contrary to popular belief, does not erase anything, but merely makes it inaccessible to Windows) for 120 GB. This will leave the last 80 GB with the sensitive data largely untouched (but the file names and allocation table will be severely affected). An unsophisticated investigator may believe that the disk's capacity is indeed that claimed by the last partition and not see the hidden data. This will not fool the experienced investigator, though. Recovering the data hidden in this manner will require software that is not commonly available.

4.11.7 The fallacy of protection through password-protected disk access

The large assortment of software programs that claim to password-protect one's computer at boot time or when it is left unattended (e.g., screen-blankers) are also ineffective. In the simplest case, unless a user has disabled the option of booting from a floppy disk (a dangerous proposition if one's hard disk crashes and one that is pointless anyway as an attacker can readily modify the BIOS to allow booting from a floppy disk), any person could bypass all these passwords and boot from a floppy disk. But even in the case when a user seems to have taken all the password-related precautions to prevent unauthorized access, these are ineffective against a forensic examination, which removes the disk from its computer, makes a copy of it (track by track and sector by sector), and looks for data without ever having to go through any of the protective barriers inserted by a user.

4.11.8 The fallacy of protection through the use of booby-trap software

The same applies to booby-trapping software, such as Don't Touch by Cybertech Group. Such software typically expects the authorized user to enter a sequence of keystrokes without any prompting when a computer is turned on; if that sequence is not entered, then the software destroys a specified file in which the authorized user is supposed to have stored the sensitive data and then erases itself as well. This scheme, too, may protect one from a nosy spouse or coworker, but not from a forensic examination because the latter never activates any software in the suspect disk. Such schemes could also backfire by causing an otherwise innocent computer user to end up with an obstruction of justice charge in some cases.

4.11.9 The fallacy that overwriting a file removes all traces of its existence

A file itself is only part of the information stored in a computer concerning that file. Also present are the following:

1. The file name (stored elsewhere).

    Hint: Do not use revealing file names, just in case you forget to get rid of the file name.

2. Information about the file. Depending on which software were used, this information can include who created it, when, when it was modified, and so forth.

3. Ostensibly temporary copies of that file created by the software in case the computer crashed while the file was being worked on. Because the computer is not clairvoyant and does not know if a crash will occur, some software products always create a temporary file.

Even if that file is deleted, it is still very much available on the hard disk until the space it occupied happens to be overwritten (or is deliberately overwritten).

Most important yet, most every hard disk sold today includes numerous sectors held in reserve. When (not if) some normally used sector appears marginal to the disk's firmware (e.g., causes occasional read errors), its data is copied to a sector held in reserve (without deleting it from the marginal sector), its logical address is assigned to that new sector formerly held in reserve, and that marginal sector is now "mothballed" with its data in it. Because it no longer has a logical address, it is not accessible by any of the many software products that purport to overwrite the disk.

4.11.10 The fallacy of encryption protection

Encryption, in and of itself, refers merely to the conversion of a readable file to one that, at best, is unreadable by anyone other then the intended recipient(s). Encryption does not deal with the following key issues, for example:

1. Is the unencrypted document or are references to it also left behind on the disk?

2. Is the encryption "key" used protected from unauthorized individuals?

3. Are there additional decryption keys (ADKs) in existence that the originator does not know about? (This was the case in the late August 1999 Advisory Circular by the highly respected CERT in connection with PGP. See Section 11.3.)

The reader is referred to Chapters 10 through 12 for a thorough discussion of commercial encryption.

4.11.11 Other protection fallacies that don't deliver

Beyond the above classical illusions of protecting sensitive documents, there can be a vast collection of tricks intended to protect sensitive files. Don't depend on them. Such tricks only deter the nontechnical casual snoop unless (1) a file is truly encrypted or hidden using good steganography, and all evidence of the unencrypted and unsteganographed file is totally eliminated (see Section 11.5), or (2) the magnetic media in question are not where they can be found by an oppressive regime. Worse than their being unreliable, such tricks make the individual using them that much more likely to receive a thorough forensic analysis of his or her computer. Such tricks are totally ineffective against a forensic analysis of a targeted computer's magnetic storage media. Ineffective tricks, which can also be used in assorted combinations, include (but are not limited to) the following:

> ▸ *Renaming a file (e.g., from supersecret.doc to virtue.exe):* This is not only ineffective but a bad idea because some forensic software (such as Encase) flag some renamed files as having been renamed (e.g., abc.jpg being renamed def.sys).

> ▸ *Compressing a file (using the standard zip software).*

Such schemes do not protect one from a forensic examination because such an examination looks at all data on a disk, regardless of each file's name, location, degree of compression, compliance with any operating system or disk filing system or lack thereof, what else it is merged with, and so forth.

Selected bibliography

Internet-accessible references on van Eck radiation

Anderson, R., and M. Kuhn, "Soft Tempest: Hidden Data Transmission Using Electromagnetic Emanations," http://www.cl.cam.ac.uk/~mgk25/ih98-tempest .pdf.

"The Complete Unofficial TEMPEST Information Page," http://www.eskimo .com/ ~joelm/tempest.html. TEMPEST stands for Transient Electromagnetic Pulse Emanation Standard.

"Electronic Eavesdropping Is Becoming Mere Child's Play," *New Scientist*, at www.newscientist.com/ns/19991106/newsstory6.html.

Moller, E., "Protective Measures against Compromising Electro Magnetic Radiation Emitted by Video Display Terminals," *Phrack*, Vol. 4, no. 44, at www.shmoo.com/tempest/PHRACK44-11.

"The Tempest Solution," http://www.ionet.net/~everett/solution.html.

Printed references on van Eck radiation

McLellan, V., "The Complete Unofficial TEMPEST Information Page," *PC Week*, Vol. 4, March 10, 1987, p. 35(2).

Russell, D., and G. T. Gangemi, Sr., *Computer Security Basics*, Sebastopol, CA: O'Reilly and Associates, 1991, Chapter 10 on TEMPEST. Available for purchase from any bookstore and online from http://www.ora.com/catalog/csb.

Smulders, P., "The Threat of Information Theft by Reception of Electromagnetic Radiation from RS-232 Cables," Department of Electrical Engineering, Eindhoven University of Technology, 1990, http://jya.com/re232.pdf.

Van Eck, W., "Electromagnetic Eavesdropping Machines for Christmas?" *Computers and Security*, Vol. 7, No. 4, 1988, http://jya.com/bits.htm.

References on optical emanations

Kuhn, Markus G., "Optical Time Domain Eavesdropping Risks of CRT Displays," *Proc. the 2002 IEEE Symp. Security Privacy*, Berkeley, CA, May 12–15, 2002. Also available online at http://www.cl.cam.ac.uk/nmgk25/..

Loughry, J., and D. A. Umphress, "Information Leakage from Optical Emanations," Vol. 5, No. 3, August 2002, http://www.applied-math.org/optical _tempest.pdf.

References

[1]   http://www.shmoo.com/tempest/emr.pdf.

[2]   Highland, H. J., "Electromagnetic Radiation Revisited," *Computers and Security*, Vol. 5, 1986, pp. 85–93, 181–184.

Why Computer Privacy and Anonymity?

"Countering computer forensics? But aren't you helping the bad people?"

No! Quite to the contrary, this is helping the good people ward off the bad people. It is also helping reduce crime by making it much harder for criminals to engage in identity theft or for thieves to steal intellectual property and legally privileged information such as medical information and attorney–client communications.

Computer forensics is not done only by or for law enforcement; more often than not, it is done by anyone with the means to do so for illegal purposes, such as stealing intellectual property, passwords, and the like.

Just as there are legitimate uses for knives and for matches, there are many legitimate uses for countering illegal computer forensics, such as the following:

1. Preventing the theft of intellectual property;

2. Preventing the theft of proprietary business documents by competitors;

3. Preventing the compromise or outright theft of legally privileged information, such as patients' medical records and attorney–client privileged communications;

4. Protecting a nontechnical freedom fighter in a patently oppressive totalitarian regime;

5. Protecting anyone from having information planted in his or her computer that can be subsequently discovered;

6. Helping lawyers defend their clients from frivolous accusations supported by contaminated evidence.

The wide availability of free and commercial software packages that promise to protect one from assorted types of unauthorized snooping are, in fact, doing most users a disservice because they lull the buyer into a false sense of security that is worse than no security: Someone who knows he or she has no security will be much more careful with what is entrusted to a computer than someone who thinks that there is security when in fact there is none. This cannot be overemphasized.

Then there is also the philosophical issue that is implicit in most civilized societies: If a youngster on a deserted island whispers sweet nothings to his girlfriend's ear, it is nobody else's business to know what was said. And that privacy should not be contingent upon the distance between the two or upon the medium used to communicate, be it two paper-cups and a string or a technologically advanced alternative.

Similarly, if a person on a deserted island wants to confide written thoughts to his or her diary, civilized society has traditionally bestowed the right of privacy to those thoughts. And that privacy should not be contingent upon the medium used to write one's thoughts, be it paper and pencil or its modern day equivalent, namely, a personal computer.

But, as members of societies, we don't live on deserted islands. Being part of a society entails numerous limitations of individual freedoms so that each society can function. Indeed, a society has the self-evident right to protect itself from individual conduct which is out-and-out harmful, such as murder, arson, and the like. Part of the implementation of such societal protection is to have early warning of a planned major crime so that such a crime can be prevented. At a minimum, any society needs to have the means to prevent the recurrence of a major crime by positively identifying the perpetrator. Just as ballistics tests can show which gun fired a bullet found in a dead body or whose DNA was at the scene of a major crime, computer forensics can and should be used if it can show conclusively who planned or executed a major crime.

In this sense, this book is highly supportive of the law enforcer who is trying to prevent a major crime, hence the lengthy chapters on effective computer forensics.

The definition of a crime is in the mind of the beholder, however. A totalitarian regime often criminalizes everything that those in power don't like, be it the expression of a dissenting political or religious thought or even a joke that treats the ruler unfavorably. Also, what is a crime one day may not be the next, and vice versa, as laws constantly change in all societies. One cannot conveniently define as a criminal anyone that any country's court has branded as one; in recent history, some regimes have made it a crime to talk about freedom, to listen to music by this or that composer, to whistle this or that tune, and so on. If the word "criminal" is simplistically defined to include anyone convicted by any court of a locally defined crime, then Christ and Gandhi would have to be included, along with Bertrand Russell, Galileo, Luther, and most other key intellectuals.

One should not forget Montesquieu's words: "There is no greater tyranny than that which is perpetrated under the shield of law and in the name of justice." Or the words of William Pitt the Younger: "Necessity is the plea for every infringement of human freedom."

Last but not least, there is theft. According to the FBI, some 319,000 laptops were stolen in 1999. Most such thefts occur at airport security gates: The laptop is placed by its owner on the X-ray machine's conveyor belt; a seemingly rushed traveler cuts to the front of the line to get through the magnetometer, but is having difficulties with keys and related items on his or her person. While that rushed traveler is being taken care of, his or her accomplice on the other end of the security gate absconds with the laptop, which has already passed through the X-ray machine. Most of these laptops must have undoubtedly included data not intended for others' eyes, such as corporate proprietary information, personal medical and financial information, and the like. The value of the loss of such data to unauthorized eyes is incalculable and usually far exceeds the value of the hardware lost. It would be nothing short of irresponsible to allow this to happen to oneself.

One should also not forget that the mere proliferation of information technology has made wholesale surveillance not only possible but also economically cost-effective. Even time-honored institutions that used to respect privacy may well not do so any more; for example, the U.S. Census, whose data was advertised as being protected, may not be so. According to the *New York Times*, the Congressional Budget Office with the help of some congressmen has been angling to get its hands on the census data to create "linked data sets" on individuals using information from the Internal Revenue Service, Social Security Administration, and Census Bureau surveys to help it evaluate proposed reforms in Medicare and Social Security (see www.nytimes.com/2000/10/23/opinion/23MONK.html).

An often-repeated adage says that if one consults a lawyer and wants justice, many a lawyer will often ask, "How much justice can you afford?" A similar situation exists with privacy and security: how much privacy and security can you afford?

5.1 Anonymity

While encryption protects the content of a file, message, or communication, it does not protect the identity of who communicates with whom.

Unlike encryption, which protects the content of a file from forensic discovery either online or offline, anonymity by its nature—in the present context—relates to the transmittal of a document from the source to its intended destination. What is to be hidden is not the content, but its author.

Far from being disreputable, anonymity is at the heart of civilized society, as evidenced from the following quotes by world-renown U.S. Supreme Court justices:

- ▶ "Anonymity is a shield from the tyranny of the majority. . . . It thus exemplifies the purpose behind the Bill of Rights, and of the First Amendment in particular: to protect unpopular individuals from

retaliation—and their ideas from suppression—at the hand of an intolerant society."
—Justice Stevens, *McIntyre v. Ohio Elections Commission*, 1996

‣ "Anonymous pamphlets, leaflets, brochures and even books have played an important role in the progress of mankind. Persecuted groups and sects from time to time throughout history have been able to criticize oppressive practices and laws either anonymously or not at all."
—Justice Black, *Talley v. California*, 1960

‣ "After reviewing the weight of the historical evidence, it seems that the Framers understood the First Amendment to protect an author's right to express his thoughts on political candidates or issues in an anonymous fashion."
—Justice Thomas, *McIntyre v. Ohio Elections Commission*, 1996

Indeed, the use of anonymous and pseudonymous speech played a vital role in the founding of the United States. When Thomas Paine's "Common Sense" was first released, it was signed "An Englishman." Similarly, James Madison, Alexander Hamilton, John Jay, Samuel Adams, and others carried out the debate between Federalists and Anti-Federalists using pseudonyms. President Harry S. Truman signed his influential 1947 essay, "The Sources of Soviet Power," as "X." Finally, the use of a pseudonym, or nom de plume, in literature has a time-honored history (e.g., Mark Twain was Samuel Clemens).

There are many flavors of anonymity, such as using a pseudonym or assuming another identity. For the purposes of this discussion, we interpret anonymity to include any technique that prevents any third party from discovering the true identity of an Internet user.

Anonymity is an obvious irritant to law enforcement and is criticized as prima facie evidence of criminal intent. For a different perspective, consider the following view by Julf Helsingius, expressed in an interview with *Wired* magazine's Joshua Quittner, coauthor of the high-tech thriller *Mother's Day*. Helsingius ran the world's most popular remailer in Finland until he retired in 1996.

> Living in Finland, I got a pretty close view of how things were in the former Soviet Union. If you actually owned a photocopier or even a typewriter there, you would have to register it and they would take samples . . . so that they could identify it later. . . . The fact that you have to register every means of providing information to the public sort of parallels it, like saying you have to sign everything on the Internet. [Law enforcers] always want to track you down.

Quite often, anonymity actually furthers the cause of law enforcement: For example, a whistle-blower may need to tip off law enforcement of a serious ongoing or planned illegal activity by his or her employer; a suicidal or homicidal individual may wish to obtain help and counseling, which he would not seek without anonymity; a drug-addicted mother of a young child may seek anonymous counseling to prevent her from using all of her financial resources to support her habit. Even some police departments are experimenting with establishing Web sites for anonymous tips about crimes; this is nothing more than an online version of the time-honored practice of anonymous crime-solver phone lines.

Less dramatic situations justifying anonymity include seeking employment through the Internet without jeopardizing one's current job, expressing religious opinions in a community that is strongly opposed to them, or placing a personal ad. Doctors who are members of the online community often encourage their patients to connect with others and form support groups on issues that they do not feel comfortable speaking about publicly. It is essential to be able to express certain opinions without revealing one's identity. In a multitude of other situations, anonymity serves a very legitimate social function.

Conversely, as with anything else, anonymity can be abused by sociopaths, who are attracted by the notion of avoiding responsibility and accountability for their actions

Many everyday activities that used to be anonymous leave electronic trails behind today. Using the lure of discounts or other benefits, the common "preferred customer" card of supermarkets, bookstores, and other vendors allows those vendors to track one's purchasing and renting preferences, even if payments are made with cash. The same applies to the use of frequent-flyer accounts, or to the use of frequent-anything accounts, and to the ever-increasing use of credit cards in place of cash.

With the ubiquitous spread of Signaling System 7 in telephony, caller ID information is available to the called party about the calling party. Blocking caller ID does nothing, in the United States, to toll-free calls made to 800 area code numbers; because the called party pays for the incoming call, the phone companies use Automatic Number Identification (ANI) to allow the called party to know who is calling, even if the calling party has disabled the outgoing caller ID feature.

E-mail records are now routinely subpoenaed by prosecutors and by attorneys in both criminal and civil cases as evidence.

And the list goes on.

As a matter of principle, many individuals have therefore resorted to technology to protect their privacy, often for privacy's own sake.

Additionally, anonymity is a matter of life and death in many societies in the case of responsible individuals expressing views that are unpopular, that the ruling party perceives as a threat, that question the status quo, or that debate religious or other topics.

5.1.1 Practical anonymity

A vast number of resources on practical anonymity are available on the Internet. One of the most useful Web sites is www.privacyresources.org/anonymity.htm.

It is important to decide up front whom one wants to be anonymous from:

1. The recipient of e-mail that one is about to send;

2. The readers of Usenet posts that one has elected to post to;

3. The Web sites that one visits on the Internet;

4. Someone in a repressive regime who is tapping one's telephone line;

5. One's ISP;

6. Someone else in one's local network, if one is in use;

7. A forensic investigator who gets hold of one's computer.

Each of these requires a different set of procedures and/or software. They are discussed, among other topics of equal relevance and concern, in separate sections in Chapters 10 through 14.

5.2 Privacy

Civilization is the process toward a society of privacy. The savage's whole existence is public, ruled by the laws of the tribe. Civilization is the process of setting man free from men.

—Ayn Rand, *The Fountainhead*

Privacy is the right of individuals to control the collection and use of information about themselves.

5.2.1 You cannot trust TRUSTe?

TRUSTe (http://www.truste.com) is a commercial organization that has set itself up as the grantor of a sort of seal of approval for online commercial entities that appear to meet some criteria for respecting the confidentiality of customer-provided information.

Can one trust that? In a word, no. One of the main failings of this scheme is that it cannot handle the cases of companies that go bankrupt and sell their assets to meet their financial obligations; those assets often include the databases of customer information that the bankrupt company had assured its customers would never be sold to anyone. The company receiving those databases does not feel bound by any commitments made by the bankrupt company. A typical example is the news item reported on the Internet on October 27, 2000, to the effect that HealthCentral.com has reportedly signed an agreement to purchase the assets of the floundering online drugstore more.com, including its customer list, and its subsidiary, ComfortLiving.com, for approximately $6 million.

5.2.2 Is privacy a right?

The United States

In the United States, there is no explicit constitutional protection for privacy.

One interpretation is that this is so because the framers of the U.S. Constitution never thought that privacy would be withheld as a self-evident individual right in the first place.

Another interpretation is that such protection conflicts with other constitutional guarantees, such as the First Amendment's protection of the freedom of expression. That constitutional amendment limits privacy in that it blocks the government from taking action to restrict expression that might compromise the privacy of others. There is also some implicit protection of select private activities, such as the practice of one's religion.

At the federal level, rights relate only to protection from the government and not from any private party, with the exception of the Thirteenth Amendment, which prohibits slavery. In general, constitutional rights do not require the government to do anything, only not to do some things.

There is some protection of privacy, but from the government only, in the Bill of Rights. The Fourth Amendment's prohibition of "unreasonable search and seizure" implies some privacy; of course, what is unreasonable is in the mind of the beholder, and the guidelines are often revised by the U.S. Supreme Court. In 1928, the Court had decreed that federal wiretapping did not amount to an unreasonable search because it did not involve a physical trespass (*Olmstead v. the United States*). This has since changed.

The Fifth Amendment prevents the government from taking private property for public use without due process and compensation. In 1984 the Supreme Court decreed that this protection extends to data, too. Even so, the protection is minimal at best because it only requires due process and compensation. It is not an outright prohibition, and like anything else in the Constitution, it applies to government actions and not to actions by private parties.

When it comes to data held by the government, the Federal Privacy Act stipulates that government agencies can only store "relevant and necessary" personal information. This stipulation is clearly quite vague and subject to abuse by unscrupulous officials.

So, in essence, what little there is of federal protection of individual privacy relates to procedures rather than substance.

Basically, if the federal government tries to protect privacy, it often ends up at odds with the First Amendment; privacy rights almost never win over the First Amendment rights of freedom of expression. As such, collection and dissemination of information, especially about government officials, is hardly ever restricted by the Supreme Court.

A case in point is the August 18, 1999, decision by a federal appeals court in Denver, Colorado, to reverse Federal Communications Commission rules designed to protect telephone consumers from having the numbers they called and the services they subscribed to used by the phone companies without the their permission. The court felt that this protection interfered with the phone companies' First Amendment right to free speech.

Laws in the United States have not kept up with the extremely rapid pace of technology developments in the last decade in the realm of data communications and storage. The Constitution is of minimal help in this regard, so a number of states have stepped in with an assortment of state laws. These laws are often vague and end up being tested in state courts time and again.

Hawaii and Louisiana make it illegal to "invade privacy," but Hawaii permits the invasion of privacy if there is a "compelling State interest." Arizona, likewise, makes it illegal for one to be "disturbed in his private affairs EXCEPT under authority of law." Alaska's 1972 constitution provides for the "right of people to privacy"; California, in 1974 considered privacy an "inalienable right," yet in 1994 it permitted mandatory drug testing of college athletes as an act that does not violate their rights.

Private individuals have almost never won law suits brought against private parties for "privacy violations."

In general, claims against nongovernment entities for loss of privacy have to be worded in terms of loss of property and use laws protecting the rights of ownership of property.

One key issue is who owns the information about one's person. Is medical information owned by the person in question, by the medical doctor, or by the hospital or insurance company? U.S. courts have often stated that the information is owned by whoever went to a lot of trouble and expense to collect and store it. Even the Supreme Court has stated that any expectation of privacy must derive its legitimacy from laws governing real or personal property.

It follows that the only substantive means that an individual in the United States can use to protect the privacy of his or her data is to encrypt it in a secure manner.

Europe

Western European countries have strong legal protection of individual privacy. Ironically, this protection is possible precisely because Western European governments have fewer legal limitations placed upon them by their respective constitutions than the U.S. government has; for example, the same First Amendment that prohibits the U.S. federal government from placing individual privacy ahead of the right of free expression prevents the U.S. federal government from enacting broad laws protecting one individual's privacy from another individual's effort to collect and disseminate information.

The European press has often been muzzled by individual governments appealing to "higher" principles. As a result, it has been possible in Europe to enact laws prohibiting the broadcasting of any "harmful programming." This very same broad European authority to intervene in the area of communications and information makes it legally possible for European governments to legislate on the privacy of individual communications and information.

European laws have explicit provisions for the protection of data and information about individuals. Such protection varies significantly from country to country in Europe, and this has already become a contentious issue: One article in the 1992 "Common Position . . . of the European Parliament . . . on the Protection of Individuals with Regard to the Processing of Personal Data" (formally approved on October 24, 1995, and to take effect in October 1998) prohibits member European countries' giving that data to nonmembers (e.g., to the United States) that "fail to ensure an adequate level of protection." This has caused the refusal of European countries to provide a lot of data to the United States and to U.S. companies.

Article 1 of the same "Common Position" document clearly states that there is a "fundamental right to privacy with respect to the processing of personal data." The fact that the European Union classifies privacy as a human right means that it will be extremely hard for it to be challenged by other conflicting laws (e.g., commercial codes).

Although individual European countries' laws related to privacy vary now, the trend is towards a uniform set of standards.

In the United Kingdom there is no written constitution, but in 1998 Parliament approved the Human Rights Act, which will incorporate a variation of the European Convention on Human Rights (ECHR) into domestic law, a process that will establish an enforceable right to privacy. Even so, on November 23, 1999, a British cryptographer, Brian Gladman, was quoted in publications stating that a component of the U.K. government may resort to covertly implanting Trojan horse software into targeted individuals' computers as a means of circumventing any encryption being used by them, in possible contravention of the 1990 Computer Misuse Act but in possible compliance with the 1994 Intelligence Services Act. Indeed, plans to intercept e-mail and Internet calls, let alone to covertly tamper with private citizens' computers, contravene the ECHR, which is the United Kingdom's version of European human rights rules.

Elsewhere

The extent of any legal protection of privacy from the government in other nations varies considerably. Even regimes with a long history of democracy tend to interpret their obligation to ensure domestic tranquility as superceding any individual citizen's right to privacy; this has the obvious potential for self-righteous abuse. As such, many countries have legislated protection of the privacy of a citizen from other citizens but not from the government itself through its law enforcement arms.

Interestingly, some languages (e.g., Greek) do not even have a word for "privacy," even though its essence may be ingrained into the culture.

Most other countries, with the notable exception of totalitarian states, have some form of a legally protected privacy of both personal records and communications. Most of these protection rights have some carefully worded exclusions in the cases of suspected but nebulously defined crimes.

5.2.3 The impact of technology on privacy

"The right to be left alone" is how a U.S. justice of the Supreme Court, Louis Brandeis, viewed privacy in 1890. And what alarmed him in the first place was the use of technological change, which in those days amounted only to the popularization of photography and of inexpensive printing to invade privacy. These were nothing compared to the electronic means openly available today to collect, sift through, and disseminate data about anyone, not to mention technologies for tracking, detecting, and identifying individuals.

There is a lot of posturing and rhetoric on all sides.

The law enforcement side of any country asserts something to the effect of "We are here to protect you. To do this we need all the tools possible to know as much as possible about everything and everyone. We want a society with domestic tranquility, free from crime" (defined as whatever conduct a state does not like), and so forth.

But this is precisely what a secret police of any totalitarian nation claims, too.

The commercial side asserts sanctimoniously that it is only trying to reduce costs through such practices as knowing everyone's preferences so that it can send customized advertising most likely to generate revenue.

The libertarian side takes the position that amounts to, in essence, "We trust neither the government nor profit-minded strangers."

The law enforcement argument can be soothingly sweet to swallow. After all, nobody can credibly take a position against law and order, as doing so evokes images of unshaved savages roaming through the neighborhoods, killing, raping, and setting fires.

The real issue is different altogether. It is a philosophical issue. In an ideal world, governments and their law enforcement arms have impeccable integrity, act always and without exception in good faith, have impeccable records of having done so, and are inherently trustworthy. In such an ideal world, it would indeed be very hard to support any objection to law enforcement omnipotence because, by definition, law enforcement would never ever do anything inappropriate or abusive. But the world is not ideal. Furthermore, there is ample documented evidence of abuse of authority in every country in the world that goes back many, many years. And such abuse of authority has always transcended the limitations of any one sick individual: It has, historically, been institutionalized. It is human nature. It is a very bad sign when a government and its law enforcement arms make the huge mental leap of confusing their own survival in power with the survival of the nation they are supposed to serve. Consider the following situations where this can occur:

1. There is a lot of internal peace and lack of crime in most totalitarian regimes. The assorted secret polices see to that. Is that really what we

want for ourselves? Sure, everybody wants to prevent crime. But at what cost?

2. To a reasonable person, crime is murder, theft, arson, and so forth. To most any government, crime is whatever conduct it does not like. In many countries it is a crime to say something negative about their leaders. In other countries, it is a crime for a teenager to have a copy of *Playboy* magazine under the mattress. In still other countries, it is a crime to oppose the great leader. As such, it is a very slippery slope when any law enforcement organization makes the claim that it is "only preventing crime" or "only enforcing the law"; it sounds legitimate, but is it? The secret police of a totalitarian regime is also "only enforcing the law."

3. Civilized societies today say, "But we are different; we have laws and courts and due process." Indeed we do, but so does any totalitarian regime. The catch is that totalitarian regimes (and even their respective constitutions, if they have one, guarantee all sorts of individual rights "except as authorized by a lawful ... (any proper-sounding verbiage can go here)...," which means that all such "rights" are the discretion of the government representative who may want to take them away as he or she sees fit.

The point being made is that there is no inherent guarantee of civil liberties in the existence of assorted institutions unless there are also built-in means to minimize the likelihood that abuses of power can pass under the banner of legal authority.

It comes down to the philosophical and societal decision of where we draw the line between law enforcement and privacy. Is the solution to have more jails and more surveillance and less privacy? Or does the solution involve sociological measures (such as tighter-knit families or instilling a sense of shame in children to act as a built-in conscience to prevent socially unacceptable conduct)?

One should not delegate such fundamental decisions to politicians and certainly not to cops but to wise people.

But this train of thought may belong to a dying breed.

Technology that makes surveillance extremely easy is here, and there is a lot more coming:

- There will be a GPS receiver in every car and in every watch, and soon there will be a chip that could be implanted in individuals.
- There will be a camera at every key location that scans passers-by and positively identifies every individual in a database.
- There will be computer and network forensics allowing a regime to identify the individual who typed every word on a keyboard.
- DNA profiling, as soon as the GENOME project advances a bit, will anticipate which newborn is likely to become antisocial (whatever

that means) and surveil him or her even more, or even exile him or her in advance of any transgression, "for the good of society."

All for the "public good" of course. But then, from which genetic pool will the new Beethovens and Van Goghs and Nietzsches and Bertrand Russells and Gandhis of the future come if everyone is prefiltered to be "good"?

One could even argue from an evolutionary-science viewpoint that this is a recipe for the suicide of the human species.

Selecteed Bibliography

Privacy news and software

http://www.privacy.net for a demonstration of what Web sites get from your browser

http://www.fipr.org for the U.K. perspective on privacy

http://www.privacyware.com for privacy-related software

http://www.cdt.org/action/doubleclick.shtml (U.S. Center for Democracy and Technology)

http://www.users.globalnet.co.uk/~firstcut/privacy.html (technical counter-measures)

http://www.privacytimes.com for privacy-related news

http://www.users.globalnet.co.uk/~firstcut/dload.html for privacy-related software

http://www.townonline.com/privacyjournal for privacy-related guidelines

http://www.vortex.com/privarch.html for an archive of postings on the Usenet privacy forum

http://www.privacyrights.org for information about privacy

http://www.privacyrights.org/links.htm for numerous additional links on privacy

http://www.andrebacard.com/privacy.html for software and links about privacy

http://www.privacyplace.com for privacy-related news

http://www.stealthyguest.com for information and software for private Web browsing

http://www.privacy.org/pi for international trends in privacy

http://www.stack.nl/~galactus/remailers/index-anon.html

http://www.anonymizer.com

http://www.cs.berkeley.edu/~daw/papers/privacy-compcon97-www/privacy-html. html

Privacy organizations

http://www.eff.org

http://www.epic.org

http://www.efga.org

http://www.privacyrights.org

http://www.aclu.org

http://www.ipc.org

http://www.rightoprivacy.com

http://www.privacy.org/ipc

http://www.computerprivacy.org

http://www.bigbrotherinside.org

http://www.aaas.org/spp/anon/links.htm

Other

[1]   According to MSNBC News Service on August 13, 2000, federal regulators from the U.S. Federal Trade Commission charged Geocities, a popular Internet company that hosts free Web sites, with misleading its 2 million members by secretly selling personal information about them to marketers.

[2]   Diffie, W., and S. Landau, *Privacy on the Line: The Politics of Wiretapping and Encryption*, Cambridge, MA: MIT Press, 1998.

[3]   "Is Your Credit Report Online? Digital Debtors: Part Deux," *News.com*, August 21, 1997, at www.news.com/News/Item/0,4,13604,00.html.

[4]   Rothfeder, J., *Privacy for Sale*, NYC, Simon & Shuster, 1992, ISBN 0-671-73491-X.

[5]   The Social Security Number Frequency Asked Questions (FAQ).

[6]   Wacks, R., "Privacy and Press Freedom," http://www.gregsonalmstorng.co.uk/raymond-wacks-privacy-and-press-freedom-271-818-826-7.html. This has a U.K. focus.

6

Contents

Practical Measures for Protecting Sensitive Information

6.1   Installing secure Windows

This is a contradiction in terms because Windows was never designed as a secure operating system, with the possible exception of Windows NT, which is secure under very rigidly controlled conditions by which no individual user abides.[1]

Even so, one can do a lot to remove a large number of security threats to one's setup.

6.2   Recommended best practices

1.   Disable the built-in microphone (present in most laptops). The easiest way is to connect a plug into the external microphone receptacle. This will disable the internal microphone, and because it is just a plug with no microphone, it will not allow any sound to get picked up and either digitally recorded on the hard disk or transmitted via a modem.

2.   Put some black electrical tape over the camera lens if a camera is built-into the computer. If one is occasionally used as an external peripheral, cover it up at all times that it is not specifically needed.

3.   Start with a newly purchased hard disk. Even huge-capacity hard disks (e.g., 120–180 GB or more) can be purchased for less that a couple of hundred dollars these days, and starting from a known clean disk is a bargain for maximizing the likelihood that one's hard disk is clean from anything

---

1.   In the now-obsolete *Orange Book*, Windows NT had received a security rating that applied only if the computer was operated under conditions that hardly any home or business user would abide by.

inappropriate. Even then, however, it is quite possible that the hard disk was sold to someone else, who used it and returned it within the grace period, before the disk was resold to you.[2]

4. After partitioning the disk for your needs and formatting it, use a DOS-based free-space wipe utility from a floppy disk (such as Zapempty from http://www.sky.net/~voyageur/wipeutil.htm) and overwrite it a few times for good measure. Better yet, use the utility WipeDrive from http://www.whitecanyon.com.

5. Install Windows (Windows NT or 2000 rather than 95/98 is highly recommended), but enter some nondescript name other than your true name during the personalization step. It is much harder to remove one's true name after the fact because the Windows registration name is saved in the Registry and is subsequently copied and used by most application software installed on a computer.

6. Obtain and use Secure Office from http://www.mach5.com/sof. This software allows you to make drafts in Microsoft Office programs (Word, PowerPoint, and so on) without leaving the massive amount of electronic trash that Microsoft sprinkles all over one's hard disk. Its user interface is very convenient, as Figure 6.1 shows.

7. Go to Recycle Bin/Properties, set the space allocated for storing files to zero, select "One setting for all drives" and "Remove files immediately when discarded" as shown in Figure 6.2. Do not put any files in

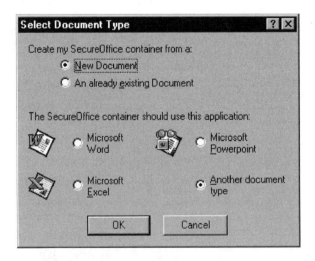

Figure 6.1   Creating a Microsoft Office document securely.

2. Purchasing a computer new is no guarantee that it has not been sold to another person who used it, saved files on it, and returned it to the store "in its original packaging" within the short time allowed by many vendors for returns. In that case it would be highly unlikely for the vendor to have reinstalled the software, let alone wiped the disk clean prior to such a reinstallation, before selling it to another buyer.

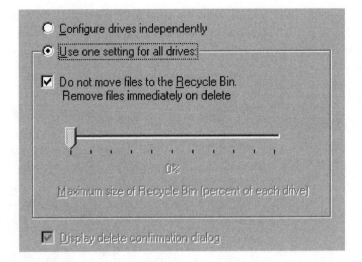

Figure 6.2 Setting the Recycle Bin not to store deleted files.

there because it is harder to wipe a deleted file (meaning one whose name has been forgotten or is not readily visible). Do not use any of the many utilities that allow one to undelete files because they work on the basis of storing "out of sight, out of mind" the files you think you deleted so that they can be retrieved.

Instead, obtain and use any of the many utilities for secure wiping of sensitive files, such as those that come with McAfee and Norton utilities.

Better yet, periodically wipe your entire hard disk (see Section 2.1.2).

Caution: Do not trust any one disk-wiping software. It may or may not do the cleaning that it claims to do. As a minimum, use two or three different disk-wiping software programs in sequence, although this can also be dangerous as the use of one disk-wiping software package may well preclude the subsequent use of a different one from being effective. Even so, the recommendation still holds because some disk-wiping software wipes the files but not their names (which are stored separately).

8. Do not allow others to use your personal computer, certainly not to install files or games. With today's extremely low computer costs, family members can easily have their own. The risks of not doing so (having a Trojan or adware/spyware unintentionally installed by a well-meaning family member in a computer that stores sensitive personal information) are just too high.

9. Do not connect your personal computer to the Internet. Ever. The risks are just too high, and you can have a computer for Internet connectivity only. Get a cheap computer on which you will store nothing even remotely sensitive or identifying, and use that to

connect to the Internet. (See Chapters 7 through 9 on preparing a computer for secure online access.)

10. Obtain, install, use, and periodically update (at least weekly) a complement of software for detecting and neutralizing a broad spectrum of malicious software. Recommended packages include the following:

   a.   Norton Antivirus.

   Caution: Do not patronize the version of this (or any other program) that requires online activation as you have no way of knowing what information gets sent out. Use, instead, software that requires no online activation. See Section 6.3.2 on this issue.

   b.   The Cleaner from www.moosoft.com. It is claimed to have superior detection of Trojans than mainstream virus-detection software packages. It is a bit quirky on Windows 98, and its online update has been having problems.

   c.   TDS-2 from http://tds.diamondcs.com.au (quirky on Windows 98 but okay on Windows NT). It, too, has a home-calling feature (to automatically check for new updates), which individual users may wish to disable.

   d.   Ad-Aware from www.lavasoftusa.com for adware detection and removal.

   e.   Who's Watching from www.trapware.com for detecting and negating spyware.

   f.   Spybot S&D by Patrick M. Kolla, also for detecting and negating software. Having two software packages for the same intended purpose is a good idea because you don't want to trust any single software package for this important function.

11. Do not print decrypted documents unless you are prepared to go through extra security steps. The problem is that anything sent to the printer is "temporarily" stored in the spool file in your disk and is then "deleted" (meaning, invisible to you but very visible to any forensic investigator).

12. Be very concerned about "system crashes." Sure, computers crash with sickening regularity, but this is much more than a nuisance: If your computer crashes during a sensitive operation (encrypting/decrypting/typing/viewing), there is a good chance that a temporary file will be left behind that one would wish had not been left behind for the benefit of forensics analysis. If the computer crashes, you must go through the following full process of securely cleaning it up, as discussed in this chapter:

   a.   Deleting all temporary files;

   b.   Wiping the slack;

      c.   Wiping all free space;

      d.   Wiping the swap file;

      e.   Wiping disingenuously chosen file names.

13.   Download, install, and use TweakUI's "paranoia" option. This is handy collection of utilities put together by Microsoft that includes the option of cleaning up the long list of electronics trails left behind by using Windows. Keep in mind that a separate version exists that works best for Windows 95/98, NT, and 2000. The main source is www.microsoft.com/ntworkstation/downloads/PowerToys/Net-working/NTTweakUI.asp; another source is http://twocows.apollo.lv/shellnt.html.

All options under "paranoia"[3] should be checked, as shown in Figure 6.3. At the same time remember that this utility deletes rather than wipes,

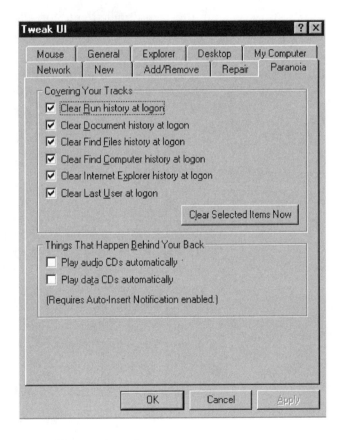

Figure 6.3 TweakUI paranoia options.

3. It is amusing that Microsoft, whose products have demonstrated such bad security over the years that the company has had to issue major security patches every few days, has used the term *paranoia* to denote a set of basic security steps everyone should take.

which means that everything is left behind for a forensic investigator unless one actually wipes the empty space of the hard disk.

6.2.1 If using Windows NT

In addition to recommendations 1 to 13 mentioned earlier in this section, do the following:

1. Create a RAM disk by using either the Microsoft-made RAM disk for NT software.

2. Convert to NTFS using the simple Windows NT command to do so. If possible, select the 512-byte cluster size so that the size of the slack (the space between the end of file and the end of cluster) is as small as possible and cannot fit and preserve much old data. This will have a slight negative impact on performance for those computer operations that require a lot of disk access.

3. Perform the steps spelled out for all versions of Windows in Section 6.1.

4. Disable print and file sharing. This is a must. If you truly need to share printers and files in a home network situation, you must make sure that you configure things accurately so that this sharing does not extend to computers outside your home network.

5. Set up the Windows NT or 2000 Registry to automatically wipe the swap file every time you power off by doing the following (in the case of Windows NT):

    a. Run REGEDT32.exe.

    b. Go to HKEY_LOCAL_MACHINE\SYSTEM\CurrentControlSet\ Control\Session Manager\Memory Management, as shown in Figure 6.4.

    c. Change the value of "ClearPageFileAtShutdown" to 1. If this parameter does not exist, add it as follows:

        i.   Value Name: ClearPageFileAtShutdown
        ii. Value Type: REG_DWORD
        iii. Value: 1

             This will become effective only after the computer is restarted.

             The above recipe works for Windows NT and Windows 2000 as well.

             Caution: There is no information from Microsoft as to just how the data is overwritten. It may or may not be adequately secure. One would be well advised (also) to wipe the Registry using stand-alone, independent software (e.g., Secure Clean, Scorch).

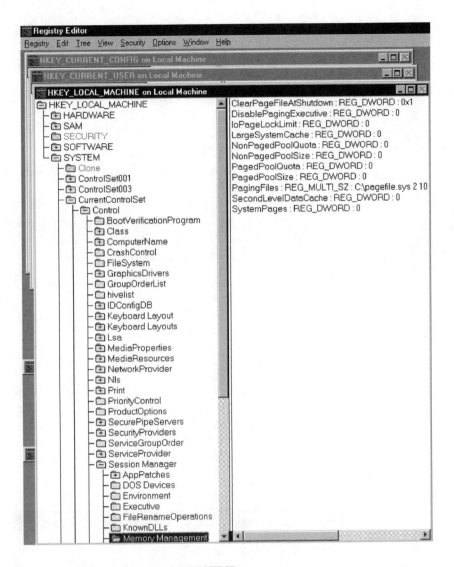

Figure 6.4 Registry editing with REGEDIT.

6. Consider getting the following security-related software, installing them, and learning how to use them:

   a. BestCrypt from http://www.jetico.com to create fully encrypted partitions on your hard drive. See also Section 6.4.2.

   b. Eraser from http://www.tolvanen.com/eraser (free software that wipes one's disk clean).

   c. PGP version 6.58ckt Build 7. In addition follow the recommendations in Section 11.3. This software's claim to fame is that it supports far longer key lengths than the mainstream PGP and is backwards compatible. Do not use the "pgp disk" option on Windows NT as it is faulty for most versions of PGP. Do not get PGP versions 7.x.

d. SecureClean from Access Data Corporation (www.access-data.com) is an excellent additional file- and swap-wiping utility. You don't want to be at the mercy of one wiping utility's weaknesses, so use this in addition to Eraser. It is very configurable, as shown in Figure 6.5.

6.2.2   If using Windows 2000

In addition to recommendations 1–13 listed in Section 6.2, do the following:

1. First and foremost, disabuse yourself of the notion that 2000 is more secure than NT; it is not. Its "encryption" option conveys a false sense of security because it is simply not secure at all from any competent forensics analyst for the following reasons:

    a. That system does not allow the swap file to be encrypted. Given what was stated in Section 2.3 about the swap file and the fact that it usually contains a lot of what one does with the computer, encrypting a file or folder but not the swap file is like locking your front door and leaving the back door wide open.

    b. System files (e.g., the Registry) also cannot be encrypted. Given what was said in Section 2.4 about the wealth of sensitive personal data placed by Windows into the Registry, leaving that unencrypted is like leaving all of one's windows in the house wide open (in addition to leaving the back door open as per (a).

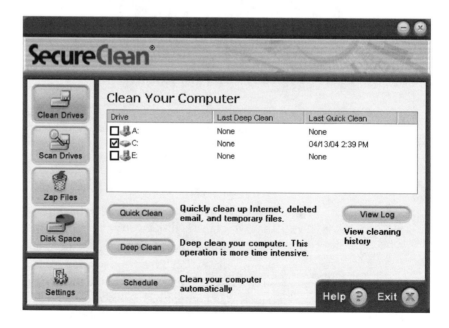

Figure 6.5   SecureClean set up to wipe data.

c.   There is no encryption of the slack in the disk. Given what was said in Section 2.2.1 about what can exist in the slack to delight the forensic investigator, this is like exposing the floor plan to the burglar of one's house for his convenience.

d.   While one can (or should, but often does not think of doing) specify that the "Temporary" folder is to be encrypted as well, the fact is that different software programs have the bad habit of using their own temporary storage locations in one's disk. As such, there is no one "Temporary" folder to protect. This is like locking one piece of jewelry in the safe but leaving the rest of them lying around for a burglar to help himself to.

e.   Even though a folder can be specified to be encrypted, and files created in or copied to it are encrypted, the folder itself is not encrypted at all, and anyone with the right access permissions can see the names of the encrypted files in it.

In view of all of the foregoing, the much-heralded "encryption" option of the Windows 2000 operating system is a useless gimmick. In fact, it is worse than useless because it will tend to instill a false sense of security in the minds of those who use it in the mistaken belief that it protects their sensitive data from forensics analysis. It does not.

2.   Do not display the last user's name in the logon sequence screen; this takes a manual step to make it happen. To disable the last-user display, go to the Local Security Policy and make the change. There is no reason why an unauthorized person should know half of your login magic words (user name) and only have to guess the other half (password).

3.   Convert to NTFS with the command-line command convert C: /fs:ntfs (if converting a drive other than C:, use the appropriate letter).

4.   Once Windows has been set up, do not log in for day-to-day usage with the administrator account or with any other account that has administrator privileges. Use, instead, one created for your use that has simple user privileges so that your system files (which require administrator privileges) cannot be accessed surreptitiously while you are using some software that has a dual malicious function. As with most any security measure, this will impact convenience: When you want to install software while logged in as someone without administrator privileges, you won't be able to, but neither will any remote hacker.

5.   Beware of Windows 2000's master file table (MFT). It has at least one entry for every file in an NTFS volume in your computer, along with extended information about each such file (date/time stamps, data content, and so forth.). Worse yet, in the interest of speed, Microsoft does not edit and compact that MFT superfile but merely appends to

it. As such, it can contain a list of files that goes back to the day you installed Windows 2000, long after you think that you deleted all references to them. By the way, if you have a huge number of files on your disk after a year or two and Windows runs out of preallocated MFT space, you will get no warning, and the directory table for the volume will crash. To prevent that, you need to hack the Registry as follows:

a. Run REGEDT32.

b. Go to HKEY_LOCAL_MACHINE\System\CurrentControlSet\Control\FileSystem.

c. Select "Add" from the Edit menu.

d. In the dialog box that comes up, enter

   Value Name: NtfsMftZoneReservation

   Data Type: REG_DWORD

   Data: (enter 3 or 4; 4 is the maximum)

e. Close REGEDT32.

   The above hack will only remove the possibility of a volume directory crash and will not fix the security problem, which is unfixable. About the only fix for the security problem is to use file names that are nonincriminating and nondescript.

6. If you elect to avail yourself of the "encryption" option in Windows 2000 (and there is really no benefit to doing so, as discussed above, other than some protection from a totally unsophisticated person that might take an interest in your computer), then at least realize that someone can still easily spoof your computer into revealing those encrypted files by logging in as an administrator through a back door as follows:

   To encrypt a folder from the command line, type CIPHER [/E| /D] [/S:dir] [/I] [F/] [Q/] [pattern or directory], where

/E Causes the encryption of the specified directories

/D Decrypts the folder and stops any further encryption

/S Encrypts all files and subfolders in that directory

/I Forces the encryption to continue even if an error occurs (normally encryption stops if an error occurs)

/F Forces encryption on all directories specified (already encrypted directories will not be encrypted again)

/Q Reports minimal information about the status of the encryption of a file or folder being encrypted

To hack into your encrypted files without your knowledge, all someone has to do is restart your computer from the Emergency Repair Disk (ERD), reinstall the Windows 2000 operating system (e.g., from the distribution CD-ROM), set himself or herself up as the administrator, and use the default file-recovery certificate that you will most likely have left in the computer.

To preclude this happening, export the default recovery certificate to a floppy as follows:

1. Log in as administrator.

2. Start/Run mmc.

3. Select "Console," then "Add/Remove."

4. Select "Add."

5. Highlight the "Certificates" option and click Add.

6. Select "My User Account."

7. Click "Finish."

8. Close and click "OK."

9. Open Certificates—Current User, Personal, Certificates in the left panel. On the right side, you will see a certificate listed. Right-click on it and select "All tasks." Export. This will start the Certificate Wizard.

10. Choose "Yes, export the private key." Click "Next."

11. Select "Personal Information Exchange" and then remove the check by "Enable strong protection" and also by "Delete the private key if effort is successful." Select "Next."

12. Enter a good password. Make sure you write it down somewhere so that it is not forgotten. Select "Next."

13. Make up a file name under which to save that key. Put a floppy disk in the computer and type A:RECOVERY.PFX

14. Select "Next" and "Finish."

15. Now you must delete the certificate on the hard disk. Right-click on the entry for the certificate and select "Delete."

16. To verify that the certificate has indeed been deleted, reboot the computer, log in as administrator, and try to read any file on the disk that has been encrypted as any user other than administrator; it should fail.

17. Install and use a RAM disk, such as the one depicted in Figure 6.6 (http://www.cenatek.com/product_ramdisk.cfm).

    Caution: Do not enable the option whereby the RAM disk is saved onto the physical hard disk just before shutting down. Doing so will negate the security benefit of having a RAM disk in the first place.

Caution: This admonition applies to all computer users, regardless of which operating system is being used and regardless of whether the computer in question is ever connected to any network: If you plan to have your computer serviced or repaired by someone else, make sure that the hard disk is removed first. The reasons should be self-evident by now.

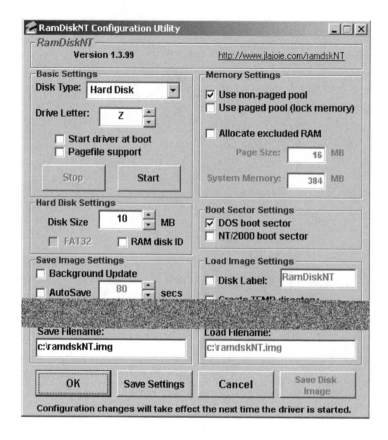

Figure 6.6 RAM disk for Windows 2000. Do not enable any of the "Save image" settings.

6.2.3 If using Windows XP

Even though Windows XP is the latest operating system, it is not recommended unless one can obtain a version that does not require online activation (e.g., one covered by a corporate license or one preinstalled by the original equipment manufacturer (OEM). See Sections 6.2.3 and 6.3.2 about the perils of online activation.

An excellent set of security recommendations in connection with Windows XP can be found at http://www.mccune.cc/SecureXP.txt and www.markusjansson.net/exp.html.

The following steps are recommended for Windows XP in addition to steps 1 to 13 listed in Section 6.2:

1. Install the latest service pack for XP.

2. Turn off autoupdates (or depend on your own personal firewall to block them). For details use XP-Antispy at http://www.xp-antispy.org/index.php?option=com_remository&Itemid=26. Information on which XP services to enable or disable can be found at http://www. blkviper.com/WinXP/servicecfg.htm.

3. Get Index.dat Suite (http://www.it-mate.co.uk/support/idsuite.asp) to clean up part of the Registry as you cannot do so from DOS if you are using NTFS (as you should).

4. Disable all services that you are not using. See http://www.markus-jansson.net/kuvat/services1.png, services2.png, and services3.png.

5. Install a personal firewall (we recommend ZoneAlarm Pro) using its most conservative settings; the firewall built in Windows XP is totally inadequate and typically offers no protection from outgoing traffic initiated by malicious software (adware, spyware) in your computer.

6. Prevent remote hackers from logging in to your computer and making changes to your Registry or to your shares (for specifics, see http://www.markusjansson.net/kuvat/lpura.png).

7. Make sure that you do not log in with administrator privileges when connected to a network (Internet or any other).

8. Install Abtrusion Protecto (http://www.abtrusion.com) to reduce the likelihood of malicious code being executed on your computer.

9. Kill NetBIOS (see http://www.markusjansson.net/kuvat/LAN2 .jpg).

10. Do not depend on XP's EFS encryption any more than you should on Windows 2000 encryption. One can reasonably expect it to have an ADK. Furthermore, it offers zero protection from unencrypted temporary files, swap files, and so forth. If you want to use EFS for good measure, at least force it to use the 256-bit advanced encryption standard (AES) algorithm. For details on how to do so, see http://support.microsoft.com/default.aspx?scid =kb;[LN];329741.

A critical security vulnerability in Windows XP allows the files in any specific directory of one's computer to be deleted if an XP user clicks on a maliciously formed URL (i.e., Web link). Such an URL could be automatically accessed by one's computer as part of reading an incoming e-mail or Usenet newsgroup posting, by going to some other Web site that contains a link to that URL in the form of a Web bug (the one-pixel dot that causes one's browser to go to the URL that the single pixel image is supposedly stored at), or through any one of a number of other ways. This security vulnerability was fixed by Microsoft on September 9, 2002, with the release of XP's first service pack. Unfortunately, that service pack caused serious problems to a number of XP users (rendering many XP computers unusable), which has caused many other XP users not to apply this service pack, thereby leaving their computers vulnerable to the above critical security problem. Microsoft subsequently released a patch that fixes this problem without requiring the installation of the troublesome Service Pack 1.

A vulnerability in Microsoft's universal plug and play (UPnP) implementation that dates back to 2002 allows an attacker to gain system-level (i.e., full) access to any default installation of Windows XP and to crash the XP computer or even to launch a denial of service attack by remotely exploiting a buffer overflow vulnerability. The threat was so significant that the FBI urged users to take steps beyond installing the Microsoft-released patch (http://www.grc.com/unpnp/unpnp.htm).

The Remote Data Protocol (RDP), which provides the means whereby Windows provides remote terminal sessions to clients, is malformed in XP. An attacker, who does not even need to be authenticated, can deliver packets to the targeted system and crash it. A fix for this was made available at www.microsoft.com/technet/security/bulletin/ms02-051.asp.

6.2.4 Heroic protective measures regardless of the version of Windows

1. If using a laptop, consider removing the hard disk and either taking it with you or storing it in a physically safe place when you cannot exercise physical control over the laptop. Most laptops' hard disks are easily removable and are inconspicuous to carry, even in a shirt pocket.

2. Consider using any of the three full disk encryption packages discussed in Section 6.4.1, but realize that they do not protect from anything (e.g., viruses/Trojans/worms coming from installed software or from connectivity to a network) while one is legitimately using the computer. They do protect, however, when the computer is off, but not from keyboard and other commercial cable taps discussed in Section 4.3.

3. Individually encrypt the files you are trying to protect.

4. Do whatever you feel would indicate to you whether your computer has been accessed in your absence. This includes not only electronic access but also physical access to its disk(s).

5. There is no sense protecting the computer if the backups (in the form of tapes, disks, or whatever) are not protected equally well. If you have backups, which you should as it is only a matter of time until your computer crashes for any one of a number of reasons, keep those backups out of reach of whomever you are (or should be) concerned can get them and cause you harm. To prevent the total loss of your data if there should be a fire on your premises, make a habit of hand-carrying your backups to a friend's house on a regular basis.

6. Do not type sensitive information:

    a. While online;

b. While in an Internet cafe;

c. When using someone else's computer;

d. When your computer screen can be seen by anyone else.

7. Purchase a keyboard as well as the keyboard cable, monitor cable, and printer cables from a store yourself. Mark them in a way that would indicate to you if they were ever changed.

8. Look for any new "adaptors" that may appear in line with any of these cables (see Section 4.3 on commercially available keyboard taps).

9. This is tedious but well worth it if the situation warrants it. Obtain a simple hash signature program, like crc.com, hash.exe, or md5.zip. The intent of any of these programs is to finger-print whichever file(s) you want to ensure are not doctored without your knowledge. The ritual for using any of these programs is as follows:

    a. You apply any of these programs to the file you want to protect. All this does is generate a few bytes on the screen that you should copy down and store securely because they represent the signature of the file at a time when you trust that file to have been unmodified by anyone. Applying these programs to a file, such as stuff.doc, is as simple as typing (from DOS) CRC [path]stuff.doc for the case of crc.exe.

    b. Whenever you suspect that someone may have doctored any such protected file, reapply the same program to that file and compare the new signature to the old, securely stored one. If they differ, the protected file has been changed.
        This should be done for all sensitive files, such as

        i. All encryption-related files, such as keys, executables, and the like;

        ii. All major system files, such as DLLs in C:\Windows\ System.

6.2.5 Last but not least

No cookbook of technical countermeasures and steps can ever take the place of common sense and sound practices (which is what OPSEC, or operational security, is all about). Self-evident blunders that can never be prevented by any technical countermeasure include, but are not limited to, the following:

1. Poorly chosen passwords, or passwords written on scraps of paper that others can find;

2. Overused and infrequently changed passwords;

3. Having a computer monitor facing an open window;

4. Leaving a computer unattended while it is on;

5. Allowing one's computer to be used promiscuously by others;

6. Storing sensitive papers or magnetic media (such as backups, recovery disks, encryption software) in locations easily accessible to others.

7. Dismissing the many security recommendations of this book.

8. Leaving a computer's hard disk physically unprotected.

The list goes on.

6.3 Additional privacy threats and countermeasures

6.3.1 Individually serial-numbered documents

Some popular software (e.g., earlier versions of Microsoft Office) have the privacy-compromising feature whereby any document saved also includes the serial number of the individual software copy that created it. This information is not displayed to the user when viewing the document but is saved nonetheless. This is known as the globally unique identifier (see www.nytimes.com/library/tech/99/04/circuits/articles/08 pete.html). It was reportedly used to identify the perpetrator of the Melissa virus.

The problem is that a savvy recipient of an electronic copy of a document (e.g., an e-mailed one or one handed over on a floppy disk or other media) or a computer forensic investigator will be able to infer additional information about the creator of the document, who may have wanted to have remained anonymous.

To protect from this, a user who wishes to remain anonymous should not provide electronic but printed copies of documents. If an electronic copy has to be given or e-mailed out, the document should first be converted to an Adobe .pdf file, image file, or equivalent.

6.3.2 Online activation and online snooping by software

The software industry, which like any industry is not a charity but a profit-making entity, has succeeded in labeling a privacy issue a "piracy" issue. The choice of the term *piracy* is not accidental as it evokes images of unshaved savages torching, pillaging, and looting the neighborhood with gleeful abandon.

One cannot and should not deny people or entities the legal right to protect and benefit from their intellectual property as long as the steps taken to safeguard this right do not violate the privacy of purchasers. As civilized individuals we would flatly refuse to allow a bookstore to install cameras in our houses so that the vendor could make sure that we didn't let our cousins read the book we just bought and observe the rest of our in-house family life as well. Yet this is precisely the problem with online activation: The software purchased snoops around our computers and then contacts the software maker online with information whose content we cannot decipher, whereupon the vendor issues an online blessing that activates the software.

Lest someone thinks that individual computer users maintain the upper hand and their rights, consider the following prose from Microsoft Passport's terms of use (http://www.theregister.co.uk/content/4/18002.html) in 2002:

> By posting messages, uploading files, inputting data, submitting any feedback or suggestions, or engaging in any other form of communication with or through the Passport Web Site . . . you are granting Microsoft and its affiliate companies permission to:
>
> Use, modify, copy, distribute, transmit, publicly display, publicly perform, reproduce, publish, sublicense, create derivative works from, transfer, or sell any such communication.
>
> . . .
>
> Publish your name in connection with any such communication.
>
> . . .
>
> The foregoing grants shall include the right to exploit any proprietary rights in such communication, including but not limited to rights under copyright, trademark, service mark or patent laws under any relevant jurisdiction. No compensation will be paid with respect to Microsoft's use of the materials contained within such communication.

Faced with public outrage and the likelihood of no sales, Microsoft quickly retracted these terms of use (http://www.wired.com/news/business/0,1367, 42811,00.html). Amusingly, the very same software, Microsoft's Internet Passport, admitted to a major security flaw that left millions of users at risk (http://www.cnn.com/2003/TECH/biztech/05/09/microsoft.flaw.ap/index. html) of data theft by hackers and thieves.

Readers may want to weigh the severe security threats posed by online activation. If the vendor offers the option of activating the software by telephone or by mail, that would be the preferred choice. Unfortunately, some software (such as the latest versions of Norton Antivirus) will only work through online activation. Users have to make their own decisions as to whether to purchase such software. In the case of antivirus software, there really is no decision to make because such software needs to call the vendor on a regular basis to download the latest virus signature information; otherwise, it is useless. One more call during installation won't matter. Most other software, however, has no business connecting with its maker.

The problem gets worse because many software packages that require no online activation take it upon themselves to periodically contact their respective parent companies over the Internet behind the user's back: Windows XP Search Assistant silently downloads files (http://www.theregister.co.uk/content/4/24815.htm) even though the user never gave Microsoft permission to do so.

6.3.3 Microsoft documents that call home

In a nutshell, a Microsoft document (Word, PowerPoint, Excel 2000) can contain an invisible "Web bug" that, when opened, can access the Internet (when one is online) and send the host name of the computer and related identifying information [1]. As the Word file is given or e-mailed to others, they become vulnerable to the same privacy-violating situation.

On the positive side, such a Web bug can be used by a company to help track leaked confidential documents and even the editing, copying, and pasting of sensitive paragraphs (that contain the Web bug) to other documents.

What makes this possible is the ability of a Microsoft Word document to link to an image file that resides at some remote Web server. Every time the Word document is opened, the Internet-enabled computer will try to get the image from the remote site. This, in turn, allows the remote site to know who is accessing the document, when, and from where.

The Web bug image need not be any larger that a single pixel. Inserting a Web bug is simple.

1. Select Insert/Picture/From File.

2. In the "File name" text box in the "Insert Picture" dialog box, enter the URL of the Web bug.

3. Opt for the "Link to File" option in the drop-down menu of the "Insert" button.

A demo of this is available at www.privacycenter.du.edu/demos/bugged.doc, /bugged.xls, and /bugged.ppt for Word, Excel, and Powerpoint, respectively. This is accessed through Microsoft's Internet Explorer.

The countermeasure is to disable cookies in the browser and to use a firewall that alerts a user to any unexpected attempt by the computer to access the Internet.

This threat is not unique to Microsoft. The generic threat can become part of practically every file format, such as MP3 music files (hotly contested by the music industry), images, and so forth.

6.3.4   The NetBIOS and other threats from unneeded network services

Most individuals use a computer that is either stand-alone or connected to the Internet. For those people there is absolutely no need to accept the default network setups that come with Windows; they include services that can only cause security-related grief.

Go to Network and Dial-up Connections. (In the case of Windows 95/98 it is under My Computer; in the case of Windows 2000 it is under Settings/Control Panel). Under Properties/Networking, disable all options except for TCP/IP (which is needed for Internet access). Specifically disable NetBIOS and any Microsoft networking.

This will take care of one the "10 Most Critical Internet Security Threats" identified by the respected SANS Institute (www.sans.org/topten.htm).

6.3.5   TCPA/Palladium

The Trusted Computing Platform Alliance (TCPA)[4] is an Intel Corporation initiative closely related to a Microsoft effort (Palladium) to embed digital-rights-management (DRM) technology into personal computers. In September 2003, Intel bowed to pressure and announced that it was rethinking this approach (code-named "LaGrande") so that Intel would not be vilified by the industry and the users.

TCPA is basically about support for hardware key storage. Every operating system/hardware environment with hardware-supported cryptosecurity mechanisms can be used to enforce DRM just as it can protect confidential information. If one can do one, one can do the other as well. The issue debated so hotly regarding TCPA, DRM, and their implications is that users want the latter but don't care about the former if it comes at the expense of freedom to use one's own computer as one likes.

Microsoft's software effort, Palladium, pastes a digital certificate on all Internet communications and encrypts the data even inside the computer processor. In the process, it takes TCP/IP, the standard Internet communications protocols, and replaces them with technology owned by Microsoft, hence the colloquial name for Palladium, "TCP/MS."

It is unknown at this stage what will happen with non-Intel microprocessors and non-Windows operating systems such as the various flavors of Unix.

The problem with this concept is in the details. If the security-administration policy of a word or image processor is remotely reconfigurable by a server to reflect changing legalities, then the police can instruct a PC to search for and report the processing of any file that contains, for example, the phrase "civil disobedience" or the words "Christ" or "Moslem." TCPA will reportedly allow a user to turn it off. The DMCA (see Section

4. For more details on TCPA and Palladium, see http://www.cl.cam.ac.uk/users/rja14/tcpa-faq.html by noted information security authority Ross Anderson.

16.4.1) and its non-U.S. counterparts criminalize the circumvention of technologies protecting copyright content.

In summary, TCPA and Palladium provide security for copyright owners but not for the user. They decrease user security by enabling remote control of an online-connected computer's security policies.

6.3.6   The vulnerability of backups

All hard disks will crash sooner or later for any one of a number of reasons. One would be totally reckless not to make regular backups. These backups, however, should be viewed as every bit as vulnerable to unauthorized viewing and analysis as the originals. In fact they are more vulnerable because

1.   They are almost always portable and easily removed from one's premises.

2.   They are rarely wiped by users, who instead either overwrite on top of the previous backup or, worse yet, simply append the changes made since the last backup, using any one of many backup-making software.

3.   They can provide an adversary with a chronological record of changes and events.

4.   In those cases where encrypted partitions are not amenable to routine backup software, one has to decrypt those partitions first, and the backups therefore often include files that are encrypted in the original.

The process of making a backup is almost always viewed as a chore (until one's disk crashes, at which point one is elated for having had the foresight to make a backup). As such, users do not usually apply security considerations to this chore.

The following list of security-motivated steps is recommended for backups:

1.   Wipe each previous backup before proceeding with the next one.

2.   Use full backups and never incremental ones.

3.   Be aware that some disk-encryption and partition-encryption software have the quirky requirement that they can only back up the encrypted portion after it has first been decrypted. This means that the backup will be extremely vulnerable. Do not use such encryption software. If your backups do contain unencrypted information that is encrypted on your computer(s), store your backups where they cannot be found by unauthorized third parties.

4.   Use a password to protect the contents of the backup. This provides no protection against a forensic attack, but does protect from casual perusal. Also, use compression, which is usually offered as an option

in the backup process, to make glancing at the contents just a bit more difficult.

5.   Always store the backups offsite at a location other than that of the computer that was backed up, preferably at some location not accessible by a potential adversary (business or personal). This will also help you save the data in case of fire at the site of the computer.

6.   Do not ever acknowledge the existence of backups to unauthorized others. Explain the existence of backup software as something you always meant to do but never got around to.

7.   Protect the backups as if they contained the family jewels. They often do.

6.4 Protecting sensitive data on hard disks

Medical professionals are usually required by law to safeguard the confidentiality of patients' records. Corporate officials and all businessmen, scientists, and other professionals must safeguard the confidentiality of proprietary information or lose business to industrial espionage. Individuals are required to safeguard their data so as to protect themselves from identity theft or face denial of any insurance coverage.

Additionally, as shown in Section 1.4.6, there are numerous ways whereby incriminating data enters most everyone's computer without the owner's knowledge or acquiescence. It follows that practically every owner or user of a computer has the legal, ethical, and practical obligation to take effective measures to ensure that his or her computer is truly cleansed in a manner that will prevent files from being seen by unauthorized eyes.

To a hammer everything is a nail, and to a law enforcer everyone is a suspect. Not surprisingly, law enforcers have been promulgating the self-serving fiction that any effort to protect confidential data implies culpability as surely as wiping bloodstains from the carpet. As shown in the preceding paragraph, nothing could be further from the truth.

Windows includes no means whereby a user can prevent a savvy data thief from stealing confidential data; worse yet, as shown in Section 2.2, Windows and Windows application software actually create a lot of files with sensitive data on a user's storage media behind that user's back.

The delete command deletes nothing; it only marks the space taken by a file in storage media as available if and when a future file might need that space.

Contrary to popular belief, the format command does not remove any data either; even though such data cannot be accessed through Windows, the data is very much intact for the benefit of forensic analysis.

Also contrary to popular belief, the FDISK and repartitioning commands also do not remove any data, even though Windows cannot access it.

Clearly the security-conscious professional has two choices:

1.   Ensure that all data in a computer is encrypted;

2. Ensure that all sensitive data is truly wiped clean before a computer is exposed to potentially hostile eyes (e.g., before selling one's computer on the used market or otherwise transferring ownership).

Encrypting individual files is not useful in protecting the confidentiality of data because Windows and Windows applications have a propensity to create and leave behind all sorts of copies of the unencrypted files; recall the discussion in Sections 2.2 through 2.4 about temporary files, the swap file, and so forth.

The professional who wants to protect the confidentiality of data in a computer must obtain and use software which encrypts the entire hard disk, end to end, on a track-by-track and sector-by-sector basis. This way temporary files, swap files, backup files, and so forth are all encrypted on the fly before being written to the disk and decrypted on the fly as needed. This process is transparent to the user. The incremental delay introduced by this on-the-fly encryption and decryption is imperceptible to the user of any of today's fast computers, except conceivably those performing the most read-/write-intensive activities, such as the processing of video files.

The reader is strongly cautioned that the full disk encryption just described is not the same disk partition encryption, which is done by such popular software as Scramdisk, E4M, BestCrypt, PGP Disk, and others. These software products take a user-specified portion of one's hard disk space (say, 1 GB) and assign it a new name (e.g., "F:/"); anything written to that partition is indeed encrypted. Additionally, such software also takes some minimal effort (which does not fool anyone) to hide the existence of such a partition unless the user activates it with a password. The problem with these schemes is that they offer absolutely no protection from temporary files (e.g., those created by Microsoft Word and other software), the swap file, or the separately saved file names being left behind in the unencrypted portion of the disk. As such, they give the user a false sense of security (which is worse than no security at all because the user will take chances he or she otherwise would not have).

6.4.1 Full disk encryption

In a nutshell, full disk encryption software negates computer forensics entirely.[5]

With their low price ($50–$150), the lack of popularity of full disk encryption[6] software is simply amazing, given how effective these programs

---

5. If one expands the definition of the term *computer forensics* to include activities that are not normally considered as part of computer forensics (such as keystroke interception, remote hacking, or van Eck radiation interception), then of course encryption of any kind does not usually negate those other activities.

6. Actually, the "boot sector(s)" of a disk cannot be encrypted because that is where the computer obtains information about how to read the rest of the disk. This sector, however, does not contain any sensitive data anyway.

are in protecting the confidentiality of one's computer files when the computer is turned off.

The user of full disk encryption no longer needs to worry about wiping individual files (temporary files, swap files). He or she also no longer needs to worry about the consequences of forgetting a laptop computer on the train, in the taxi, at the hotel, or anywhere else—a problem with potentially deadly consequences if that laptop belongs to an employee of the security services.

At the same time, a full-disk-encrypted computer offers no protection when it is turned on by the authorized user who knows the password. Once the computer is turned on by an authorized user, it is as if there is no encryption at all. If that computer is left on while the user steps out of the room, or even while that computer is connected to a network, it is every bit as unprotected as a conventional unencrypted computer.

In those cases, the savvy professional must deploy additional protective measures, such as the following:

1. Encryption of individual sensitive files (patient records, tax returns, and so on);

2. Use of partition encryption, discussed in detail in Section 6.4.2;

3. Use of firewalls, malicious mobile code protection software (a.k.a. antivirus software[7]), and online settings intended to minimize vulnerability to online threats (see Chapters 7 through 9).

Currently the three most recommended software packages for full disk encryption are

1. SecureDoc by WinMagic of Canada (http://www.winmagic.com) which is Federal Information Processing Standards (FIPS) certified;

2. SafeBoot by Control Break International in the United Kingdom (http://www.controlbreak.net), which is also FIPS-certified;

3. DriveCryptPlusPack by DriveCrypt in Germany (http://www.securestar.com).

All of these use 256-bit AES encryption. There is even a hardware-based device, SecureIDE, by Abit Company (www.abit.com.tw) that curiously uses only 40-bit DES encryption, which is totally inadequate.

This author experimented at length with the first of the above software packages with the following results:

---

7. Actually, over and above the semantic distinction between viruses, Trojans, and worms, some of the most popular antivirus software is not nearly as effective in protecting from Trojans, adware, or spyware as some other software that specializes in detecting those nonvirus threats. The reader is referred to Sections 7.4.1, 9.2 through 9.4, and 9.17 for a discussion on the best complement of software to protect from the different classes of malicious mobile code.

1. The software does indeed encrypt the entire disk as advertised (with the necessary, but inconsequential, exception of the boot sector).

2. Not surprisingly, the software conflicts with software that wants to write on that boot sector. This includes legitimate software (e.g., programs that allow one to boot from one of many operating systems on the disk, such as System Commander), as well as ill-behaved software such as the new batch of activation-required software (see Sections 6.2.3 and 6.3.2), which use the boot sector to enforce the producers' means of preventing a user from making (legal or bootlegged) copies of such software.

3. The computer worked flawlessly and encryption was transparent to the user as long as one did not use disk-defragmenting software (such as Windows 2000's own disk defragmenter) or disk-wiping software (such as Eraser, discussed in Section 2.1.3). In those cases the computer crashed but was rebooted with no apparent lingering aftereffects. One could argue that one does not need entire-disk-wiping software at all if one uses full disk encryption. Disk defragmenting, however, is very much needed periodically, regardless of whether there is full disk encryption or not.

6.4.2   Encrypting disk partitions

Disk partition encryption is also known as on-the-fly encryption. Software programs include BestCrypt, E4M, Invincible Disk, PGPDisk, SAFE Folder, ScramDisk, Flycrypt. F-Secure File Crypto, SafeHouse, seNTry 2000, and S to Infinity. The most popular ones are BestCrypt, E4M, PGPDisk, and ScramDisk. See Section 6.4.2 for details.

Reference

[1]   http://www.privacyfoundation.org/advisories/advWordBugs.html.

Basic Protection from Computer Data Theft Online

A few years back, TV viewers in Germany were shown how an unsuspecting Internet user, who had accessed a seemingly innocuous Web site, had his own hard disk looked at and actually modified by that Web site! In particular, the seemingly innocuous Web site searched the unsuspecting Internet user's hard disk, found that he was using a particular software for online banking, and remotely modified its "to do" list. The next time the unsuspecting user connected to his bank with that software for his regular online banking session, unbeknownst to him, he directed his bank to make a payment to the account of the hackers running that seemingly innocuous Web site he had browsed a few days earlier.

There are numerous ways whereby the files in one's computers can be viewed, changed, or deleted by a remote third party if one is connected to the Internet. Some of these involve remote hacking through any one of a multitude of security weaknesses in Windows and Windows applications software. Others use adware (a.k.a. spyware) installed by unsuspecting users of assorted software packages that call (their) home and report on a user's hard disk contents (see Chapter 9, particularly Section 9.19). Still others use commercial keystroke-capture software or hardware that also calls home and reports on a user's keyboard strokes (see Sections 4.3 and 4.4). Still others exploit one's use of wireless Wi-Fi connectivity (see Section 13.2). The list goes on and on.

Unless one has plugged each and every possible way that information can be remotely accessed from one's computer, one's computer files can be read, modified, deleted, or even added to without one's knowledge. "But I am using a firewall, and this cannot happen to me," one might say. Not true in most cases! Despite its name, a firewall is not an impenetrable barrier; depending on just exactly what it does and how it is configured, its protection could range from none to some (see

Section 9.18). Firewalls are, at best, permeable membranes that can be exploited; some enterprising software programs, for example, try to avoid detection of their surreptitious access to the Internet by timing it to coincide with times that one is already sending data to the Internet through the Web browser (port 80). Others masquerade as legitimate-sounding system software so that when one's firewall asks the user for permission for what seems like a legitimate system function to access the Internet, most users will readily grant it on a permanent basis, incorrectly assuming that this access is legitimate and innocuous.

Chapters 7 through 9 will expose the most common ways whereby one's privacy can be compromised while online and spell out specific ways of defeating those threats to one's security and privacy. The reader must appreciate, however, that different ways of compromising one's privacy online can easily be developed and that there is really no future-proof way of positively ensuring that one can never have his or her files looked at, modified, or deleted by unauthorized others from afar. One must stay current with evolving threats and take the appropriate countermeasures in the future.

It is for this reason that a security-minded user is advised to use two different computers: The "good" one should never be connected online. The other one can be inexpensive; it should be used only for online connection and should contain nothing sensitive.

Both computers should be subjected to the same security-related procedures detailed in this book to ensure confidentiality of private information. The computer reserved for online use should be subjected to additional precautions (detailed later in this chapter) because it is vulnerable not only to physical forensics but also to unauthorized online access of its contents. As an example, encrypting the entire hard disk (an option strongly recommended in Section 6.4.1) is totally ineffective for an online computer because the disk has to be functioning in its decrypted state while online.

Any data to be transferred between these two computers (e.g., a recently downloaded file intended for the offline computer) could easily be transferred through a removable disk (e.g., floppy, Zip, USB key).

Alternately, one can opt for having a single computer with removable, bootable hard disks so that one can boot with and use one disk for secure offline use and another disk for risky online use. Removable, bootable drive mounts are available for conventional hard disk drives.

Adding security-related protective measures always results in varying degrees of inconvenience, much like having a lock on one's front door results in the inconvenience of having to carry a key and unlock the door each time one wants to enter. Each user will have to decide for him- or herself whether the security benefits derived from each of the detailed steps recommended in the rest of this chapter are worth the associated inconvenience they introduce. Such a decision can only be made personally because each individual has different security needs: A freedom fighter in a repressive regime has different security needs from a teenager in a free society who uses his or her computer mostly to play computer games and who never uses it online.

7.1   Protection from which of many online threats?

The importance of answering this question up front cannot be overemphasized. In normal life, too, one takes different protective measures outdoors to protect one's self from, say, malaria carrying mosquitoes as opposed to pickpockets as opposed to heavy rain.

One's privacy is exposed online to the following threats:

1. Malicious remote Web sites that attempt to read (or write to) one's hard disk from afar;

2. Adware installed on one's computer that calls home;

3. Commercial keystroke-capturing software/hardware that calls home;

4. Remote attempts to hack into one's computer from afar;

5. A nosy ISP;

6. A tap on one's telephone by a private detective or other entity;

7. A hostile virus/Trojan/worm.

Each threat requires a different set of protective measures. Most protective measures can work in conjunction with each other.

It must also be appreciated that some protective measures may raise one's profile and, in essence, invite even more intrusiveness and inquisitiveness into one's affairs. An individual who prances around a disreputable part of town with a briefcase visibly handcuffed to his hand is inviting far more unwanted attention and trouble than the same person dressed in clothes that match the environment and carrying whatever it is he or she is carrying in a concealed pocket. Similarly, an online computer user in a totalitarian regime would be unwise to connect with a fully encrypted connection as a matter of principle just to browse the latest posting of antique furniture on Ebay. Each security-conscious user will have to use good judgment and common sense in deciding what technical security, if any, to use.

7.2   Installation of Windows for secure online operation

When personalizing Windows during installation, use a nondescript, rather than a true, name. Numerous remote threats can readily view the name and other personalized information one enters when installing Windows. This personalized information gets saved in the Registry (see Section 2.4) and is very hard to remove in some cases (as, for example, in the case of Microsoft Office). Many other applications read that personalizing information and copy it into their own personalization sections.

Caution: In an effort to reduce software piracy, Microsoft has shifted to a software distribution system that requires one to register online. If one does not, the software stops functioning after 50 uses. This registration has to be done from each computer that the software is installed in, as it entails an abstract of that computer's configuration.

Caution: Up until (and including) Office 97, Microsoft embedded the individual serial number of the particular copy of Microsoft Office on many documents created by Microsoft Office. The electronic copy of such document (i.e., a software copy on a disk or even the file sent by e-mail to a recipient) would therefore include that serial number, which would be traceable to the purchaser, regardless of what funny name was used on the computer during installation. A means for disabling this annoying feature was made available—amusingly by Microsoft. This feature has reportedly been discontinued as of Office 2000. Whose latest releases, however, have introduced the more dangerous requirement that one "register" the software online, or it stops functioning after 50 uses.

Intel's notion behind individually identifying serial numbers in each microprocessor was to help facilitate e-commerce by preventing fraud. It was an implementation doomed to fail because it is easy to hack and alter: The software that reads this serial number and relays it via the Internet can readily be doctored to show a fake serial number. This concept has been abandoned by Intel.

When installing application software, there is no also reason why one must enter a true name to be saved on one's disk that remote unauthorized individuals can retrieve.

Caution: A very small percentage of shareware enabled by sending the vendor a credit card number utilizes a scheme whereby the enabling code is derived from that user's credit card name and works only if the user enters that true name in addition to that enabling code.

Caution: Any software that requires a serial number or other code to be entered to validate it is traceable to its point of sale. If a credit card was used to buy it, it is linked to that credit card as well. Putting aside the serious legal issues involved, an individual in a totalitarian regime whose software bears a serial number that is traceable to a freedom-related foundation or to a buyer in an opposing regime could easily find him or herself in serious political trouble.

7.3   Online security threats and issues

7.3.1   Web browser hijacking

Through the use of scripts (ActiveX, JavaScript, and so on), software or a remote site takes it upon itself to modify one's Web browser settings to, for example, add shortcuts to one's "favorites" list in Internet Explorer and/or to change the default Web site that one's browser goes to every time one activates it—thereby informing that new default Web site every time one activates one's browser online. Even AOL had started placing "free.aol.com" in Internet Explorer's trusted sites security zone and bypassing security settings. United Parcel Service (UPS) apologized to 200,000 customers in 2001 for switching their home page to that of UPS (http://news.com.com/2100-1023-253074.htm?legacy=cnn).

At a minimum, one should disable ActiveX, JavaScript, Java, Visual Basic Script, and any other script in one's Web browser. Better yet, if one is using Internet Explorer (a bad idea from a security perspective because it is integrated with the operating system, writes onto the Registry, and has been acknowledged by Microsoft itself on an almost weekly basis to have a never-ending string of security vulnerabilities), go to Control Panel/Internet Options/Security, reset the security level to custom and disable all of the options in that entire list.

Additional countermeasures for this include any of the following:

1. Installing Browser Hijacker Blaster from www.wildersecurity.com/bhblaster.html, whose settings page is shown in Figure 7.1.

2. Installing Guard-IE freeware (guardIE34b314.exe).

3. Installing spyware blaster (http://www.javacoolsoftware.com/spywareblaster.html), which also handles numerous other online security problems and is recommended.

4. Installing IE-Spyad (a Registry file) from http://www.staff.uiuc .edu/~Ehowes/resource.htm#IESPYAD. It adds a long list of known domains to the Internet Explorer's restricted zone; once IE-ADS.reg

Figure 7.1 Browser Hijack Blaster to prevent browser hijacking.

is merged into the Registry, many of the usual tricks against Internet Explorer hijacking can be defeated.

5. Installing Settings Sentry from http://www.spywareinfo.com/downloads/spyblocker/settings+sentry.php, whose setup page is shown in Figure 7.2.

6. Using StartPage Guard from http://www.spywareinfo.com/downloads/spg, whose setup settings options are shown in Figure 7.3.

7. Using Spybot S&D from www.safer-networking.org.

Figure 7.2 Settings Sentry configuration.

Figure 7.3 StartPage Guard to prevent Web page hijackings.

7.3.2 The romantic e-card and related con schemes

Just as kids should never accept candy from strangers, Internet users should never install software e-mailed to them by anyone, not even friends, unless one has first verified that the e-mail was really sent by that friend and not by someone else masquerading as that friend—and even then.

A particularly odious example is the "Lover Spy" e-mail, pictured in Figure 7.4, which one can purchase and e-mail to a loved one (http://www.spy-ware-remover.com/HwEasy). Once installed by the un-suspecting recipient, it e-mails to the sender all of the recipient's com-puter activities on a regular basis. Not a good way to nourish a loving relationship.

7.3.3 E-mail bombs

In this scheme, the attacker subscribes the victim to numerous e-mail lists; attackers can use Web crawlers and scripts to fill in thousands of forms in very little time. The intent is to get the victim's e-mail account to receive hundreds to tens of thousands of e-mails per day, forcing the victim to change e-mail addresses. The current practice deployed by some e-mail lists to send the victim a single e-mail asking for confirmation prior to subscrib-ing that victim to the e-mail list is of minimal help as it still results in an e-mail to the victim by each such e-mail list administrator.

About the only protection from this to be extremely judicious about giv-ing out one's e-mail address. As a minimum, one should never post any-thing on any Usenet newsgroup with one's true e-mail address.

Figure 7.4 Remotely mailed spying software.

One convenient preventative approach is to subscribe to a service such as www.cotse.com; if one's e-mail address is, say, abcd@cotse.net, then anything sent to *****@abcd.cotse.net goes to one's e-mail box. One can, therefore, give e-mail address xxx1@abcd.cotse.net to one untrusted entity, qwer@abcd.cotse.net to another, and so forth; then, if any of them gets abused, selectively disable any one or more of these (e.g., xxx1, qwer) without affecting the rest.

7.4   Software to enhance online security

7.4.1   Junkbuster

Junkbuster (http://www.junkbuster.com) is a highly recommended free software that can be merged with both Netscape's Communicator/Navigator and Microsoft's Internet Explorer.

It blocks banner ads that match its frequently updated block file, and it deletes unauthorized cookies and other unwanted header information (such as which Web site one was referred from, which browser one is using[1]) that is exchanged between Web servers and browsers.

Proxomitron is a similar free software package of comparable scope.

7.4.2   SurfSecret

SurfSecret (http://www.surfsecret.com) helps enhance anonymous Web browsing by periodically destroying cached files and information that a Web browser collects in one's disk while one is browsing the Web. If not periodically destroyed, these cached files mirror a user's online browsing (see Figure 7.5).

7.4.3   Assorted cleaners of browsers

At the end of any online browsing session, browsing software has collected a considerable amount of stored tidbits of information, such as sites visited, cookies collected, and so forth. Rather than purchase one piece of software for each Web browser and other software that one is using, it is simpler and more effective to get a software package, such as one of the following, that cleans up after the digital litter left behind by many pieces of software:

1.   Secure Clean (http://www.whitecanyone.com);

2.   Window Washer (http://www.webroot.com);

3.   Tracks Eraser (http://www.acesoft.net);

---

1.   Because an attacker benefits considerably from knowing which software and version one is using, a JunkBuster user has the option of having his or her browser declare it is using a different browser than it is in fact using. Also, the referring Web site can be changed to a nondescript one of the user's choice.

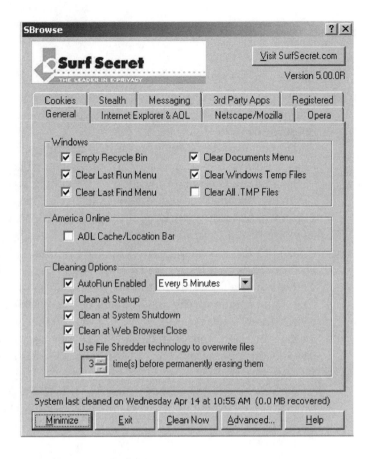

Figure 7.5   SurfSecret configuration.

4.   Evidence Eliminator (http://www.evidenceeliminator.com).

It is recommended that one use in succession at least two different packages from the list above as each has its share of weaknesses.

Secure Clean appears to be the most effective; however, it tends to freeze when it comes across a file to be removed that has odd characters in its name (such as the little rectangle that Windows occasionally inserts).

Window Washer is excellent as long as one downloads the many free plug-ins that work with it and as long as one enables the overwriting function (called "bleach" in that software).

Once the cleanup of such litter is completed, one should also worry about the fact Windows itself leaves a lot of electronic litter behind, especially when (not if) one's computer crashes. One should also, therefore, use software to clean up data that may have been left behind in temporary files, in the swap file (see Section 2.3), in the slack (see Section 2.2.1), in the Windows sectors that store file names, and in unallocated disk space. Perhaps the best software for so doing is Eraser (http://www.tolvanen.com/eraser), although some of the software programs listed in the section above also claim to perform some of these functions as well.

7.5   Basic do's and don'ts

7.5.1   Don'ts

Do not give access to any computer that you connect online to anyone else.

Do not allow software of suspect origin to be tried or installed on your computer, especially a computer that you connect to the Internet or any other network.

Do not open any e-mail sent to you by someone you do not know, and most certainly do not open any attachments to such e-mail.

Do not use Outlook or Outlook Express; they have been involved in far too many documented security incidents. Use some other software such as Eudora (free from www.eudora.com) instead. The same goes for Internet Explorer; use a Netscape or Opera browser instead.

Do not use any Web browser for either e-mail or for Usenet newsgroup reading. They are not secure enough.

Do not enable HTML in the software that you use for e-mail or Usenet newsgroup reading. This is to enable online tracking of your activities by third parties.

Do not open your e-mail or Usenet messages online. Go offline after downloading them and then open them. This is to negate Web bugs (see Section 9.4).

Do not be online unless you have to be. When composing or reading a Microsoft Office document, for example, you should be offline; this is also to negate Web bugs.

Do not register online or allow any software to register on line. Unless the software won't work unless you register it, do not register it at all. If you must register it, tell the vendors that you do not use the Internet and get them to accept your registration by mail or over a regular telephone call.

Protect your e-mail address almost like your social security number and do not give it out except to individuals you know well.

Do not register with any online service or group that wants to list you or your interests in any directory.

Do not use Wi-Fi (see Section 13.2) unless you are aware of the major security risks that it brings and are willing to accept them.

Do not post to Usenet groups using your true name or use your true e-mail address.

Do not ever leave your hard disk in the computer if you have your computer serviced or repaired.

Do not leave your computer on and online unless you are sitting in front of it, even if (especially if) you have a high-speed connection (xDSL or cable modem).

Do not store your e-mail (especially copies of outgoing e-mail) for long. Thin it out to the minimum that you absolutely must keep and convert that into an encrypted form for storage in a removable disk that you can keep in a nonobvious place that will be known only to yourself.

Keep in mind that, for all practical purposes, whenever you do something with your computer, someone is sitting right behind you and is dutifully noting everything you see or do. As such, do not see or do things with your computer that can land you in jail in your particular country. If you are a freedom fighter or a religious activist and must use a computer, learn all the security-related issues first (all of them are spelled out in this book) before you risk life and limb; you owe it to those who have trusted you.

7.5.2   Do's

Use a good virus-protection software package and update it at least weekly. Norton AntiVirus used to be the best, but it now requires online registration, which is inadvisable for any software as you really have no idea what information is being sent to the vendor.

Additionally, use a good Trojan detector such as The Cleaner (http://www.moosfot.com).

Additionally, use a good adware detector and remover, such as Ad-aware from http://www.lavasoftusa.com.

Additionally, use a good spyware detector, such as Spyware Search and Destroy from http://www.security.kolla.de.

Additionally, use a good firewall software with its most conservative settings (including specifically disallowing all scripts, such as JavaScript). Zone Alarm from http://www.zonelabs.com (a part of Checkpoint Software Technologies as of late 2003) is recommended. Set the firewall to forbid any software in your computer from acting as a server. Be very suspicious when your firewall informs you that some software is trying to connect to the Internet and deny permission unless you know and approve of such connectivity.

Periodically (meaning at least once per month, and certainly immediately after any computer-related activity that might be frowned upon by a regime) defragment your disk(s) and also wipe the disk(s) as per Chapter 2.

Depending on your situation, consider deploying the means described in the next two chapters for intermediate and advanced protection.

Get in the habit of using only encrypted e-mail with those with whom you routinely communicate. There are numerous simple ways of doing so described in this book. When you do, compose your plaintext e-mail in RAM-disk (see Section 6.2.2), then encrypt it and store on hard disk only the encrypted version. The reverse holds for incoming, encrypted e-mail.

If traveling with your laptop, remove the hard disk and have it carried separately, preferably by another person that you may be traveling with, who should clear customs ahead of you. This will drastically reduce damage from theft, as well as the motivation of those in the country you are traveling in to spend much time sifting through what may be your company's proprietary data.

Practical Measures for Online Computer Activities

All Web browsers, in their default settings, engage in the annoying practice of volunteering to each and every Web site visited the following information:

1. The type and version number of the browser being used via the http_user_agent environmental variable. This is a bad idea because it makes it that much easier for a malicious remote Web site to know exactly how to exploit one's browser's unique security weaknesses. Also, some Web sites make a marketing statement by refusing to deal with this or that Web browser.

2. The referring page, that is, the Web site visited just prior to the current one being visited.

Additionally, a Web browser has to send the user's current IP address as well, which remote sites record. This is a (partly) necessary evil because the remote site has to know where to send the information asked for. (The "partly" qualifier alludes to the fact that one can use a proxy; see Section 9.6).

In addition, Web browsers have a long history of many security bugs that allow hostile remote Web sites to take full control of one's computer from afar, depending on how a user has set the Web browser up.

The following in specific suggestions applicable to all browsers and e-mail software:

1. Download, install, and use JunkBuster from http://www.junkbuster.com (freeware). You can then set it up to show that your Web browser is, say, Gameboy64 and that the last Web site you visited was http://www.forever_virtuous.com or some such.

2. Disable all autocomplete features, such as autocompletion of Web addresses and especially of passwords.

3. If you use Web browsers for e-mail or Usenet reading, disable HTML-enabled e-mail and Usenet message reading, in addition to disabling cookies. HTML-enabled e-mail and newsgroup readers can be exploited to tie a cookie to a specific e-mail address and using that information, Web sites and third-party advertising entities can collect information about the sites one frequents (e.g., insurance sites, adult sites, cosmetics sites), plus sell one's e-mail address to others.

4. Visit one of many Web sites that do an online security analysis of your setup and tell you what can be obtained from your computer. One such site is http://privacy.net/analyze. Another one is Shields Up at https://www.grc.com. These sites probe your online setup and inform you of any security holes in your setup that you should close.

8.1   Netscape Navigator/Communicator

1. Make sure you use a 128-bit version. Until recently, when U.S. export regulations on encryption were relaxed, non-U.S. users had to be content with a lower-grade encryption version. This is no longer the case.

2. Create (at least) two different user profiles, a public one and a private one. If one needs to prevent others from finding that two (or more) profiles belong, in fact, to one and the same person, then one should not have more than a single profile on a single computer because the two (or more) profiles can become discovered during computer forensics (offline or online).

    Use the private one to connect to any site you do not trust (which should be just about every site except, perhaps, your employer's). For that private one, disable cookies, java, JavaScript, Smart browsing, "what is related," and Smart update; there is nothing "smart" about them. Quite the contrary, they expose you to security vulnerabilities.

    For the public profile, enable the minimum features that are required for it to function with the sites you trust and use it only for those sites.

    If you want to use Netscape for encrypted e-mail (not recommended), then you must get a security certificate from any one of the many companies that make them. It is recommended that you use Thawtee Company because it is free and every bit as good as the for-pay ones. The procedure is self-explanatory: Click on the lock icon on the top line of the Netscape browser.

    By the way, there is an easy way to copy over the security certificate(s) you have created from one profile to another. Go to Program

Files/Netscape/Users and open the folder containing the profile for which you already obtained the security certificate. Copy the following three files to the other profile's folder(s):

a. cert7.db;

b. key3.db;

c. secmod.db.

The same procedure can be used to copy the security certificates you got using one computer to another computer using Netscape as well. Keep in mind that one cannot use the same certificate for both Netscape and Internet Explorer (the use of which is strongly discouraged due to its numerous security flaws, anyway).

3. Install and Use JunkBuster (see Section 7.4.1). For the private user profile, select the following preferences (under Edit/Preferences):

a. Set the home page to http://internet.junkbuster.com/cgi-bin/show/proxy-args.

b. Set Navigator to start with "home page" (see Figure 8.1).

c. Under "proxies," select "manual proxy configuration" (see Figure 8.2). Then, under "view" enter the word "localhost" in both the HTTP and the Security windows and the number "8000" under both ports for these two (see Figure 8.3).

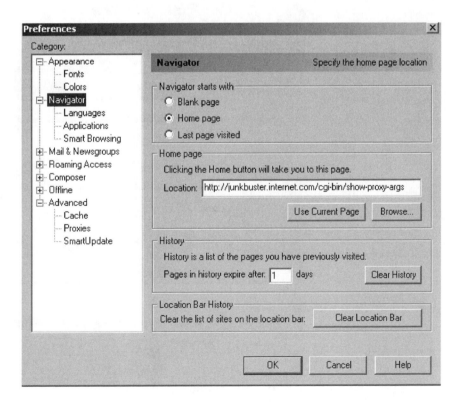

Figure 8.1 Home page settings for Netscape.

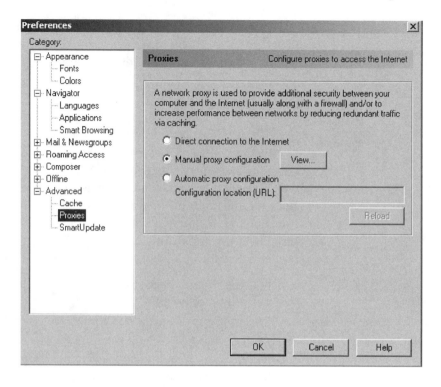

Figure 8.2   Navigator proxy settings detail.

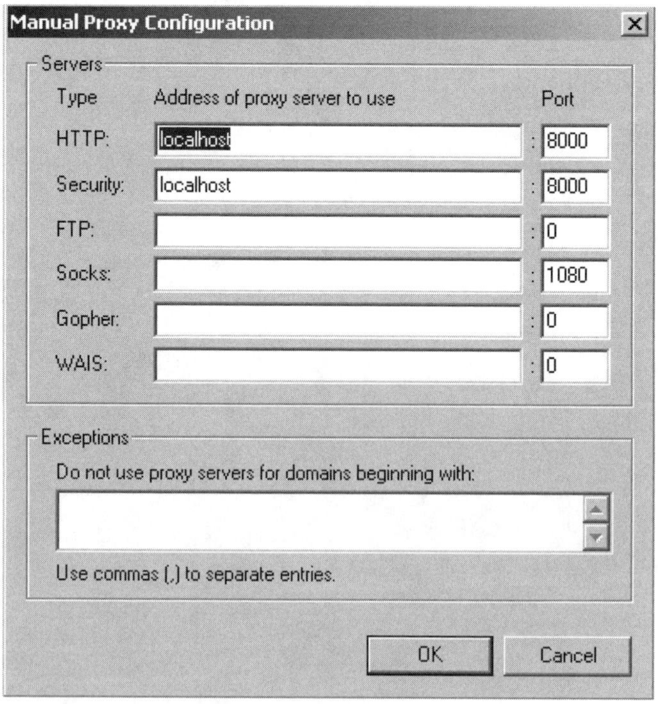

Figure 8.3   Navigator proxy settings further detail.

4. Anonymize and clean-up the configuration. From a security perspective it is preferable not to use Web browsers (especially Internet Explorer) for e-mail at all. Use a dedicated e-mail program instead, (such as Eudora). Integrating the e-mail function into a Web browser exposes the e-mail functionality to many of the security weaknesses of the Web browser, which, in the case of Internet Explorer, are overwhelming and have been responsible for the massive damage caused by infamous malware, such as the I Love You virus from the Philippines and most others.

   a. Under Mail Identity, leave all spaces blank or fictitious.

   b. Do the same with mail servers and news servers. Under Advanced, disable Java, JavaScript, style sheets, and cookies. Enable only the "automatically load images" option.

   c. Under Advanced/Cache, set disk cache to zero and memory cache to not much more than 1,024 KB. Clear both.

   d. Double-click on the "cache" folder. Delete all files in it. Remember that this is useless until you wipe the disk (see Chapter 2).

5. Remove the instant messaging capability. Unless you use AOL as your ISP or AOL Instant Messenger (AIM) for instant messaging (any instant messaging is not a good idea at all from a security perspective because it works by broadcasting your being online every time you go online); get rid of that feature. Because Netscape is now owned by AOL, AOL is pretty tightly integrated with Netscape and requires a few steps to get rid of.

   a. Find the location where Netscape keeps its user-related files. It is usually in C:\ProgramFiles\Netscape\Users. Click on the folder for whatever you have named you private profile.

   b. Remove AOL/AIM altogether as follows:

   Step 1: Go to Program Files/Netscape/Communicator/Program and delete any folder titled AIM.

   Step 2: Remove all references to AOL and AIM from the Registry because some of them install the AIM software and icons on Netscape every time you boot, even if you have removed the shortcuts. Be very careful when editing the Registry; any carelessness or errors can render the computer unbootable. It is best to make a backup copy of the Registry (see Section 2.4.3) before editing the Registry, especially if you have not been editing the Registry on a routine basis. Proceed slowly and carefully.

   Step 3: Run REGEDIT.

   Step 4: Go to Edit/Find and search for the string "AOL". Delete each entry obviously referring to AOL. Make sure you do not inadvertently delete any entry where the "aol" has nothing to do with America Online.

Step 5: Repeat this Edit/Find and deletion for the string "AIM". Here you must be even more careful not to delete strings having nothing to do with America Online's AIM, such as Application X-aim, EudoraImport, AphaImageLoader, or DataImport because all of these entries are needed by other software.

Step 6: Repeat this Edit/Find and delete for the string "America Online".

Step 7: Go to Program Files/Netscape/Users. For each user profile you have (if you don't have more than one, then go to the "Default" folder), find and remove all occurrences of the AIM icon named launch.aim. Reboot, double-click on the Netscape icon (or run the Netscape software) and exit from it. Now go to the same location(s) where you deleted the launch.aim file and make sure it is not there. If it has miraculously been recreated, it means that your clean up of the Registry missed some references to AOL, AIM, and America Online, and you must redo it.

6.   Remove the netscape.hst and fat.db files. These are two files created by Netscape that have no redeeming value. From the moment that Netscape is installed, it keeps a record of the user's online and offline activities using the browser. The netscape.hst file is the surfing log; fat.db identifies the files in the browser cache, which is usually a huge collection of HTML pages and image files. These files are mildly encrypted and may appear essential to the uninitiated, but can and should be deleted; even more important, because Netscape will create new cache files after the old ones are deleted, one should take the following steps to prevent that from happening:

Step 1: Find netscape.hst and fat.db and delete them. They sit in each and every user profile folder (Program Files/Netscape/Users/...).

Step 2: Create new text files (File/New/Text) in each of the exact locations where the old ones were deleted and call them netscape.hst and fat.db respectively and save them.

Step 3: Right-click on each of those two files, select properties, and make each a read-only file. This will prevent any records about your Netscape usage from being stored on disk.

Step 4: Periodically recheck those files to make sure that they continue to have a size of zero and are read-only files. Netscape updates and some well-meaning software that cleans up Netscape's trails often remove the read-only feature.

7.   Get Rid of cookies for good.

Step 1: Search for, find and delete cookies.txt. There is one in each user profile, just as there is a copy of netscape.hst in each profile. By the way, Netscape's "Do not edit" warning does not mean that the file cannot or should not be edited. Edit it anyway.

Step 2: Right-click on that file, select properties, and make it read-only as well. This will prevent any cookies from being written. This is an additional layer of protection beyond what is provided by JunkBuster. (Note: Because cookies are stored in RAM memory during an online session and are only written to disk at the end of each online session, the above scheme will prevent the writing of cookies to disk but will not prevent the coming and going cookies during any one online session. Junk-Buster and the configuration of Netscape will do that).

8. Delete some more hidden threats. Go to Program Files/Netscape/Users. For each user profile you have (if you don't have more than one, you merely have to open the folder named "Default"), do the following:

Step 1: Right-click on the pab.na2 file, select "open with," and open with any text editor, such as Notepad. Look at whatever is in ASCII text. If you feel that it contains too much information about your system or past usage of Netscape, then

Step 2: Go to Edit/Select All and delete it all.

Step 3: Save the empty file.

Step 4: Right-click on the saved empty file, select "Properties," set it to read-only status (so that Netscape will not add to it later on), and click "Apply."

You may be amazed that these .na2 files often contain such sensitive information as verbatim copies of e-mail sent long ago, lists of Usenet newsgroups visited, and so forth.

Step 5: Do likewise for any other file with the .na2 suffix in each and every one of your user profiles.

9. Remove the shockwave plug-in. If you have the shockwave plug-in for Netscape, get rid of it; if not, don't get it. It has been associated with numerous security compromises.

10. Most important yet, when done, defragment the disk and go through a secure wiping (see Chapter 2) to remove in reality what was essentially merely marked for deletion before.

8.2 Microsoft Internet Explorer

It is not recommended that you use Internet Explorer at all because of its seemingly never-ending litany of security-related weaknesses. Still, you may want to keep it for specific tasks such as Windows updates that Microsoft refuses to provide through other browsers unless you are willing to download the required security updates as executable files form the Microsoft Web site (a recommended option).

Microsoft's business-based arguments notwithstanding, there is a funda-mental security problem when a Web browser is integrated with the operat-ing system. This is also the position of the author of the security software products NSClean and IEClean (that remove the electronic trails left behind on one's disk by Netscape and Internet Explorer, respectively), who wrote the following back in 1996:

> The greatest risk of all on the Internet however comes from the integration of browsers into the operating system itself. At one time, browsers were external applications which did not have hooks directly into the computer's operating system. JavaScript applets were kept isolated from the operating system entirely which meant that the only risks to privacy were those vol-untarily or unwittingly given up by the user. . . . Now we are faced with the Internet Explorer product [being tied] directly into the operating system where no walls of separation will exist which will serve to protect the user against unauthorized rummaging through the most personal and private parts of their computers.

If you absolutely insist on using Internet Explorer, then at least do the following:

1. Get the latest version of it.

2. Disable cookies from session to session.

3. Go to Start/Settings/Control Panel and select the "Internet Options" icon.

   a. Under Address, enter http://internet/junkbuster.com/cgi-bin/show-proxy-args (Figure 8.4).

   b. Under History, set the days to zero, and clear history.

   c. Under Internet Options/Content/Personal Information/Auto-complete, disable all autocomplete options. This stops Internet Explorer from gathering this information but does not delete information already gathered. To delete such preexisting infor-mation, use Clear Forms/Clear Passwords and General/Clear History. Then wipe the disk clean using the procedures shown in Chapter 2.

   d. Important: Under Security/Internet, select the custom level and disable everything, except (if you absolutely need them) file downloads and font downloads. In particular, make sure that you disable all scripting and all ActiveX options. See Figures 8.5 to 8.7.

   e. Under Connections, find the profile with which you access your ISP, select it, and click on "LAN Settings." Under "Proxy server" enter the word "localhost" in the "Address" field and the number "8000" in the "Port" field (Figures 8.8 and 8.9). Then click Advanced and make sure that this shows up under both

Figure 8.4   Setting the Junkbuster filter in Internet Explorer.

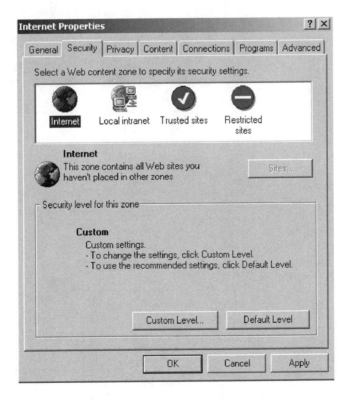

Figure 8.5   Panel for improving Internet Explorer security.

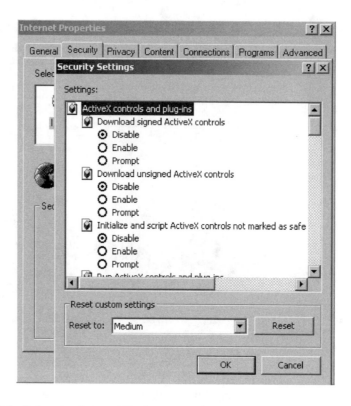

Figure 8.6   Enhancing Internet Explorer security.

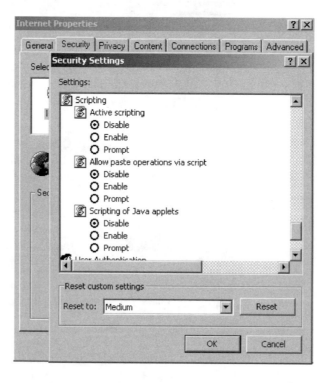

Figure 8.7   Disabling mobile code and scripts in Internet Explorer.

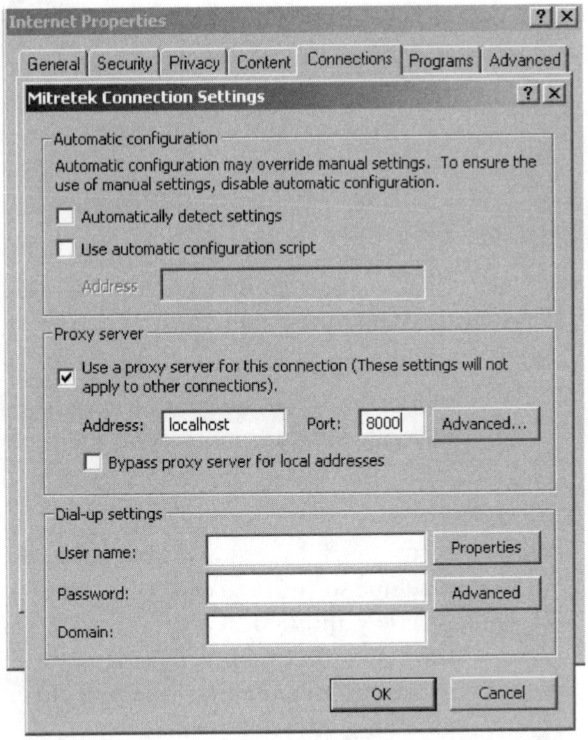

Figure 8.8   Setting up a local proxy to filter hostile content.

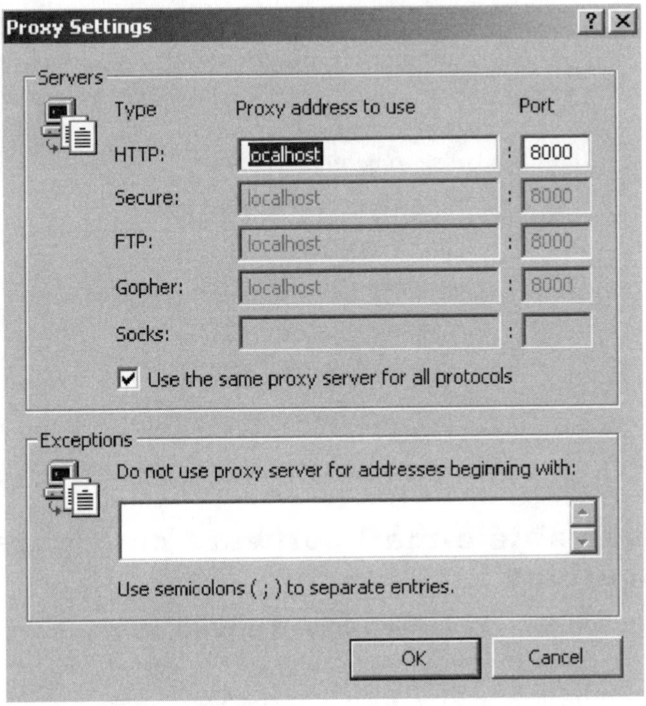

Figure 8.9   Further settings for the local proxy.

the "HTTP" and the "Secure" type; click the "Use the same proxy for all protocols" option.

    f.   Under Programs select an HTML editor other than Internet Explorer, such as Netscape, because Internet Explorer has been found to have serious security problems when hostile HTML code tries to execute commands in your computer.

4.   Click on the Security tab. Disable JavaScript.

5.   Click on the Advanced tab. Double-click on Java VM and uncheck all three options.

6.   Disable SSLv2 and enable only SSLv3. SSLv2 has also demonstrated vulnerability to some attacks which result in your having no encrypted connection despite the presence of the little locked lock icon.

7.   Consider using Secure2surf from http://www.netmenders.com/secure2surf. Microsoft's Internet Explorer uses Microsoft's Virtual Machine software to enforce more Internet accountability, which is precisely antithetical to online privacy. It places all Internet traffic in the region between restricted sites and trusted sites. A security-conscious user needs to put them all, instead, in the not-trusted bin, and this software does that.

8.   If you are using the shockwave plug-in for Internet Explorer, get rid of it. If not, don't install it. It has been associated with numerous security problems.

9.   If you use software, such as SCORCH, to wipe specific files from your computer on shutdown (or on start-up, which is not recommended because it could be too late then, as far as hostile computer forensics is concerned), then add the following files and folders to the list of those to be wiped:

        C:\WINDOWS\cookies*.*

        C:\WINDOWS\history*.*

        C:\WINDOWS\Temporary Internet Files\

        C:\WINDOWS\Recent\

        C:\WINDOWS\TMP\

        C:\WINDOWS\TEMPOR~1*.*

8.3   Desirable e-mail software configuration and modifications

8.3.1   Free Web-based e-mail offers that require JavaScript: don't!

In late August 2000, a major security flaw was discovered in Web-based e-mail that affected well over 100 million users. Users could not defeat it by merely changing passwords. The problem was based on a well-known Web browser vulnerability that allowed stealing a "session cookie" from a Webmail user; this could be done by sending an HTML message to the intended victim with an embedded image file containing some JavaScript code. While users could protect themselves by disabling JavaScript in their browsers, some ill-designed Webmail systems refuse to function if a user has done so. For this reason alone, users should avoid any Web-based service that requires one to have enabled JavaScript, Java, or ActiveX.

Messages sent through Yahoo!, Hotmail, or other such popular accounts, including instant messaging software such as ICQ and AIM are just as accessible to employers and government as conventional e-mails (see http://news.cnet.com/news/0-1007-200-2924978.html).

With the notable exception of www.cotse.com, which is highly recommended,[1] even Web sites that sanctimoniously promote privacy are not to be trusted.

Hushmail, for example, hosted two tracking networks on its Web site: doubleclick.net and valueclick.net. One can avoid these sites by creating a firewall rule set that denies access to doubleclick.net, valueclick.net, and valuenet.com and by abiding by the rest of the recommended security-related procedures in Chapters 7 through 9.

Ultimate Anonymity, another site that pontificates about the virtues of anonymity, is a division of Cyber Solutions that is reported to be a bulk e-mail provider. If one follows the links from www.cyber-so.nu to www.cyber-so.com, one reads, "Broadcast your ad and even include an image if you desire to as many as 200 newsgroups at a time, twice a week, using methods to ensure your ads remain intact and undisturbed by Usenet cancelbots for a full month."

8.3.2   Outlook and Outlook Express

These programs are not recommended due to the following security problems:

1.   Response to HTML cannot be disabled in many versions. This is a fatal flaw.

2.   Numerous Trojans and other malware have exploited Outlook and Outlook Express to cause virus-containing mail to be sent from one's computer to all e-mail addresses in one's address book.

8.3.3   Eudora e-mail software

Go to Tools/Options and do the following:

---

1. The reader must keep in mind that any ISP has to comply with a court order from a court having authority over that ISP. As such, no ISP can (nor should) condone out-and-out illegality; nor can it (or should it) shield a subscriber from prosecution for flagrant illegality. At the same time, ISPs can be (and should be) expected not to accommodate frivolous or illegal requests by overzealous investigators on fishing expeditions.

1. Under Attachments, select anything other than the default, after having created a folder such as C:\abracadabra\hocuspocus. This prevents a Eudora security weakness from being exploitable. See Figure 8.10.

2. Under Viewing mail, uncheck the "Use Microsoft viewer" option to prevent another known security weakness in Eudora. See Figure 8.11.

Figure 8.10   Eudora e-mail attachments vulnerability.

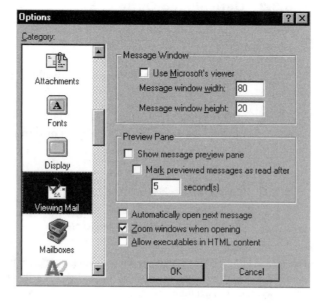

Figure 8.11   Eudora message viewer vulnerability.

3. Important: Under Viewing mail, disable the option that allows executables in HTML content. See Figure 8.11.

4. By the way, you may elect to opt for having all incoming and outgoing e-mail copies stored in a fully encrypted volume, rather than keeping them in the open for the world to see. To do this you must first create such encrypted volumes (see Section 6.4.2, for example, for a discussion SCRAMDISK, which uses encrypted volumes).

Caution: Users of Eudora should be advised that, like many other software such as Adobe Photoshop, it calls home (the Eudora server) every so often behind a user's back. The manufacturer claims that this is done merely to find out if a new version of the program is available. Regardless, users would be well advised to disable this dubious feature in all software. Luckily, the Eudora Web site has instructions on how to do so. To disable this undesirable attribute, copy and paste the following text into the message window of a new message in Eudora:

```
DontShowUpdates=1
```

This text will show up in blue as a URL. Hold down the Alt key and click on the URL. A window will appear asking one to click "OK." Click "OK."

Caution: Users of PGP encryption should not use the PGP plug-ins for either Eudora or Outlook/Outlook Express. Instead, encrypt the clipboard and cut and paste the ciphertext into the e-mail software program's window. The danger is that the Outbox saves on the hard disk—under some conditions—both the plaintext and the ciphertext; this is about the worst-case scenario from a security perspective.

8.4   Secure e-mail conduct online

The following represents a list of recommendations to save you grief in connection with the use of e-mail.

▸ Get in the habit of using encryption for all of your e-mail. It is really not onerous to do so any more. You have numerous choices. By far the most effective e-mail encryption available to anyone worldwide is the use of PGP. Download PGP 6.58 CKT Build 7 available from numerous online sources (do a Google search for the latest, as they change all the time), but do not install the PGP DISK option, which is defective in most PGP versions. You can use it with any e-mail software you have. Once installed and set up correctly (see Section 11.3 because the default set up may not be the secure one), all you have to do to encrypt messages is type them using a text editor on a RAM disk (see Section 6.2.2). Never save them to disk, but Edit/Copy them onto the clipboard, invoke PGP to encrypt the clipboard, and Edit/Paste them into the message window of whichever e-mail software you are using (even a Web-based free e-mail account such as those provided by yahoo.com, netscape.com, or hotmail.com).

▶ Get rid of the bad habit of storing old e-mail forever, especially outgoing ones (you are not as culpable for what others e-mail to you as you are for what you e-mail to others). Even large corporations that have taken notice of how other corporations have been stung by the content of employee e-mail are now professing "hard disk storage limitations" as a legitimate-sounding excuse for policies whereby all e-mail is permanently removed from corporate records after rather short periods. ("Get rid of," of course, means not merely to delete—which does nothing—but to wipe the disk clean as per Chapter 2.)

▶ If you absolutely must keep some old e-mail, then move it to a folder for that purpose and encrypt that entire folder's contents, realizing that in most countries you can be compelled by law enforcement to decrypt it. Consider hiding the fact that such a folder exists by using steganography (see Section 11.5), or even physically shipping it (encrypted, of course) to a trusted friend in another country for storage on your behalf. See Chapters 10 through 12 on encryption for the numerous options available.

▶ Have at least two e-mail accounts: a public one (where you will inevitably receive junk mail), which you can obtain freely from numerous providers, and a jealously guarded personal one that you give only to trusted correspondents. Even the personal one should not have your true name as part of the e-mail address. Do not cross-contaminate the two. Here again, www.cotse.com comes in very handy; if your account name is, say, abcde@cotse.net, then any e-mail sent to ****@abcd.cotse.net (where **** can be anything you like) will be delivered to you. This way, you can give your e-mail address as, say, user24@abcde.cotse.net to someone you don't trust. If the address is abused, you can have Cotse bounce back as undeliverable any subsequent e-mail sent to that made-up address ("user24").

▶ For your personal e-mail account, sign up with any one of many e-mail forwarding entities, such as www.cotse.com or www.IEEE.org (for IEEE members only), or with one your own professional organization or college offers that will forward your incoming e-mail to your "real" account. Give only that go-between's e-mail address to your friends so that when you do change your ISP for whatever reason, you don't have to notify any of your correspondents (but only that go-between e-mail forwarding service). In addition, you get an extra layer of insulation from assorted online crackpots.

▶ If you do use encryption for your e-mail, as is highly recommended, do not use a form that allows you to read the messages that you yourself have composed and sent. In other words, do not use S/MIME because the locally saved copy of your outgoing e-mail is also decryptable by the sender, and do not use any symmetric encryption, such as DES; use PGP instead (see Section 11.3). This is to make it impossible for you to possibly comply with any demand to decrypt outgoing e-mail and to limit your alleged culpability to incoming e-mail only (which you should overwrite soon after reading, by the way, and not keep for posterity as it can only cause you grief). If you are concerned (as you should be because you really do lose all control of your e-mail after you have sent it) about what an intended recipient may do with your e-mail (e.g., print it out, paste it into another e-mail that goes out unencrypted to third parties), then you should consider using one of the handful of new commercial schemes that control (with varying degrees of success) your e-mail's fate even after it is on its way to the intended recipients. See Section 8.4 on this topic.

• Never reply to unsolicited junk mail that offers to remove your name from its distribution list as this will confirm that your e-mail address is valid and will subject you to more junk e-mail. Unsolicited e-mail is a societal, not a technical, problem; laws to ban it will be about as effective as laws to ban bad weather. The best you can do is to give your e-mail address only to trusted individuals. Give the rest disposable Webmail addresses and dispose of them when the amount of unsolicited e-mail becomes too annoying.

• Do not access any e-mail attachments unless you have already installed an antivirus software that checks attachments, and it is current, and you know the sender, and you are expecting such an attachment from the sender. Most e-mail-propagated viruses/Trojans/worms come as e-mails that have hijacked the e-mail address of a sender you trust. If all of the above conditions are met, use safe software for opening some kinds of attachments, such as Word Viewer in the case of Microsoft Word files. If the e-mail does not meet those qualifications, delete it without opening the attachment, and then go and overwrite the attached file (which usually stays in your disk even after you delete the e-mail that brought it).

• If you use Eudora for e-mail, perform the bug-fixing steps listed in Section 8.3.3.

• Most important of all, always keep in mind that unless you encrypt your e-mail and also hide the "from whom" and "to whom" information from whomever you are concerned may be intercepting your e-mail (now or through forensics in the future), do not compose e-mail that you would not want used against you in a court of law. Even if you do encrypt your e-mail, you still have no control over what the intended recipient does with it, and it could still haunt you in the future.

• If, for whatever reason (such as by virtue of being the publisher of the newspaper of the political opposition in your country), you are the likely target of extensive surveillance by those with the means to do so, then do the following:

1. Forget about using e-mail for your sensitive communications needs.

2. Consider establishing an account with an out-of-country ISP and establishing an encrypted (128-bit SSL; see Section 9.7.1) connection with that ISP before anything else. Alternately, you can use a local ISP and simply connect to the Web site of an out-of-country commercial entity that offers end-to-end SSL encryption between its site and your computer, such as https://www.rewebber.com or https://www.cotse.net.

    Caution: Most so-called anonymous remailers, such as www.anonymizer.com, are not recommended at all because they have one or more of the following security shortcomings:

    a. They may not remove your IP address from what is sent; even though the e-mail received by one may appear to be coming from god@heaven, the IP address and the rest of the information in the detailed header (see Section 8.5) of the message pretty much give away where it came from.

    b. They may not be establishing an encrypted connection between your computer and theirs, leaving you vulnerable to local interception and to snooping by your local ISP.

    c. They may be keeping a copy of all traffic going through them, which can be subpoenaed by the authorities of the country where that remailer is located.

    d. Pseudonymous remailers (which assign you a pseudonym in place of your true e-mail address so that others can respond to you through that remailer), too, are vulnerable to a subpoena from their local judicial systems and will reveal who said what to whom and when. This, in fact, happened with a Finnish remailer (anon.penet.fi) a few years ago.

3. Consider the use of encrypted concatenated remailers (Mixmaster, etc.) through the use of programs like Private Idaho or Jack B Nimble, available for free worldwide and discussed in more detail in Sections 9.6 and 9.15. Keep in mind that the use of such schemes stands out like the proverbial sore thumb if someone is keeping tabs on your online activities; however, they do protect the content of your messages as well as the "from whom" and "to whom" information.

8.4.1 Self-protecting e-mail

"Today's e-mail, tomorrow's legal evidence."

Getting rid of incoming e-mail and of locally kept copies of outgoing e-mail is not simple. Some e-mail software packages (such as Outlook an Outlook Express) tend to store e-mail in assorted proprietary condensed ways whereby one cannot simply identify a single file that contains just one piece of e-mail so as to get rid of it. Instead, one has to depend on the good graces of each such piece of software to respond to a user's request to delete an e-mail that one would rather not keep on one's disk. (This usually places that particular e-mail in yet another location on the hard disk corresponding to the trash folder of the e-mail software that one needs also to get rid of).

If, despite all the vulnerabilities discussed in this book, one persists in not insisting on encryption for all incoming e-mail, one can work around the security vulnerabilities of e-mail software by asking correspondents to send e-mail as an attachment rather than as text in the body of the e-mail. In that case, the attachment is a file that can be overwritten and wiped clean as needed by the recipient.

For e-mail whose text is in the main body, as is the case with the vast majority of e-mail, about the only effective strategy is to customize one's e-mail software to store incoming e-mail and the e-mail software's trash folder on a RAM disk (see Section 6.2.2). This is not easily done with most e-mail software that tends to store files within its own subdirectory in the Program Files folder.

In the case of Eudora Pro, change the "Target" line under Properties for the Eudora shortcut icon on one's desktop to the following:

E:\Mailbox\Eudora.ini

where:

"E:\" is the name of whichever drive is used for the RAM disk (it can be D:\ or whatever else);

"Mailbox" is whichever name one wants to give to the folder (which must have been created in advance for the occasion).

If that is not possible, then do the following:

1. Delete incoming e-mail.

2. Delete the same e-mail from the e-mail software's Trash folder.

3. Proceed with a full disk defragmentation.

4. Follow up with a full disk wiping (slack, free space, and swap file) (see Chapter 2).

All this pales in comparison with the potential headaches from outgoing e-mail for the following reasons:

1. Unlike incoming e-mail for which the recipient is not legally liable, outgoing e-mail is the sender's full legal responsibility.

2. Once outgoing e-mail has left, the sender loses all control of it and is at the mercy of its intended recipients.

3. E-mail can end up in the wrong recipient's hands through many possible ways:

    a. The sender inadvertently clicked on the recipient directly above or below the name of the intended recipient in the sender's local address book.

b. The sender mistyped the recipient's e-mail address, and the e-mail was rerouted by the receiving host to the "e-mail post-master" there (this is common in universities), who read it in an attempt to figure out who it was for and forwarded it to numerous possible intended recipients "just in case."

c. The Internet erred, as it often does, and directed an e-mail to the wrong place.

Even under the best of circumstances, when the e-mail goes only to its intended recipient, the sender has still lost control of that e-mail. The recipient can forward or redirect it to others, can print it and keep or send copies to others, can take portions of out of their context and paste them into e-mails to others (possibly after having altered the material), and so on. This is not unlike the priest's saying in a sermon, "The Devil wants you to think that 'God is dead'," which a newspaper headline reports as "Priest says in sermon that 'God is dead'."

In more practical terms, a corporation may understandably want to ensure that its internal, confidential, and proprietary e-mails do not leave its confines. There is a need, therefore, for a means whereby e-mail

1. Can only be read by the intended recipient;

2. Cannot be printed or electronically copied.

The first requirement is easily met with public-key encryption (see Section 10.2.3). The message is encrypted to the public key of the intended recipient, who is the only one who can read it.

The second requirement is vastly more difficult to meet because depends on the receiving computer's unknown capabilities and operating system:

1. To prevent printing, the receiving computer's "Print Screen" function must be disabled.

2. To prevent editing, copying, and pasting, the receiving computer's e-mail software itself must be changed.

A handful of commercial solutions to this conundrum have been marketed:

1. Cryptolopes (from Cryptographic Envelopes) (www.research. ibm.com/people/k/kaplan/cryptolope-docs/crypap.html): This IBM effort was transferred to Lotus in late 1997. The initial version, Cryptolope Live Server, was to allow Web publishers both to protect and to sell data on the Web.

2. Secure Information Management System 2.0 by TriStrate (www. tristrata.com): This software solution runs on any TCP/IP network intended to provide end-to-end file, e-mail, and VPN security. It is integrated with MS Exchange, Outlook, and Lotus 4.1–4.6.

3. Disappearing from Disappearing Inc. (www.disappearing.com/faq3. html): Very perceptively, that company's own product description states that it cannot protect against someone's defeating the purpose of its product by doing a screen capture, screen print, and the like, but is intended for the situation when "all parties are interested in a private exchange."

4. Content Guard by Xerox Corporation (www.contentguard.com/ productmenu.htm): This product converts documents from many popular file formats to encrypted self-protecting documents without requiring consumers to install any client-side software to access the protected documents. If this is indeed true, then the product is unlikely to be particularly secure because protected documents could end up in the swap file or be captured by screen-capture software.

5. SafeMessage by AbsoluteFuture Company (www.safemessage. com): This software has the interesting twist of facilitating the sending of e-mail as encrypted packets point-to-point that bypass e-mail servers completely. It requires the recipient to have SafeMessage software installed and to have logged onto the server at least once.

6. PageVault by Authentica Company (www.authentica.com): Like many other systems, it requires the installation of a full infrastructure that includes a dedicated server for PageVault-protected e-mail.

All of these schemes take one of the following approaches:

1. Requiring that e-mail be only in the form of a specific attachment type that requires a particular software (provided by that vendor) to view and that has no edit/copy/paste or print functions;

2. Requiring that all e-mail be stored in a trusted central server and that access to it be allowed only to individually authenticated users using vendor-controlled software that can neither edit/copy/paste nor print;

3. Requiring a separate infrastructure of servers, databases, and so forth within an organization dedicated to handling the self-protecting e-mail only.

Clearly, none of these approaches is practical to use for e-mailing to the world at large, although they may be tolerable for a closed group such as tightly knit organization or corporation. Worse yet, if one thinks of it, it becomes apparent that there really cannot be a technical solution to the problem of preventing an authorized e-mail recipient from copying the e-mail and further disseminating it at will: An e-mail recipient can always snap a photograph of the screen, print it, run it through commercial optical character recognition (OCR) software, and convert it into a plain old e-mail that can be disseminated worldwide on the spot.

The only real fix is never to e-mail verbiage from which one would not like to have pieces taken out of context and displayed on the front page of the local newspaper, show up on an overzealous law enforcer's desk in a repressive regime, or appear on an opposition lawyer's desk in a litigious society.

The problem of loss of control of outgoing e-mail is essentially the same as the problem of DRM. There, too, the creator of content loses control once that content is delivered to its recipient. If one were able to solve the DRM problem with technical means (one can't), one would also solve the problem of loss of control of e-mail.

8.4.2   Accessing e-mail from anywhere on Earth

One does not have to dial into one's own ISP to retrieve one's e-mail. One can dial into any ISP anywhere on earth and retrieved one's e-mail from any other POP3[2]- or IMAP4-based e-mail server.

To access one's e-mail from anywhere using most any e-mail software (e.g., Eudora, Netscape), one only has to configure that e-mail software with the particulars of one's own ISP, namely:

▸ POP3 e-mail server name (e.g., incoingmailserver.myISP.com);

▸ SMTP e-mail server name (e.g., outgoinge-mailserver.myISP.com);

▸ Login name;

▸ Password.

At that point, one can launch one's e-mail software, and it will dutifully retrieve one's e-mail, plus send whatever e-mail one wants to send.

Caution: Unless an encrypted connection is used,[3] doing this allows one's e-mail address and password to be seen by anyone along the way from where one is to where one's ISP is. If one is not using a service provider that offers an encrypted connection option, like www.cotse.com, one should at least use a password that is not amenable to a playback attack (i.e., being used by whomever intercepted it). This is possible, for example, when using the SecureID tokens (which produce a different string of numbers every few seconds) or some challenge/response scheme. Of course, use of such schemes requires that the service provider supports them.

Caution: If one is using someone else's terminal to do this (e.g., hotel terminal, Internet cafe) one has no assurance that everything being sent and

2. All e-mail servers use either POP3 (the post office protocol) or IMAP4 (the improved mail protocol) unless they are of the type that requires a user to access e-mail through the Web, which is usually done by the free e-mail accounts only).

3. http://www.cotse.com and a handful of other service providers offer the option of a fully encrypted connection from anywhere in the world for receiving and sending e-mail. This can be done not only through a Web SSL connection but also through the use of some client e-mail software such as Eudora.

received (including passwords) is not being captured by the owner of that terminal.

Finally, it is worth mentioning that, for those cases when one does not have access to an ISP, where ever one happens to be (e.g., a foreign country), and if one's home ISP does not have a local number that it can be accessed from that location, one may want to consider subscribing to a handful of services that offer worldwide access to one's ISP. These include, for example, www.ipass.com and www.gric.com.

8.5 E-mail forensics and traces: the anonymity that isn't

Just because an e-mail says that it was sent by God@heaven does not mean that it was. It is extremely simple for a sender simple to fudge the sender's ID merely by temporarily entering any old e-mail address for him- or herself in the configuration of the e-mail software. It is just as easy for the receiving person to use an editor and change the sender's name to anything at all and then save the incoming e-mail.

In addition to the message itself, every e-mail has a header that amounts to a sequential list of how the message came from the originator to you. This header normally complies with the standards set in Internet RFC 822. True, some parts of it (although not all) can be deliberately modified by a sender who wants to cover his or her identity. In fact, most people do not know how to do this in a way that can escape detection by a competent analysis of that header. Of course, the recipient can remove the entire header; this would be effective only if the remnants of the original header were also wiped from the disk, and the ISP that delivered the e-mail (over whom a user is unlikely to have any control) had also deleted all audit records about that e-mail.

When the sender's e-mail is sent, the sender's e-mail software (e.g., Eudora, Netscape) adds some information to the header:

1. A Message-ID assigns a string of symbols that is unique to that message (e.g., Message-Id: 678901234.0123@fakedISPname.com).

2. An "X-Mailer" line gives the name of the e-mail software (e.g., X-Mailer: QUALCOMM Windows Eudora Pro Version 4.2).

3. The date/time when the e-mail was created or sent, which can be faked because anyone can set his or her computer to show any time at all (e.g., Date: Fri, 18 Sept 2000, 12:10:04 –0400). The offset (–0400) is the time difference from universal time in London. A minus sign means west of Universal Time (UTC) (or GMT, as it used to be called).

Next, the e-mail goes to the SMTP server of the sender's ISP, which adds a new line to the header that starts with "Received:" It shows the following:

1. From whom the e-mail was received (you in this case) (e.g., Received: from fakedISP.com (trueISP.com [3.4.5.6]);

2. The real IP address of the sending computer, shown in parentheses, just in case the "From" address was faked by the sender;

3. By whom it was received (e.g., by nameofsmtp.com (3.4.5/3.4.5) with SMTP id ABC12345), where "3.4.5/3.4.5" is the version number of the SMTP server's software, and the "with" part shows the protocol used (SMTP in most cases);

4. The date and time when this happened (e.g., Fri, 18 Sept 2000 12:20:02 −0400), where the date/time has to be later than the date/time stamp of when the message was composed or sent, unless the sending computer's clock was not set correctly, which in and of itself does not imply any misdeed.

Next, the e-mail received by the sender's mail server goes through a few go-between Internet nodes on its way to the mail server of the intended recipient. Each such go-between adds lines to the header showing

1. From whom it is was received;

2. By whom it is was received;

3. Date and time.

For example:

```
Received: from nameofsmtp.com (nameofsmtp.com [9.8.7.6])

by firstgobetween.com (6.7.8/6.7.8) with SMTP id DEF67890

Fri, 18 Sept 2000 12:25:07 −0400
```

Eventually the e-mail arrives at the mail server handling the account of the intended recipient, which adds its own lines to the header, plus an additional one with the notable difference that the "From" header does not include a colon after the name of the header:

```
From fakedname@fakedISPname.com Fri Aug 18 12:27:43 −0400

Received: from lastgobetween.com (lastgobetween.com [1.3.5.7])

by recipientmailserver.com (2.4.5/2.4.5) with SMTP id DEF67890

for recipient@recipientISP.com; Fri. 18 Aug 2000 12:27:43
−0400
```

Because most people don't want to be bothered with all of the above detail in their incoming e-mails, most e-mail software hides it, but the user can opt to see it. In Eudora Pro, for example, the user simply clicks on the "Blah blah" icon.

Of all these header lines, the only lines one can believe are those added by go-between hosts that one can trust. Worse yet, a savvy sender can cause fake lines to be added to the long header to further obfuscate things. One can only detect the existence of such faked lines (some times), which does not help identify the true sender of an e-mail.

The clues to look for in identifying faked "Received from" header lines include basically anything that deviates from the standard detailed above, which is an uninterrupted concatenation of

```
Received: from sending_server [(sending_host_name
sender's_IP_address)]

by receiving_server [(software_version)]

with mail_protocol and id [for recipient_name]; date
```

One needs to do the following:

1. Check the dates and times to ensure logic and consistency;

2. Check for extraneous information and lines in the above sequence;

3. Check for illogical server names and locations for the purported sender's location;

4. Check for incorrect syntax, as per above;

5. Look for any deviation from the norm above;

6. Look for relay sites.

"Relay sites" are the SMTP servers sites other than one's own ISP. Most (but not all) ISPs reject outgoing e-mail that does not come from their own account holders. The use of a relay site means nothing in and of itself; it merely suggests the increased likelihood that someone is trying to cover his or her tracks a little (although there are far more effective ways of so doing, as per Sections 9.6, 9.15, and 11.5 on anonymity).

Relay sites are shown explicitly in the header:

```
Received: from relaysitename.com (RELAYSITENAME.COM
[123.456.789.12])

by receivingsite.com (1.2.3/1.2.3) with SMTP if ABC12345

for recipientname@hisISP.com; Fri, 18 Aug 2000 12:22:41 -0400
```

One can at least verify if the relay site referenced indeed relays outgoing e-mail by accessing it and sending a test message to one's self. This can be done, for example, through the Telnet program by accessing port 25 of that site, at which point the response from that site might be

```
220 relaysitename.com SMTP Sendmail 1.2.3/1.2.3; Fri, 18 Aug
200012:53:31 -0400
```

Using Telnet, type

```
HELLO your_own_site.you_own_domain
```

This should evoke the response

```
250 relaysitename.com Hello your_own_site.your_own_domain [IP
address]
```

You can then specify

```
MAIL FROM: your_name@your_own_site.your_own_domain
```

You should get a response like

```
250 your_name@your_own_site.your_own_domain… Sender ok
```

Then you state that you want to send mail to yourself by entering

```
RCPT TO: your_name@your_own_site.your_own_domain
```

If that site indeed relays mail, it will respond with

```
250 your_name@your_own_site.your_own_domain Recipient ok
```

If it does not, it will respond with

```
250 your_name@your_own_site.your_own_domain We do not relay
```

Type QUIT.

If one's intent is to hide the IP address of the originating computer, finding a relay that does so is one way of doing this. This is one main reason why unsolicited e-mail is unlikely ever to stop; anyone can sent e-mail through unsuspecting "sendmail" servers in this way and thereby totally hide the originator's identity.

One could argue that the sendmail server is likely to keep records of such access. This would not hinder the originator because the originator could easily be in a totally different country and, furthermore, could be accessing that sendmail server through a public computer terminal, an unsuspecting person's insecure Wi-Fi AP, and so forth.

For other ways to hide the IP address of the originating computer, see Sections 8.5.2, 9.6, and 9.15 on various aspects of anonymity. More information on how to read e-mail headers can be obtained from http://www.stopspam.org/e-mail/headers/headers.html. Also, the interest reader will find a lot of specific information on tracing suspect e-mail at http://www.happyhacker.org/gtmhh/gtmhh2.shtml.

8.5.1 Tracking suspect e-mail

Numerous software packages—some free and some for pay—make it extremely easy for one to learn all there is to know about any Internet server, either by its name or its IP address.

One excellent such free software is NetLab from http://members. xoom.com/adanil/NetLab, which offers all network-search options one would need, such as Finger, WhoIs, Ping, Trace, and PortScan, as can be seen in Figure 8.12.

As one can readily see, it offers numerous functions for searching Internet-related issues about servers and users.

A similar software product openly available to anyone is Sam Spade, available at http://www.samspade.org/ssw.

Even without any special software, to find the domain name of a site by knowing its IP address, one can go to http://www.net.princeton.edu/ tools/dnslookup.html, http://ipindex.dragonstar.net, or http://combat.uxn .com.

To get more information one can then go to http://www.networksolu-tions.com, www.arin.net/intro.html, and www.arin.net/whois/index.html.

For non-U.S. servers, one can go to http://www.ripe.net/db/whois.html, www.ripe.net/cgi-bin/whois (for Europe and Middle East), and http:// www.apnic.net/apnic-bin/whois.pl (for Asia/Pacific).

To get information on individuals in the United States, three of the most prolific sources of information are http://www.cdbinfotek.com in Santa Ana, California and, http://www.digdirt.com (both require a subscription and a legitimate business reason for requesting such information).

Information publicly available can also be obtained online from, among others,

- http://www.whowhere.com;
- http://www.four11.com;

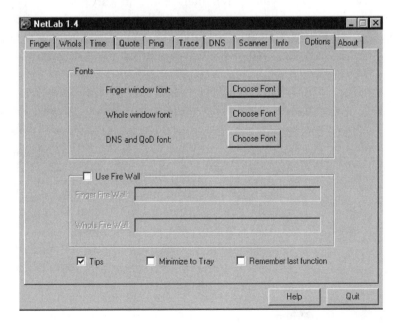

Figure 8.12   NetLab options.

- http://www.555-1212.com;

- http://www.bigfoot.com;

- http://www.switchboard.com;

- http://www.infospace.com;

- http://www.iaf.net;

- http://www.findme-mail.com (available in four languages);

- http://www.phonebook.com.

A "how to find people's e-mail address" set of procedures is also available online at http://www.qucis.queensu.ca/FAQs/e-mail/finding.html.

8.5.2   Sending anonymous e-mail: anonymous remailers

Introductory information about forged e-mail addressing can be obtained from http://smithco.net/~divide/index.html and http://happyhacker.com/gtmhh.

Anonymous and pseudonymous remailers are computers accessible through the Internet that hide one's true identity from the recipient. They are almost always operated at no cost to the user and can be found in many countries.

A pseudonymous remailer replaces the sender's true e-mail address with a pseudonymous one affiliated with that remailer and forwards the message to the intended recipient. The recipient can reply to the unknown originator's pseudonymous address, which, in turn, forwards it to the true address of the originator.

Anonymous remailers come in three flavors: cypherpunk remailers, mixmaster remailers, and Web-based remailers. The header and "From" information received by the intended recipient give no information about how the originator can be contacted. One can concatenate two or more such remailers.

For additional privacy, cypherpunk remailers support layered public-key PGP encryption, which amounts to the following:

- The message, including the e-mail address of the intended recipient, is first encrypted with the public key of the last remailer that will be used before the intended recipient receives the e-mail.

- This entire encrypted package, plus the e-mail address of the last remailer above, is then encrypted with the public key of the remailer to be used just prior to the last remailer.

- This process of layering encryption is repeated for each and every remailer that the originator wants to route the message through. This is depicted in Figure 8.13.

When the end result is sent by the originator to the first remailer, that remailer peels off the outer public-key-encryption layer (which is all he can

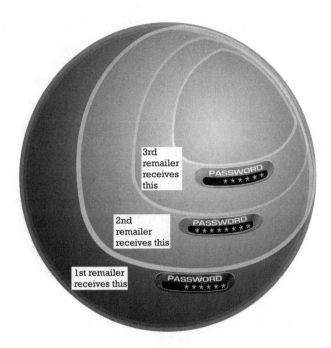

Figure 8.13 The essence of concatenated anonymous remailers.

decrypt) and finds inside a message encrypted with the next remailer's public key and its e-mail address for forwarding.

This process is repeated as the message goes from remailer to remailer until the last remailer is reached, which then forwards it the intended recipient.

The implementation of all this is automated and is very easy for the originator of a message. Two popular such implementations, Private Idaho and Jack B. Nymble, contain current lists of remailers and take care of the tedious ritual of placing the various layers of encryption on the message, using the correct public keys in the right order, and so forth.

Jack B. Nymble can be obtained from numerous sources on the Internet, such as http://www.skuz.net/potatoware.

Private Idaho can be obtained from numerous sources on the Internet, too, such as http://www.skuz.net/Thanatop/contents.htm (lots of help on setting it up), http://www.eskimo.com/~joelm/pi.html, and http://www.itech.net.au/pi.

An excellent set of detailed instructions on setting up a secure pseudonymous e-mail operation using, for example, Private Idaho (version 2.8 or later is required) is available at http://www.publius.net/n.a.n.help.html.

If additional help is required, one can also see http://www.dnai.com/~wussery/pgp.html and the Usenet newsgroup alt.privacy.anon-server.

Quicksilver can be obtained from http://quicksilver.skuz.net.

In practice, the process works well as long as a message is not routed through more than a handful of remailers; as the number increases, so does the probability that nothing will emerge on the other end.

It has been argued that there is no good technical reason why some remailer traffic is lost. Some have suggested by way of explanation that some "anonymous" remailers are, in fact, operated by governments that have an interest in monitoring such traffic and, perhaps, in deliberately and selectively deleting mail to particular destinations or causing selective denial of access by flooding the system.

Cypherpunk remailers (also known as Type I remailers) receive the message to be forwarded, strip away all headers that describe where the message came from and how it got there, and send it to the intended recipient (which can be an e-mail address or a Usenet newsgroup). Conceivably, someone with access to such a remailer's phone lines could correlate the incoming and outgoing traffic and make inferences.

Mixmaster remailers (also known as Type II remailers) get around some of the security problems of conventional and cypherpunk remailers. They use stronger encryption, as well as numerous procedures to frustrate traffic analysis, such as padding a message to disguise its original length and adding a pseudorandom delay between the time a message reaches the remailer and when it leaves that remailer.

While extremely secure, even Mixmaster remailers are not foolproof in providing impenetrable anonymity under all conditions. For example, a concerted effort could detect a correlation between sender A sending an encrypted message through remailers and receiver B receiving a message at some variable time afterwards. Problems of this nature can be solved with appropriate procedures and processes and not with technology alone. Also, the fact that most such remailers' encryption keys change very infrequently for logistical reasons makes them more vulnerable than one might otherwise think.

The process of using mixmaster remailers can be quite simple if one elects to use a GUI such as that offered to paying members by www.cotse.com. In that case, however, the user is vulnerable to the service provider who may be compelled by an in-country court order to provide security services with the records.

Web-based anonymizers, too, come in different flavors, ranging from a straightforward Web-based version of a conventional anonymizer to ones where the connection between one's computer and that anonymizer is itself encrypted with 128-bit encryption using the standard SSL encryption built into all late-vintage Web browsers.

Internet anonymity can be achieved through a multitude of means other than remailers. These include, but are not limited to, the use of public Internet terminals (e.g., ISPs' sales booths, public libraries, Internet cafés).

The reader is strongly urged to read the extensive information available on the subject at http://www.dis.org/erehwon/anonymity.html and at http://www.stack.nl/~galactus/remailers/index-mix.html, which is dated but useful, before being lulled into a false sense of security through half-measures.

Also, to check periodically for any new developments with some of the following Usenet newsgroups on the subject, check the following:

- alt.anonymous;
- alt.anonymous.e-mail;
- alt.anonymous.messages;
- alt.hackers;
- alt.security.keydist;
- alt.security.pgp;
- comp.security.pgp;
- comp.security.pgp.announce;
- comp.security.pgp.discuss;
- comp.security.pgp.resources;
- comp.security.pgp.tech;
- misc.security;
- sci.crypt;
- sci.crypt.research.

Caution: Some remailers are allegedly operated by or for law enforcement or governments. If they are, then one should not use a single remailer for anything, but a concatenation of numerous remailers located in different countries. The biggest vulnerability is posed by the very first remailer in the chain (which knows where an e-mail is coming from) and the very last one (which knows where it is going).

Caution: With the recently discovered PGP weakness of ADKs (see Sections 11.3.8 and 11.3.9), one should be even more careful about the choice of the remailers used.

Caution: The use of anonymizing remailers for routing encrypted e-mail is an obvious irritant to local law enforcement. One should balance privacy benefits against the likelihood of attracting attention from a repressive regime's interceptors.

Offerers of anonymous or pseudonymous e-mail services include the following:

- https://www.cotse.net;
- https://www.replay.com/remailer/anon.html;
- https://www.ziplip.com/sp/send.htm;
- http://209.67.19.98/lark2k/anonymail.html;
- http://www.MailAndNews.com;
- http://www.graffiti.net;
- http://www.ureach.com (one of the few big-name e-mail services that hides the sender's IP address from the recipient)[4];

---

4. Even so, one should not forget that a service provider can always be compelled by a court order to reveal the true IP address of a user of its services.

- http://pintur.tripod.com;
- http://www.cyberpass.net;
- http://www.ultimate-anonymity.com;
- http://www.surfanon.net (for anonymous Web browsing);
- http://www.secure-ibank.com.

Caution: Setting up an account with any one of the many Web-based free e-mail services under a pseudonym does not guarantee any e-mail anonymity to speak of.

Such "free" e-mail services keep detailed logs of the IP address from which they were contacted each time, and these records can be subpoenaed along with the logs of the ISP identified there to show exactly to whom a pseudonym belongs.

Anyone who needs true anonymity in e-mail is strongly advised to opt for the concatenated remailers with layered encryption just described in detail in this section.

8.5.3   General network tracing tools

Perhaps the easiest way to find information about the identity of IP addresses, about hosts, and about use of such tools as TraceRoute and Finger is to use the free services provided by www.cotse.com/iptools.html. Alternately, one can obtain and use one's own software tools, such as NetLab from http://members.xoom.com/adanil/NetLab.

CHAPTER

9

Contents

Advanced Protection from Computer Data Theft Online

9.1 Virus/Trojan/worm protection

This protection is an absolute must have, whether or not one goes online, because malicious mobile code often comes through CD-ROMs, floppy disks, and the like. There are numerous software packages available that provide this service on a low-cost yearly subscription basis. It is important is to do the following:

1. Update the virus-detection signature files at least every week. Whereas in the past it used to take days or weeks to exploit a security vulnerability, it now takes hours; as such, last week's virus protection is often not current enough.

2. Set up the configuration so that the software checks incoming e-mail, especially any attachments, as they come in online. Also to do automatic scans of files on inserted floppy disks, in addition to doing periodic scans of one's hard disk no less than, say, once per month.

3. Subscribe to a mail list service, such as the one from CERT at Carnegie Mellon University, that sends e-mail when a serious new security problem has been discovered and suggests effective fixes. To be added to that mailing list, send e-mail to cert-advisory-request@cert.org and include "SUBSCRIBE *your e-mail-address*" in the subject of your message.

4. Disable HTML in the e-mail client software. HTML makes some incoming e-mail look pretty, but it is also a major avenue for malicious code to sneak in.

At the risk of oversimplifying a complex situation, Webopedia defines a computer virus as "a program or piece of code that is loaded onto your computer without your

159

knowledge and runs against your wishes. Viruses can also replicate themselves. All computer viruses are manmade."

A Trojan is a program that pretends to be or do one thing, but in reality damages your data or sniffs your system for personal data. Back Orifice and Back Orifice 2000 are among the most notorious such programs. The term comes from the huge wooden horse parked, according to Homer's *Iliad*, by the Greeks as a gift outside the city of Troy. At nighttime, the horse's wooden belly was opened from the inside to let the hidden Greek soldiers out, who proceeded to attack Troy.

A worm is "a program or algorithm that replicates itself over a computer network and usually performs malicious actions, such as using up the computer's resources and possibly shutting the system down."

Virus detection software does a credible, but inadequate, job of detecting Trojans. Trojans are best detected with dedicated software packages, such as The Cleaner from www.moosoft/com.

9.2   Protection from keyloggers

9.2.1   Protection from keystroke-capturing software

Numerous software packages detect and eliminate many (but not all) keystroke-capturing software programs in common use. However, given the large number of these programs, such as Keykey, discussed in Section 4.4, that are openly available on the Internet, there is no one easy way to detect and eliminate all of them from one's computer. Given the major security threat that such programs represent, however, one would be well justified in taking the time needed to weed such programs out and, better yet, to minimize the likelihood that they get into one's computer in the first place. The latter can only be done by adhering to the following standard security measures:

> ‣ Do not open e-mail attachments unless you know for a fact who sent them and why. The fact that the sender's e-mail address is that of a friend means nothing as it can be faked. In fact, the most troublesome recent worms (Melissa and I Love You) hijacked one's computer, looked up the list of friends' e-mail addresses in Outlook/Outlook Express, and sent them e-mails ostensibly coming from the hijacked computer.

> ‣ Do not download and install assorted software from the Web from sites with unknown or dubious agendas. Check first with a privacy-minded Usenet forum such as alt.privacy for any postings about them.

> ‣ Do not allow others to insert floppy disks (or CD-ROMs or USB keys or any other media) of unknown origin into your computer.

> ‣ Do not allow others to use your computer in your absence.

Some antivirus and anti-Trojan software detect some (but not all) of the keystroke-capturing software. Alternately, one can manually search for such software by simply searching the hard disk for any software running in the background that one cannot recognize. One has to do this often enough to spot what is unusual and also to have started doing so when the computer was known for a fact not to have any such software running on it.

To detect what software is running in the background, do the following:

1. Use WinPatrol from http://www.billp.com/winpatrol, which will also alert you every time a new program wants to run behind your back.

2. In WinNT/2000, type Ctrl-Shift-Esc.

9.2.2 Protection from keystroke-capturing hardware

The best (and perhaps the only) protection is to prevent it from being installed (through physical security) or at least to detect (through physical inspection) if it has been installed. Such devices cannot be detected through software schemes. It follows that if you are patronizing someone else's computer (e.g., at an Internet cafe or hotel), you have zero assurance that your passwords and everything else you type are not being recorded. The same applies to hidden overhead cameras.

9.3 Protection from commercial adware/spyware

There is an obvious commercial incentive for companies to know as much about an individual as possible, so that customized advertising can be sent to him or her. Because many individuals wisely do not volunteer much information about themselves to total strangers in these days of rampant identity theft, and because personal computers nowadays contain a fairly accurate representation of their respective owners identities, many companies have taken it upon themselves to steal as much information as they can about a person from his or her computer anyway. This unauthorized stealing of information from individual PCs for marketing purposes is enabled by the fact that when their PCs are connected to the Internet, most users have no idea what information is going out. This is made possible through the following.

1. When filling out online registration forms for software, the user may think only that information manually entered by the user is going out when in fact a digest of one's entire hard disk is often sent. Even reputable large companies have been caught red-handed engaging in this practice. Do not ever fill out online registration forms or allow software to register itself online. Never. Do not do online activation of software; if you must use such software (which, on philosophical grounds, you may not want to do at all), do the activation by talking to the vendor over the telephone.

2. Some marketing companies (such as Predictive Networks at http://www.predictivenetworks.com) engage in a business practice whereby the participating ISP provides the marketing company the individual users' Web browsing habits. This involves not only free ISPs where this tracking has become the norm, but also regular ISPs that one pays for by the month.[1]

3. There is often hidden functionality in a large collection of software packages that scouts one's hard disk, collects whatever information it feels like, and relays it on the sly and without the user's knowledge when the unsuspecting user is online on the Internet. These are known as "adware" or "spyware."

This threat is made particularly bothersome by an odious new law called the Uniform Computer Information Transactions Act (UCITA), which has been already passed in Maryland and Virginia. This legislation allows companies to spy on a consumer's computer to make sure that all license requirements are obeyed. Companies will be able to remotely turn off the software if they feel that the terms of the license have not been abided by, without notifying the user. Finally, licensors can require that individual users not publicize flaws in their software and also that no legal action be taken by the buyer of the software except in the form of a mediation in the jurisdiction of each such company's choice.

A typical example, according to Steve Gibson of Gibson Research Corporation (http://grc.com), is Real Network's Real Download, Netscape/AOL's Smart Download, and NetZip's Download Demon in their default configurations.

> "Every time you use one of these utilities to download any file from anywhere on the Internet, the complete URL address of the file, along with a unique ID tag that has been assigned to your machine and—in the case of Netscape's Smart Downloadonly—your computer's individual Internet IP address, is immediately sent to the program's publisher. This allows a database of your entire personal file download history to be assembled and uniquely associated with your individual computer . . . for whatever purpose the program's publisher may have today or tomorrow."

---

1. According to Predictive's privacy policy, "Predictive Networks uses digital silhouettes to match Internet content and advertising with appropriate subscriber recipients. As a result, subscribers receive information that appeals to their current needs and interests. To develop a digital silhouette, the Predictive Network analyzes URL click-stream data, such as Web pages visited, and date and time of visit." "To optimize the format of the content delivered to subscribers, the anonymous digital silhouette may include specifications about the subscriber's computer, such as processor type, browser plug-ins and available memory." "Predictive Networks urges subscribers to consult their ISP before opting out, as doing so may affect their Internet service and/or their Internet service rate." For more information, one can look at "Start-Up's Tracking Software Sets Off Privacy Alarm," by Jom Hu, CNET News.com, May 1, 2000.

According to Gibson,

> Aureate/Radiate and Conducent Technologies [have] advertising, monitoring, and profiling software [that] sneaks into our machines without our knowledge or permission. Comet Cursor secretly tracks our Web browsing, GoHip hijacks our Web browser and alters our eMail signatures . . . and many other hopeful and exploitive newcomers on the horizon. When confronted with their actions, such companies invariably say "read the fine print, what we're doing is spelled out there and the user agreed."

It must be emphasized that some adware programs leave the secretly installed utility (that periodically sends out such information) even after the original software that installed this utility has been removed from one's disk.

A long list of software programs that, according to Gibson, engage in the practice of periodically sending information about some of the user's habit out over the Internet can be found at http://grc.com/oo/spyware.htm and includes the popular CuteFTP utility.

The best protection against such adware is provided by Ad-aware by Lavasoft (http://www.lavasoftus.com) and (not "or") the Spybot Search and Destroy freeware by Patrick M. Kolla.

Because there is a vast sea of software available, perhaps the best protection, in addition to the above, is to install and use a network packet sniffer, which observes what gets sent out from one's computer over the Internet. This is recommended only for those who have—or are willing to invest the time to acquire—a thorough understanding of TCP/IP and IP. (See an excellent source of additional information in the 738 page "TCP/IP Tutorial and Technical Review" written by the IBM International Technical Support Organization; it is available freely as a 3.2-MB Adobe Acrobat file that can be downloaded, along with others, from http://grc.com/oo/packetsniff.htm.)

There are numerous packet sniffers available, such as the SpyNet Sniffer from eEye (http://www.eeye.com/html/Products/Iris/overview.html), the CommView v2.0 sniffer from Tamos Software.

9.4 Protection from Web bugs: an insidious and far-reaching threat

A particularly insidious threat is the use of invisible images on a Web page that are as small as only one pixel ("pixel" is shorthand for "picture element") square. What makes them invisible is that they can be made to match the exact color of the background. When one receives e-mail or browses a Web site with such an HTML invisible image (or even looks at any HTML-enabled document with such embedded HTML code), one's client software requests and receives all images in that e-mail or Web site, including the image with the invisible pixels, which resides in some remote server. That remote server (which could be operated by some nation's security services) will know right away which specific IP address has looked at a given Web site or at a specific e-mail or at a specific Usenet newsgroup posting. Worse yet, anyone that the trapped e-mail, Web site, Microsoft document is forwarded to who looks at that file will also dutifully—and unknowingly—report to and identify him- or herself to that remote server.

The threats from this technique are far reaching:

 ▸ It can track which IP address reads which Usenet newsgroup posting and when.

 ▸ It can track which IP address is accessing which HTML-embedded document and when.

 ▸ It can track which IP address is reading an e-mail, thereby tying e-mail address to an IP address.

 ▸ It can tie a Web browser cookie to an e-mail address so that the remote Web site will learn the identity of the person who visits it.

 ▸ It can track whether an e-mail is forwarded, to whom, and when it is read by that new recipient.

 ▸ It can act as a watermark to uncover the identities of the members of a network of like-minded individuals.

The best defense against this security threat consists of multiple steps:

1.   Disable HTML in one's e-mail client software. (If your e-mail software does not allow this—as is the case with many versions of Outlook, Outlook Express, and Netscape software, do not use such software for e-mail or Usenet Newsgroup reading.)

2.   Do not read e-mail or Usenet newsgroups online. Download, disconnect, and then read what you downloaded.

3.   Do not perform any activities online that do not require online connectivity. Word processing, spreadsheet preparation and editing, PowerPoint slide editing, and so forth should never be done online.

4.   Have a firewall that will alert you to any attempt to establish outbound connectivity and disallow it.

9.5   Using encrypted connections for content protection

SSL is easy to use for connecting to Web sites. Make sure that you disable SSLv2 because it has been shown to be easily compromised to convert the connection to an unencrypted one without any visual indication to the user. (SSL is now called TLS, an Internet standard; even so, millions of people have known it as SSL and this old name is likely to prevail).

In a nutshell, SSL implements public-key encryption (see Section 9.7.1) without the user having to do much of anything. In the Web browser context it achieves two goals:

1.   It encrypts communications all the way from one's Web browser to the server being accessed. Anyone along the way is unable to view the contents, although any interceptor can readily see the identities (the IP addresses) of these two end points.

2.   It authenticates the remote server (say, American Express, Amazon, or whatever) to the individual Web-browsing person. Actually it only authenticates the remote Web hosting service to the user; this Web hosting service may or may not be operated by the commercial entity that one is transacting with. In other words, if you are in an SSL connection with company XYZ hosted by Web hosting service ABC, your encrypted connection ends at company ABC.

SSL does not authenticate you, the individual user, to the remote service.

Item (2) above brings up an interesting question: How do you make sure that when you think that you are connected to, say, Microsoft.com on an SSL connection, you are not, in fact, connected to some man-in-the-middle hacker who acts as a go-between and intercepts all of your traffic before forwarding it (if he or she forwards it at all)?

The answer depends on whether or not the certificate of the suspect remote site is or is not digitally signed by one of the certificate authorities (or their designees; see Figure 9.1) that your Web browser considers to be beyond reproach by virtue of the fact that these certificate authorities' own certificates came with your Web browser.

If the remote site has elected to create its own self-certified certificate, you will be asked whether you want to accept that certificate this one time or forever after.

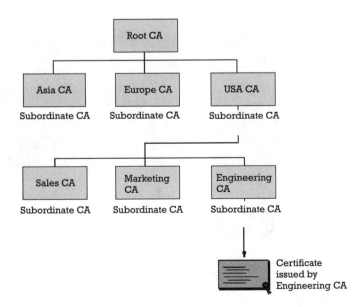

Figure 9.1   Certificate authorities' web of trust. (Courtesy of Netscape.)

Once you accept it, it will go into your list of accepted certificates, which you can readily peruse; in the case of Netscape, you click on the little security lock icon on the top pull-down menu (see Figure 9.2).

For connecting to the office from home, a hotel, or an Internet cafe, use some variant of VPN that your office hopefully has had the foresight to implement. The options are as follows:

1. *Point to Point Tunneling Protocol (PPTP):* This is Microsoft's proprietary protocol, which has been superceded by Layer 2 Forwarding (L2F). Its security has been questioned by noted cryptographer Bruce Schneier (http://www.counterpane.com/pptp-pressrel.html); also, it uses a fixed port for its connections, and this port has been blocked by service providers and nations that don't like users to use PPTP.

2. *IP Security Protocol (IPsec):* This is a far better protocol. The problem with it is that it was designed by committee and the result is too complicated, the manual that comes with it is too confusing, and most organizations shy away from it. Needless complexity is the enemy of security.

3. *Custom VPN packages offered by a few vendors, such as Virtual Transmission Control Protocol (VTCP):* VTCP uses randomly selected, high-number ports for its connections and is therefore much harder to identify or block.

For connecting with an encrypted connection directly to another user for file transfers, one should consider using Secure File Transfer Protocol (FTP) or Secure Shell (SSH) (http://www.ssh.com). There are numerous vendors of software packages that enable this. For more details on SSH, see Section 9.8.

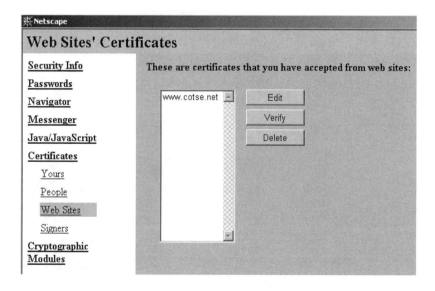

Figure 9.2 Checking which self-issued certificate sites you have accepted.

9.6   Using proxy servers for anonymity

A proxy server is a go-between between one's computer and whichever server one connects to through the Internet. Depending on the specifics of a proxy, it can serve numerous needs:

1. A lot of people use proxies just to get around slow, nonoptional ISP caching (content stored locally to avoid having to get it from the Internet each time); in so doing, one can get speed improvements even if the proxy used is on the other side of the world.

2. Others establish an encrypted connection with an out-of-country proxy as a means of defeating local censorship or local monitoring. Once connected to a proxy, one can do all other Internet activities in a manner that is not observable by anyone in the path between the user and the proxy. Of course, the fact that one has established an encrypted connection to an out-of-country server will be very much visible to the local service provider and security services, and this is unlikely to endear one to the local regime.

3. Still others use a proxy in order to prevent a Web site that one looks at from knowing who is looking at it. Because Web browsers broadcast a lot of information about a Web surfer, and especially because there are countless ways whereby a hostile Web site can retrieve any and all information from one's browser, the motivation to prevent all that is self-evident.

4. Still others elect to use proxies to post anonymously to Usenet forums to avoid the—sadly inevitable—result of ending up on numerous advertisers' lists or receiving harassing e-mail by assorted strangers.

5. Some proxies allow easier Internet access for the visually impaired: ea.ethz.ch:8080 is one notable example. Still others translate Web pages into languages that the user may understand; for example, mte.inteli.net.mx:3128 translates English Web pages into Spanish and zip-translator.dna.affrc.go.jp:30001 translates English Web pages into Spanish. As such, the often-heard assertions by law enforcement that proxies are only used by those with criminal intent are totally without merit.

Setting up a proxy on one's browser is quite simple. In the case of Netscape, go to Edit/Preferences/Advanced/Proxies, select "Manual proxy configuration," click "View," and fill in the blanks in accordance with the instructions of the particular proxy you want to use.

In the case of a local proxy (meaning, software in one's own computer that assumes a go-between filtering role, such as JunkBuster), one merely needs to enter the word "localhost" in the "Address" blank for both the "HTTP" and "Security" fields, and the number "8000" in the blank for "Port."

Web sites that provide current lists of proxy servers of all sorts or that provide information about a particular proxy include the following:

- http://www.webveil.com/matrix.html (highly recommended);
- http://www.webveil.com/proxies.html;
- http://tools.rosinstrument.com/cgi-bin/fp.pl/showlog;
- http://www.somebody.net;
- http://www.egroups.com/community/proxy-methods-list;
- http://mylad.newmail.ru/howto.htm;
- http://proxys4all.cgi.net/public.shtml.

Internet users from oppressive regimes should prefer out-of-country proxy servers, which are ephemeral and unlikely to have been identified as proxy servers by such regimes. Even so, using them involves the considerable risk of incurring the regime's wrath.

Caution: Most of the proxies one can find at proxys4all (http://proxys4all.cgi.net) actually mask very little and give a false sense of security because they reveal the IP address of the originator to the Web site being visited.

Remember that a remote proxy is nothing more than an untrusted go-between. That server will know precisely who you are (because it must know your IP address to forward to you whatever it is you are browsing through the proxy), and it will also know what you are browsing. Proxy servers usually do keep logs of who did what and when, and such logs can be subpoenaed by the local (to the proxy) authorities whose interest will be piqued by the mere fact that you are using a proxy, especially one that encrypts its connection with you. As such:

1. Try to use a proxy from a suitable country other than your own.

2. Keep in kind that that the lifetime of a proxy is very iffy. Many survive for just one day; others for years. You need a continuously updated list of current ones that you can get as shown above.

3. Be very suspicious of proxy servers that require you to enable JavaScript because they can then see a lot in your computer that they really have no reason to see.

4. Do not overuse any one proxy; spread your online communications over different proxies, preferably located in different countries.

5. If you don't (and you shouldn't) trust any one proxy to protect your privacy, consider chaining proxies. According to a posting by Anony-mouse (which has since been sold) on February 5, 1999,

   - Record your own current IP address (you can get it, for example, by going to www.tamos.com/bin/proxy.cgi, or by typing netstat—n.

   - Go to the Anonymizer form at www.anonymizer.com/surf_free. shtml and enter www.tamos.com/bin/proxy.cgi into the form's box and press the Enter key. This will take you to http://www.tamos. com/ bin/proxy.cgi.

» Now look at the URL displayed for the page http://anon-free.ano-nymizer.com/www.tamos.com/bin/proxy.cgi.

» That prefix (http://anon-free.anonymizer/com) is the prefix that you must write ahead of any URL you want to chain through Ano-nymizer in the future, for example: http://anon-free.anonymizer .com/www.cnn.com.

» Also notice the IP address shown (209.75.196.2); it is the identity that Anonymizer gives out instead of your real IP address.

Equivalently, you can go through other combinations, such as Ano-nymicer as follows:

» Go to the Anonymicer form at http://www.in.tum.de/~pircher/ano-nymicer and type http://www.tamos.com/bin/proxy.cgi into that form's box (and hit Enter).

» This takes you, again, to http://www.tamos.com/bin/proxy.cgi; yet, if you look at the URL shown for that page, you will see http://www. in/tum.de/cgi-bin/ucgi/pircher/anon-www.pl/www.tamos.com/bin/ proxy-cgi.

» The prefix http://www.in.tum/de/cgi-bin/ucgi/pircher/anon-www.pl is the prefix that you should write in front of whichever URL you want to go to through Anonymicer.

A good current reference of the status of many free Web-based proxies can be found at http://www.webveil.com/matrix.html. It provides about 10 long pages full of detailed information on the current status of such proxies.

For additional information about the strengths and weaknesses of prox-ies, one may consult the following sites:

» http://www.ijs.co.nz/proxies.htm;

» http://www.ultimate-anonymity.com (don't believe the name of the site);

» http://tools.rosinstrument.com/proxy/proxyck.htm;

» http://proxys4all.cgi.net.

One can find numerous others by searching on the keyword "proxy."

9.7 Using encrypted connections to ISPs for content protection

The initial connection to one's ISP when one logs in is never encrypted. What could (and should) be encrypted is what happens afterwards:

1. In the simplest case, one can connect to any one of many Web pages that support SSL (see Section 9.7.1), and this will establish an end-

to-end encrypted connection between that Web server (which may be on the other side of the Earth) and one's computer. This prevents anyone else from becoming privy to the content of the data flow. Of course, the primary ISP will know where one has connected to, but not the content of any subsequent information flow.

2. Many corporate computing centers have established secure means whereby employees can log-in to the corporate network from afar. This is useful for traveling employees and those who work from home. This means is known as a VPN (Chapter 12), and it amounts to connection which is also end-to-end encrypted between the individual's computer and the remote server. It shares many of the characteristics of SSL above, but many of the technical details are quite different.

3. Encrypted e-mail with or without attachments can always be sent through unencrypted connections. All that is observable to the ISP or anyone else is the outer envelope (i.e., who is sending something to whom). If anonymous remailing techniques are used (see Sections 8.5.2 and 9.6), then that information is not very helpful to an interceptor or ISP, except in a negative sense because it raises the profile of the sender as someone who may be "up to no good" and worthy of more detailed surveillance.

4. Encrypted voice connectivity is a reality using free software (www.fourmilab.ch/speakfree); see Section 10.2.5.

9.7.1 SSL

SSL (now officially referred to as TLS, which is an Internet standard) is a protocol developed by Netscape that allows end-to-end encryption between one's browser and the Web site one visits.

An SSL connection is verified by looking at the little lock icon on the lower left side of Netscape, as shown in Figure 9.3.

Caution: Recent work at Dartmouth College showed that a malicious remote site can paint your screen to make the lock look locked even when the connection is totally unencrypted.

The process of using Web-browser encryption to send and receive encrypted e-mail is quite straight forward from within either Netscape's or Microsoft's browser:

1. One connects to any of a handful of popular certificate-issuing organizations, such as Verisign (http://www.verisign.com), which charges about $10 per year, or to Thawte (http://www.thawte.com), which gives free certificates even though it has been bought out by Verisign.

2. After installing this certificate, one can subsequently exchange encrypted e-mail with others who have also gone through the same ritual.

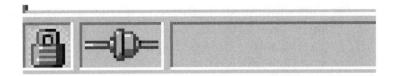

Figure 9.3 Visual indication of an SSL-encrypted connection on Netscape.

Caution: SSL mail does not encrypt the "From" and "To" information or the "Subject" line. Also, outgoing SSL-encrypted e-mail is encrypted so that the sender can also read it after it has been sent. It follows that a sender can be compelled by local authorities to decrypt that mail. By comparison, a user of PGP (which is highly recommended as a superior alternative for e-mail encryption; see Section 11.3) cannot decrypt outgoing e-mail encrypted for some intended recipient who is the only one that can decrypt it.

9.8 SSH

SSH is simply a piece of software that allows one to connect to another computer over a network and to do so securely over inherently unsecured channels such as the Internet. As such, it is a secure replacement to Telnet's rsh, rlogin, and rcp, familiar to old-timers in the Internet world. There are over 2 million SSH users around the world.

SSH is now the de facto standard for remotely logging in to a computer. It solves three key problems of Telnet-based login:

1. Weak authentication based on IP addresses that can be spoofed or reusable passwords that can be sniffed;

2. No privacy as packets can be sniffed and the content of the communication, notably including the log in userid and password, can be seen by unauthorized persons;

3. No integrity protection as connections can be hijacked.

Without SSH, the content of Telnet-based communication between machines can be readily intercepted. This includes passwords as well as all data.

SSH foils such interception by optionally encrypting the packets and by only allowing connections between computers that trust each other by virtue of their IP addresses. Rivest-Shamir-Adelman (RSA) public-key technology, initially published in 1978, is used for the authentication. SSH never trusts the network. Of course, SSH is not a cure-all; it only protects from the three problems listed above.

There are two incompatible versions: SSH1 and SSH2.

There are plenty of software packages available that implement SSH; some are even free to download.

The interested user is encouraged to use SSH in place of FTP between Internet-connected individuals. It is dependable, secure, and easy to use. One can browse through frequently asked questions (FAQs) on SSH at any of the following sites:

▸ http://www.employees.org/~satch/fq/ssh-faq.html;

▸ http://www.tigerlair.com/ssh/faq/ssh-faq.html;

▸ http://www.onsight.com/faq/ssh-faq.html;

▸ http://www.ayahuasca.net/ssh/ssh-faq.html (in the United Kingdom);

▸ http://member.ctinets.com/~dhackler/ssh/faq/ssh-faq.html (in Hong Kong);

▸ http://www.cs.univ-paris8.fr/ssh/faq/ssh-faq.html (in France).

9.9   The failed promise of peer-to-peer clouds

During the last 4 to 5 years, a number of independent efforts started—and largely failed—whose basic theme was that an online user could hide in the anonymity afforded by large numbers of concurrent users whose data packets were to be shuffled through a collection of nodes.

The most notable of such efforts the following:

1. The well-regarded (for its technical skills) group Cult of the Dead Cow had promised "peekabooty" over the last 3 or 4 years as a peer-to-peer scheme for defeating interception. The effort has been discontinued.

2. The British libertarian group http://www.m-o-o-t.org had also been promising a bootable CD that would shield users from the invasive power of the British RIP Act.

3. The German J-A-P effort has been extensively reported in numerous Usenet posting in the alt.privacy forum to have been compromised by the German authorities.

4. A commercial effort by a Canadian firm, Zero Knowledge, ended within days after the September 11, 2001, tragedy.

Not all of these efforts were entirely the same. The British m-o-o-t effort emphasized leaving no data on one's computer that could be forensically found and analyzed.

The rest of the efforts emphasized a cloud of nodes plus encryption.

The basic idea behind these schemes has been that a user who is stuck behind a censoring firewall can connect to any point in a "cloud" of many users and that, unless an oppressing organization manages to shut down all the computers in this ad hoc network, it cannot be defeated. Access to the network could be attained by any means, such as posting a message on eBay, an ICQ message, an HTML access, and so forth; a reply could be made by a different scheme.

The problems with this concept are as follows:

1. A censor could block access to all the known nodes (e.g., IP addresses, e-mail addresses) of the cloud that a user is likely to know of and access. Those attempting access to the blocked nodes could be arrested. Worse yet, a censor could not block access but observe, monitor, and eventually arrest all who make access.

2. A censor could create rogue servers pretending to be volunteers helping the cause of freedom.

3. If known APs were to be blocked by a censor, then the users would likely go to "circumventor" nodes, thereby identifying such circumventor sites to the monitoring censor.

Is there a fix? Yes, but clouds are not the way. They are a viable solution to a different problem, that of preventing traceback from a destination site, not to the problem of preserving the anonymity of a freedom-minded individual operating inside a repressive regime.

A possible fix is for the freedom-minded user to have a personally trusted out-of-country site (or sites) from which to request locally banned information in an encrypted or steganographically hidden manner.

9.10 Caller ID traps to avoid

Most countries of the world have leap-frogged interim technology and have migrated from the mechanical "Stromberg Carlson" routers of telephone calls to the latest implementation of what is known as Signaling System 7 (SS7). This all-electronic system allows one to offer such popular features as caller ID, selective call rejection, call forwarding, and so forth. What may not be as evident is that identification of the origin of a telephone call is instantaneous in all cases. Caller ID blocking (i.e., when a subscriber thinks that he blocks his own phone number from being forwarded downstream) is an illusion; the number is still forwarded all the way except—in some cases—that it is not seen by the called party. In many cases (such as when calling a toll-free number, where the called party pays for the call and is presumed to be entitled to know whose call he is paying for), Automatic Number Identification (ANI) which is separate from caller ID, ensures that the called party knows the caller's phone number regardless. The same applies when calling emergency numbers or some government offices); caller ID blocking does absolutely nothing.

The bottom line is that the initiator of an Internet dial-up connection, whether the call is local or international, is immediately identifiable, and there is nothing that the caller can do about it other than to use someone else's telephone.[2] This applies to cellular calls as well.

---

2. Some bill-collection agencies faced with the obvious "problem" of having their calls ignored by those they are trying to reach have been reported to be using equipment that allows them to cause a different number to be displayed on the called party's caller ID box.

9.11 Traps when connecting online from a cellular phone

A tourist from a Western country to a totalitarian one might mistakenly think that an Internet connection through a cellular phone, while on such travel, will provide anonymity and untraceability. Nothing could be further from the truth.

As stated above, a cellular phone enjoys no more safety from being identified than any landline telephone. With the increasing interest in offering position-location services for emergency purposes (and any country's law enforcement's insatiable appetite to know everything about everyone), cellular phones can not only be listened to with the same (or greater) technical ease as regular landline telephones, but can be geolocated with an accuracy of a few hundred feet using commercial technology implemented by the cellular telephone companies that are now required to comply with the U.S. CALEA[3] requirements.

In the case of Global System for Mobile Communications (GSM) cellular telephones, the identity of the subscriber is not in the telephone instrument itself but in the subscriber identification module (SIM) card, which is a small smart card that can be used with any GSM phone anywhere in the world. If the SIM card corresponds to a user registered within the country where the phone is being used, then that country can know everything about that user unless that user purchased the SIM card and add-on airtime anonymously at some local kiosk, which is commonplace these days worldwide. If the card corresponds to a user registered with some other GSM country, then the country where that GSM phone is being used will only know which is the issuing country. Even then, however, the location of the GSM phone can again be pinpointed to within a few hundred feet using commercial technology.

About the only anonymity one can have with cellular phones is through the vastly popular business model whereby a buyer purchases a phone (usually a GSM phone) with a prepaid number of air minutes. Such purchases are usually anonymous or pseudonymous as the selling vendor and GSM service providers are protected from unpaid charges since the phone will stop functioning when the prepaid limit is used up. Such accounts are almost always usable only within the country that sold them.

9.12 Traps when using FTP

FTP is the standard way of downloading files from the Internet. It is also an option for any two individuals for sending and receiving such files by interjecting a go-between: The sender FTPs the file to some interim "parking space" such as an ISP or a Web site; the intended recipient is then notified

---

3. The Communications Assistance for Law Enforcement Act, passed by the U.S. Congress in October 1994.

and retrieves that file from its parking space. This two-step process provides some insulation between the sender and the recipient; a freedom fighter in a repressive regime could, for example, use this to avoid being associated with the other party to the communication. The danger is that this file now sits in some third site (the parking site). Unless it is protected by encryption, which may be alerting in and of itself (in the freedom fighter in a repressive regime scenario, for instance), there are security risks from this process.

FTP software can be obtained freely from many sites, such as www.cuteftp.com.

Caution: CuteFTP is one of a number of software packages identified as adware or spyware in the sense that they also install a file in one's computer that, unbeknownst to the user, periodically contacts the maker or the software through the Internet.

9.13 Using instant messaging schemes

In one word, don't. Despite their appeal and popularity, instant messaging schemes are a can of security worms.

Instant messaging is a very popular class of software applications that notify online users right away if any one them is online and allows one-on-one (or many-with-many) textual communications between them. It is very convenient.

It is also a security disaster. There are easy ways whereby one's instant messaging identity can be highjacked by someone else. Also anything typed becomes a matter of record for a long time to come. Finally, one may well not wish to advertise to the world when he or she is or is not online or what one's IP address (hence whereabouts) is.

These comments apply to all Instant Messenger application software, such as AOL's Instant Messenger, the Yahoo messenger, the MSN messenger, and so forth. Depending on the version used, many are vulnerable to crashing and even running a program on your computer if they receive a malicious "buffer overflow" message.

Also, regardless of the message, one never really knows who is on the other end of the line. Finally, since all messages typed back and forth are unencrypted, they are eminently interceptable and are routinely intercepted by many countries' law enforcers looking for assorted predators.

9.14 Pitfalls of online banking

A few years ago, the German "Chaos Club" demonstrated on German national TV how a popular online banking program was doctored remotely by a malicious Web site to cause it to direct the user's bank to send payment to a hacker's account. This underscores the fact that if a computer goes online to the Internet, unless its user has taken the many protective measures spelled out in this book, any of its files are vulnerable to being read, stolen, or modified. To that extent, online banking is vulnerable for merely having its files exist on a vulnerable computer.

In addition, one should ensure that the encryption used employs key lengths that are

1. No shorter than about 3,000 bits if public-key encryption is used (as is likely the case);

2. No shorter than 128 bits if symmetric encryption is used or if a symmetric session key is used.

Because this level of technical detail is unlikely to be shown in such software intended for nontechnical users, one may wish to ask before using such software; even if the encryption uses acceptably long keys, there is no assurance that it is implemented properly.

If the same online banking software was available outside of the United States prior to the liberalization of the U.S. encryption exportation laws in CY2000, users should be concerned that it uses weak encryption (in order to be exportable at that time).

Caution: Some banks use online customers' social security numbers as that customer's ID for all Web-based banking. This is an outrageous violation of privacy and a practical nuisance because, for example, it precludes a customer from having more than one online account with that bank.

In the final analysis, the online banking user's only real protection can be a clause that indemnifies and protects the user in case of a problem caused by unauthorized use of the online banking software. Because banks have no control over that, however, it is unlikely that a user will get such legal protection. The best a user can do is to secure his computer, which is what this book is all about.

9.15 Secure Usenet usage

Where are Usenet messages stored? They are not stored in any one big computer. As one (anyone) posts a message to any of the more than 100,000 different Usenet forums, that message goes out right then and there to the world. Hundreds of thousands of computers that "listen" to Usenet postings will capture it and store it for varying lengths of time if they are set up to capture messages to that particular forum.

It is never a good idea for one to post using a true name on Usenet forums for the following reasons:

1. Unless the topic has absolutely no political, religious, cultural, or other implication and unless the prose used has absolutely no barbs, it is inevitable that some person(s) reading it may take exception to its contents. Given how easy it is to "e-mail-bomb" someone (i.e., to subscribe the victim to a few thousand mail lists each of which generates some 100 messages a day, which are e-mailed to each member of the mail list, thereby clogging one's e-mail beyond belief and

rendering one's account unusable, one should not post messages that could offend anyone.

2. Even if the topic is totally clean (e.g., posting a technical question on how to deal with a technical problem in Windows), one will end up in spammers' (e-mail advertisers) list, whereupon one's e-mail box will again start getting clogged with messages offering instant wealth, sex, miracle cures, and the like.

It follows that because Usenet can provide an extremely useful source of quick technical advise (e.g., when some popular software or hardware misbehaves and one is at a loss as to the cause), the only way to post a question (e.g., "my software xyz seems to crash the computer under these conditions; does anyone know of a fix?") and avail oneself of this vast resource is to post anonymously or pseudonymously.

But merely looking at what others have posted on this or that Usenet newsgroup can incur the wrath of select law-enforcement zealots in one country or another. As with anything that is a network activity (such as the Internet), there is no such thing as a "passive" act. "Merely browsing" is a very active endeavor in that it amounts to asking one's ISP to fetch and send to the subscriber the specific documents that the subscriber wants to see. In merely looking at Usenet postings, therefore, a user must again be anonymous.

Here again one must ask oneself, Anonymous from whom?

1. From the readers of the posted Usenet prose around the world?

2. From the in-country ISP who may well be in collusion with local ambitious law enforcers? If so, it is unwise to read—let alone write to—Usenet forums that deal with a topic that is taboo in-country for religious, political, or other reasons.

3. From someone who might get physical access to one's computer for forensics purposes to use against that person?

The X-No-Archive: yes flag in the header of a Usenet posting is not to be depended on. It is honored by only a small percentage of services. For all practical purposes, Usenet postings last forever, hence the need to post anonymously (or not at all).

Even anonymous posting is not enough: Usenet postings do identify the poster's server unless one has had the foresight to use remailers. Once the supposedly anonymous poster's server has been identified, a court (or security organization) having jurisdiction or influence over that server can compel that server to identify the user who made the posting.

Using Mixmaster remailers for posting to Usenet forums is about as secure as one can get (though nothing is beyond compromise). It can be done through the use of dedicated software (JBN, pidaho.zip) or through some ISPs' GUI, such as Cotse (http://www.cotse.net) shown in Figure 9.4.

Alternately, one can send posting as e-mail as follows:

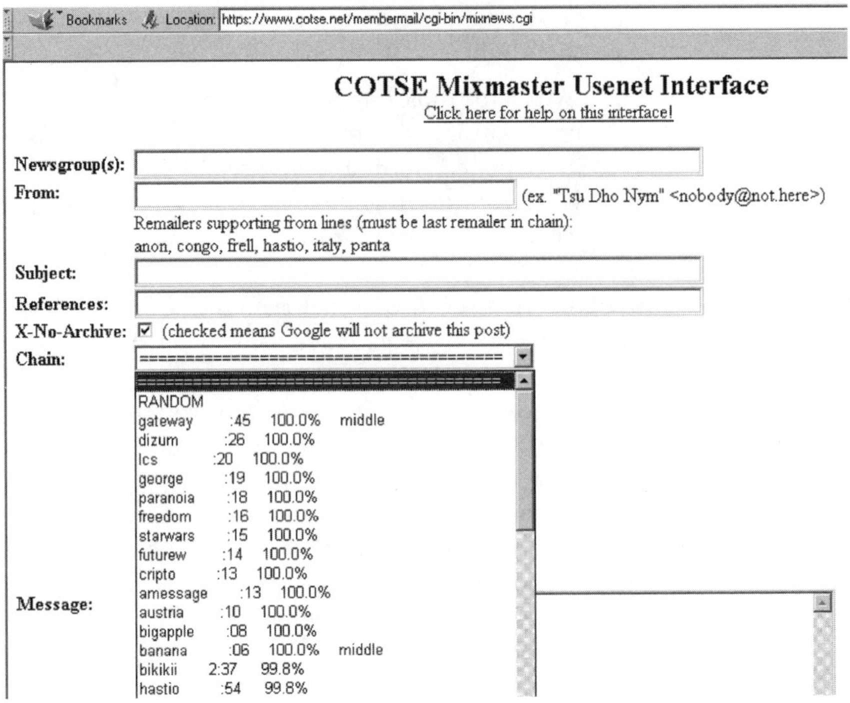

Figure 9.4 Interface for anonymous posting to Usenet.

```
To: mail2news@anon.lcs.mit.edu
Newsgroups: alt.whatever (enter the Usenet newsgroup to post
to)
Subject: (enter subject)
X-no-archive: yes
(message goes here).
```

9.15.1 Anonymity from other Usenet readers

Item (1) above is easy to take care of in an amateurish fashion but not so easy to handle in a professional fashion. Merely altering the userid and e-mail address in one's Usenet software before composing and sending a Usenet message will cause the message to be posted with the assumed name; this is only a fig leaf, however because the IP address of the sending entity is not disguised.

It is far better to post through any one of many anonymizing remailers that accept postings to newsgroups, such as

▸ http://www.cotse.net;

▸ http://www.MailAndNews.com;

▸ http://www.zedz.net;

▶ http://209.67.19.98/lark2k/anonymail.html (hides the IP address of the sender).

plus, of course, Private Idaho, and so forth. for facilitating the use of Mixmaster remailers without the need for trusting a server.

Alternately, one can use services that allow Usenet posting from e-mail, such as "Mail2News" (http://canal3.hypermart.net/mail2news.htm). Of course, unless one is willing to place full faith in such services' discretion, it is best to combine this with e-mail from a reasonably untraceable source, such as from a public library, Internet café, and so on. Mail2News gateways come in numerous flavors, such as Web-to-News, and E-mail-to-News.

9.15.2 Anonymity from one's in-country ISP

Anonymity from one's in-country ISP is harder to achieve.

Certainly one's ISP, who—unless end-to-end encryption is used—can see everything that the subscriber types and sees on his or her screen. The issue is "would the ISP bother to monitor subscribers' Usenet usage?" The answer is an emphatic "yes" under any of the following common conditions:

1. If the ISP is served with a court order to log a user's online activities, an ISP will always comply. Unless a user is running his own news server (not common, but quite possible), an ISP will have the ability to record all of user's Usenet activities.

2. If the subscriber has been giving an ISP a very hard time in terms of complaints, it is human nature to expect that individuals at the ISP can spy on that user out of curiosity or even vengeance. If that user's Usenet activities then turn out to be ones that local law prohibits, then the ISP can tip off local law enforcement by stating that a "routine" or "preventive" maintenance uncovered that conduct (so as to preclude appearing to have violated any applicable privacy acts and have the evidence thrown out of court). Software for doing such "routine maintenance" does exist; for small ISPs that may not have it, it is a simple matter to write a few lines of code to end up with the same selective data collection; most ISPs that offer access to Usenet require individual authentication of users before such access is granted, anyway.

3. *Posting to* Usenet messages is almost always monitored and recorded by most ISPs because they are often blamed for the content of what is posted.

If one merely wants to minimize (as opposed to eliminate) the likelihood that the local ISP will monitor a subscriber's Usenet access, then the subscriber can use Usenet service offered by servers other than his or her own ISP—preferably in a different country. Such servers include, for example:

▶ http://www.newsfeeds.com;

- http://www.altopia.com;
- http://www.ctservice.de/taker/cgi-bin/anon-www.cgi/http://ctservice.de/ taker/news;
- http://www.uncensored-news.com;
- http://liberty.banhof.se;
- http://www.GUBA.com;
- http://www.newshog.com;
- http://www.newsnerds.com;
- http://www.nuthingbutnews.com;
- http://www.vip-news.com;
- http://www.Supernews.net;
- http://www.randori.com.

Most of the above servers require a fee, and some offer anonymous access. The user is cautioned, however, that one should not depend on the "anonymity" promises of a for-fee news-server because:

- Any server must comply with the in-country court orders to retain logs (such as the IP address showing where it is being accessed from and any other identifying information).
- Unless the communication is end-to-end encrypted (using SSL for example), a user's online activities are still perfectly visible to that user's local ISP.

Because one's ISP sees everything that goes in and out of a subscriber's computer, the only fix is to establish an SSL connection (See Section 9.7.1) with a remote Web site (preferably out of the country and hence out of reach of the local constabulary) that will accept posting to an ISP; once the SSL connection has been established, the in-country monitors are left with nothing to read other than the fact that a user being monitored has connected to an out-of-country Web site with an encrypted connection. This will protect the content of the ensuing communication, but is guaranteed to raise the user's profile that much higher in the eyes of the frustrated local investigator.

Remote Web sites that accept SSL connections include:

- https://www.cotse.net;
- https://www.rewebber.com.

An excellent list of URL sites for anonymous posting can be found at www.fen.baynet.de/~na1723/links/links10.html.

9.15.3 Usenet privacy in oppressive regimes

Item (3) above falls within the category of general counter-forensics discussed throughout this book. An easy to follow step-by-step set of instructions on "nym" (pseudonym) creation that allows one anonymity in Usenet postings as well as in e-mail can be found at http://www.stack.nl/%7Egalactus/remailers/nym.html ("Nym Creation for Mere Mortals").

Finally, there is the common sense approach to posting anonymously to Usenet: sitting in front of the keyboard of some publicly accessible computer, such as that at a public library, at a university, at an "Internet Café," at a Computer show where they have terminals online, etc.

Caution: There is a lot of material available online for free downloading that is positively illegal to download and view in this or that country; one country may criminalizes the popular cartoon character Pokemon, another criminalizes nudity, another criminalizes postings that criticize the regime in power, and so on. This applies to Web sites and especially to the Usenet forums, many of which are on topics that strain credibility, are positively distasteful to even the most broad minded person, and test one's level of tolerance. It is always best to browse Usenet forums and Web sites through an SSL connection to an out-of-country go-between proxy server, so as to avoid incurring the wrath of local enforcers of local morality and political correctness.

9.16 Ports to protect from

For a stand-alone computer that is not connected to any other computer through a network such as the Internet, ports are not an issue and do not apply.

When a computer is connected to other computers through a network, however, some way must be agreed upon for each to know how to communicate with the others. This is analogous to a room full of people who want to communicate: Each has a different name. Similarly, for the telephone network to work, each telephone has to have a different number. In the case of the Internet, each connected computer's unique number is its Internet Protocol, or IP, address, which is a string of 12 numbers separated into four groups of three numbers each.

Individual computers, unlike telephones, can do many different things, such as browse the Web, send and receive e-mail, transfer files using FTP, and so forth. As such, each computer that deals with other computers has to have a "switchboard" function to direct each incoming "telephone call" (data packet, in this case) to the correct "extension" inside the multifunction-capable computer. Ports are the computer equivalent of a telephone switchboard's inside extensions.

Because most computers that want to communicate with other computers have a set of standard functions (referred to as services) that they all perform (such as e-mail, FTP, Web browsing), it makes sense that agreements have been made [1] as to which port does what. This way, a remote computer that sends e-mail, for example, knows up front not only to whom to send it (the IP address) but also which port to send it to.

There are three ranges of ports:

1. The well-known ones from 0 to 1,023;

2. The registered ones from 1,024 through 49,151, which a number of "services" use, but which are also used for many other purposes;

3. The rest of them (used for private functions and also dynamically allocated by some software such as some VPNs) in the range from 49,152 through 65,535, to which no service is supposed to be assigned.

Complete lists of all the ports in the first two categories can be readily downloaded from many Internet sites, such as http://isi.edu/in-notes/iana/assignments/port-numbers; these lists are well over 100 single-spaced typewritten pages long. Similarly, http://advice.networkice.com/advice/Ecploits/Ports has hyperlinks to descriptions of various ways that some ports have been exploited.

The commonly used "legitimate" ports are the following:

*   HTTP 80
*   HTTPS 443
*   SMTP 25
*   POP3 110
*   FTP 20-21
*   TELNET 23
*   REALAUDIO 1090
*   ICQ 4000
*   NEWS SERVERS 119
*   DNS 53
*   IRC 6667
*   VDOLIVE 7000

Open Service Ports for Windows NT, Terminal Server, and Exchange Server include the following:

*   Functionality UDP TCP IP
*   Browsing 137, 138
*   DHCP Lease 67, 68
*   DHCP Manager 135
*   DNS Administration 139
*   DNS Resolution 53

- Exchange Administrator 135
- Exchange Client/Server Comm. 135
- File Sharing 139
- IMAP 143
- LDAP 389
- LDAP (SSL) 636
- Logon Sequence 137, 138 139
- MTA—X.400 over TCP/IP 102
- NetLogon 138
- NT Diagnostics 139
- NT Directory Replication 138 139
- NT Event Viewer 139
- NT Performance Monitor 139
- NT Registry Editor 139
- NT Secure Channel 137, 138 139
- NT Server Manager 139
- NT Trusts 137, 138 139
- NT User Manager 139
- Pass Through Validation 137, 138 139
- POP3 110
- PPTP 1723 47
- Printing 137, 138 139
- RPC 135 135
- SMTP 25
- WINS Manager 135
- WINS Registration 137
- WINS Replication 42

However, a port is an open gate to the outside world and is therefore also exploitable as a pathway for a malicious outsider to penetrate one's computer. It follows that any computer connected to the Internet (or any other network) should have all ports closed (meaning that the computer will ignore all attempts from either the outside or, as an option, even from mischievous software on the inside, to get data through those ports), except for those that are absolutely required to do whatever function has to be performed; in fact, this is precisely what some firewalls do.

137, 138, and 139 are NetBIOS ports. Simply unbind NetBIOS from TCP/IP in your network settings. Not only do you not need them, but they are a security concern. It may require a reboot to make the change effective.

Run netstat -a from command prompt and make sure that NetBIOS ports are now closed.

The Web site http://members.cotse.com/helpdesk has a complete port listing guide, as well as a lot of other useful information.

The port numbers that are used mostly by Trojan and intrusion programs and that should therefore be closely watched can be found at http://www.doshelp.com/trojanports.htm.

A highly recommended detailed presentation of each individual main port's vulnerabilities and legitimate functions can be found at http://www.robertgraham.com/pubs/firewall-seen.html.

9.17 Sniffers

A sniffer simply monitors and selectively records the data flow through a choke point. It can be used by a hacker to steal passwords, and it can also be used by an individual to detect if information is leaving his or her computer without permission (e.g., caused by adware, spyware, or Trojans).

Most sniffers are primarily intended to debug (find flaws and correct them) network problems.

They include the following, among others:

1. RealSecure, for SunOS, Solaris, and Linux (http://ww.iss.net/RealSecure);

2. Snoop for Solaris;

3. Etherfind for SunOS 4.1x.

For DOS-based systems, one can use the following:

1. Gobbler for IBM DOS computers;

2. EthLoad v1.04 for Ethernet monitoring (ftp://ftp.germany.eu.net:/pub/networking/monitoring/ethload/ethld104.zip);

3. PacketView by KLOS Technologies, Inc.;

4. Microsoft's Net Monitor;

5. Analyzer.exe for Windows 95/98/NT/2000 (http://packetstorm.security.com/sniffers);

6. Anger.tar.gz (a challenge/response sniffer—see below—by L0phtCrack (http://packetstorm.security.com/sniffers);

7. Aps-0.14.tar.z, COLD, coopersniff01.zip, dsniff, and a vast number of others, all available through http://packetstorm.security.com/sniffers.

It is not possible to detect the presence of a sniffer on one's network through software unless the sniffer is (unwisely) programmed to advertise its presence. The only real protection from a sniffer is to ensure that only encrypted data passes through it.

If the concern is only about a sniffer detecting passwords being sent, this can easily be remedied by using an authentication system where a different password is needed every time. This, of course, requires that the server one is connecting to supports the feature. This can be done by using the following:

1. SecureID tokens (a small device like a garage door opener that generates a different set of numbers every few seconds to be used as the password). The remote host has to have a duplicate of this device so that it can verify that the numbers entered as the password are the correct ones. Such devices are usually used in conjunction with a PIN number so that if the device itself is stolen, the thief cannot gain access. One of many such vendors is Security Dynamics in Cambridge, Massachusetts.

2. A software solution based on challenge-response. The authorized user has a piece of software that accepts a random challenge (in the form of a few random symbols sent) by the server that one is trying to log on to. This challenge is different every time. The software computes the response using a cryptographic algorithm and sends it to the server, which has a duplicate of that software and verifies that the correct response was sent to the particular challenge. A typical implementation available worldwide is S-Key (ftp://ftp.nrl.navy.mil/pub/security/nrl-opie).

9.18 Firewalls

A firewall, despite its name, is a semipermeable membrane that, depending on how good the particular implementation is, prevents most (but not all) undesired data from crossing it, whether it's coming into to one's computer (such as malicious attacks) or going out of one's computer (such as adware that call home to report on a user's activities). One of its key functions is to protect one's ports (see Section 9.16) from unauthorized access; it has numerous other functions as well.

The need for even an imperfect firewall is quite apparent to anyone who has monitored intrusion attempts from random Internet users. The most common such attempts are

1. Port-scanning by others of one's ports. Would-be intruders with Sub7 typically scan port 27,374, while others scan just about any port they find open. If one has used ICQ, Napster, or other such software that essentially broadcasts one's IP address to others, many such others will routinely port-scan one to find (and exploit) vulnerabilities.

2. Unauthorized outgoing messages being sent by adware/spyware (see Section 9.3) that have been surreptitiously installed on an unsuspecting average user's computer.

There can never be any standard as to what a firewall must do or how well because a firewall merely implements an organization's (or individual's) security policy, and these differ across the board.

A firewall can be a stand-alone piece of hardware, such as a full-blown computer or a dedicated box, or it can be software in one's computer, or both.

Information on firewalls beyond what is provided in this section can be found at an archive maintained at http://lists/gnac.net/firewalls.

"Frequently Asked Questions about Firewalls" can be downloaded from http://www.interhack.com/pubs/fwfaq.

An excellent technical overview of firewalls can be downloaded from http ://www.boran.com/security/it12-firewall.html and is highly recommended.

A list of technical references on firewalls that goes beyond the scope of this book can be found at http://www.cert.org and is also highly recommended reading.

Most commercial concerns use pricey firewalls, such as Checkpoint, which recently bought out the very maker of the very popular firewall Zone Alarm in December 2003 and which has 40% of the market, and Cisco, which has 23% of the market. Others include IBM's Lotus Firewall for Windows NT, Network Associates Gauntlet, AltaVista's Firewall97, Raptor Eagle NT 4.0, Ukiah's NetRoad Firewall for NT, and numerous others.

There are four basic kinds of firewalls, although most commercially available products are hybrids of these four basic kinds:

1. *Packet filtering:* This is the simplest and most common. Packets are filtered based on user-provided criteria, such as where the packets are coming from or going to. As an example, packets that appear to be coming from known potential threats are prevented from passing through. Because the "From" portion (or any other portion, for that matter) of a packet header can readily be spoofed by any hacker, this is not a foolproof protection. No modification to a user's existing software is needed.

2. *Stateful inspection:* This corrects some of the most glaring weaknesses of packet filtering firewalls by looking at sequences of packets and making decisions based on such sequences. As an example, acknowledgment (ACK) packets that have not been preceded by a SYN packet with the right sequence packet can be blocked at the user's discretion. This type of firewall, too, requires no change on the user's existing software. The popular Checkpoint firewall is of this type and in fact claims the rights to the term *stateful inspection*, with the addition of advanced features such as network address translation (NAT), which partially hides one's protected network true addresses from an untrusted network. (NAT is not a security mechanism; one can send packets through a NAT device. In practice, however, a NAT device protects from most unsophisticated cyber-attacks). LanOptics's Guardian 2.2 also uses this approach.

3. *Application proxy:* This amounts to a go-between, or proxy, and checks all requests for everything that is trying to go through a firewall, compares them against its list of what is allowed and what is not, and acts accordingly. In other words, it operates at the Application Layer and, as such, it requires the setting up of a separate such proxy for each application, such as FTP, and each custom application such as IP telephony (see Section 10.2.5) requires its own such proxy.

4. *Circuit-level gateway:* This is similar to the Application Proxy firewall above. The firewall first authenticates the end points in an Internet Transmission Control Protocol (TCP) connectivity and then allows TCP and User Datagram Protocol (UDP) data to go through between those two points. The best such firewalls use a standard developed by the Internet Engineering Task Force (IETF) called SOCKS (version 5 is the latest).

As with the testing of anything that is security-related, one can never in clear conscience pronounce what is being protected as secure. About all one can do is try to reduce the known vulnerabilities. This applies to firewalls as well.

Firewalls are not a cure-all. If one's computing system, for example, allows a trusted person to bypass a firewall in order to do system maintenance from afar, then the firewall cannot be blamed if that loophole is compromised.

Firewalls cannot protect well against most viruses because there are far too many ways whereby viruses can enter one's computer. Accordingly, one would be well advised to invest in the minimal cost of antivirus software as well.

Also, a firewall that allows encrypted traffic to go through (e.g., encrypted e-mail, VPN; see Chapter 12) cannot possibly protect from the content of such encrypted traffic.

A firewall offers no protection against an insider threat.

9.18.1 Personal software-based firewalls

Software personal firewalls worthy of notice include the following:

1. Symantec's Norton Internet Security package (www.symantec.com) bundles the firewall function with optional functions such as cookie blocking, parental Web control, and so forth. Its high-security option is quite effective; its parental Web control, like most all Web filters, is annoying and easily defeatable by any teenager by routing Web browsing through anonymizing proxies. Unfortunately, it is now sold in a manner that requires online registration, which is highly undesirable from a security perspective because a user has no control over what information is being sent to the company online.

2. NetworkIce's BlackIce Defender (http://www.networkice.com) is really less of a firewall and more of an intrusion-detection piece of software. It is intended to bounce intruders off one's computer.

3. Zone Labs's free ZoneAlarm (http://www.zonelabs.com), in a nutshell, allows the user to specify which program(s) can access the Internet and locks all others out. Even though Zone Alarm seems to be the most effective in preventing outbound unauthorized communication, it is not a guarantee of online security. (See http://grc.com/su-leaktest.htm for a benign program that tests if one's computer alerts one that some software is trying to call home.) There is no easy fix for programs that use legitimate ports, such as port 80, which is used by Web browsers, other than eliminating such programs from one's computer in the first place. (See Section 9.3 on adware.)

   Caution: After installing it, uncheck the default "I want to check for updates automatically" in the "Configure" option.

4. McAfee Personal Firewall (http://www.mcafee.com) is what has become of the personal firewall by Signal9. It continues to be a reasonably good firewall.

5. Although it is not a firewall per se, one is highly encouraged also to consider using a small software application called WinPatrol from http://www.billp.com/winpatrol. It alerts the user any time any new software starts running behinds one back in one's computer (such as adware) and asks the user specifically to permit or not permit this to happen. It can also readily display a list of what is running in the background.

9.19 Software that calls home

Depending on their sophistication, detecting such software programs ranges from easy to very hard. Such software includes keystroke loggers.

As with any security issue, it is far easier to prevent the intrusion in the first place (through the safe-computing practices detailed in Part II of this book) than it is to remove the software after it has installed itself in one's inner sanctum.

Software programs such as Regrun and Winpatrol can alert one to programs that start automatically at Windows start-up without one's knowledge.

One would be well advised to visit http://www.sysinternals.com/misc.htm#autoruns to obtain autoruns.exe, which searches system locations that can launch programs at start-up.

One should also visit http://grc.com/su-leaktest.htm to download a small benign test program that checks if one's computer does or does not prevent most software that call home.

If one suspects that some software is calling home (i.e., connecting to some remote site through the Internet when one is online), one should go to the DOS prompt and type netstat -a. This will show if there are any connections being made beyond what one expects. Interpreting the results takes some getting used to, especially if one is using proxies and firewalls that do address translation, so one should do this routinely to get used to the display when there are no surreptitious communications out of one's computer.

Reference

[1]   Postel, J., "User Datagram Protocol," STD 6, RFC 768, USC/Information Sciences Institute, August 1980.

Contents

Encryption

There are so few who can carry a letter of any substance without lightening the weight by perusal.

—Cicero to Atticus, 61 B.C.

10.1 Introduction

In the beginning, there was the mattress under which to hide things. And then, there was the safe, for those who could afford one. Since personal computers became popular, potent encryption, previously reserved for governments, militaries, and spies, suddenly became available to everyone

There are two distinct situations when one wants to hide the contents of a file (in the generic sense, which includes an image, a sound, a text document, and so forth.) from someone: when the file is in the possession of unauthorized persons, and when a copy of the file is being transmitted through channels that one has no control over. In older days, files were always in the possession of authorized persons even when being physically carried from one place to another, and file encryption was all that was needed. Since the advent of electronic communications, files can be sent almost instantaneously over channels that one has no control over, such as the Internet or even a direct telephone-to-telephone connection. This has brought about the need for encrypting traffic at the channel level so that individual files need not be encrypted (even though one can certainly do that as well and, in fact, would be well advised to do so).

This chapter and Chapter 11 deal with individual file encryption. Because, clearly, individual file encryption also protects that file while it is in transit, this book emphasizes individual file encryption. Chapter 12 deals with encryption of all traffic over a given channel, which aspires to protect even files that have not been individually encrypted.

There have always been legitimate reasons for confidentiality beyond protecting the affairs of state, for example, to protect commercial trade secrets (such as those that have propelled the United States to technological excellence), medical records, and so on. The laws in practically all countries have even protected some material from the eyes of the state itself; for example, attorney–client communication is privileged (but confessions made to psychotherapists and the clergy are not, at least not in the the USA. The confession is one of a crime that has been or is likely to be committed).

Until about 20 years ago, the means available to nongovernmental individuals and groups for protecting secrets amounted to physical protection: placing things inside safes or in other hiding places. For most commercial and private needs, this used to be good enough because a tangible physical object, such as a document or an occasional magnetic recording, was being protected.

The transformation of society during the past decade to one that is entirely dependent on computers has resulted in the conversion of most of those sensitive physical objects into computerized data. In addition, the increasing acceptance of telecommuting has caused such sensitive information to be sent from one facility to another with increasing frequency. Finally, the sheer volume of sensitive corporate and personal information has increased vastly as a result of the use of e-mail, which is treated by most as a substitute for phone calls rather than as the permanent written record that it actually is.

It is self-evident that there is a legitimate need for technology to protect sensitive data in personal and office computers. Indeed, there is a way to meet this need: potent encryption.

The problem is that like a kitchen knife, which can be used to slice bread or as a weapon, potent encryption can be used legitimately or illegitimately to hide what courts and governments, rightly or wrongly, may want to see.

For example, an employee with access to highly sensitive corporate information would find it very easy to transfer that information to a floppy diskette or to one of the new USB-port "dongles" that can hold the equivalent of a few hundred floppy diskettes' worth of data, encrypt it, remove it, and pass it to a competitor. It would be very difficult for any evidence of this to be produced in a court of law. Conversely, a brutally totalitarian regime would very much like to be able to decrypt a file containing the names of the members of the underground opposition.

In the past, armed with a court warrant (or often without one in some regimes), a state could easily force open a safe. Today, however, it is eminently possible for any individual anywhere in the world to use encryption, which is openly available worldwide, to encrypt text, voice, images, and anything that can be computerized in a manner that cannot be broken by any physical force. (The term *unbreakable* is unfortunate because, with the encryption of the One Time Pad, no encryption is provably unbreakable; it is only a matter of how long it would take to break it. Perishable information needs encryption to work only for the useful life of that information. On the other extreme, brute-force cryptanalysis of openly available encryption has been shown to require computers to work for many times the expected life of the Sun.) This amounts to an involuntary transfer of massive power from the state to the individual. Its social impact has not yet been fully felt.

Not surprisingly, every government in the world has been scrambling for ways to limit the spread of this new tool, citing assorted lofty principles. From a sovereign state's perspective, the existence of the Internet is bad enough in that it makes censorship extremely difficult. Adding strong encryption to the brew makes the end result downright threatening to most governments.

Repressive regimes have realized the threat posed to their longevity by the use of strong encryption by dissident groups. Democratic regimes, too, have realized the potential threat to social order posed by the use of unbreakable encryption to facilitate out-and-out criminality, as well as to facilitate far lesser transgressions such as transmitting content deemed inappropriate by a state.

10.2 Availability and use of encryption

The sole purpose of encryption is to render a sensitive document ("plaintext") unreadable to all except those authorized to read it. This protection need not necessarily last forever; tactical information, whose usefulness to an adversary vanishes after some length of time, need not necessarily remain unreadable forever. This truism is often forgotten in debates about the relative strengths of various encryption algorithms and key lengths.

An attack on encrypted material is not limited to brute-force attacks (i.e., exhaustive searches of all possible decryption keys). More often than not, it amounts to cheating; that is, it is an attack brought about through ways that the user never thought of. In other words, there is a lot more to protecting a sensitive plaintext than the encryption algorithm itself, as the following questions reveal:

- Has a copy of the plaintext been inadvertently left behind on one's computer?
- Has the decryption key been compromised?
- Is it possible that the encryption software being used has been compromised?
- If a password is used to enable the decryption key, is it easier to find that password than embarking on brute-force cryptanalysis?

Unless each different file encrypted by a given sender (or sent to a given recipient by many senders) is encrypted in a different manner (using a different key, a different encryption method, or both), the person attacking the encrypted file has a strategic advantage: If he or she can somehow read one such file from a given sender or to a given recipient, that person can probably read many other encrypted files from the same sender or to the same recipient. This amplifies the infrastructure-related weaknesses of the encryption process (how people handle keys, procedures, and so forth).

Today, engineers who may be very competent in their respective fields but who have minimal experience in cryptography often implement encryption in software as an afterthought. What may seem to be an unbreakable scheme to the author of an encryption algorithm may well be (and has often turned out to be) an implementation with serious exploitable weaknesses. Brute-force cryptanalysis is only one of many possible attacks on an encryption system; other attack approaches include the following:

- Exploiting the use of untested proprietary algorithms. In general, only those encryption schemes that have successfully withstood the concerted analysis and assessment of experts over many years are to be used; the rest may seem secure until proven otherwise (or until they, too, have successfully withstood a similar scrutiny).

- Exploiting weaknesses in the choice of the password itself. If a password is used, it should be secure. A password should offer as much difficulty to a cryptanalyst as the encryption algorithm itself. Passwords should not be just a couple of dictionary words. A dictionary has less than 100,000 words in it. To get a password that is no more vulnerable to a brute-force dictionary attack than a 128-bit key, one would need about eight words randomly chosen from the dictionary.

- Exploiting the hardware on which the encryption algorithm is used. The hardware should itself be secure. In 1995, the timing attack became popular. In summary, it allowed someone with access to the hardware to make useful inferences from the precise time it took to encrypt a document using a particular class of algorithms. One can enlarge this class of attacks to include any externally observable hardware phenomenon, such as power consumption, unintentional radio-frequency (RF) radiation, and so on. This class also includes an assessment of any electronic paper trail left behind if the hardware is caused to fail in the middle of an encryption or decryption.

- Attacking the trust models. Except in a small percentage of situations, the sender and intended recipient of encrypted messages never meet each other in person to exchange encryption keys; instead, they rely on third parties and processes that may well contain exploitable weaknesses.

- Exploiting the all too common human tendency to take shortcuts and to bypass security procedures in encoding and decoding sensitive documents.

In view of the above, the odds favor the person attacking an encrypted file unless the person being attacked is very well informed in the ways of information security.

10.2.1 Old-fashioned encryption

Interestingly, provably unbreakable encryption was available long before computers entered the scene, even though the concept was not formalized until the middle of the twentieth century. A conceptually simple, yet potent, encryption scheme known as the one-time pad could be used by anyone willing to go through a manual process that is, however, quite onerous for long messages. Basically, one substitutes each symbol in a message to be encrypted (the plaintext) with another symbol, using a pre-agreed-upon conversion known to both the sender and the intended recipient and never to be used again (hence the name "one-time pad"). For example, both individuals can agree to substitute the first letter of the plaintext with the sequence number in the alphabet of the first letter of the first page of a certain edition of Mark Twain (e.g., "A" is 01; "B" is 02), the second letter of the plaintext with the sequence number in the alphabet of the second letter of the second page of the same book, and so on.

Amusingly, a one-time pad offers an interesting way of defeating a demand by authority to decrypt a file: One can readily create and "reluctantly surrender" a fake one-time pad key which will convert that same encrypted document to something totally innocuous, like an excerpt from the Bible or the Bill of Rights.

The solutions to these problems have opened up a Pandora's Box of new problems, new solutions, and a few hopes. Anyone today can obtain powerful encryption from the Internet or from software stores. It is of two fundamentally different kinds: symmetric and public key. Symmetric encryption refers to the fact that the same key is used to encrypt and to decrypt a message. The sender and the recipient must somehow find a secure way to share such a key. Public-key encryption refers to the fact that one key is used to encrypt a message, but a different key (which cannot be mathematically inferred from the first) is needed to decrypt that message.

Just like medicine, bad encryption looks like good encryption on the surface; one cannot tell the difference. "Proprietary," "secret," and "revolutionary" schemes that have not withstood the scrutiny of cryptanalysts over time should never be trusted, as they could be extremely easy to break or could have a backdoor; the same goes for encryption with recoverable keys or that is exportable. However, as already stated, since the liberalization of U.S. laws on the exportation of encryption around 2000, being exportable no longer implies weak encryption; it only means that the United States saw the folly of trying to control encryption and gave up on attempting to do so. Some other countries have not reached that level of maturity and still have all sorts of inescapably ineffective controls on encryption within their borders.

10.2.2 Conventional (symmetric) encryption

This is old-fashioned encryption, which is actually not old-fashioned at all because it is at the heart of even modern public-key-encryption implementations. Contrary to popular belief, public-key encryption (Section 10.2.3) encrypts files with conventional symmetric encryption; public-key encryption encrypts only the key of the symmetric conventional encryption used so that the authorized recipient can decrypt the symmetrically encrypted files. This is so because public-key encryption is much, much slower than conventional symmetric encryption.

The most popular algorithm for symmetric encryption is DES, which was developed in the 1970s and is still in extensive use worldwide, especially in the banking industry. It is a block cipher (64 bits/block) using 56-bit keys. By now, there is an extensive amount of open literature on DES cracking.

Double DES (encrypting the already DES-encrypted output with a different key) does not add any measurable strength against brute-force cryptanalysis to the end result; in fact, double encryption of most block codes is generally acknowledged to add little security. Triple DES, however, substantively improves the resistance to cryptanalysis of the end result, making it a highly secure algorithm, albeit slower than others. It is noteworthy that most so-called Triple DES implementations, however, use only two keys, not three: The first encryption uses key #1, the second uses key #2, and the third uses key #1 again. A true triple-key implementation should be used.

Other encryption algorithms from which a computer user is often asked to select include the following:

> International Data Encryption Algorithm (IDEA) uses a 128-bit key and was developed by ETH Zurich in Switzerland. Its patent is held by Ascom-Tech, but noncommercial use is free. It is considered to be a good algorithm for all, except possibly the most well-funded, attacks. It is used, among others, in PGP and SpeakFreely (voice encryption).

> Blowfish is a 64-bit-block-size block code having variable key lengths from 32 bits up to 448 bits. Developed by Bruce Schneier in 1993, it is also considered to be one of the best algorithms. Over 100 products use this algorithm already.

> Twofish is a more recent encryption algorithm reputed to be very strong, but which has not yet had the benefit of withstanding the concerted efforts and review of cryptanalysts.

> RC4 is a very fast algorithm of unknown security, which can accept keys of arbitrary length. Key lengths shorter than about 40 bits result in encrypted output that is relatively easy to break.

Numerous other symmetric codes exist, many of which have historical value.

DES is headed for the dustbin. In October 2000, a new data encryption standard, Rijandel (or Rijndael), named after its three creators, was selected in the United States as the AES.

10.2.3   Public-key encryption

In conventional (symmetric) encryption, the same key is used to encode a message and subsequently to decode it. This has numerous practical disadvantages:

- The problem of secure key distribution is compounded every time the keys are updated.
- Unless a voluminous one-time pad key is used, the repeated use of the same key for encrypting multiple different plaintext files favors the cryptanalyst.

An ingenious scheme that solves these problems (and introduces some new ones) was proposed in 1976 by Diffie and Hellman. It was reportedly devised earlier, in the early 1970s, in the United Kingdom by James Ellis, Clifford Cocks, and Malcolm Williamson. It allows two entities, which never have the opportunity to exchange keys in some secure manner, to communicate with full encryption nonetheless.

In a typical implementation, assume that both Mr. A and Mr. B have a copy of openly available software that implements public-key encryption. Initially, each directs his respective (identical or just compatible) copy of the software to create a key. What gets created (ideally using manual user input for true randomness) by each is a pair of keys. It is significant that, in each pair, one key cannot be mathematically inferred from the other. The crucial concept is this: A file encrypted with one key of each pair can only be decrypted with the other key of that same pair. The implications of the last statement are far-reaching in that they allow:

- Encrypted file exchange between two entities without the need for any secure means to exchange keys;
- Sender authentication, also known as digital signature;
- Message integrity authentication.

This is shown in Figure 10.1.

Assume that Mr. A and Mr. B both elect to publicize any one of the keys of the pair each generated and appropriately name that publicized key as the public key. They each retain under tight control the other key in their respective pairs and each calls that his secret key. If Mr. A wants to encrypt a message that only Mr. B can read, Mr. A uses Mr. B's public key (which has been made available to anyone). That message can only be decoded by the

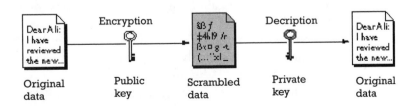

| Original data | Public key | Scrambled data | Private key | Original data |

Figure 10.1   Public-key encryption. (Courtesy of Netscape.)

other key in the pair, namely, Mr. *B*'s secret key. The converse process (an encrypted message by Mr. *B* to Mr. *A*) is clear. What has been achieved is that Mr. *A* and Mr. *B* can now exchange encrypted files without the need for any secure means to exchange keys.

Sender authentication (digital signature) is just as easy: Mr. *A* sends any message he wishes to the world after encrypting it with his secret key. The world uses Mr. *A*'s public key to decrypt that message, thereby validating that it could only have come from Mr. *A*.

Message authentication (validation that the message received is indeed an unaltered copy of the message sent) is also easy: The sender (Mr. *A*, for example) performs a digital summary ("digest") referred to as a cryptographic hash function on his outgoing plaintext message (an elaborate version of a checksum) before encrypting it. This cryptographic hash function, such as the very popular Message Digest Version 5 (MD5) (developed by RSA, it extracts a digital digest from a file of arbitrary length into a 128-bit value) and Secure Hashing Algorithm (SHA) (published by the U.S. government, hashes a file into a 160-bit value), compresses the bits of the plaintext message into a fixed-size digest or hash value of 128 or more bits. The hash function is such that it is extremely difficult to alter the plaintext message without altering the hash value. The sender then does the following:

- Encrypts the plaintext with the intended recipient's public key;
- Encrypts the above hash value with his own secret key;
- Sends both to the intended recipient.

The intended recipient then:

- Decodes the received plaintext using his own public key;
- Decodes the received checksum digest by using the sender's public key, thereby confirming sender authenticity;
- Compares the received checksum with one that he performs locally on the just-decrypted plaintext, thereby confirming message integrity.

This is depicted in Figure 10.2.

Public-key encryption has been a part of any Web browser for the last few years for automatically providing end-to-end encryption between an Internet user and select Web sites (e.g., when sending credit card information to an online vendor for a purchase through a Web browser, or when sending e-mail using the standard S/MIME protocol and a security certificate that one can obtain from online commercial vendors or that can be created locally by some software).

Public-key encryption is not without shortcomings. It is orders of magnitude more computationally intensive (read: slower) than conventional symmetric encryption. As a result, practically all implementations use the following trick, which involves using both conventional symmetric encryption and public-key encryption for the same message:

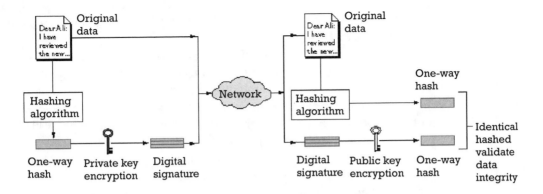

Figure 10.2 Message integrity authentication. (Courtesy of Netscape.)

1. Encode the outgoing plaintext using strong conventional symmetric encryption, such as IDEA, Blowfish, or Triple DES, and a locally generated symmetric-encryption key.

2. Encode only that locally generated symmetric-encryption key with public-key encryption.

3. Send both of the above to the intended recipient. In addition, perform the ancillary functions just described for permitting message authentication and sender authentication.

The obvious question that comes up then is, If the symmetric-encryption algorithm used is such-and-so and its key length is x bits, what is a good public-key-encryption algorithm, and how many bits should its key have so that both are of equal strength? A good 128-bit block code like IDEA is roughly comparable in resistance to brute-force cryptanalysis to a 2,304-bit public-key-encryption algorithm like RSA.

Another shortcoming of public-key encryption is that it is subject to the same logical conundrum as any encryption when the two parties to the communication have not had a secure channel to allow each to confirm the identity of the other. If Mr. B receives a public key (or a conventional symmetric key) ostensibly coming from Mr. A, Mr. B has no way to confirm that this key does not, in fact, belong to a third party (Mr. C, the so-called man in the middle). There is no technical fix for this logical conundrum: Mr. A and Mr. B must find some independent way of verifying that the keys indeed belong to each other as claimed.

One of the most commonly used public-key algorithms is RSA. Its security is based on the difficulty of factoring the products of large prime integers. At present, a key length of at least 2,048 bits is generally considered secure enough for the next decade; key lengths of 1,024 bits are no longer considered adequate for the foreseeable future. However, RSA has been claimed to be somewhat vulnerable to chosen plaintext attacks (namely, when known plaintexts and the corresponding RSA-encrypted ciphertexts are available to a cryptanalyst) and to timing attacks. For a good assessment of key lengths see [1, 2].

The most popular implementation of public-key encryption is PGP. (See Section 11.3 for details on installing and using PGP securely.) Philip Zimmerman created PGP as a sociopolitical statement that potent encryption should be widely available. It has now become a mainstream product of a reputable corporation, although freeware versions continue to be available from the Internet throughout the world.

Like all implementations of public-key encryption, PGP uses strong, conventional, symmetric encryption (typically 128-bit IDEA, but more recent versions can accommodate the 256-bit AES encryption as well) to encode plaintext with a session-specific key, then uses public-key encryption to encode that key. This means that any two encryptions of the same plaintext to the same recipient will be different.

Even though it was stated above that a 128-bit IDEA encryption is comparable to a 2,304-bit public-key encryption, one should use a public key that is longer than this 2,304 value because in PGP breaking the symmetric-encryption key (e.g., IDEA) compromises a single message, whereas breaking the public-key encryption compromises all messages to a given recipient.

Over the years, there have been numerous versions of PGP. Not all versions are compatible with the others. Early versions of PGP were made for DOS, whereas late versions are for 32-bit operating systems. PGP has been ported to numerous non-Windows operating systems as well, such as Apple OS and Unix.

10.2.4 Elliptic-curve encryption

The architecture of typical microprocessors is not efficient for software implementations of encryption. Although this is not a problem for personal computers, it is a problem for new classes of handheld devices needing encryption, such as the wireless version of 3Com's Palm Pilot. A new class of encryption algorithms, known as elliptic-curve encryption, appears to provide encryption strength equal to that of the earlier-mentioned ones but using a smaller key and an arithmetic that is easier on microprocessors than either symmetric or public-key encryption and requiring far less memory. Being a new type of encryption, its security must withstand the concerted scrutiny of experts before it is accepted.

10.2.5 Voice encryption online

Until only a few years ago, the Internet was viewed as a means of exchanging text messages and files. Today it is also handling a vast amount of voice and even slow-scan-video traffic.

Telephony over the Internet started as a fringe underground technical application. Today it is a legitimate mainstream industry; even well-established telephone companies have begun to use it and to offer it to their non-Internet customers. Communications between Internet users are free. Communications to or from non-Internet-connected parties are billed at rates lower than those of the conventional telephone companies.

In countries where the telephone service has been a government-protected monopoly, this has been viewed as a revenue threat. Attempts to eliminate it have been unsuccessful. (Section 10.2.5 deals with Internet telephony at length.)

In addition, conventional broadcasting of audio (speech and/or music) has also taken off, totally undermining the control that governments used to have over licensing radio broadcasting within their respective territories. In fact, Internet "radio" has a worldwide reach, unlike local conventional RF broadcasts, and can be done with no budget. This has caused understandable consternation on the part of repressive regimes used to being able to control the news media.

Merging powerful encryption with digitized telephony over the Internet was an inevitable, simple step. Indeed, anyone today can use fully encrypted voice communications with any other user connected to the Internet. Perhaps the most advanced, yet totally free, software is Speak-Freely, available worldwide (www.fourmilab.ch/speakfree). Its latest version allows users to select IDEA, DES, or Blowfish encryption, or a combination of the three. Unlike some mainstream nonencrypted voice-over-the-Internet software, such as the technically impressive Internet Phone by Vocaltec Communications, which routes the data through its own servers, thereby opening a possible security weakness, SpeakFreely and some other software, such as PGPfone, allow Internet users to communicate directly and with strong encryption as a built-in option.

10.3 Attempts to control against encryption

Practically every organization needs discipline to function, be it the military, the church, a government, or a commercial organization. This, in turn, implies a "stovepipe" organizational structure to ensure command and control. The Internet undermines this time-honored structure by allowing low-level subordinates to bypass the entire chain of command to communicate with any level of management. As if that were not threatening enough to traditional organizations, such communication can be encrypted.

The forcefulness of most governments' opposition to the use of encryption by individuals, however, suggests a more fundamental reason why governments have been so opposed to it: the loss of the ability of a state to exercise censorship. Even the most enlightened and democratic regimes have topics that are patently disallowed. Even the most staunch opponents of censorship have no problem supporting censorship of what they consider "obviously offensive," even if it is victimless. Depending on the country, such topics could be related to religion, to criticism of the head of state, to sexuality, and so on. Ultimately, censored topics follow from religious or political taboos. Encryption by individuals makes censorship unenforceable, and this loss of control is unacceptable to most sovereign states, sort of like having two rude guests at your dinner table who whisper secrets into each other's ears.

Given the dual use of both the Internet and of encryption for legitimate goals, goals that offend individual governments, and also for out-and-out criminality, most governments engage in a triple-pronged counteroffensive to limit the use of encryption on the technical, legal, and social fronts.

10.4 Legal issues

On the legal side, there have been enactments of a flurry of new laws intended to criminalize numerous acts related to strong encryption.

The interested reader can find a country-by-country summary of laws on encryption at www.epic.org/reports/crypto2000. As previously stated, the United Kingdom has enacted legislation, known as the RIP Act, which permits the police to compel a person to decrypt an encrypted file or face a two-year jail term. Worse yet, its Clause 16 requires the recipient of such a demand to "keep secret the giving of the notice, its contents and the things done in pursuance of it" under penalty of a five-year jail term. This law's definition of encryption is extremely broad and includes what some consider a mere "data protocol." Along similar lines, the Clinton administration drafted the Cyberspace Electronic Security Act (CESA), which would have given officials the ability to use search warrants or court orders to access encryption keys.

This class of approach, which sounds simple on the surface, has two fatal flaws:

1. If the very commonly used public-key encryption has been used to encrypt a file to an intended recipient, the sender is physically unable to decrypt that file; only the intended recipient can. That is the nature of public-key encryption.

2. If a commonly occurring crash of one's hard disk containing a conventional symmetric key has occurred, one is again physically unable to decrypt a file.

On August 20, 1999, the *Washington Post* reported that the U.S. Justice Department had prepared a request to Congress to enact laws to authorize federal investigators to enter private residences and offices secretly in order to override encryption programs on personal computers covertly. This could turn into "Spy vs. Spy," according to the director of George Washington University's Cyberspace Policy Institute; knowledgeable computer users could take countermeasures.

The October 1999 version of the U.S. CESA bill would allow police to present a text in court, claim that it was the decrypted version of an encrypted file, but not require the police to show how it had been decrypted. As cryptography expert Bruce Schneier of Counterpane Internet

Security points out in his October 1999 Cryptogram, a free monthly electronic newsletter sent by this company to anyone who requests it

This means that the police could present decrypted plaintext in open court, but refuse to reveal to the defendant how that plaintext was obtained. This, of course, means that the defendant can have a hard time defending himself, and makes it a lot easier for the police to fabricate evidence. The ability to receive a fair trial could be at stake.

In Australia, according to Attorney General Daryl Williams's spokeswoman Catherine Fitzpatrick, a bill passed in December 1999 and waiting for the largely ceremonial approval of Australia's governor general before it becomes law allows the attorney general to authorize legal hacking into private computer systems, as well as the copying of data and even the altering of data to conceal surveillance, as long as the attorney general has reasonable cause to believe that it is relevant to a "security matter." It also authorizes "reasonably incidental" activities. Greg Taylor, vice chairman of Electronic Frontiers Australia, views this bill as "getting around the problems that strong cryptography presents law enforcement" in that "now they can attack the problem at the source before the data even gets encrypted." Also, according to Taylor, such a law "opens to question all computer evidence if there has been the potential for legalized tampering of it."

Unlike most any other human institution, the Internet is inherently transnational in nature. While any nation could elect not to allow the Internet within its borders, a simple assessment of the economic benefits that it brings has caused practically every nation on Earth, including the most repressive ones, to connect to the Internet. Besides, keeping the Internet out is no more feasible than wishing the wind away; any country's citizens can access the Internet through foreign ISPs by merely dialing them up. This applies to a considerable degree to the situation when individual countries have elected to filter out select Internet material.

10.4.1   Crypto laws around the world

Some countries control cryptography's export; others control its import; still others control its use; some control a combination of the above.

The importation of cryptography is controlled to varying degrees by Vietnam, France, most of the former Soviet states, and a handful of other governments. The exportation of at least some kinds of cryptography is controlled to varying degrees by the United States, Canada, Australia, New Zealand, France, the former Soviet states, and a few others. The use of cryptography is controlled to varying degrees by the former Soviet states and to a lesser degree by France, Italy, South Africa, and a few others. In the United States at present, the use of cryptography of any strength is legal, but its export is controlled by the following:

> ‣ The Arms Export Control Act (22 U.S.C. 2778), which does not mention cryptography, but empowers the president to designate any items to be included as "defense articles" or "defense services";

- The International Traffic in Arms Regulations (ITAR), which explicitly mention cryptography as being heavily controlled;

- Munitions Control Newsletter #80 (a 1980 newsletter elaborating on the application of cryptography export regulations to scientific and technical speech vis-à-vis the First Amendment);

- Numerous Commerce Department export guideline documents, which do not mention cryptography per se but apply whenever the State Department passes jurisdiction of some specific cryptography export matter to the Commerce Department.

The Coordinating Committee for Multilateral Export Controls (COCOM) was an organization of 17 member states (Australia, Belgium, Canada, Denmark, France, Germany, Greece, Italy, Japan, Luxembourg, the Netherlands, Norway, Portugal, Spain, Turkey, the United Kingdom, and the United States; additionally, Austria, Finland, Hungary, Ireland, New Zealand, Poland, Singapore, Slovakia, South Korea, Sweden, Switzerland, and Taiwan were cooperating members), whose purpose was to control the export of items and data that were viewed as dangerous to particular countries. In 1991 COCOM, with the notable exception of the United States, allowed the export of mass-market and public-domain cryptography. In March 1994 COCOM was dissolved, and in 1995 it was replaced by the Wassenaar Agreement between (as of last count) 32 countries (Argentina, Australia, Austria, Belgium, Bulgaria, Canada, Czech Republic, Denmark, Finland, France, Germany, Greece, Hungary, Ireland, Italy, Japan, Luxembourg, the Netherlands, New Zealand, Norway, Poland, Portugal, Republic of Korea, Russian Federation, Slovak Republic, Spain, Sweden, Switzerland, Turkey, United Kingdom, Ukraine, and the United States).

It is significant that the Wassenaar Agreement is not a treaty, which therefore cuts out review by any country's legislature.

The laws pertaining to encryption in various countries are quite convoluted in that they are full of exceptions and qualifications (e.g., based on the number of bits, on whether or not it is "for personal use," and so on), which are periodically revisited and changed. In Sweden, for example, encryption importation and use is free, and so is its export to all but a few countries; the authorities may search one's premises for the decryption key but may not compel one to assist in one's own investigation by providing that key to the authorities.

10.4.2   Can encryption bans work?

Can encryption bans be effective in their intended purpose? No, for the following simple reasons:

1. The penalty for using encryption (if caught) is likely to be far lower than the penalty for openly disclosing what was deemed sensitive enough to have warranted encrypting it. This is similar to the situation where, even though lying under oath in any court is a crime (if

one is caught), people still routinely lie under oath simply because the penalty for admitting to a more serious crime by not lying is often much higher.

2.   There is a class of openly available techniques, known collectively as steganography, that allows anyone to hide data in plain view, whether encrypted or not. Such techniques often make the issue of banning or not banning encryption irrelevant.

3.   Detection of the existence of sophisticated encryption can be impossible. Who can prove that the innocuous sentence, "The temperature in the garage was 75 degrees," means "Meet me behind Joe's garage on July 5"? Who can detect new advanced custom-designed steganography schemes?

4.   The existence of the Internet makes it easy for encryption technology to circumvent bans on its proliferation. Indeed, former U.S. attorney general Janet Reno is alleged to have stated so in writing in a May 1999 letter (openly available on the Internet) to the German federal secretary of justice, Herta Doubler-Gremlin, in which she allegedly stated, "The use of the Internet to distribute encryption products will render Wassenaar's controls immaterial."

5.   Banning software encryption is unenforceable against savvy users. In most (though not all) countries, one can bring encryption software in a diskette to any one of many publicly available computers connected to the Internet, such as public libraries or Internet cafes, and transmit the encrypted files quite anonymously to a recipient who can retrieve them in a similar manner just as anonymously. Obtaining encryption software in the first place can easily be done in the same manner, anonymously, through thousands of Internet servers that openly provide a large collection of such software.

6.   Potent encryption is available indigenously in dozens of countries; as such, controls on exporting it from select countries are pointless. In fact, the big to-do about attempts to ban encryption may be having an effect opposite to what was intended because individuals who may not have otherwise been sensitized to the vulnerability of their plaintext material are now aware and may be encrypting what they otherwise would not have.

The bans on the exportation of encryption are even less effective in their stated goals, even though the stated goal of making encryption unavailable to terrorists is laudable. It makes good sense for a country to ban the exportation of something that it alone possesses or it alone can create and that could be used against it; it makes no sense for any one country to ban the export of what other nations produce locally too. Potent encryption is available indigenously in many countries, notably including the United States, Israel, Russia, France, India, Ireland, and Australia in addition to some 30 other countries as well.

A recent survey conducted by George Washington University's Cyber-space Policy Institute identified 805 products (hardware and software) that use encryption developed in 35 different countries. That same study states that "on average, the quality of foreign and U.S. products is comparable" and that

> in the face of continuing U.S. export controls on encryption products, tech-nology and services, some American companies have financed the creation and growth of foreign cryptographic firms. . . . With the expertise offshore, the relatively stringent U.S. export controls for cryptographic products can be avoided since products can be shipped from countries with less stringent controls.

The technicalities of U.S. law pertaining to the exportation of encryption, while understandable in a legal and historical context, make the ban on the exportation of encryption even more porous. While it is illegal in the United States to export potent encryption in software form without the appropriate license, constitutionally guaranteed rights make it perfectly legal to export the source code of that same encryption if it is printed on paper. The printed source code is optically scanned across the ocean using standard OCR tech-nology, then compiled into the same executable code that it was illegal to export directly. This has, in fact, been done legally on a number of well-documented occasions.

The concept of escrowed encryption, where a third party accessible by the state would be able to decrypt material belonging to a user, seemed rea-sonable from the perspective of a government that presumes itself to be trustworthy, but unreasonable from any user's perspective. The arguments against it are basically the following:

- A citizen often does not trust the government.
- Even if a credible case can be made for the government to obtain the decryption key to read a particular document, it is difficult to see how that key, once obtained through escrow, cannot be copied and used by the government to look at other documents by the same user in the future without building a credible case for the need to do so, or conceivably to impersonate the user.

The counterargument by some government representatives to the effect that "escrowed keys should be a welcome service to a user in case he loses his own decryption keys" has been invariably met with polite bemusement.

Today, even governments are backing away from the concept of escrowed encryption for the following reasons:

- Those who matter most to law enforcement (narcotraffickers, terror-ists, and so forth) are most unlikely to oblige law enforcement officials by using encryption that is openly advertised to be readable by the government.

‣ The transnational nature of the Internet requires a global key-escrow system. This is not palatable to sovereign states with their own equities to protect.

‣ Steganography and related data-hiding techniques that can conceal the mere existence of files, whether encrypted or not, make the debate almost irrelevant.

‣ The logistics of who keeps which escrowed keys, who has authority to demand the release of such escrowed keys to whom under which conditions, and so on become unmanageable for vast numbers of encryption keys.

As a result, escrowed encryption is basically dead in the United States and in practically all other countries. As of May 1999, for example, the U.K. prime minister's office has abandoned a similar proposal; a report by the House of Commons Trade and Industry Select Committee on the Electronic Commerce Bill, concluded that "U.K. electronic commerce policy was for so long entrapped in the blind alley of key escrow that fears have been expressed that the United Kingdom's reputation . . . for electronic commerce is now severely damaged."

Worse yet, the notion of escrowed encryption seems to have backfired in two ways:

1. Individuals who would not have otherwise encrypted their data due to their former lack of awareness of the threats have now been sensitized to it by the extensive press coverage of escrowed encryption and now routinely encrypt their data.

2. Entire nations have realized that escrowed encryption where the keys are kept by another nation is an obvious threat. In early 1999, in a reversal of its position on encryption, the German government actually started encouraging its citizens and businesses to use strong, unescrowed encryption. According to a report released in early 1999 by the German Federal Ministry of Economic Affairs and Technology,

Germany considers the application of secure encryption to be a crucial requirement for citizens' privacy, for the development of economic commerce and for the protection of business secrets. The Federal Government will therefore actively support the distribution of secure encryption. This includes in particular increasing the security consciousness of citizens, business, and administration.

In a departure from the U.S. position, this report stated that it understood that encryption can be used to criminal ends but that the need to protect the economic concerns of that nation took precedence.

The reader may misconstrue the above verbiage as slanted in favor of libertarian privacy at the expense of the legitimate concerns of law enforcement. Quite the contrary is true. The point being made is that some legitimate concerns of law enforcement can only be met through provably effective means and not through simplistic and ineffective cosmetic measures such as provably ineffective attempts to ban encryption.

It is, perhaps, due to the realization of all of the foregoing that in September 1999 the U.S. government came up with a new policy that removes many of the bureaucratic burdens to companies wanting to export encryption. A one-time review of each encryption product is still required, though, before it can be exported; this has caused the cynics to suspect that only products with an identifiable weakness may receive the requisite export license. Furthermore, this new policy will have little practical impact because the most contentious encryption, namely, freeware encryption, is not affected by it. This policy is hotly debated because, among other reasons, it does not adequately define key terms in its provisions, such as what a *low-end user* or a *government-affiliated buyer* is (e.g., Is Fiat, the well-known private automaker, which has a substantial investment from the Italian government, a *government-affiliated entity*?). It also interprets the term *retail* as excluding sales over the Internet, and so on.

At the same time, the new policy criminalizes the refusal of any individual to surrender a decryption key in response to a court order; yet, providing the authorities with such a key is inherently impossible for public-key-encrypted files sent to anybody else because only the intended recipient (and never the sender) can decrypt such files. Furthermore, the new policy exempts law enforcement from having to disclose how a decrypted version of a document was obtained. This has obvious legal implications when, for example, the defense questions the authenticity of such documents.

10.5 Societal issues

On the social side, there have been numerous strong campaigns by various law enforcement organizations to demonize the Internet, anonymity, and encryption. Some regimes have branded the Internet "an American imperialist tool" allegedly out to corrupt the moral fiber of their societies. Others have taken offense at the fact that most Internet activities are in English; some have even criminalized the operation of Web sites on their soil if such sites are solely in English. Still others have been outraged by the availability of this or that on the Internet, be it nudity, religious commentaries considered blasphemous, political discourse viewed as threatening or critical of a regime, and so on. Nearly all regimes, including democratic ones, have taken offense at the free flow of encrypted data that could contain any of the above or could be facilitating terrorism or other acts generally deemed criminal.

Encryption has been equally demonized with simplistic arguments of the type, If you have nothing to hide, then you do not need encryption; ergo, if you do use encryption, you are up to no good. This argument ignores the legitimate national and societal needs for protecting trade secrets, privileged attorney–client information, patient medical records, and so on in the face of a huge number of documented attacks on such computerized data.

10.6 Technical issues

On the technical front, there have been public reports even in responsible journals, such as *Business Week*, of extensive ongoing government activity in intercepting digital communications. Given the minimal, if any, likelihood of any effectiveness in banning encryption, governments appear to have concluded that a much more effective tool would be to capitalize on the fact that most traffic is in fact not encrypted and to try to derive information from massively expanded monitoring of the unencrypted traffic. Even in the case of encrypted traffic, a lot of information can be derived from what is almost always unencrypted: Who is communicating with whom and when. The only exception to this is if traffic uses concatenated anonymizing remailers.

According to A. Oram in his August 1998 article "Little Known International Agreement May Determine Internet Privacy" (http://www.oreilly. com/people/staff/andyo/ar/cypto wassenaar.html), the International Police (Interpol) decided to implement a system known as ENFOPOL, intended to access any and all kinds of electronic transmissions, specifically including the recently launched (and more recently bankrupt) Iridium global satellite phone system.

On October 16, 1999, however, it was reported that ENFOPOL was being scrapped by the member states. Even so, according to a November 8, 1999, Telepolis (Germany) report by C. Haddouti, ENFOPOL plans remain integrated into Article 11(b) of the European Legal Aid Agreement. That article stipulates "remote access" of national monitoring measures "regarding telecommunications connections on a state's own territory under engagement of national service tenderers by means of remote control in another member state which has the appropriate ground station." It also stipulates that all telecommunications member service offerers make "possible the execution of national monitoring arrangements." Article 12 of the same legal-aid convention stipulates that another member state can be obligated to make a technical monitoring of telecommunications traffic in real time or deliver monitoring recordings already existing.

Independently, for the last few years, a number of Internet Usenet forums (the bulletin-board-like newsgroups on the Internet) and even reputable media organizations such as ABC News have been alleging the existence of a multinational surveillance network named Echelon. In June 1999, Duncan Campbell, a British investigative journalist, submitted a report ("Interception Capabilities 2000") to the European Parliament's Science and Technology Options Assessment (STOA) panel assessing that panel's concern about such a network. Following that report, the Australian government confirmed its participation in it in related interviews.

According to Campbell's report, a law enforcement–oriented organization, the International Law Enforcement Telecommunications Seminar, is involved in coordinating and sponsoring related activities. A different report, "An Appraisal of Technologies of Political Control," dated January 6, 1998, authored by Steve Wright of the Omega Foundation, a British human rights organization in Manchester, England, and written for a research unit of the European Parliament department for the STOA, asserts that "Echelon ... [is] a global surveillance system that stretches around the world." Public inquiries about it have been made by numerous politicians on both sides of the Atlantic, such as Representative Bob Barr (R-Georgia, and a former federal prosecutor) and Glyn Ford, a British Labor Party member of Parliament. According to the U.S.-based Federation of American Scientists Internet Web site, Echelon "searches through millions of interceptions for preprogrammed keywords on fax, telex and e-mail messages."

In his book *Secret Power*, Nicky Hager asserts that this system facilitates the "monitoring of most of the world's telephone, e-mail, fax and telex communications" and that "it is designed primarily for nonmilitary targets," thereby "potentially affecting every person communicating between (and sometimes within) countries." He asserts that "every word of every message intercepted gets automatically searched—whether or not a specific telephone number or e-mail address is on the list."

Independently, according to a spokesman for the U.S. National Security Council (NSC), a 160-page draft plan by the NSC calls for setting up a Federal Intrusion Detection Network (FIDNet) that would monitor traffic on both government and some commercial networks as a means of safeguarding the United States's critical information infrastructure. According to a counsel for the Washington, D.C.–based Center for Democracy and Technology, this network would also monitor citizens who visit federal Web sites and might involve tracking e-mail, use of certain computer programs, and remote access to government as well as commercial networks. The same counsel has stated that the chances that FIDNet will be established are good.

On a much smaller scale, of course, it is certainly well within any one country's power to use its own laws (or influence) to require select ISPs to track and report on the activities of specific clients or to use criteria to identify users meeting particular online profiles.

If large interception systems do, in fact, exist, then one can understand why encryption, which negates them, is disliked so intensely by governments involved in such systems.

10.7 Countermeasures

The right and, indeed, the obligation of any responsible government to protect its citizens from terrorism and from out-and-out criminality are unquestionable. The only issue is how to do this effectively without trashing the very institutions in which a democratic government takes justifiable pride.

Political correctness makes discussion of countermeasures to surveillance inappropriate in polite company. The philosophical positions between those who advocate state interception of personal data and those who oppose it have had the rigidity of religious debates that ultimately appeal to nebulous higher principles for their justification. In practical terms, the law enforcement side has the benefit of the power of the various laws. The privacy-protection side has the benefit of technology, which evolves and allows numerous creative ways of negating interception, let alone decryption.

At issue is not merely whether two individuals should have the ability to communicate information that the state cannot decipher, but whether individuals and organizations should have the ability in the first place to encrypt and store encrypted information that the state cannot decipher.

The two main classes of techniques that have evolved to defeat attempts by nations either to ban encryption or to force the disclosure of decryption keys are (1) steganography, which hides the mere existence of a hidden file (see Section 11.5), and (2) anonymity, which hides the author or originator of a file (see Sections 8.5.2, 9.7, and 9.15).

10.8 State support for encryption

In March 1999, the French government, which had been strongly against the use of potent encryption by the public in the past, issued a decree specifically encouraging its use by French citizens. In May 1999, Germany surprisingly announced that it would actually promote the use of potent encryption throughout Germany, even though this would hamper eavesdropping by law enforcement. Because the Wassenaar Agreement is not binding on its member states, the federal minister of Economic Affairs and Technology recently released a report stating that Germany "considers the application of secure encryption to be a crucial requirement for citizens' privacy, for the development of electronic commerce, and for the protection of business secrets." In fact, this document also states that "for reasons of national security, and the security of business and society, the federal government considers the ability of German manufacturers to develop and manufacture secure and efficient encryption products indispensable."

In other words, Germany now considers the use of strong encryption by its citizens as something that furthers, rather than hinders, the interests of its national security. Indeed, the German Ministry of Economics and Technology, to its credit, is now actively sponsoring and funding the development of encryption software known as GnuPG, whose "innards" (source code) will be openly available for inspection to anyone who wishes to satisfy himself or herself that there are no hidden features; it will also be knowingly unbreakable by that government (or anyone else, for that matter).

The motivation for both of these fundamental policy changes seems to have been the realization by individual countries that the protection of their respective data from each other outweighs law enforcement concerns.

Independently, Canada's minister of industry, John Manley, announced on October 1, 1999, that the Canadian government would not seek to regulate the domestic use of encryption and would restrict exports only as far as Canada's Wassenaar obligations require. The Irish government has announced the same policy.

To their credit, Hong Kong police were reportedly handing out the pro-encryption sticker shown in Figure 10.3 during the 1999 Internet Convention.

The significance of these transcends the boundaries of any one nation: The global interconnectivity of the Internet makes it extremely easy for encryption software to travel between countries despite controls. If one or more major countries elect not to enforce encryption controls, then the effectiveness of attempts to control encryption software by any country becomes highly questionable.

10.9   The future of encryption

No matter what wondrous encryption schemes come along in the future, one should never lose sight of the fact that the specific process of encrypting information is only a small part of what needs to be done to protect that information from the eyes of someone having no authorized access to it.

The availability of computers to implement the encryption arithmetic has actually made the overall problem of protecting something through encryption more difficult and not less. This is so because the complexity of the operating systems of contemporary computers has created a plethora of

Figure 10.3   Hong Kong police support for encryption.

exploitable security weaknesses once a sensitive plaintext has been accessed by a computer. Many openly available modern (and certainly future) cryptographic algorithms are adequately strong in and of themselves. Instead, the real weaknesses are in the following:

- The handling, processing, and removal of the unencrypted plaintext in the computer;
- The propensity of modern user-friendly operating systems to do things without one's knowledge, such as create housekeeping files, swap information between memory and hard disk, and so on;
- The human tendency to cut corners, such as enabling "fast key generation" in public-key-encryption systems (which is based on factoring large prime numbers in favor of precomputed prime numbers) or using easy-to-remember weak passwords;
- The vulnerabilities created by connecting a computer to a network;
- The vulnerabilities created by running untrusted software in the computer, such as some software downloaded from the Internet and bootlegged software from friends, which could quietly steal passwords and keys;
- The vulnerability introduced by doctored encryption software;
- The serious vulnerability of ensuring that a key (whether the public key in public-key encryption or the key in conventional symmetric encryption) indeed belongs to the person one thinks it does;
- The serious vulnerability of securely distributing a conventional symmetric-encryption key.

10.10   Quantum cryptography

The basic precepts of quantum cryptography were discovered in the early 1970s. In the 1980s, Charles Bennett of IBM and Gilles Brassard of the University of Montreal published a number of papers on the subject; they gave a demonstration of it in 1989.

Quantum cryptography is not an encryption algorithm. Instead, it is a means for the secure distribution of a key using single photon transmission and for the creation of such a random key. The basic idea is that, according to Heisenberg's uncertainty principle, the communicating photons cannot be diverted from the intended recipient to the interceptor without disturbing the communications system to the point of creating an irreversible change in the quantum states of the system.

Because the secret key cannot be intercepted without evading detection (because the interception of the photons will raise the error rate of the key above an alarm threshold), it can be viewed as a secure means of encrypted communications over open channels. As such, the fundamental security of quantum key distribution (QKD) is based on the fundamental principles of quantum physics. The optical distribution path can be free space or optical fiber.

Numerous teams have been working on quantum cryptography for the last decade, including teams at various universities such as Johns Hopkins in the United States and the University of Geneva; at U.S. national laboratories such as Los Alamos; and in the corporate sector at companies such as British Telecom.

The lack of overwhelming interest in the deployment of the technology has not helped expedite the progress. This underscores a significant point: Encryption strength today is where it is because there is no need for it to be any stronger. Unless some cryptanalytic breakthroughs occur that challenge the fundamental mathematical assumptions behind modern encryption, such as the difficulty of factoring large prime integers, it is quite easy to increase encryption strength by merely adding bits to the encryption key; this would increase the brute-force cryptanalytic effort required nearly exponentially.

10.10.1 Quantum computing

According to the late Nobel Laureate Richard Feynman and others, binary numbers can be represented by orthogonal quantum states of two-level quantum systems; a single bit of information in this form was then called a "qubit." Having more than one qubit, quantum logical gate operations can be seen as the building blocks for a quantum computer. The advantage over conventional computer architectures is that the quantum gate operations can be performed simultaneously rather than serially. Cryptanalysts' interest was piqued in 1994 when it was shown that this "quantum parallelism," if implemented in a practical "machine," could factor the products of large prime integers, which are the basis of many (but not all) cryptographic algorithms today.

Despite extensive work in academia and the national labs, quantum computing is nowhere close to resulting in a practical reality for the following reasons:

- It is difficult to engineer the quantum states needed.
- Even if created, those quantum states lose their coherence properties (which are necessary for quantum computing) when interacting with the environment.
- It is difficult to engineer the means to read out the end quantum states that contain the result of a computation.

Elaborate work-arounds to the problems above are continuing to evolve. Realistically, a practically useful device for factoring large prime numbers cannot be expected for at least a decade or more.

Even if prime number factoring becomes a reality, however, numerous other encryption algorithms do not depend on prime number factoring for their strength, such as one-time pads or quantum cryptography, to cite a couple. As such, quantum computing will not spell an end to encryption as its proponents have claimed on occasion in the literature.

10.11   DNA-based encryption

The first step in this technique is to convert each letter of the alphabet into a different combination of the four bases that make up the DNA. This is followed by synthetically creating a piece of DNA spelling out the message to be encrypted in addition to short marker sequences at both ends of the DNA chain. Finally, this can be slipped into a normal fragment of a human DNA strand of similar length. The end result can be dried out on paper and cut into small dots. Only one DNA strand in about 30 billion will contain the message, making the detection of even the existence of the encrypted message most unlikely; for this reason, DNA-based encryption is basically a data-hiding technique that is the modern equivalent of the microdot of World War II fame.

10.12   Comments

Governments have been trusted with the obligation to protect their citizens from terrorism and from out-and-out criminality but not to use that power to squelch dissent by labeling it as criminality. Controlling encryption is not an effective means of meeting this obligation and may actually hurt vital economic national interests; some Western governments have recently realized this and are now actually encouraging their citizens to use strong encryption.

The increasing and vital dependency of modern society upon computers makes the protection of corporate and personal sensitive information through potent encryption a matter of national economic survival. Furthermore, there is an increasing legitimate need to continue protecting the confidentiality of such personal information as attorney-client-privileged information, medical data, and the like through strong encryption.

While cryptography, like anything else, can be used for illegitimate purposes (e.g., to hinder valid investigations by the police), the fact that it is also used to prevent crimes and make society safer is often overlooked by law enforcement officials interested merely in getting evidence to result in a conviction at all costs.

To be sure, there are situations where there is a legitimate need for specific third parties to have a way to read an encrypted file (whether through escrowed keys, backup keys, or other means): These include work-related employee documents in an organization, as well as some personal records (e.g., life-insurance information) in case one dies and a spouse needs to access that information. In the case of data encrypted for transmittal to an intended individual recipient, it is hard to conceive of any justification for a third party to have any right to see that data; this is merely an extension of one person's right to whisper a secret in someone else's ear. The distance between the first person's mouth and the second person's ear should have no bearing on the right to keep private what is being transmitted.

The indigenous availability of potent encryption in most of the world's nations and the global interconnectivity provided by the Internet makes the control of software encryption an unattainable goal. Independently, the development of data-hiding techniques, motivated by the commercial applications of digital watermarking, will continue. Effective data-hiding techniques will make the debate about encryption irrelevant.

While encryption, just like other technologies such as commercial tele-communications, automobiles, and assorted devices, can be used for terrorism and criminality, outright banning of any of these technologies is ineffective and has a major negative economic impact on any nation. The alarmist prose used by today's law enforcement to solicit support for banning encryption is rather unconvincing; if one were to change only a few words, that same prose could have been used in the 1930s to claim a need to ban horseless carriages and the telegraph ("criminals escape using horseless carriages . . ."; "criminals conspire and communicate at the speed of light using the telegraph . . .").

The solution may lie in criminalizing the use of encryption in the commission of generally recognized, serious, criminal acts only and in actually encouraging its use in all other activities.

Selected bibliography

General encryption

Curtin, M., "Snake Oil Warning Signs," Ohio State University, at cmcurtin@interhack.net.

Kosiur, D., "Keep Your Data Secure from Prying Eyes: An Encryption Primer," http://www.sunworld.com/swol-03–1997/swol-03-encrypt.html.

"The Passphrase FAQ," http://stack.nl/-galactus/remailers/passphrase-faq.html.

Schneier, B., *Applied Cryptography*, 2nd ed., New York: Wiley, 1996.

Schneier, B.,"Security Pitfalls in Cryptography," *Counterpane Systems*, at http://www.schneier. com/ essay-pitfalls.html.

On DES cracking:

http://www.replay.com/mirror/cracking-des/chap-l.html.

http://cryptome.org.

On other encryption cracking:

http://www.stack.nl/-galactus/remailers/index-crack.html.

Encryption software and algorithms

On blowfish algorithm:

ftp://ftp.psy.uq.oz.au, ftp://ftp.ox.ac.uk.

On elliptic-curve encryption:

Smart, N., et al., "Elliptic Curves in Cryptography," *London Mathematical Society Lecture Notes,* Cambridge, England: Cambridge University Press, 1999.

On hashing algorithms:

ftp.funet.fi:/pub/crypt/hash.mds/md5.

ftp.funet/fi:/pub/crypt/hash/sha.

http://www.esat.kuleuven.ac.be/-bosselae/ripemdl60.html.

On PGP:

http://www.pgp.com

http://www.pgpi.com for the United States and international versions, respectively.

On PGP versions:

http://www.stat.uga.edu/.-rmarquet/pgp and www.paranoia.com/-vax/pgp versions. gif.

On public-key encryption:

http://www.cesg.gov.uk/about/nsecret/possnse.btm.

On voice encryption:

http://www.speakfreely.org.

Legal controls on encryption

ftp://ftp.cygnus.com/pub/export/export.html.

http://cwis.kub.nl/-frw/people/koops/cls-sum.htm.

http://cwis.kub.nl/-frw/people/koops/lawsurvy.htm.

http://www.dfat.gov.au/isecurity/pd/pd 4 96/pdlO.html.

On applicable U.S. laws:

ftp://ftp.cygnus.com/pub/export/aeca.in.full.

ftp://ftp.cygnus .com/pub/export/itar.in.full.

On cryptography in Europe:

http://www.modeemi.fi/-avs/eu-crypto.html.

Technical countermeasures by governments

Markoff, J., "U.S. Drafting Plan for Computer Monitoring System," *New York Times,* July 28, 1999, http://www.nytimes.com/learning/general/featured-articles/ 990729thursday.html.

"They're Listening to Your Calls," *Business Week,* May 31, 1999, pp. 110–111.

Data hiding and steganography

http://ise.gmu.edu/-njohnson/Steganography.

http://www.jjtc.com/Steganography.

http://www.psionic.com/papers/covert/covert.tcp.txt.

http://ww2.umdnj.edu/-shindler/telemedicine.html.

Future trends in cryptography

Bancroft, C., C. T. Clelland, and V. Risca, "Genomic Steganography: Amplifiable Microdots," *Fifth International Meeting on DNA-Based Computers*, Massachusetts Institute of Technology, Cambridge, MA, June 16–17, 1999.

On quantum cryptography:

http://p23.lanl.gov/Quantum/images/gcrypt.gif.

References

[1] Lenstra, A. K., and E. R. Verheul, "Select Cryptographic Key Sizes," *Journal of Cryptology: The Journal of the International Association for Cryptologic Research, October 27,* 1999, http://security.ece.orst.edu/koc/ece575/papers/cryptosites.pdf.

[2] Key Management Guideline—Workshop Document, draft, October 2001, http://csrc.nist.gov/encryption/kms/key-management-guideline-(workshop).pdf.

CHAPTER

11

Contents

Practical Encryption

11.1 Introduction

By now, it must be quite clear from the vast number of ways that sensitive information can be left behind on one's hard disk that the odds are stacked in favor of the computer forensics expert. This is as it should be for civilized societies that must defend against out-and-out criminality, the evidence of which may be hidden in computer files.

However, there are perfectly acceptable situations, like those listed as follows, in which honorable individuals may want to maintain the privacy of their files and protect themselves against malicious computer forensics.

▸ An individual in a patently repressive, totalitarian regime, or a regime known for its intolerance of religious or other individual preferences, who feels the need to keep overzealous investigators from either planting incriminating evidence on his or her computer or otherwise manipulating stored data;

▸ An individual who connects his or her computer to the Internet or to any other network and who is therefore vulnerable to having his or her confidential files stolen, vandalized, or otherwise accessed without authorization by any savvy hostile remote site;

▸ A businessperson who travels with a laptop that contains proprietary corporate information of interest to an unscrupulous competitor;

▸ A professional who stores information entrusted to him or her by his or her clients, such as a physician, a mental-health practitioner, or a lawyer;

▸ An individual who stores legitimate personal information in his or her computer, such as tax returns and personal correspondence;

‣ An individual entrepreneur who uses his or her computer to store confidential lists of clients, creative new designs, ideas for which patent protection has not yet been applied, copyrighted material, and so on;

‣ An individual who uses his or her computer to store intellectual property, such as scientific publications, laboratory test results, and artistic creations.

Because the odds are stacked in favor of the computer forensics examiner, a user who falls into one of the above categories may elect to take the safe, yet easy, way out by having his or her entire hard disk encrypted. This will do away with most of the subtleties and threats detailed in this book, including the following:

‣ The proclivities of Windows to create temporary files all over one's hard disk;

‣ The difficulties of keeping track of entries made by Windows 95/98/NT in the Registry and the difficulty of cleaning the Registry (see Section 2.4);

‣ The swap (paging) file;

‣ The data stored by assorted applications software in nondescript files on one's hard disk (e.g., Network Navigator/Communicator's netscape.hst file);

‣ The data left behind in cluster tips, or slack (see Section 2.2.1).

And so on.

11.2   Entire-disk encryption

Encrypting the entire disk is quite different from creating an encrypted file or an encrypted disk partition, such as can be done with PGP-disk, Scram-Disk, E4M, and others discussed in this chapter. These schemes do not negate most computer forensics searches, although they do provide a hiding place for some files.

Encrypting an entire disk is not a panacea, however. One is still vulnerable to all of the following threats, which carry through from the normal Windows-user list of threats:

‣ Commercial keyboard-capturing software (see Section 4.4);

‣ Commercial keystroke-capturing hardware (see Section 4.3);

‣ Commercial hardware for intercepting van Eck radiation (see Section 4.7);

‣ All online threats while one is connected to a network such as the Internet at which time the encrypted hard disk is just as accessible to the remote malicious hacker as it is to the legitimate user sitting in front of the keyboard;

> ‣ Adware/spyware that calls home via the Internet after it has been installed (see Section 9.3).

Even so, this is a far smaller and more manageable list of vulnerabilities than if it were to include the threats posed by computer forensics after physical possession of one's hard disk by an adversary.

There are three promising commercial solutions to the problem of encrypting an entire hard disk:

> ‣ SafeBoot from Fischer International Systems Corporation in the United Kingdom. This software has been acquired by Control Break Europe Computer Security Consultants (www.controlbreak.co.uk). It is compatible with Win3.lx, 95/98, and NT. As an option, it can work with a smart card through one's PCMCIA port or a smart card reader that works through one's floppy disk drive using that company's SmartySmart card reader/writer.

> ‣ SecureDoc from Winmagic Corporation (www.winmagic.com) in Canada. This program allows authentication from password to hardware token, biometrics, and PKI, commencing at preboot time. It utilizes public-key cryptographic standard PKCS-11. According to Winmagic's Web site, SecureDoc has achieved validations for Common Criteria, FIPS 160-1 Level 2, and SecureDoc's FORTEZZA-based version is claimed to be the only hard disk–encryption software certified by the National Security Agency (NSA) to safeguard U.S. government secret information.

> ‣ Drive Crype Plus Pack (DCPP) from www.drivecrypt.com.

Full-disk-encryption software may have problems with conventional software that accesses disks at the sector level, such as disk-defragmenting software and disk-wiping software. The latter is not needed for disks encrypted in their entirety except as a second layer of defense in case one does not fully trust the disk-encryption software and suspects it may have a backdoor entry. This author has used Winmagic's SecureDoc and found it to work satisfactorily; not surprisingly, it crashed during disk defragmenting with the popular defragmenting software Diskeeper, and it also crashed during disk wiping with Eraser. It rebooted with no problems, however.

11.3 Encrypting for e-mail: PGP

If all of the personal computers in the world—260 million—were to work on a single PGP-encrypted message, it would still take an estimated 12 million times the age of the universe, on average, to break a single message.

—William Crowell, former deputy director, National Security Agency,
March 20, 1997
http://www.McCune.cc/PGP.htm.

PGP[1] is an encryption program available over the Internet worldwide at no cost. A commercial version is also available for purchase. A detailed list of FAQs about PGP can be found at http://www.cryptography.org/getpgp.htm and www.pgp.net/pgpnet/pgp-faq. Additional information about it can be found at the following Web sites:

- http://www.cryptorights.org/pgp-help-team/hello.html;
- http://www.mit.edu:8001 /people/warlord/pgp-faq.html;
- http://www.freedomfighter.net/crypto/pgp-history.html.

Official PGP documentation in several languages can be found at these Web sites:

- http://www.pgpi.com;
- http://www.geocities.com/Athens/1802 (German);
- http://www.geocities.com/SiliconValley/Bay/9648 (French).

PGP started as a political statement by its creator, Phil Zimmerman, to make encryption available to everyone. Unlike versions available for purchase, whose source code (the human-readable sequence of steps that it performs) is often not made available, all of the many free versions have made the source code universally available for analysis and scrutiny. It is considered an extremely good piece of encryption software, and all known attempts to break (cryptanalyze) PGP-encrypted cipher have failed.

At the same time, no encryption software can protect a user from sloppy usage, specifically the following:

1. PGP, like any encryption software, encrypts and decrypts. It is not a security suite (except for commercial versions, which are not recommended) intended to take care of the inherent security flaws of Windows or DOS. Similarly, it does not protect a user from himself or herself, such as the user's forgetting to wipe the unencrypted plaintext version of a message that was (foolishly) stored on hard disk.

2. PGP, like most any encryption software program, does not counsel the user not to use easily guessable pass phrases such as one's name or birthday.

3. PGP, like most any encryption software program, presumes that the user is versed in the many security precautions discussed in this book (e.g., commercial software or hardware that can capture a pass phrase entered on a keyboard). The reader is referred to the condensed list below of such gotchas!

A false sense of security is far worse than no security at all because a false sense of security motivates one to entrust a computer with information,

---

1. The best authority on PGP is Tom McCune. He has an extensive online set of tutorials on PGP, along with current information and relevant links. http://See www.mccune.cc/PGPpage2.htm#Why.

while a person who believes that there is no security will act as if there is no security. Because of this, the reader is strongly cautioned to understand the ancillary ifs, buts, and howevers outlined next before assuming that encryption will meet his or her needs.

As with all software that has evolved over more than a decade, PGP has gone through numerous versions, not all of which are compatible with the others. The interested reader is referred to http://www.paranoia.com/^-vax/pgp versions.gif for a list of such compatibilities; knowledge of such is really not necessary, however, as shown next.

Caution: PGP, like many encryption products, makes it very clear in its encrypted outputs that PGP was used. This may be highly undesirable if one is in a situation where the mere use of PGP is incriminating. For those cases, one can use Stealth v1.1 by Henry Hastur (http://www.unicom.com/pgp/s-readme.html), which removes the telltale headers from a PGP-encrypted message (and allows the intended recipient to add them back before decrypting a message). This is not foolproof, however, as PGP-encrypted messages have a structure that, to the trained eye, immediately reveals that PGP was used. A user would be well advised to use steganography as the outer envelope of an encrypted message in such cases.

Caution: Due to its importance, this admonishment is repeated. Users of PGP encryption should not use the PGP plug-ins for either Eudora or Outlook/Outlook Express (in fact, Outlook/Outlook Express should not be used at all, with or without PGP, due to its long history of security flaws announced by Microsoft in its many security warnings). Instead, encrypt the clipboard and cut and paste the ciphertext into the e-mail software program's window.[2] The danger is that the outbox saves on the hard disk, under some conditions, both the plaintext and the ciphertext; this is about the worst-case scenario from a security perspective.

Caution: Avoid using encryption plug-ins for e-mail software, be it a Web browser or anything else. While no evidence of actual exploitation exists, it is quite possible for a smart-enough plug-in to compromise the security of the encryption in any one of numerous ways.

Encryption, like any human activity that involves discretion, should avoid the following pitfalls of vanity or the force of habit:

1. Avoid the temptation to name your PGP public key with your true name or e-mail address because this information is available to everyone who comes across a file encrypted to your public key. Name your public key, instead, as something like "Someone" at

---

2. Easier yet, use the Current Window feature of Windows; see Tom McCune's excellent tutorial at http://www.mccune.cc/PGPpage2.htm#usecurrent, where a shortcut is shown for this cut-and-paste ritual. The session key then evaporates into thin air. Because the session key is unique to each encryption and is random, you can encrypt the exact same file to the exact same recipient, and you will end up with two totally different-looking end results, both of which will be perfectly valid.

whoever@wherever.com. Reserve the use of PGP for sensitive matters and not for socializing with strangers.

2. There really is no good reason to post your PGP key to any server whatever; instead, create a brand new PGP key pair to meet a specific need, send that public key to the intended correspondent, and upon completion of the desired communication, destroy that key pair.

3. Do not use the PGP feature of "signing" or "validating" others' keys, and do not allow others to do that to your public key either. The reason is that all the signing and validating information is openly readable by anyone who gets your public key (that is the whole purpose of signing/validating someone else's key), which would reveal your network of associates and correspondents to anyone.

11.3.1 How PGP works

PGP uses a combination of conventional (symmetric) and public-key encryptions (see Sections 10.2.2 and 10.2.3); this is standard for most programs using public-key encryption. Specifically:

▸ Upon initial installation (and at any time thereafter), PGP creates a public- and private-key pair. You provide (by whatever appropriate means) to the intended recipient the public-key part and store the private key securely (see Figure 11.1).

▸ To encrypt a file, you need the intended recipient's PGP public key, which he or she must first have provided to you by some appropriate

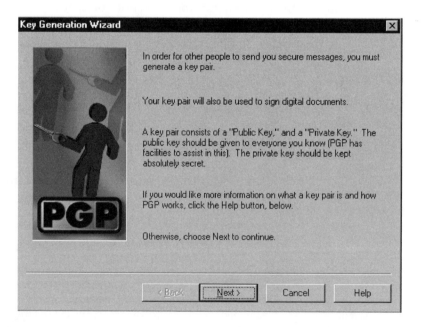

Figure 11.1 PGP key generation.

means. The software will ask you "to whom shall this unencrypted file be encrypted?" and you provide that information.

▸ Because public-key encryption/decryption is much slower than conventional key encryption, PGP dreams up a conventional encryption session key, which it uses to encrypt the file in question. It then encrypts that session key using public-key encryption with the public key of the intended recipient and sends out both the conventionally encrypted ciphertext and the public-key-encrypted key for that conventionally encrypted text.

▸ As an option, you can digitally authenticate your message so that the recipient knows that it really came from you. This is done as follows: Your copy of PGP will first form a brief digital summary of your message and encrypt it with your private key. This becomes part of the overall encrypted file to be sent. On the receiving end, if the recipient who has your public key can decrypt this digital summary, it could only have been encrypted by you with your private key (or else it wouldn't be decryptable with your public key). As a side benefit, the intended recipient's PGP compares the digital summary you sent with the one he or she generates locally on your decrypted file; if the two are identical, the message was not doctored by anyone along the way.

▸ Given that one way for someone to break encryption is to try many possible keys until he or she hits upon the correct one, and given that the easiest way to tell that one has is if readable text comes out, PGP in essence prerandomizes what is to be encrypted in a manner that is transparent to both the sender and the recipient.

Once installed, PGP usage is easy and intuitive; all one has to do is to click on the PGP icon on the lower right corner of the screen, at which time a self-explanatory list of options appears (see Figure 11.2).

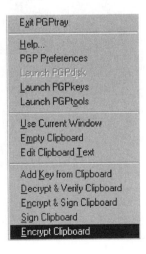

Figure 11.2   PGP primary menu.

11.3.2 Do's and don'ts of PGP installation and use

Windows version

Here is a list of do's and don'ts of PGP installation and use for Windows.

▸ Do not accept the default "faster key generation" option; uncheck it (see Figure 11.3).

▸ Set the "temporary" disk to be a RAM disk (see Section 6.2.2) so that no interim steps get written onto the hard disk.

▸ It is recommended that the public keys and especially your own secret keys not be stored on the computer (see Figure 11.4), but on a floppy disk or USB key that is carried separately if needed and is stored in a physically secure and especially nonobvious location when not needed.

▸ Do not use plug-ins for assorted e-mail programs. Instead, to encrypt, write the plaintext in RAM disk using a simple text editor such as the one that Windows provides to create a new text file (see Figure 11.5). Select Edit/Cut and then use PGP's "Encrypt Clipboard" option. Edit/Paste into the text window of your favorite e-mail program. To decrypt, Edit/Cut from your e-mail program's inbox; then select "Decrypt & Verify Clipboard" (see Figure 11.6). Then make sure that

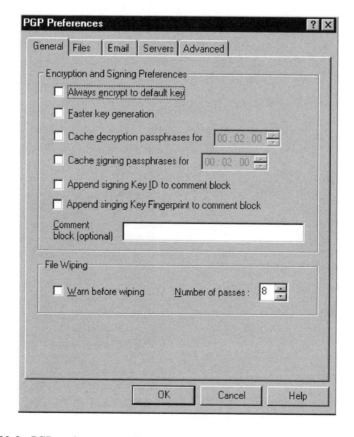

Figure 11.3 PGP preference setting.

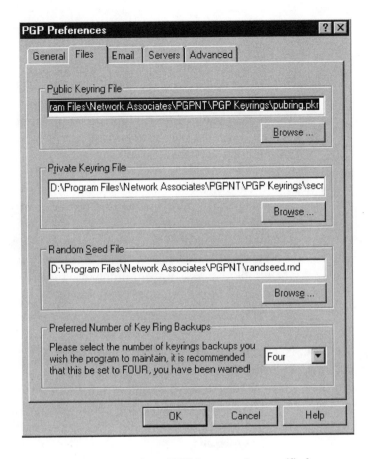

Figure 11.4   Secure off-site storing of PGP keys can be specified.

Figure 11.5   Creating a new text file in RAM disk.

Add Key from Clipboard
Decrypt & Verify Clipboard
Encrypt & Sign Clipboard
Sign Clipboard
Encrypt Clipboard

Figure 11.6   Encryption/decryption options.

you key the "Empty Clipboard" option to minimize the likelihood of plaintext spillage into the swap file (see Figure 11.7).

Caution: It is debatable whether the most secure versions of PGP are the older DOS-based ones or the newest Windows-based ones; strong arguments can be made for both sides. The DOS-based PGP versions obviously do not have to contend with Windows's numerous security vulnerabilities (e.g., swap file, temp files, likelihood of keystroke-capturing software). The Windows-based versions have longer key-length options and a number of bugs have been removed. This author is strongly in favor of the DOS versions and against the Windows versions of any software that deals with security and privacy. Windows has far too many security vulnerabilities that the user has no control over.

› When using PGP from within Windows, do not use the error-prone plug-ins for a handful of popular software programs, such as Eudora or Outlook Express. Instead, simply use the little icon on the lower-right corner of the screen and do the following:

  › In the case of encryption, copy the plaintext file to clipboard, opt for "encrypt clipboard," then Edit/Paste the (encrypted) clipboard contents into the message window of whichever e-mail program you are using.

  › In the case of decryption, Edit/Copy the encrypted file from the e-mail onto the clipboard, opt for "decrypt and verify," read it, and do not save it. Then make sure you overwrite the e-mail that carried this message.

› Abide by the recommendations provided in Chapter 6 about setting up Windows securely, particularly the following:

  › Have enough physical RAM memory so as to set the virtual memory to zero. This prevents any sensitive data, such as passwords, from ending up on disk.

  › Ensure that your computer has no software or hardware enabled that can capture keyboard strokes (see Sections 4.3 and 4.4). If what you are doing is particularly sensitive, it would not hurt to keep the possibility of an overhead hidden camera in mind.

DOS version

The DOS version is preferable from a security perspective because it is not vulnerable to the many security problems of the Windows environment;

Figure 11.7 Cleaning the clipboard from plaintext.

however, like all DOS programs, it requires the use of unintuitive commands.

▸ Create a RAM disk (see Section 6.2.2).

▸ Print out and read the lengthy document that comes with the software; it is highly informative, though a bit verbose. Do not be intimidated by its length or apparent complexity; once you become accustomed to using PGP, you will find that it takes only a few seconds to encrypt or decrypt a file.

▸ After installing PGP, go to the folder where it resides, find config.txt, open it with a text editor, and set the temporary directory to point to that RAM disk letter. This will prevent the writing of sensitive information on the hard disk and will also speed up the program's execution.

▸ PGP uses several special files for its purposes, such as pubring.pgp and secring.pgp, the random number seed file randseed.bin, the PGP configuration file config.txt, and the foreign-language string-translation file language.txt. These special files can be kept in any directory by setting the environmental variable PGPPATH to the desired pathname. If using MS DOS, the following command must be inserted in the standard autoexec.bat file using any text editor, assuming that these files are in C:\PGP\:.

```
SET PGPPATH=C:\PGP
```

PGP for Windows

There are numerous PGP versions for Windows and not all are compatible with each other, although a lowest common denominator can usually be found that most versions can handle. A compilation of which version does what can be found at http://staff.uiuc.edu/%7Eehowes/pgp-summ.htm.

The reasons for the large number of versions are mostly legal:

1. Until recently, RSA public-key encryption was covered by patents in the United States but not abroad; accordingly, U.S. versions shied away from including RSA.

2. Until recently, U.S. law viewed encryption as a "munition," and its export was largely illegal. This was an unenforceable law and U.S.-only versions of PGP found themselves outside the United States within minutes of their release in the United States.

3. There have been a few efforts to commercialize PGP that tried to compete with the free versions n the basis of additional features not present in the free versions. The biggest concern with commercial versions is security: Their source code is almost never released, and they are usually bloated with features, which makes the software code too long to review for security vulnerabilities even if it were to be given out.

The user unwilling to deal with the DOS versions is advised to consider the Cyber Knights Templar (CKT) versions (e.g., pgp 6.58ckt) available from numerous sources that one can find by doing a keyword search on "6.58ckt," such as at ftp://ftp.zedz.net/pub/crypto/pgp/pgp60/pgp658_ckt.

The source code of these versions is available for inspection if one is so inclined, and one can even compile one's own version from that source code. Their main claim to fame is that they support very long public-key lengths (up to over 16,000 bits), which should offset any concerns about the predicted cryptanalytic strength of quantum computing if and when it comes about. They now also support 256-bit symmetric encryption (e.g., Twofish, AES).

A listing of numerous sources for various PGP versions can be found at www.staff.uiuc.edu/%7Eehowes/soft13.htm.

The latest commercial PGP version, as of the time of this writing, is PGP 8.02. Although it now has full Windows XP compatibility, there are still some issues with PGP Disk, and this author is unimpressed with it for the following reasons:

1. It buries the all-too-important method of generating nonstandard key sizes.

2. It has a licensing structure that requires paying a fee every year or the paid version reverts to the free version.

3. It has no command-line PGP executable option.

4. It does not allow one to edit the version string.

To its credit, this commercial version has been released and made available for peer-review purposes, but it is not open source (i.e., it cannot be incorporated into one's own product or be distributed by third parties).

Both DOS and Windows versions

Here is a list of do's and don'ts for PGP installation and use with both DOS and Windows.

> Get your PGP copy from a trusted source, such as http://www.pgpi. com or (for the long keys) www.ipgpp.com. Just because the version you got from an unknown source appears to work well and be compatible with PGP messages going in and out, that does not mean it has not been compromised. It is quite possible, for example, for a version to select the encryption keys from a list of, say, 100 keys only, as opposed to a repertoire of a quadrillion choices or more. The end result would still be compatible with every PGP message going in or out, and it would also be trivial for an interceptor to break merely by trying 100 keys.

> Follow the simple instructions about validating the integrity of the file you just downloaded [usually this amounts to checking a cyclic

redundancy check (CRC) or hash value, which in PGP parlance is the digital signature].

▸ Make sure that whatever you compose to be encrypted is composed on RAM disk and not on magnetic disk. If it is sensitive enough to warrant encryption, it has no business being on a magnetic disk where it can be found.

▸ Select a key length of no less than 1,024 bits. If compatibility with other unknown users of PGP is not an issue (and it shouldn't be because you don't know "unknown" people and thus cannot trust they are who they say they are—see Section 11.3.4 for a discussion of the man-in-the-middle problem), opt for a key length of 2,048, 4,096, 8,192, or even 16,394 bits. The Windows versions from CKT (www.ipgpp.com) support very long keys. Expect the time it takes to generate those keys to be quite long if you have a slow computer, but key generation is only done once and generation time does not reflect how long it will take to encrypt or decrypt files later on.

▸ Select a pass phrase that is truly not guessable or amenable to a brute-force dictionary attack by the numerous commercially and freely available software programs on the Internet.

▸ Do not store PGP files, and certainly not the "key ring" files that contain your secret key, on the hard disk. Instead, store them on a floppy disk, which should be kept separately in a physically secure place. Make sure that you specify in your setup where PGP is to look for those files.

▸ Do not publish your public PGP key anywhere; doing so is pointless and dangerous. A recently discovered bug in PGP allows one to doctor up your PGP public key so that any messages encrypted with it can be decrypted by ADKs. Because you don't want to be dealing with total strangers anyway, due to the man-in-the-middle problem, there is really no reason to publish your PGP key. Simply give it to the select few with whom you want to communicate using PGP.

▸ Do not accept someone's PGP public key from the Internet unless you have some independent way of verifying that it truly belongs to whomever it is alleged to belong and has not been altered. This, too, is to prevent the man-in-the-middle problem.

▸ Do have at least two PGP key pairs, one for low-trust communications and one for high-trust ones. For highest-sensitivity communications, create a key pair immediately, use it, and destroy it securely shortly thereafter.

▸ Delete (read: overwrite) PGP key pairs on a regular basis (at least monthly, but preferably more often) so that you could not possibly be compelled to decrypt this or that file by anyone after a few days (or minutes if you are a member of the opposition in a repressive regime).

- Depending on the level of threat you think you may face, you may also want to consider periodically verifying that your copy of the PGP software and public and private keys have not been altered. You can do this by running CRC or some other hashing program on your files. Make sure that you keep those CRC or hash values in some secure place that the would be attacker of your files cannot find.

- Do not opt for encrypting an outgoing message to yourself as well as to the intended recipient. (This may be phrased as a "Save outgoing files" option, which is not desirable at all because it makes you able to comply with a demand to decrypt a file sent.) In other words, uncheck the option "Always encrypt to default key" (see Figure 11.8).

- You can reencrypt an already-PGP-encrypted file for additional security, but this is really pointless if you have abided by the recommendations of Section 11.3; if you have not abided by them (e.g., not protected against keystroke-capturing software), then encrypting a file a hundred times over will not make it any more secure.

- Keep in mind that a PGP-encrypted file does not hide the fact that it is a PGP-encrypted file, as shown in the partial message reproduced in Figure 11.9. Because of this, it may attract unwanted attention on its way to the recipient. To get around this, consider steganography (see Section 11.5).

- Also keep in mind that neither a PGP-encrypted e-mail nor any other encrypted e-mail hides the "From" and "To" information. If this is an issue, consider the information on anonymity in Sections 8.5.2, 9.6, and 9.15.

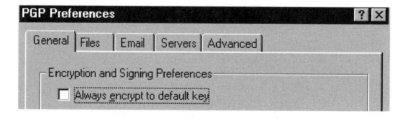

Figure 11.8   Defeating forced decryption of outgoing PGP messages.

```
-----BEGIN PGP MESSAGE-----
Version: 6.0.2CKT b-6

qANQR1DBw04DQ2KWr5oNP8EQD/4gFs+jLMFB204gSg5uDbrsAKzdBZPY9nqfzFIT
cF63/rK3KgMJcYpZcnTe+LuRiFyD4WB6N/CpEVapyFTFx0AdKVb2g5YXm9ZVxzMd
cRKnRFqG2p8Mqs3KNmtSOWSoP77Cg7R78vKL44z/mviSxmhXiBKgwwFbfcVFEqB2
P1OFfYm5z1isNstu+XtgzlfRb7wllcqb91fCRdnGVX40a+ApD/LhMLtxksR8QEJM
```

Figure 11.9   PGP files stand out.

- Keep in mind that no encryption software protects from someone who can make inferences based on the mere fact that encrypted messages are being sent (or received), when some other publicly observable event, such as activity by freedom fighters in a repressive regime, occurs.

- Never keep both an encrypted and a decrypted version of the same file.

- If you have an attachment to a PGP-encrypted e-mail using your favorite e-mail software, the attachment will not be encrypted by default; you have to encrypt it separately prior to attaching it as follows:

  - From Windows Explorer (or any other way) select the file you want to encrypt; it could be an executable file or any other type. Edit/Copy.

  - From the little PGP lock icon in the tray on the lower left, select "Encrypt" (or "Encrypt and sign," if you wish to sign it too).

  - Select and drag the intended recipient's name to the lower window of PGP. Click OK.

  - The PGP-encrypted file will be saved as a new file in the same folder where the unencrypted one was. Use the "Attach file" option of your favorite e-mail program. Do not Edit/Paste (See Figure 11.10).

An excellent set of FAQs is available at www.pgp.net/pgp-faq and at http://cryptography.org/getpgp.txt; a much better collection of facts and advice is available through the acknowledged PGP guru, Tom McCune, at www.McCune.cc.htm.

11.3.3   The need for long public keys

It has been estimated in papers available on the Internet (see www.inter-hack.net/people/cmcurtin/snake-oil-faq.htmi) that a 128-bit symmetric key is about as resistant to brute-force cryptanalysis as a 2,304-bit RSA public key; the corresponding equivalences for various key lengths are reported in Table 11.1.

Some (amazingly, even the revered originator of PGP) have inferred incorrectly from this that the public-key length need not be longer than 2,304 bits. This is incorrect: If someone were to break the symmetric session key of PGP (see Section 11.3), then only that one encrypted file would be compromised. However, if one were to break the public key of PGP, then all encrypted files to that recipient would be compromised. Because of this, the

video.exe   video.exe.pgp

Figure 11.10   PGP-encrypting any file, including executables.

Table 11.1   Bit Equivalences

Symmetric Key Size (bits)	Public-Key Size (bits)
56 bit	384 bits
64 bit	512 bits
80 bits	768 bits
112 bits	1,792 bits
128 bits	2,304 bits
256 bits	~15,000 bits

Note: This table is predicated on the dubious assumption that a brute-force attack is the likely cryptanalytic threat to PGP.

public-key length should be much stronger than the symmetric key, that is, much longer than 2,300 bits. It is for this reason that if 128-bit symmetric encryption is used in one's PGP, this book recommends PGP key lengths of 4,096 or longer; if 256-bit symmetric encryption is used (as this author recommends), a 16,384-bit public-key-encryption key length should be used. This is possible with the CKT versions of PGP.

At the same time, users should realize that if they want to be compatible with the majority of other PGP users, the use of ultralong keys will have to be reserved for those who have PGP versions that can handle long keys.

11.3.4   The man-in-the-middle problem

The man-in-the-middle problem has nothing to do with PGP per se; it is a logical security problem inherent to all public-key-encryption schemes. If you receive an e-mail (or floppy disk or other document) with a public key that claims that it belongs to Mr. *XYZ*, this in and of itself does not prove that it belongs to Mr. *XYZ*, even if you can exchange messages with Mr. *XYZ* using it. The key could very well belong to Mrs. *ABC*, who receives your message to Mr. *XYZ*, decrypts it, and reads it (because what you think is Mr. *XYZ*'s public key belongs, in fact, to Mrs. *ABC*). Then she, in turn, encrypts it with Mr. *XYZ*'s public key and sends it on its way without Mr. *XYZ* being any the wiser. The reverse path works just as well.

You need to have some independent way of verifying that a key stated to belong to *XYZ* does in fact belong to *XYZ* and not to some go-between, or man in the middle. Such an independent verification depends on the specifics of the situation.

If you know *XYZ* personally, you could talk with him on the phone, and he could confirm, "The key that goes like this [here he could read the public key aloud to you, which is OK because it is public] is mine."

If you don't know *XYZ* personally, you can use someone you trust to vouch for the fact that this is the case. This, in fact, is the basis of authenticating a public key among people who do not know each other: a "web of trust," where each person in the Web trusts another person, who trusts another, and so on, that the key belongs to *XYZ*. This is formalized in PGP by having each person in the web of trust "sign" (digitally) a key for the person that they can vouch for.

In practice, nobody pays too much attention to this web of trust, and the only way for you to know for a fact that a key belongs to *XYZ* is for you to find some independent way of satisfying yourself that the key in fact belongs to *XYZ*.

11.3.5 DH or RSA?

Many versions of PGP allow the user to select between Diffie Hellman (DH) and RSA encryption [1]. (Actually, PGP uses a variant of DH known as El Gamal.)

DH's security is based on the difficulty of factoring and computing discrete logarithms [2] (the "Discrete Logarithm Problem"), whereas RSA is based on the difficulty of factoring large numbers into the prime number components (the "Prime Integer Factorization Problem" [3]). Both were covered by patents that have expired (DH's patent expired on September 6, 1997, and the RSA patent expired on September 20, 2000). Because of this, both algorithms are now in the public domain. This is significant because the main reason why there have been so many versions of PGP has to do with the fact that the RSA patent was in force in some countries but not in others.

The benefits of DH over RSA are as follows:

1. A longer RSA key (in terms of the number of bits) is required to result in the same security as a given-length DH key [4].

2. DH has the benefit of a more solid mathematical foundation. This is not to say that RSA keys are weak, however.

3. If someone were to forcibly obtain your DH-using PGP key, he or she would be able to read your e-mail but would not be able to impersonate you by digitally signing outgoing e-mail because a different algorithm, the Digital Signature Standard (DSS), is used for that. RSA keys, by comparison, perform both functions.

The disadvantage of DH in PGP implementations is that it is more amenable to the recently discovered weakness whereby an ADK can be inserted by a third party (see Sections 11.3.8 and 11.3.9).

11.3.6 DSS?

DSS is an algorithm for generating a fixed-sized (1,024 bits) digital summary of a message of arbitrary length to allow detection of any alteration of the message. It is considered safe for another couple of decades. Even though a 1,024-bit key may appear to be weaker than, say, an 8,000+-bit DH key, PGP does not use DSS for encryption, but only for message authentication.

Of more concern should be the fact that according to the open literature (e.g., www.scramdisk.clara.net/pgpfaq.html), DSS keys suffer from a weakness known as "subliminal channels" [5]. This is a term used to denote the existence of unintended pathways that can leak information an adversary would find advantageous.

11.3.7 Selecting the Symmetric Encryption Algorithm

AES-256,International Data Encryption Algorithm (IDEA), CAST-128, and Triple DES are all very secure algorithms and are well implemented in PGP. The choice comes down to compatibility with the version of PGP that one's correspondent is using. While CAST-128 is about twice as fast as IDEA, which, in turn, is about three times as fast as Triple DES, it really does not matter in typical usage of an average-length message every few days.

Both CAST-128 and IDEA are 128-bit algorithms, and they are about equally secure. AES exists in both 128- and 256-bit versions. IDEA has been around for longer, and there is more comfort factor associated with its use, but some minor patent issues make it free only for noncommercial use.

Triple DES is often implemented with only two, rather than three, different 56-bit keys (encrypt with key #1, decrypt with key #2, which causes further encryption because it is the wrong key, and reencrypt the result with key #1 again). This is a sloppy and totally unnecessary shortcut, which does not save any computation time. In the case of PGP, Triple DES is implemented with the full three different keys. There is debate as to whether its effective equivalent key strength is 168 bits or 112 bits; the latter is associated with the assumption that a "meet-in-the-middle" cryptanalytic attack, a specific attack documented in the open literature that exploits the specific construction of Triple DES, is possible.

11.3.8 A minor flaw in PGP

In August 2000 there was a big to-do [6] about a discovery of what has really been common knowledge among software-encryption professionals: If a hostile entity gets hold of one's public key, that public key can be downright changed (the man-in-the-middle problem, explained earlier) or (and this was not as well known) altered so that messages encrypted with it can be decrypted by others in addition to the intended recipient.

This is nothing new. The trouble started when a major company that started making PGP for profit had the most unfortunate idea of increasing PGP's appeal to the corporate marketplace by providing an ADK so that an employee's supervisor could also decrypt the employee's incoming, PGP-encrypted messages. In fact, some versions of this PGP for corporate customers were openly advertised as having this feature, which appealed to law enforcement as well.

A PGP user not savvy about the technical details of PGP at a fairly esoteric level is most unlikely to spot the existence of such ADKs in his or her
public key. Worse yet, and this is where PGP can be rightfully blamed, there
are ways in most versions between 5.5 and 6.5.3 whereby such ADKs can be
added by third parties onto one's public key at a later time (e.g., when one's
public key is stored in a public-key directory server), thereby enabling such
third parties to read messages encrypted to that unsuspecting user's public
key.[3]

For this to happen, the following conditions have to be met:

1.   The attacker has gained access to the victim's public PGP key. This
     can be done if that key is deposited in a public-key directory server,
     something that Section 11.3 has already advised against, or even if
     that public key is merely stored on a computer that is connected
     online to the Internet or is physically accessible by others; in both
     cases all the files in the computer are vulnerable, specifically includ-
     ing encryption keys.

2.   The attacker knows how to add the ADK and repost or replace the
     doctored public key where the undoctored one was before.

3.   The attacker can either access incoming e-mail sent to the victim
     (physically, by a tap, or any other way described in Chapter 7) or has
     modified the e-mail software to send e-mail to the attacker as well.

New versions of PGP (such as PGP v6.5.8) are reputed to have fixed this
bug. This may lull one into a false sense of security because the logical
conundrum of any encryption key has not been and cannot be fixed: One
has to have some independent means of verifying that an encryption key
does indeed belong to the person it is supposed to belong to and has not
been modified.

Some have stated that PGP's hubris in having claimed for so long that it
is unbreakable has been punished and that PGP has irrevocably lost the confidence of users. Perhaps the opposite is true: Users and would-be users
have had a crash course on the logical and procedural weaknesses of any
encryption. As a result of that forced, new awareness, any encrypted communications will now be that much more secure.

Users of PGP 6.*x* for Windows and Mac OS can easily test for the presence of ADKs in a certificate by right-clicking on the certificate and selecting

---

3. Adding an ADK can, reportedly, be done from the command line by adding the following line in the pgp.cfg
   file:

       ADKKEY=OX28A635C6 [put the ADK here]

       7ENFORCEADK=ON

   Now create a new key in the usual manner with the command pgp-kg.
   Add the ADK to this new key with the command pgp-kg+ADDKEY=Ox28a653c6+ENFORCEADK=ON.
   The author has not verified this process.

"Key Properties." If the ADK tab is present, the key has one or more ADKs and might be a malicious certificate. There is no easy way of finding ADKs in the Unix command-line version of PGP 5.*x* or 6.*x*.

To negate the ADK threat, do the following:

1. Never post a PGP public key anywhere. First of all, do a quick CRC or hash check on it. Then hand-carry it to the intended other user with whom one needs to exchange secure e-mail or send it by secure e-mail; in the latter case, the recipient should do a quick CRC (or hash or PGP-digital-signature) check of the received public key and compare the result with you through some independent means whereby you and he or she can ensure that you are talking with the right other person.

2. Never store a PGP public key (let alone the PGP private key) on a computer that either goes online or can be accessed by others. Store it on a floppy disk in a secure place.

3. For particularly sensitive communications, create a PGP key pair for that occasion only. Destroy it afterward.

4. If at all possible, do not use any of the Windows-based PGP versions because of the difficulty of mitigating Windows's numerous security problems. Instead, use the DOS versions (2.3.a through 2.6.*x*) available from the Internet worldwide. If you really want to use the Windows-based versions, consider applying a repair tool from www.pgp.com/other/advisories/adk.asp.[4]

PGP, like any complex software, has its share of peculiarities, which are not exactly flaws. A compilation of these oddities is available at http://www.angelfire.com/pr/pgpf/pgpoddities.html.

11.3.9 PGP weaknesses

Another PGP weaknesses is the fact that it does not protect one from making unsound decisions, such as the following:

1. A user can select an easily guessable password.

2. A user can leave copies of unencrypted text on the hard disk.

3. A user may not elect to verify independently that the public key he or she is using does, indeed, belong to the person to whom it is alleged to belong.

---

4. The technical subtlety that the PGP repairl.0 fixes is this: ADKs added to PGP keys in some versions can escape detection because they are appended after one digitally signs his or her public key, thereby eluding detection because the digital signature still validates the public key despite its having been doctored. An ADK should never sit outside the hashed part of the self-signature of the sender.

4. A user may elect to use a very short-length public key.

5. Pass-phrase entry is susceptible to keystroke capture (see Sections 4.3 and 4.4).

6. A user may forget to encrypt and end up saving or sending unencrypted text.

7. PGP does not encrypt or wipe the swap file; the user must do that.

8. PGP does not ensure wiping of buffers; the user must do that.

11.3.10 Other uses of PGP

In addition to its classic use for encrypting e-mail, PGP is highly desirable in two additional roles:

1. Encrypting real-time voice over the Internet through the use of the free SpeakFreely software (see Section 10.2.5).

2. Setting up an encrypted peer-to-peer network using PGPNet. One can use PGPNet to create a VPN in a peer-to-peer setting. This requires knowing the IP addresses of the parties involved, which is easily found by each such party by, for example, entering the ipconfig /all command (Start/Run, then enter the above command).

11.4 Encrypting one's own files: Encrypted disk partitions

Any business person or responsible individual who wants to protect the privacy of digitized files from unscrupulous competitors, from overzealous prosecutors in totalitarian regimes, and from thieves of intellectual property must contend with two classes of threats:

1. Theft of data while in transit (e-mail);

2. Theft of data while in storage on one's computer.

PGP, discussed in Section 11.3, being public-key-encryption-based, is primarily intended for e-mailing encrypted messages or attached files to another party. Of course, one can always encrypt to one's own public key and save the encrypted output locally; by so doing, however, one surrenders one major benefit of public-key encryption (when properly set up), which is that the sender is mathematically unable to decrypt a file that he or she has encrypted to an intended recipient's public key and, hence, cannot be forced to do so.

A number of encryption products are available, the intended purpose of which is to encrypt files for one's own use. The most common are:

▸ BestCrypt;

> E4M ("encryption for the masses");

> FlyCrypt;

> F-Secure FileCrypto (part of the F-Secure Workstation Suite);

> Invincible Disk with Data Lock;

> PGPDisk (the only part of PGP that is not recommended, due to bugs; while versions of PGP since v6.02 have ostensibly corrected the problem, this author has had continuing difficulties with PGPDisk in later versions as well);

> SAFE Folder;

> SafeHouse;

> S to Infinity;

> McAfee PC Crypto;

> ScramDisk.

BestCrypt's configuration panel (see Figure 11.11) is quite intuitive and straightforward, and it has received good reviews from the "typically picky" users that post on the various Usenet forums related to computer security and privacy.

The best of these encryption products, which also happens to be free, is ScramDisk, assessed at length here. The interested reader is encouraged to see a comparison of most of these products in S. Dean's article "On-the-Fly Encryption: A Comparison" at http://www.fortunecity.com/skyscraper/true/882/ Comparison_OTFCrypto.htm.

ScramDisk is still available worldwide (including from www.scram-disk.clara.net) and is intended primarily for encrypting files for one's own use. As with most PGP versions, its source code has been made available for review and scrutiny. The versions for Windows 95/8/Me have been free; the versions for NT/2000 used to be available for a fee but are no longer sold as the software's author has joined the Drive Crypt firm (recently renamed Secure Start), which now sells a commercial version (whose source code is not available for inspection), called Drive Crypt 4.

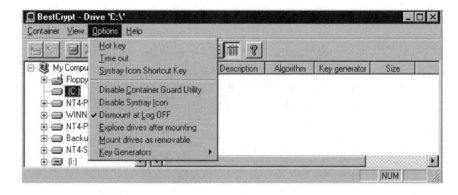

Figure 11.11   BestCrypt configuration panel. (Courtesy of Jetico.)

Scramdisk can use any one of a large number of established reputable encryption algorithms, and it is considered an excellent software product. Figure 11.12 depicts the ScramDisk user interface.

Caution: As with any encryption software, one should be very concerned that a keystroke logger can capture the pass phrase or encryption keys used, thereby rendering all such encryption useless in its intended purpose. One such program, KeyKey (see Section 4.3), was able to capture ScramDisk (v2.02h) passwords entered even in the protected "red-screen mode."

As its own Web site succinctly states,

> Scramdisk is a program that allows the creation and use of virtual encrypted drives. Basically, you create a container file on an existing hard drive, which is created with a specific password. This container can then be mounted by the Scramdisk software, which creates a new drive letter to represent the drive. The virtual drive can then only be accessed with the correct pass phrase. Without the correct pass phrase the files on the virtual drive are totally inaccessible.

> Once the pass phrase has been entered correctly and the drive is mounted the new virtual drive can then be used as a normal drive, files can be saved and retrieved to the drive and you can even install applications onto the encrypted drive.

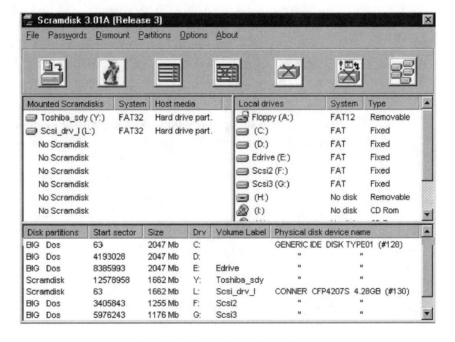

Figure 11.12   Scramdisk user interface for encrypted disk partitions. (Courtesy of Shaun Hollingworth.)

ScramDisk goes beyond the conceptually simple task of encrypting one's files by including the following functionalities intended to conceal the fact that it is being used:

1. It is computationally infeasible to prove that a large file held on a drive is a ScramDisk virtual disk container without knowing the pass phrase. The ScramDisk container files do not have to have a standard file extension and contain no file headers that indicate the file is anything but random data.

    Caution: While this is true, the Registry of a computer on which ScramDisk has been installed contains unmistakable evidence to that effect.

2. Unlike the Windows versions of PGP, some of which are about 8-MB long, the ScramDisk executable program is very small and can be carried on a 3.5-inch floppy disk.

The following key points are of direct interest to any potential user of ScramDisk:

▸ Passwords are protected from ending up on the swap file.

▸ ScramDisk files cannot be identified as such, but an investigator can infer as much from the presence of telltale installation files in one's computer. Although Scramdisk-encrypted files look like random data, a user should have a plausible story as to what that random data is. One could, for example, create a digitized long file of, say, an old 33-rpm audio disk (and not from a CD because of the identifiable high quality of the CD recordings), and one can seamlessly append the ScramDisk file to it. Regardless, one must have a believable reason as to why there is a large file of random data on one's hard disk.

▸ ScramDisk partitions are readily identifiable for what they are. Don't use them.

▸ To obscure some of the most obvious telltale evidence of ScramDisk, one should rename the device driver (sd.vxd) to something plausible, such as drv45gx.dll. Do likewise for the executable portion of ScramDisk. Also, make sure that there is no scramdisk.ini anywhere; this is created only if one alters the standard configuration of Scram-Disk, in which case that file, too, should be suitably renamed. The reader is cautioned, however, that these are very simplistic steps that any competent investigator will readily see through. Half measures can get one in worse trouble than no measures as they suggest an intent to mislead.

▸ ScramDisk volumes have the .svl file-name extension, but one can name them anything at all.

▸ Because ScramDisk counts the number of times that a volume has been mounted along with the time and date that this occurred (albeit in encrypted form), the user may well wish to prevent this by making the volume file a read-only file.

▸ Do not use the "fast shutdown" option in Windows 98 Second Edition. Disable this option if using Windows 98 Special Edition.

▸ Use the "red screen" option for password entry. It defeats some (but not all) keyboard sniffers openly available. This works only for the standard QWERTY keyboards and not others (such as Dvorka, French, German, or other).

▸ Use the latest version of ScramDisk. Older versions have a security weakness that allows one to reset the passwords of an encrypted volume to the original ones when the volume was created.

▸ Do not leave the computer on unattended after dismounting a ScramDisk volume.

▸ Consider availing yourself of the security benefits of a (free) companion utility called SecureTrayUtil from www.fortunecity.com/skyscraper/true/882/SecureTrayUtil.htm.

▸ If you use ScramDisk's steganography option, select the 4/16-bits option and not the 8/16-bits option.

11.5 Steganography

In our youth, most of us delighted in writing secret messages on a piece of paper with lemon juice as ink, then using our parents' iron for the really useful purpose of rendering the lemon ink visible. What made it more fun was if the paper we used had a perfectly innocuous letter written on it to disguise the existence of the secret message.

For applications other than entertainment, the microdots of World War II fame are well known. In earlier years, leaders often wrote secret messages to distant recipients on a messenger's shaved head and then waited for that messenger's hair to grow before sending him on his way. Some popular printed images, which suddenly reveal a previously invisible three-dimensional image when stared at long enough from the right distance, are yet another example of a technique for hiding information in plain view. These techniques are collectively referred to as steganography, which is a means of hiding data.

Unlike encryption, which disguises the content of a message and often does so in an alerting manner unless additional steps are taken, steganography hides the existence of the message. Computers are clearly well suited for implementing a broad collection of techniques with the same purpose: to hide information in plain view. The types of techniques that can be used are limited only by one's imagination.

There is nothing inherently disreputable or subversive about steganography. It is just one example of a class of information technology techniques known as data hiding, and there is even a very proper annual international professional conference on the subject. Also, it is the technical basis for digital watermarks, namely, hiding a digital watermark on a copyrighted image or in a sound file in a way that will not "wash out" if such files are tinkered with.

Openly available software programs, available worldwide, for implementing steganography tend to take advantage of three classes of techniques:

1. If one were to change the least-significant bit of most digitized samples of a sound file, the ear certainly would not notice. One can therefore hide one bit of sensitive information for every digitized sample of sound. The resulting file would still sound the same and would be no bigger and no smaller than the file with which one started.

2. If one were to change the least-significant bit of a digitized value that represents the brightness of a picture element ("pixel"), the eye would most likely not notice the change in brightness change by 1 out of a typical 256 levels, let alone if it is by one of over 32,000 levels. Typical images use 256 levels of brightness and hence 8 bits per pixel for black and white or, in the case of color images, 8 bits for each of the three primary colors (red, green, and blue) for each pixel. It is simple arithmetic to show that one can hide a lot of data in a typical image of 1,024 × 768 pixels. The image in Figure 11.13 depicts the concept.

3. One can also hide data in normally unaccessed portions of a computer disk (floppy or hard disk). Such portions include the free space (which usually includes so-called deleted files), the slack (the space

Figure 11.13   One steganography concept: data hidden in an overt image.

between the end of a file and the end of a cluster), and normally un-used tracks on a disk.

While the concept of steganography sounds very appealing on the surface, it is not the panacea it may appear to be. This is so for two basic reasons:

1. Having on one's computer—or, worse yet, sending via the Internet—many innocuous images or sound files can be quite alerting unless one's normal daily activities are such that warrant this content and conduct (e.g., being a musician or a painter or a professional photographer). If such files are coupled with the existence of steganography-related software discovered on one's computer, then one will be hard pressed to come up a believable explanation other than perhaps claiming to be a steganography enthusiast who experiments with evolving concepts in this field.

2. While images and sound files used to hide steganographically hidden files may look natural to the eye and sound natural to the ear, they are not necessarily undetectable by special mathematical techniques devised to home in on their weaknesses. This is discussed in more detail next.

The most commonly used steganography software tools, which are available worldwide, include the following:

- Hide and Seek by Colin Maroney;
- Steganos (shareware) by Demcom (initially authored by Fabian Hansmann);
- StegoDos by an anonymous author;
- White Noise Storm by Ray Arachelian;
- S-Tools for Windows by Andy Brown;
- Jpeg Jsteg;
- Stealth by Henry Hastur;
- Steganographic File System (SFS) for Unix computers by R. Aderson et al.

The encryption software ScramDisk (see Section 6.4.2) also includes the option of hiding a file with steganography.

Each of these software packages has its own strengths and weaknesses; it is not the purpose of this book to do a comparative evaluation. For such an assessment, the reader is referred to numerous publications on this topic by Neil F. Johnson of the Center for Secure Information Systems at George Mason University.

Numerous commercial steganography packages, such as Invisible Systems Pro by East Technologies (http://www.east-tec.com/ispro/index.html), are now entering the marketplace. Caution: Practically all of the commercially and openly available steganography tools are not safe against steganalysis, the science of determining if an innocent-looking file contains steganographically hidden information (see Section 11.5.2).

11.5.1 Practical considerations in steganography

The extent of the detectability of a file that contains steganographically hidden information is, amusingly, somewhat proportional to the popularity of the software package. The more extensive its usage, the more resources are devoted to detecting its footprint. Steganography is treated by law enforcement like a virus: Once it hits the market in a significant manner, tools are developed to detect it.

Conversely, if a new method were to be devised privately and used sparingly, chances are that its existence would never become alerting enough for it to be subjected to scrutiny that could lead to techniques for its detection. As an example, a recent telemedicine-related article discusses hiding a sensitive file in the images of echocardiograms. With a little imagination, one can conceive of steganographic techniques having nothing to do with either image or sound files. As another example, the reader is referred to an interesting paper, "Covert Channels in the TCP/IP Protocol Suite" (http://www.watermarkingworld.org/WMMLArchive/0011/msg000I5.htm l) by Craig H. Rowland of Psionic Company, which discusses hiding information in TCP/IP packet headers.

From the perspective of the traveling businessperson who would rather not alert a prospective data thief to the existence of valuable information on his or her computer, the steganographic strength of the software being used is far less important than maintaining a low profile and not attracting attention. This applies even more if one uses steganography in e-mail from countries with knowingly repressive regimes. While it would be plausible for one to explain sending a couple of digitized photos of the local scenery to the family at home, sending the exact same photograph every day at 7 p.m. would raise suspicions even in the mind of the most unimaginative interceptor.

11.5.2 Detecting steganography: Steganalysis

Users of some amateurish steganography software, satisfied by their own inability to detect the existence of hidden information, assume that nobody else can do so either. The result of this dangerous self-deception is that law enforcement can reap the benefits of information that would never have been entrusted to a particular steganography software program if its users knew just how alerting it was.

Whether the existence of a steganographically hidden file is visible to the eye or perceptible by the ear should never be the criterion of steganographic strength. Instead, the sole criterion should be whether or not mathematical tools can be deployed on a file to determine if it includes steganographically hidden data.

Steganalysis is a potent tool for law enforcement that is only now beginning to find its way, slowly, into the toolbox of computer forensics experts. Interestingly, the identical tools can be used to identify the existence of perfectly legitimate digital watermarks placed on copyrighted material by their owners to identify illegally proliferating copies. This is rapidly becoming big business in music, photography, and literary prose as more and more of such copyrighted content is traded over the Internet.

Because there is no single steganography scheme, there is no single steganalysis scheme. Some steganographic schemes can be readily detected, while others cannot. Due to the nature of steganography, this will remain the state of affairs: New steganographic software programs will continue to be developed, and as soon as they become popular enough to pique the interest of law enforcement, steganalysis software will follow, and the cycle will be repeated.

Steganography is viewed as a serious threat by some governments as evidenced by the fact that one sees on the Internet mention that even the U.S. Air Force's Research Laboratory has subcontracted with Binghamton University's Center for Intelligent Systems and WetStone Technologies to "develop algorithms and techniques for detecting steganography in computers and electronic transmissions, as in digital imagery files, audio files, and text messages." According to the Air Force Research Lab site, "The goal is to develop a set of statistical tests capable of detecting secret messages in computer files and electronic transmissions, as well as attempting to identify the underlying steganographic method. An important part of the research is the development of blind steganography detection methods for algorithms."

11.5.3 Other ways that steganography can be detected

Clearly, if the original unmodified file (image or sound) used as a cover by the steganography software is available to an investigator, then all one has to do is a bit-by-bit comparison with the suspect version in order for the existence of steganography to become apparent. For this reason one should never use commonly available digital files (such as sound files from CDs, or classical images from the Internet) because the difference would stand out right away.

Independently of the above, most of the steganography software available on the Internet modifies the least-significant bit of a color image, often an 8-bit color image. To understand the problems caused by this simplistic scheme, one must first understand the notion of the "palette," the list of allowable colors; changing the least-significant bit in 8-bit images often results in a color that is not in the original palette. Using 24-bit images allows one to get around this problem somewhat, but at the cost of dealing with an image that takes much more space on the disk and hence much more time to send.

Numerous least-significant-bit-based steganography tools have been shown to be detectable in an excellent paper by Neil F. Johnson, "Steganalysis of Images Created Using Current Steganography Software," at http://debut.cis.nctu.edu.tw/ryklee/Research/Steganography/Sushil-Jajodia/IHW 98.html.

Shortly after the United Kingdom passed the RIP law, which empowers authorities to demand that one surrender the decryption key to a file, numerous countermeasures appeared on assorted Usenet forums about ways to defeat the spirit of that law. One such message, for example, urged readers to fill their hard disks with digital noise so as to inundate the British authorities with suspicious files that, in fact, contained nothing at all.

Another message proposed the scheme whereby one would have two one-time-pad keys for the same encrypted message: One key (which would be surrendered to the authorities upon demand) would decrypt the suspect file into something totally benign, such as a passage from the Bible; the other key (the existence of which would never be disclosed) would decrypt the exact same suspect file into the true hidden content. Because a one-time pad is really a simple one-to-one transformation, then

Ciphertext = One-Time-Pad Key 1 + True Sensitive Message   (11.1)

Ciphertext = One-Time-Pad Key 2 + Passage from the Bible   (11.2)

Hence:

One-Time-Pad Key 2 = Ciphertext − Passage from the Bible   (11.3)

As soon as one creates the ciphertext from (11.2), one uses (11.3) to create the bogus one-time pad to be surrendered upon demand while keeping silent about the existence of Key 1.

11.5.4 Recommendations for maintaining privacy through steganography

Here are a few recommendations on how to maintain privacy through steganography:

1. Do not use the software commonly available over the Internet.

2. Read paper on steganalysis such as the tutorial at http://www.krenn.nl/univ/cry/steg/article.pdf.

3. Realizing that some regimes take extreme exception to anyone hiding things from the eyes of the state, ensure that you have a very good explanation for the presence or transmittal of whichever files you use to hide others through steganography.

4.   Have a good explanation with respect to why your hard disk contains steganography software. Remember that even if you remove such programs (with the Software Add/Remove feature of Windows), they usually leave traces behind in the Registry; it goes without saying that the removed files must be wiped, as per Chapter 2).

11.6 Password cracking

Passwords are used to protect the following:

1.   Documents created with popular commercial software (e.g., Microsoft Word and WordPerfect).

2.   Public encryption keys (as in PGP). Because the keys in public-key encryption are much longer than in conventional encryption (see Chapter 10) and one cannot possibly remember the hundreds of random symbols of a typical public key, such keys are activated by entering a smaller password. Clearly it is far easier for one to try to crack a shorter sequence of symbols (the password) than the much longer sequence (the key).

3.   The document itself, encrypted with conventional encryption. Conventional encryption, such as IDEA, typically uses 128 bits (128:7 = 18 alphanumeric symbols). One can try to remember it, if it is a sequence that can be remembered. A 128-bit password, if (and only if) it is a truly random sequence of 128 bits (ones and zeroes), cannot be found through exhaustive search; the number of possibilities is simply too great ($2^{128} = 3.4 \times 10^{38}$; i.e., 34 followed by 37 zeros). Even if a computer tries a billion different keys every second, it will take 1.08×10^{28} years to go through all the keys. By comparison, the life left in the Sun is a mere 10 billion years. However, if one unwisely selects those 128 bits to be a sentence like "I hate passwords" (which is about 128 bits long), then an adversary would not find it too difficult to break it using openly available dictionary-search software and a cheap personal computer.

In password selection, as with anything else, technical knowledge is no substitute for common sense.

Numerous password-cracking software programs that basically do exhaustive searches of dictionary words are available through the Internet. Additionally, companies such as Access Data Corporation in Utah (www.accessdata.com) sell software that breaks the password protection of such popular programs as PKZip, WinZip, Word, Excel, WordPerfect, Lotus 1–2–3, Paradox, Q&A, Quattro-Pro, Ami Pro, Approach, QuickBooks, Act!, Pro Write, Access, Word Pro, DataPerfect, dBase, Symphony, Outlook, Express, MSMoney, Quicken, Scheduler+, Ascend, Netware, and Windows NT server/workstation.

Most people tend to use passwords that they can easily remember, such as permutations of family member names, birth dates, and so on, often abbreviated or spelled backward.

The following password-cracking software tools are openly available on the Internet:

- wordcrk.zip (attacks passwords of Microsoft Word documents);
- c2myazz.zip (spoofs Windows NT passwords);
- pwdump.zip (dumps the hash function values from NT.sam files);
- Pwdump.zip (obtains password information from the sam file);
- Samdump.zip (same as above);
- Pwlcrack.zip (obtains password information from memory);
- Pwltool.zip (attacks .pwl files);
- 95sscrk.zip (attacks Windows NT passwords);
- Winpass (breaks Windows screensaver passwords);
- Wfwcd (attacks passwords used in Microsoft Word);
- Wpcracka (same as above, but for WordPerfect files);
- sharepw.c (attacks Windows 95 share passwords);
- sharepwbin.c and exe (attacks Windows 95 share passwords);
- Glide (decrypts .pwl files);
- Crackerjack (cracks Unix passwords on PCs).

At the time of this writing, all of the above were downloadable from www.cotse.com/winnt.htm.

Openly available on the Internet is the following list of backdoor CMOS BIOS passwords:

Award bios

Award
AWARD_SW
SW_AWARD
AWARD?SW
LKWPETER
lkwpeter
j262
j256

AMI BIOS

AM
AMI
A.M.I.
AMI_SW
AMI?SW

Other BIOS

Syxz
oder
Wodj
bios
cmos
alfaromeo

It follows from the foregoing that one should choose a password that is both easy to remember and long enough to be at least as hard to break through known means as a 128-bit truly random sequence of bits. If one goes through a little arithmetic, this amounts to 107 truly random alphabetical letters if no distinction is made between uppecase and lowercase. That is not easy to remember either. And this is precisely why passwords that can be remembered are breakable and truly random encryption keys are not.

Clearly, the more random the password, the better. But the more random the password, the harder it is to remember.

Do not do the following:

 • Use phrases from poems or stories.
 • Depend on the password protection of commercial software such as MS Word, WordPerfect, and so on, but use full-blown encryption instead.
 • Use phrases from common foreign languages.
 • Use words, names, or dates that are related to your family and that others could figure out with minimal effort.
 • Use the same password for more than one piece of software.
 • Use the same password for a long period of time (beware of keystroke capture, as per Sections 4.3 and 4.4).
 • Write the password or pass phrase down on anything.

Do do the following:

 • Select a pass phrase that includes upper- and lowercase letters in unexpected places, as well as punctuation marks and numbers.
 • Select a pass phrase that cannot be remembered, yet which you can reconstruct. For example, the tenth word of the eleventh page of the first 22 books on your bookshelf in the precise order that the books are arranged. If an assertive intruder ransacks the books, the password is gone forever (or you can claim that it is).
 • Abide by the security precautions listed in Chapters 6 through 9 to preclude the possibility that your prized pass phrase may have been captured on your hard disk (in the swap or slack or by keystroke-capturing software).

The interested reader is referred to an excellent paper on the subject, "The Passphrase FAQ," at http://www.stack.nl/—galactus/remailers/pass-phrasefaq.html.

11.7 File integrity authenticity: digital digests

Given the ease with which it is possible to alter any digital document, there is an obvious need for ways to detect such alterations in such situations as the following:

1. *E-mail text.* There is all the difference in the world between a message to one's stockbroker that directs him or her "Buy 10 shares of stock" and one that says "Buy 10,000 shares of stock."

2. *Encryption software.* One would clearly like to know if the encryption software that is being trusted with sensitive information has been doctored since the time when it was known to be good.

Simply running a checksum that detects whether the number of "ones" is even or odd is not good enough.

A mathematically more elaborate version of a checksum is CRC. A mathematical operation is performed on the entire digital file of interest, and a digital summary is generated in the form of a sequence of a few numbers. An additional advantage of CRC over a checksum is that it is order sensitive, meaning that the strings "ABCD" and "DBCA" will produce totally different digital summaries. The odds that two different digital files can be created that will have the same CRC digital signature are about 1 in 4 billion.

Indeed, CRC is exactly the technique used by most hard disk drives to check on the integrity of every sector (a sector has 512 bytes). The CRC value is computed (and stored along with the data) when the data is stored in that sector, and it is recomputed when the data is read from that sector. If the two CRC values differ, then there has been a disk read/write error.

One can readily obtain crc.com through a vast number of servers from the Internet. It is in the public domain and free.

Caution: Early versions of CRC had flaws.

CRC checks were developed to detect accidental, not intentional, changes in data, and they serve that purpose very well.

Given the odds that CRC can be theoretically spoofed (1 in 4 billion is not all that small a probability when it comes to security), an even more robust mathematical algorithm has been replacing it: the MD5 hash. "Hashing" refers to the process of obtaining a digital digest or summary from a digital file. MD5 is an upgrade from MD4, which has been reported in the open literature to be broken [7].

The MD5 hash has 16 symbols (bytes) and is therefore $16 \times 8 = 128$ bits. It was originally developed by RSA, and it is in the public domain now. The odds that two files can be concocted that have the same MD5 hash digital signature are about 1 in 10^{38} (i.e., one in 10 followed by 37 zeros).

Software programs for computing the MD5 hash of a file are also available from multiple sources on the Internet by doing a keyword search for "MD5." The reader is strongly encouraged to download and use such software to verify the integrity of key files (such as encryption-related ones). It is a simple process, and it is well worth the minimal effort to do it. The savvy user should first determine the MD5 (or CRC) value of each and every sensitive file of interest, label and store those digital digests in some safe place other than the computer on which the files themselves reside, and periodically recheck by recomputing the MD5 or CRC values of the same sensitive files and comparing.

A better algorithm yet for digital message digests is SHA-1. Its output is 160 bits, and it has withstood the scrutiny of competent specialists. It is offered in both PGP and S/MIME, but it is roughly twice as slow as MD5 to compute, all else being equal.

11.8 Emergencies

11.8.1 Protecting sensitive data from a repressive regime

Obviously, in an emergency there is seldom time to wipe magnetic data from disks and tapes. Wiping (overwriting) a typical 120-GB hard disk can take hours. The only viable safe practice is not to write unencrypted sensitive data on data-storage media in the first place. There are two alternatives, which are not mutually exclusive:

1. All keyboard input should go to RAM and not to magnetic media. This means one should do the following:

    a. Direct all temporary files to a RAM disk (Section 6.2.2). If using software that sets its own location for temporary files, consider using some other software. For example, instead of using Microsoft Word, use Secure Office, discussed earlier in this book. Ideally, do not use Windows at all; use MS DOS instead and a RAM disk. Because file names often get stored in locations other than, and in addition to, those associated with the files themselves, do not use file names that are descriptive of the content.

    b. Make sure that you have enough RAM and that there is no swap file because the swap file would negate the very reason for having a RAM disk in the first place, which is not to have something written on the hard disk.

2. If sensitive data must be stored in magnetic media, it must be encrypted automatically on the fly and not as a separate step that one would have to do manually. This means you must do the following:

a. Use full-disk-encryption software (see Section 11.2). This way, anything written to disk is encrypted, specifically including the swap file, the Registry, and the slack (see Section 2.2.1).

b. As an alternative, use MS DOS and a simple text editor with no smarts (i.e., no temporary files and no activities running without a user's knowledge), rather than any version of Windows, work with a RAM disk on the sensitive files, and encrypt all things that are to be saved. In the worst case, you can turn the computer off and anything not encrypted will disappear.

11.8.2 A word of caution

The following point has already been made and cannot be overemphasized. Resources in even the most repressive regime are limited; everyone cannot be surveilled physically all the time. However, technology today makes it possible for most regimes to surveil the Internet and other telecommunications activities of everyone all the time (through automated procedures that scan for preprogrammed suspect activities or words. It follows that one should not attract attention to oneself by engaging in such readily observable alerting activities as routine use of encrypted e-mail (when today hardly any users encrypt their e-mail), exchanging inflammatory e-mail with others on topics that the local regime considers threatening, posting inappropriate messages in Usenet forums, frequenting Web sites and forums that a local regime finds offensive, and the like.

If you travel to repressive regimes, avoid bringing your own computer for use with respect to anything that could land you in a local jail. For your communications needs, consider patronizing other's computers, such as public libraries or Internet cafes (to see if one is available in a given area, check http://www.cyber-cafe.com/icafesearch.asp) and carry your encryption software in an encrypted floppy disk.

11.8.3 Getting discovered as a desirable persona

Realistically, no one personifies pure virtue. Because of this, it behooves one to have some carefully crafted "secret" that can be "reluctantly" surrendered to overzealous computer forensic investigators so that they do not go away empty handed, and mostly so that they can feel satisfied that they have done their job and there is no need to pursue a forensics investigation further. Such a surrenderable secret must be one that is believable and mildly embarrassing, but not one that would land you in jail. There is an even greater importance to having such a sacrificial lamb: It helps explain the reason for having encryption software in the first place.

And what if you live in a totalitarian regime and find strong evidence that your computer has been compromised? Obviously, there can be no one-size-fits-all advice because the prudent course of action would depend entirely on the specific circumstances. You would be well advised, however, to view this as the opportunity that it is and not as a cause for alarm. It is an opportunity because you have been provided with a direct pipeline to the regime, and you can use this pipeline to ensure that the image you present to the regime, or to whoever is monitoring you on its behalf, is precisely the one that you want to present and not the one that the totalitarian regime might suspect. Not too many suspects have this opportunity!

So, do not disable whatever mechanism you have discovered is monitoring your computer habits. Leave it alone, and let it monitor and inform on that side of your life that you want to advertise. Clean all of your magnetic media of anything remotely incriminating. This may also be a good time to plan a politically correct and graceful exit to another country.

Selected bibliography

Steganography

Anderson, R., (ed.), "Information Hiding: First International Workshop," *Lecture Notes in Computer Science*, Vol. 1174, New York: Springer-Verlag, 1996.

Anderson, R., and F. Petitcolas, "On the Limits of Steganography," *IEEE Journal on Selected Areas in Communications*, Vol. 16, No. 4, May 1998, pp. 474–481.

Aura, T., *Invisible Communication*, EET 1995, Technical Report, Helsinki University of Technology, Finland, November 1995, at http://deadlock. hut.fi/ste/ste html.htmi.

Bender, W., et al., "Techniques for Data Hiding," *IBM Systems Journal*, Vol. 35, Nos. 3 and 4, 1996, pp. 316–336.

Johnson, N. F., and S. Jajodia, "Exploring Steganography: Seeing the Unseen," *IEEE Computer*, Vol. 3, February 1998, pp. 26–34.

Petitcolas, F., R. Anderson, and M. Kuhn, "Attacks on Copyright Marking Systems," *Second Workshop on Information Hiding*, Portland, OR, April 1998, pp. 218–238.

Steganalysis

Kuhn, M., "Watermark and Steganography Analysis Tools," 1997, http://www.cl.cam.ac.uk/-fapp2/watermarking/image-watermarking/stirmark.

Sanders, D., "Stegodetect," steganography detection software tool, 1997.

"unZign," watermarking testing tool. (See http://altern.org/watermark.) Information available through unzign@hotmail.com, 1997.

Steganography software

Arachelian, R., White Noise Storm&trade (WNS), shareware, 1994, at ftp://ftp.csua.berkeley.edu/pub/cypherpunks/steganography/wns2IO.zip.

Black Wolf: StegoDos, Black Wolf's Picture Encoder, v0.90B, in the public domain, ftp://ftp.csua.berkeley.edu/pub/cypherpunks/steganography/stegodos.zip.

Brown, A., "S-Tools for Windows," shareware, 1994, ftp://idea.sec.dsi.unimi. it/pub/security/crypt/code/s-tools4.zip.

Digimarc Corporation, PictureMarc&trade, MarcSpider&trade, http:/www. digimarc.com.

Hansmann, F., Steganos, Deus Ex Machina Communications, www. steganography.com.

Hastur, H., Mandelsteg, ftp://idea.sec.dsi.unimi.it/pub/security/crypt/code.

Kutter, M., and F. Jordan, JK-PGS (Pretty Good Signature), Signal Processing Laboratory at Swiss Federal Institute of Technology (EPFL), http://ltswww. epfl.ch/,kutter/watermarking/JK PGS.html.

Machado, R., EzStego, Stego Online, Stego, www.stego.com.

Maroney, C., Hide and Seek, shareware, ftp://ftp.csua.berkeley.edu/pub/ cypherpunks/steganography/hdsk4lb.zip (version 4.1), http://www.rugeley. demon.co.uk/security/hdsk50.zip (version 5.0), www.cypher.net/products (version 1.0 for Windows 95).

MediaSec Technologies LLC, SysCop&trade, http://www.mediasec.com.

Repp, H., Hide4PGP, at http://www.rugeley.demon.co.uk/security/hide4pgp. zip.

Signum Technologies, SureSign, at http://www.signumtech.com.

Upham, D., Jpeg-Jsteg, at ftp://ftp.funet.fi/pub/crypt/steganography.

Passwords

Reinhold, A., "Diceware: (A Passphrase Generation System)," http://world. std.com/-Renhold/diceware.html.

RFC1750 Randomness Recommendations for Security, http://www.clark.net/ pub/cme/html/ranno.html.

Schneier, B., *Applied Cryptography*, New York: Wiley, 1994.

Ward, G., "Creating Passphrases from Shocking Nonsense," http://www.cert.lu/ cert-web/security/bibliography. html.

Williams, R. T., "A Simple Random Noise Source," July 1, 1995, posted to sci.crypt and alt.security.pgp, http://www.finerty.net/pjf/crypto/passphrase.txt.

References

[1]   Simpson, S., "PGP DH vs. RSA FAQ," http://www.scramdisk.clara.net/pgpfaq. html.

[2]   Tsiounis, Y., and M. Yung, "On the Security of El Gamal-Based Encryption," *PKC 98, LNCS*, Berlin: Springer-Verlag, 1998, http://citeseer.nj.nec.com/tsiounis98 security.html.

[3]   Menezes, A. J., P. C. van Oorschot, and S. A. Vanstone, *Handbook of Applied Cryptography*, Boca Raton, FL: CRC Press, 1997.

[4]   Schlafly, R., "Re: El Gamal vs. RSA," sci.crypt USENET posting, March 11, 1999.

[5]   Young, A., and M. Yung, "The Dark Side of 'Black-Box' Cryptography or Should We Trust Capstone?" *Crypto '96*, 1996, pp. 89–103.

[6]   Senderek, R., "Key Experiments: How PGP Deals with Manipulated Keys, An Experimental Approach," August 2000, http://Senderek.de/security/key-experiments.html.

[7]   RSA FAQ v4, 1998, http://www.rsa.com.

12

Link Encryption: VPNs

If one could count on having phone lines dedicated exclusively to one's private use, then one would only have to worry about wiretapping. But leased phone lines are very expensive and even the largest industrial conglomerates are foregoing such lines and moving to the Internet, where circuits can be shared as a means of drastically driving costs down. This was the bottom line behind the migration from switched circuits to packet switching. The latter is like the post office where individual pieces of mail ("packets" in the digital case) get sent through a vast network, which routes them to their destination through whichever path is most appropriate at any one time.

Given the notorious insecurity of Internet paths, organizations and individuals have wished for VPNs, that is, technical means whereby one can use inexpensive public networks such as the Internet, yet have end-to-end encryption. Such networks are "virtual" in the sense that they act as if they were dedicated private networks when in fact they are not. The physical connection is dynamic in that it may well change several times during a data transmittal, yet the users are unaffected by this because the data packets will arrive at their destination regardless.

There is a lot of hype and mystique about VPNs; in a nutshell, all they do is to encrypt all data before it gets put in the standard Internet packet en route to that packet's destination and decrypt it at the other end.[1] This way, one has end-to-end encryption for anything that gets sent down the pipe by the sender to the recipient.

Some 70% of large businesses today use VPNs for all inter-office traffic.

---

1. The term "tunneling" is also used synonymously with VPN; it is just another way of saying that one takes the unencrypted data, encrypts it, encapsulates it inside the normal IP packet, and sends it to its destination as if one had a private tunnel to that destination.

A VPN connection has to provide much more than mere encryption of the content of the communication; it has to provide four elements:

1. Authentication of the sender (to prevent spoofing);

2. Access control (to prevent unauthorized access);

3. Confidentiality of the content of the data;

4. Guarantee of message integrity (i.e., to ensure that the data cannot be modified in transit).

Figure 12.1 depicts the concept of a VPN.

The VPN client is simply the sending computer; the VPN server is the receiving computer. Either one can be part of a local area network (LAN).

There are numerous ways of implementing the above concept for encrypting data in transit. The first one, popularized by Microsoft, is the "Point-to-Point Tunneling Protocol" (PPTP). It uses TCP port 1723, which makes it easy for some nations and some ISPs to block[2] that port and hence PPTP.

PPTP is built into Windows, and it is free and easy to set up and use. There is a negative side, however:

1   It is a proprietary protocol. The receiving server is almost always a Windows NT computer.

2. Its security has been questioned by noted cryptographer Bruce Schneier (see www.counterpane.com), who easily broke early

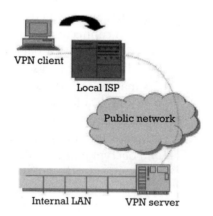

Figure 12.1   The VPN concept.

---

2. In fact, many high speed ISPs do block this port for residential accounts, claiming that VPN is a business activity and that users should pay the business rate (which is higher) if they want to do VPN. In practice, this limitation is silly because there are other VPN software packages that use randomly selected ports for each connection, thereby precluding an ISP from blocking the activity as an ISP cannot block all ports if it expects to stay in business.

versions of it. Its 128-bit encryption key is derived from the user password, which means that an attacker would only need to attack the user password and not the full 128-bit encryption space.

3. It provides no means for encryption key management.

Microsoft's PPTP has been largely superceded by nonproprietary protocols, such as the following:

1. L2F, the heir apparent to PPTP;

2. Layer 2 Tunneling Protocol (L2TP). which is an improvement upon L2F in that it includes rate control to L2F.

Both L2F and L2TP can function over non-IP networks such as Frame Relay, Asynchronous Transfer Mode (ATM), X.25, or Sonet, and they use much stronger encryption than PPTP; in fact their encryption is derived from yet another VPN implementation known as IPsec (see Section 12.2).

12.1 Split tunneling

This is a security nightmare for organizations that have implemented VPNs to allow employees to connect securely to the organization's server from wherever these employees happen to be (e.g., home, traveling).

The problem is depicted in Figure 12.2. If the remotely located computer (e.g., an employee's personal computer or laptop) is tinkered with by the employee to allow concurrent Internet connection to the commercial Internet in addition to the connection to the corporate VPN server, then the

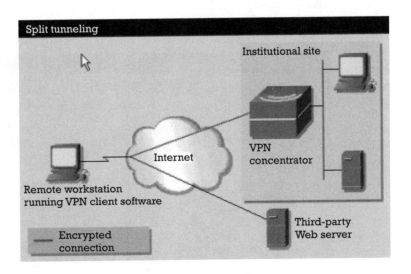

Figure 12.2 Split-tunneling security problem.

employee's computer can be used by malicious Internet hackers as a bridge to access the inner sanctum of the institutional site.

This tinkering amounts to a very simple modification: In a typical setup, the default gateway to the Internet is set up to be the ISP's router, in this case, the institutional site's chosen server address (see Figure 12.3).

If the above selection is unchecked and the employee specifies his or her own remote network gateway, then the employee can establish and maintain a connection to the commercial Internet in addition to the VPN connection to the employer's trusted databases. This is about as bad a security vulnerability as there can be as far as the VPN server at an institutional site is concerned.

12.2   IPsec

IPsec is a set of protocols agreed to by the IETF, the respected organization that develops standards for the otherwise chaotic Internet. Unlike PPTP, it is an open protocol and its intent is again to provide the four security elements needed from a VPN connection (authentication, access control, confidentiality, and message integrity). Additionally, IPsec offers the capability to prevent data replay (e.g., to prevent someone from recording a banking transaction and then playing it back again and again until the victim's bank account has been depleted) and allows verification of the sender's address and identity.

IPsec was born out of efforts to secure the next-generation Internet known as IPv6, but IPsec is also usable on today's IPv4 Internet as well. It can easily be integrated with the existing Internet infrastructure and can be transparent to the user.

IPsec has been available since the early 1990s, so why is it not everpresent today? Numerous reasons have offset the fact that IPsec is the best VPN scheme:

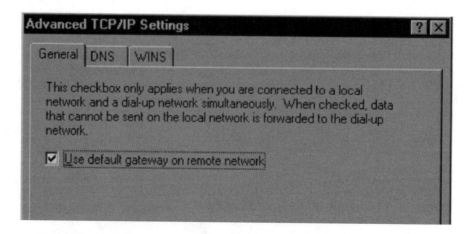

Figure 12.3   Setting that prevents split tunneling.

1. Since IPsec was first developed, SSL (see Section 9.7.1) became very popular for encrypting online transactions and even securing e-mail. This removed a lot of pressure for the need for IPsec.

2. IPsec was primarily intended for IPv6, which was itself created primarily because the world was rapidly running out of Internet addresses (IP addresses). In the meantime, a technique known as Network Address Translation (NAT) was developed which removed the shortage of IP addresses for the foreseeable future by allowing internal networks connected to the Internet to have their own internal IP addresses and not to need IP addresses from the dwindling pool.

3. Different vendors' IPsec gear often does not work with other vendors' IPsec gear due to a lack of standardization.

4. Unlike, say, AES, where there was individual competition, IPsec is the classic outcome of a team effort where everyone feels strongly about having his or her contribution included in the end result. As a result, IPsec offers four different ways of doing the same thing and is needlessly complex. Complexity is the enemy of security; there are too many options and too many things can go wrong in any given implementation.

5. IPsec documentation lacks a statement of the problem and an overview of how it goes about solving that problem. Instead, it reads like an encyclopedia without a unifying purpose.

6. Some of its protocols (AH, rather than ESP) are incompatible with NAT, which is the de facto reality today, not only in organizations but also in most individuals' home networks.

12.3 Summary

VPN implementations, whether by PPTP, L2F, L2TP or IPsec, do indeed provide the individual who connects to the appropriate server through such connections adequate security from wiretapping, and the individual does not have to worry about individual file encryption as a protection from wiretapping on that particular connection. But this solves the institutional organization's security problem with geographically dispersed employees; it does not really address the individual's concern about protecting the content of a file or communication from any and all threats, such as the following:

1. Confiscation of or unauthorized attempts to view sensitive files while they are in the possession of the individual;

2. Interception by the ISP or by wiretapping while that file is being transmitted to another individual rather than to an organization's VPN server.

Selected bibliography

VPN tutorials

http://compnetworking.about.com/library/weekly/aa010701a.htm.

http://www.homenethelp.com/vpn.

http://www.alliancedatacom.com/vpn-tutorial.htm.

http://www.dwtechnology.com/lsns97/Lsn97_1.asp.

IPsec tutorials

http://www.networkmagazine.com/article/DCM20000509S0082.

http://portal.acm.org/citation.cfm?id=352601&jmp=indexterms&dl=portal&dl=ACM.

http://tricolour.net/freeswan/oclug2003-01-30/toc.html.

Security of Wireless Connectivity: Wi-Fi and Bluetooth

13.1 Background

Wireless connectivity for computers has had a colorful history. Because the cellular industry has had an established infrastructure in place, it has had an obvious advantage over any competitor without such an infrastructure in place—such as the now defunct Ricochet network in the United States.

Cellular Digital Packet Data (CDPD) is a data-transmission technology developed for use on the "old" analog cellular system known as the advanced mobile phone system (AMPS) in the 800- to 900-MHz range. It transmits data in packets and offers data transfer rates of up to 19.2 Kbps (usually much lower), as well as better error correction than is possible using conventional modems on an analog cellular channel since modems were designed with error-free copper wire lines in mind and error-prone wireless channels.

As digital cellular systems evolved, digital-data capabilities did too. General Packet Radio Service (GPRS) is the current data-communications standard for GSM and runs at speeds up to 115 Kbps (usually much slower in practice). Not to be left behind, competing digital cellular systems in the United States, such as time division multiple access (TDMA) used by AT&T and code division multiple access (CDMA) used by Sprint PCS, advanced their own data-communications schemes with roughly comparable performance.

The latest entrant, Evolution Data Optimized (EVDO), is considered a third generation (3G) cellular technology with a maximum predicted throughput of 2.4 Mbps, which declines with distance from the cellular tower and, as with all cellular-based systems, with the number of users on the network. As of late 2003, it is being offered in the United States by Verizon Company and in South Korea by SK Telecom.

Cellular service providers have yet to find the long-sought killer application that will motivate users to use the high bandwidths promised by 3G cell phones, such as EVDO. The novelty of being able to take and send a photograph with a cell phone wears thin pretty fast. Indeed, the 802.11 technologies[1] described next already offer much higher data rates than even 3G cellular telephony; worse yet for the cellular providers, 802.11 technology can easily support telephony via the Internet itself.

13.2   The 802.11 technologies

As with many technology offerings, their commercial success depends less on the technical merits and more on the pricing packages. Integrated System Digital Network (ISDN), a wired technology, died in the United States because the telephone companies insisted on billing by the minute and by the amount of data handled; users migrated en masse to the much higher-speed Internet access provided by cable TV companies that offered a flat rate. The telephone companies, whose twisted-pair copper wires cannot even approach the bandwidth capability of cable TV's coaxial cables and fiber optic lines, were forced to take heroic technical measures and came up with the digital subscriber line (DSL) for which they began charging usage-independent flat rates.

Similarly, largely as a result of cellular telephone service providers' insistence on billing Internet users by the minute and by the amount of data handled, alternate technologies became popular that do not force users to keep an eye on their watch and on the amount of data they send or receive. These alternate technologies, initially standardized by the Institute of Electrical and Electronic Engineers (IEEE) as standard 802.11, were not anticipated for use for public access to the Internet, but for wireless LANs, so as to eliminate the expense of installing data cables all over a small building or house.

Standard 802.11 was initially developed in 1997 for a throughput of 1 to 2 Mbps. Then, 802.11b became a standard in 1999 with a throughout of 11 Mbps in the 2.48-GHz band. This was followed by 802.11a[2] in 1999 with a 54-Mbps maximum throughput (actually 2 to 30 Mbps in practice) in the 5-GHz band; 802.11g with 54 Mbps in the 2.48-GHz band; and 802.11x and 802.11i, which are being finalized at the time of this writing to take care of a number of security-related flaws in the 802.11b,a,g implementations. All use international scientific/medical (ISM) frequency bands, which require

1. "802" is the general designator for network standards; "11" is the family of standards governing wireless LANs.

2. The 5-GHz ISM allocation is not only less crowded with other services (baby monitors, cordless phones, and so on.), but it is also much broader and allows for at least eight simultaneous 802.11 channels versus three simultaneous channels in the 2.48-GHz ISM band. An additional 255 MHz in this band already available in Europe will become unlicensed in the United States.

no licensing. The 2.48-GHz band is shared with baby monitors, wireless home links, cordless phones, and the like.

Other competing standards include the following:

> 802.11e, which offers quality-of-service (QoS) guarantees;

> 802.11f, for interaccess point communications;

> 802.11h, which supports European requirements for 802.11a.

802.11 devices can be configured in either a peer-to-peer mode or in the much more common fixed-access-point mode where an AP (or base station) is set up where there is wired connection to high-speed Internet, and 802.11-equipped computers gain wireless access to it.

Since the end of 2003, at least half of all corporate laptops have wireless LAN connectivity, according to Gartner/Dataquest (http://www.idc.com). Research from IDC estimates that by there are already more than 54 million Wi-Fi users in the world, 28 million of whom are in the United States.

Contrary to popular belief and the claims made on the packages of 802.11 devices, the range figures provided mean absolutely nothing. The range depends on the following

1. The gain of the antenna on both ends of the link;

2. The terrain in between the two communicating stations;

3. The quality of the design and engineering of the devices (e.g., sensitivity and selectivity of the receivers, transmitter power output that reaches the antenna);

4. The exact nature of any obstructions between the transmitter and the receiver (California-style stucco walls with a built-in chicken-fence wire that severely attenuates radio signals? Wet cement?);

5. The extent, specific technical details, and precise location of any interfering radio sources in the vicinity, such as baby monitors, poorly designed microwave ovens, arc-welders, diathermy machines, cordless phones, and the like.

And herein lie the major security vulnerabilities of any wireless data line to be discussed in this section:

1. Such links can be intercepted from a distance far greater that the range over which they are operated, as long as the interceptor has a better antenna and is at a reasonably good location (such as a high-elevation building a mile away or in a car parked a few blocks away). Because there are no wires, there is no smoking gun leading to the interceptor. This is the idea behind the popular practice of war driving whereby individuals drive around town with their 802.11-equipped laptop computers seeking (and obtaining) free access to any 802.11 networks that have not been adequately secured.

2.   Such links can readily be jammed by anyone using home-brewed transmitters built for this purpose.

In a stroke of marketing genius that is technically laughable, the concept of Wired Equivalence Protocol (WEP) was created for 802.11 devices. In fact, the security of wireless devices can never be equivalent to wired networks because of the two reasons just mentioned, even if the design is technically superb. In the case of 802.11a,b,g devices, the specs and implementation are so bad from a security perspective that the WEP concept has been an embarrassment that is rapidly being shoved under the carpet and replaced with a new security set of standards, Wi-Fi Protected Access (WPA).

13.2.1 WEP insecurity

WEP does not provide end-to-end security but only attempts to secure the wireless portion, and very unsuccessfully at that. Out of the box it comes with no security enabled, which is most unfortunate, as most users have neither the know-how nor the inclination to tinker with the 802.11 devices they have just bought.

WEP aimed to provide the following:

1.   Authentication. The media access control (MAC) address is the supposedly unchangeable (but actually very changeable) unique electronic serial number of each network interface card and node in a network. WEP can be configured to deal with only the MAC addresses that the user specifies during the optional customization at installation time.

2.   Confidentiality. This is achieved through encryption. Sadly, the encryption implementation for WEP is laughable.

3.   Integrity.

When activated, most 802.11a,b,g APs broadcast their Service Set Identifier (SSID) to the world; unless the user has bothered to change it during the optional customization, the SSID is the same for all units of any manufacturer, which allows the war driver to infer the rest of the technical parameters of the unit. Some newer units wisely allow one the option of disabling the broadcasting of the SSID until a client unit transmits a request for service; depending on whether the system has been configured for open or closed authentication, the AP will or will not allow access to a client unit seeking access with an old SSID. Amusingly, even in the closed authentication mode, where the client unit has to send the same SSID as that of the AP, the AP obliges by broadcasting the SSID anyway.

If encryption is enabled, which it almost never is, a challenge-response handshaking ritual allows only users with the correct encryption key to join

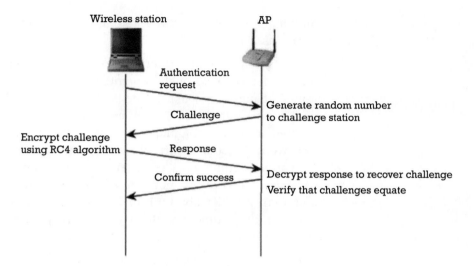

Figure 13.1   Handshaking protocol in Wi-Fi.

in, and all subsequent communications with those users are encrypted. The specifics of the handshaking are depicted in Figure 13.1.

Notice that this ritual does not identify the AP to the client wireless user in any secure way; anyone can masquerade as the AP, and this makes the entire ritual vulnerable to a classic man-in-the-middle attack.

The use of symmetric encryption of up to 128 bits is fine in theory, but the implementation is a shining example of how not to implement encryption:

1. In the interest of making the manual entry of up to 128 bits of an encryption key less tedious, many implementations allows the user to enter a keyword of the user's choice, such as the user's first name, which is then converted into the encryption key. Anyone with the same manufacturer's device (conveniently broadcast in the SSID) can try a handful of plausible keywords and gain access. The 128-bit encryption has been reduced to making a few reasonable guesses as to the keyword used.

2. The encryption used is the standard RC4 algorithm by MIT's Ron Shamir, which exclusive-ORs data with the pseudorandom stream created by a built-in linear shift register using 40-104 (and not 128 as commonly believed) keys. The "128-bit-key" illusion comes from adding these 104 bits to the 24 bit initialization vector (IV), which is sent unencrypted as clear text for the benefit of any interceptor. Indeed, the cryptanalytic attack is so well known that it has been reduced into a script available over the Internet. The IV itself is (in at least one major vendor's products) set at 24 zeros; even when it isn't, the shift register is short enough that the ostensibly pseudorandom

output of the shift register repeats often enough to aid in the breaking of that code.[3]

3. 802.11 specifies no means for encryption-key management. Those readers familiar with public key interface (PKI) know all too well how problematic key management and key distribution are. WEP keys can be introduced (if they are introduced at all) that never change, or that are not unique, or that are factory defaults (such as "password"), or that are trivial (such as one's name or birth date). Similarly, enterprise management of the WEP cases is very cumbersome because WEP does not scale well to a large number of devices and users. Additionally. WEP keys are often shared in a large network for a long time with the obvious consequences if one link is compromised.

4. The same IV is used in all devices by a given manufacturer. This results in identical key streams for all devices in a network. Also, the IV is short (24 bits), which means that the pseudorandom sequence repeats often (see footnote 3). And it is transmitted in the clear, too!

5. A noncryptographic checksum (actually a CRC digital digest) acknowledges packets with the correct CRC value. This can be exploited by an attacker who systematically modifies packets and CRC, sends the CRC to the AP, and looks for acknowledgement.

6. Contrary to popular belief, increasing the encryption key length above 128 will not solve the security problems of WEP because, as shown above, the security problems are with the IV. As such, 802.11g and 802.11a are no more secure than the popular 802.11b. There are numerous products peddled on the Internet for breaking 802.11 WEP security.

13.2.2 War driving and war chalking

War driving (a term based on the movie *War Games* where a teenager sets his modem up to dial a large number of random phone numbers to identity which were answered by a modem, a.k.a. "war dialing") amounts to driving

---

3. For the mathematically inclined, practically all modern encryption schemes need a pseudorandom sequence. They are most easily generated with a linear shift register having some number of taps whose sum is fed into the input of the shift register. If (and only if) these taps are at the right places in an n-stage linear shift register, then one can get the full $2^n - 1$ stream of bits from the shift register before the entire sequence coming out of it repeats. This is known as a "maximal linear sequence." If an interceptor knows or can guess where these taps are placed, the number of stages of the shift register, and the value (1 or 0) entered into each stage when the shift register is started up (the IV), then the interceptor can duplicate the shift register and negate all encryption based on it. Ideally, one would like to have a truly random source of bits (as opposed to a pseudorandom one), such as one based on the time between emissions of particles of a radioactive decay source or on the amplifier noise (thermal or $1/f$) of a semiconductor. This is quite easy; the practical problem is that this truly random source has to be duplicated at both ends of the communications link, which means that it cannot be truly random.

down the street looking for SSID broadcasts, at which time one attempts to obtain access to the 802.11 network one has stumbled onto. If successful, and depending on how insecurely that network has been configured, the war driver gains free access not only to the Internet but also to the networked computers and their files themselves. Free access to the Internet is not as innocuous as it may sound; consider the possibility that the war driver may engage in some illegal act (e.g., sending a threatening e-mail to the president or engaging in online fraud), which will be traced back to the unsuspecting penetrated wireless network.

War chalking is based on the Depression-era practice when homeless people would use chalk to mark compassionate households that offered food to the hungry so that others would know to go there too. In the 802.11 context, the term refers to chalk marks that indicate to war drivers where free Internet access can be obtained without the knowledge of the owner of the wireless network. War chalking is more than a passing fad; www.warchalking.org has a vast listing of relevant hot spots around the world, plus numerous helpful pointers. From an Internet communications privacy and anonymity perspective, such a database can be priceless.

13.2.3 Using Wi-Fi while traveling

Wi-Fi popularity is expanding at an unforeseen rate, much to the consternation of cellular telephone companies that had hoped to capture the revenue from "road warriors" in hotels and airports and coffee shops. Figure 13.2 shows a chart from Source Analytics that attests to this explosive worldwide growth.

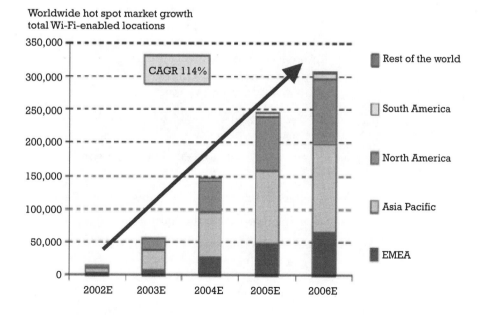

Figure 13.2 Market for Wi-Fi.

The problem with this is that a vast number of Wi-Fi users are exposing themselves to huge security vulnerabilities for the following reasons:

1. Most of the hundreds of thousands of hot spots operate in a default mode of no encryption. The person using a laptop across the room from you in a hotel, airport, or coffee shop may busily be reading all of your incoming and outgoing traffic unless you have the foresight to connect with either SSL or VPN, either of which applies encryption on top of whatever you are communicating.

2. Most of the users of Wi-Fi have not bothered to disable file sharing in their computers or to unbind TCP from everything else in their protocol settings. As a result, they are vulnerable to anyone in the network having access to the files on their Wi-Fi connected computers.

Interestingly, although (or perhaps because) the number of Wi-Fi hot spots is exploding, there is no evidence that vendors are making any money from it. Users are increasingly expecting to use it at no charge. Some vendors view the provision of Wi-Fi service as a means of attracting customers to the vendors' main money-making business, such as selling coffee (select Starbuck's), selling food (select MacDonald's stores), or renting rooms to businessmen (select hotels). As such, vendors are not much interested in the security aspects of Wi-Fi.

13.2.4 WPA

WPA is the long overdue fix to WEP. It is a significant improvement over WEP, but it will take time before the vast number of 802.11b devices and APs in the field are replaced with WPA ones.

WPA is an improvement over WEP in the following ways:

1. RC4 encryption key is constructed from the hashed value of a WEP key and a serially increasing IV, as opposed to concatenating the shared WEP key and vendor's IV.

2. Instead of a simple 32-bit CRC check, WPA uses a CRC check plus a message integrity code.

3. Encryption is no longer optional. Algorithms supported include AES.

4. It offers increased security against replay attacks.

5. It offers improved authentication through a two-step process.

6. It eliminates the currently known WEP flaws and makes it easier to upgrade both clients and APs.

WPA is not a cure-all. It does not address the key-distribution problem, it has a somewhat degraded performance compared to WEP, and it is not widely used yet.

Also, as of summer of 2004, WPA is still a temporary protocol that has not been officially recognized by the IEEE yet. Even so, Microsoft offers a download for WPA drivers for Windows XP only.

For these reasons, the specific countermeasures discussed in Section 13.2.5 are recommended.

13.2.5   Securing 802.11

It is realistically impossible to give a quantitative estimate of the "goodness" of each of the security measures proposed here. One cannot even give a measure of the effectiveness of a lock in one's front door in the abstract: The effectiveness depends on the neighborhood, on whether or not one leaves the backdoor open, on whether the house is a target because of a local belief that it contains valuables, and so forth.

At best, one can view the suggestions below as "recommended best practices," just as one would recommend the—now commonplace—recommendations in physical and personal security.

1. Place the wireless AP in a low-elevation room such as the basement to minimize its interceptability from any credible distance outside the premises.

2. If possible, forego WEP altogether and use the new WAP standard.

3. Disable file sharing in the networked computers so as to provide an additional layer of difficulty for a war driver who may penetrate your wireless LAN.

4. Disconnect Internet access when not using it to prevent a war driver from conducting illegal activities on your Internet account that will incriminate you and for which you will be legally liable.

5. Power off the 802.11 AP when not using it.

6. Change the manufacturer's default SSID and keep changing it on a regular basis.

7. Disable SSID broadcasting.

8. Disable the promiscuous mode and require SSID matches.

9. Enable MAC authentication. This is no cure-all; it only delays the determined attacker's success as the attacker has to wait until an authorized computer sends a packet.

10. Enable 128-bit encryption.

11. Enter the encryption key manually, not through a guessable keyword, and keep changing it on a regular basis.

12. Use Network Address Translation (NAT) with Dynamic Host Configuration Protocol (DHCP) (i.e., get a DHCP-enabled switch between the high-speed Internet connection and preferably one with a built-in stateful inspection firewall). Enabling NAT is also not a cure; it simply hides some information of use to an attacker. It does not thwart an attack but only delays its success.

13. Use a software firewall (such as Zone Alarm) at its most conservative settings.

14. Do not depend on 802.11 WEP encryption. Use your own encryption on top of 802.11 (e.g., PGP); that is, use Application Layer security.

13.3 Bluetooth wireless link security issues

Named after the tenth-century Danish king Harald Bluetooth and now standardized as IEEE 802.15, Bluetooth was intended to replace the finicky infrared (IR) links and some of the many cables connecting computers with peripherals and extensions. It is also used as a network access link, and this creates a lot of the security issues because the Bluetooth link can be used as the entry point to compromise an entire network.

The standard was developed by Ericsson, Nokia, IBM, and Toshiba in 1998, and some 2000 companies have joined in since then. Bluetooth has gained acceptance in Europe and the East, but has never gained any commercial success in the United States

As with 802.11b and 802.11g, Bluetooth uses the 2.4-GHz ISM unlicensed frequency band which is not quite "international": Whereas there are 79 channels available for use in Europe and the United States, there are only 23 channels available for use in most other countries.

Data rate is only around 720 Kbps, which is slow compared to 802.11, but eight times faster than the typical serial ports of computers. Unlike 802.11, Bluetooth signals change frequency (frequency hop) 65,000 times per second, which is fast even by military standards. This makes it harder to intercept or to jam. Also unlike 802.11, it uses forward-error-control coding to reduce the bit-error rate.

Bluetooth devices use stronger authentication and encryption than 802.11 devices. One should keep in mind that the question, Is it strong enough? cannot be answered in the abstract. Strong enough for what? Under what operating conditions? Assuming what capabilities of the attacker?

Bluetooth is viewed as a short-range link and has three classes of devices, one of which (class 1) can have ranges comparable to those of 802.11:

1. Class 3: 1mW;

2. Class 2: 1–2.5mW;

3. Class 1: up to 100mW.

A given master device, roughly analogous to an AP in 802.11 lingo, can communicate with up to seven active slaves. If more connectivity is needed (e.g., in a meeting with many Bluetooth-equipped laptops), up to 10 "subnets" can be grouped into "scatternets." A single master can also accommodate up to 255 inactive slaves.

13.3.1 Bluetooth security threats

Like any network security threats, Bluetooth security threats include disclosure threats (e.g., identification and tracking of a user or interception of the content of a communication), integrity threats (e.g., spoofing, malicious change of the data, or man-in-the-middle attacks), or denial-of-service threats (such as disruption of the link or the entire network).

As with any wireless network, physical security is unable to cope with a link that does not obey physical boundaries (unless it is in a shielded Faraday Cage). Interception can occur from distances far greater than the operating range of the link, and there will be no smoking gun to incriminate the interceptor.

Bluetooth can be configured in any one of three security modes, two of which offer no security to speak of:

1. Mode 1. No security. This mode allows any Bluetooth device to initiate communications with a device operating in this promiscuous mode.

2. Mode 2. No Bluetooth security, but software applications implement their own security (if any). In practical terms, this means that any outside device can still connect, but it may not be able to access the software applications.

3. Mode 3. This is the only secure mode in that it enables both authentication and encryption.

Device authentication uses a 48-bit physical device address. Once connected, Bluetooth devices exchange a challenge/response based on a shared secret and encryption that is between 8 and 128 bits,[4] depending on local legal restrictions to facilitate government interception.[5] The encryption cipher is "E0," which is considered to be quite acceptable.[6] If authentication fails, the waiting times for retry increase exponentially so as to frustrate an exhaustive search attack.

Bluetooth authentication is not intended to replace network authentication if a Bluetooth device is used for network access. One should use end-to-end encryption on top of Bluetooth security in such cases, such as IPsec, PPTP or its heirs apparent L2F and L2TP. Red Fang, a Linux program

---

4. Encryption key size (between 8 and 128 bits) is negotiated between two units, each of which has its own maximum allowed key length, as well as its own minimum acceptable key length. If there is no common ground, key-length negotiation may fail.

5. The verifier issues a 128-bit challenge to the claimant. The claimant then applies encryption using the challenge, its own 48-bit Bluetooth address, and the current link key and returns to the verifier the 32 most-significant bits of the 128-bit result. The verifier confirms the response, and this concludes the authentication.

6. Just like 802.11 with its use of RC4 encryption, E0 also requires an IV; this one is a digital hash derived from a pseudorandom number, the link key (described in Section 13.3.1), and a byproduct of the authentication procedure.

developed by Ollie Whitehouse to demonstrate Bluetooth security weaknesses, sends queries over a large range of addresses until the targeted unit replies. This narrows down the search range to the address space of a single chip vendor, a task that can be completed within an hour and a half. Version 1.2 introduced a new anonymity mode countermeasure to defeat Red Fang.

Bluetooth devices intended to communicate securely (Mode 3, above) are brought close to each other in what is called a bonding session. The process is started by pushing a button on each of them that allows them to share a link key (the shared secret) which can be used in the future by each to generate a new encryption key for each such future session.

Note the following:

1. This bonding does not authenticate users but only the devices. To authenticate the user, there is an option for a user to enter a PIN each time a link is established; this PIN is usually stored in nonvolatile memory, which is a source of concern because any unauthorized user can use it as well.

2. If this link key is intercepted during bonding, the interceptor can compromise all subsequent communications to either of these bonded devices.

There are two major types of link keys:

1. Unit keys, generated by a single Bluetooth device independently of any other devices. These are used when a single master wants to broadcast securely to a number of slaves. This key is stored in nonvolatile memory, with the obvious security problems that result.

2. Combination keys, generated for each new pair of Bluetooth devices using link keys. These are preferred and more secure.

The number and types of possible attacks on Bluetooth security are numerous:

1. Many vendors' Bluetooth devices default to sharing all files with any Bluetooth device that knows a given device's address.

2. Unless configured otherwise, battery operated Bluetooth devices that are flooded with over-the-air requests will keep replying no until their batteries run out.

3. A malicious authenticated receiver that does not acknowledge a request will force the sending Bluetooth device to keep sending until its battery runs out.

4. Once the 48-bit ID of the Bluetooth device has been associated with someone (or with some organization), that individual and his or her

activities can be tracked. The ID is sent in an unencrypted header with every message.

5. The PIN code option poses a usability problem. Having to enter it twice every time one connects two devices is irksome; having to do so for a piconetwork of many devices is unbearable. Not surprisingly, some 50% of Bluetooth devices with PINs are set to "0000."

6. There is no elegant way to generate and distribute PINs.

7. There is no way to blacklist a Bluetooth device that has been compromised so as to prevent it from receiving information.

8. The Bluetooth-enabled devices themselves are usually insecure; microphones can be enabled remotely, and Trojan malware (e.g., BO, BO2K, Netbus) can be installed.

9. Bluetooth devices are vulnerable to the following attack: If devices A and B negotiate to use device A's unit key as their link key and, later on, device C communicates with device A and also uses A's key as its link key, then device C can fake its own device address in the future, calculate the decryption key, and eavesdrop on any communication between A and B. Device C can also authenticate itself to A as being B or to B as being A.

10. Bluetooth devices are also vulnerable to a replay attack. If an attacker records all 79 channels between two devices (say, a PDA and a wireless router at a bank), then the attacker can play back the PDA's transmissions causing the bank to honor each transaction and empty the user's bank account.

11. In the default discoverable mode, Bluetooth units respond to inquiries made by other devices and transmit their identities in response to an inquiry. A user can be tracked this way with more precision and less expense in custom equipment than the user of a cell phone.

12. Because Bluetooth devices do not register when joining a network, they are invisible to network administrators who cannot manage such devices centrally.

13.3.2   Recommended steps for enhancing security of Bluetooth devices

▸ Use combination keys, never unit keys.

▸ Configure the Bluetooth device to use only Mode 3.

▸ Perform any bonding procedures in a secure environment only.

▸ Require that PIN numbers be enabled, changed frequently, be nontrivial, and, if allowed, consist of more than four digits.

▸ Disable the storing of PIN numbers in the nonvolatile memory of Bluetooth devices (or on little papers taped on the devices).

‣ When using Bluetooth devices to connect to a secure network, use additional authentication and encryption (such as IPsec, PPTP, or Application Layer security) on top of whatever Bluetooth offers.

Selected bibliography

Wi-Fi security

http://www.wi-fiplanet.com/tutorials/article.php/1495811.

http://www.pcworld.com/news/article/0,aid,109482,00.asp.

http://www.informationweek.com/story/showArticle.jhtml?articleID=108081 86.

http://www.infoworld.com/article/03/01/10/030113newifisec_1.html.

http://www.smallbusinesscomputing.com/webmaster/article.php/1498861.

Bluetooth security

http://www.niksula.cs.hut.fi/~jiitv/bluesec.html.

http://www.vnunet.com/News/1151614.

news.zdnet.co.uk/communications/wireless/0,39020348,39145886,00.htm.

http://www.palowireless.com/bluetooth/security.asp.

maccentral.macworld.com/news/2004/02/11/bluetooth.

CHAPTER

14

Contents

Other Computer-Related Threats to Privacy

Even if a computer is defined as a box with a keyboard, mouse, and screen, numerous threats to privacy are introduced by its application beyond the purposes of a personal computer. Realistically, a computer is defined not by its shape today, but by its function; as such, the term includes PDAs and a plethora of other electronic devices that perform extensive digital computations. Such other devices' computational power often exceeds that of the mainframe computers of yesteryear, despite their deceptively small physical size. The threats to privacy posed by such computer-based devices are formidable, as will be shown below.

14.1 Commercial GPS devices

The GPS network consists of 24 satellites in half-geosynchronous altitude (i.e., 11,000 nautical miles up) in three orbital planes so that at least three, or preferably four, of them can be "seen" from most any part of the world at any one time. The requirement for four satellites follows from the fact that there are four unknowns to be derived (three positional coordinates plus time), which requires the simultaneous solution of four equations. These satellites continuously transmit radio signals that when received and processed by any suitable receiver, allow the user of that receiver to infer his or her position in all three dimensions. Depending on the specifics of the GPS receiver (e.g. whether it is authorized to receive the very accurate P code or only the tenfold less accurate C/A code, whether it avails itself of correction signals sent from terrestrial transmitters, and whether it does any integration or averaging of successive estimates of position), the accuracy ranges between approximately 100 feet and a fraction of a foot.

In addition to the wide commercial availability of GPS receivers for motorists, pilots, sailors, hikers, and so forth, anyone can also purchase GPS-based devices intended to be implanted in someone's vehicle (or boat, or suitcase, or anything else) for the purpose of covertly tracking the precise travel pattern of whatever the covert GPS device has been planted in. The old-fashioned art of physical surveillance is passé since the job has been taken over by this commercially available, self-contained device.

Such devices are available from numerous sources:

1. Followit at http://www.findware.co.uk/gpstrackingdevices/surveillance_tracking.htm and http://www.goandtrack.com/hardware/coverttracker.htm;

2. Cartracker II from http://www.pimall.com/nais/cartrack.html (see Figure 14.1);

3. ProTrack from http://www.securitywholesalers.com/cat/protrak_gps_covert_vehicle_tracking_system_1122191.htm;

4. Other implementations, such as those from http://www.comstrac.com and elsewhere.

Besides being physically detected and removed, such devices can be defeated by preventing them from receiving the GPS signals by wrapping them, for example, in any conductive material such as common aluminum foil. Doing so, however, would be readily detected and recorded as a loss of signal by these devices. A preferred alternative may be to relocate these devices, if possible, to another container, vehicle, or person as appropriate.

Overt variants of this include the ankle bracelet forced by some courts upon individuals and the wristwatch-like device "in galactic blue" (Figure 14.2) that parents can place on their children's wrist. These watches are available from numerous retailers, such as http://www.spygear4u.com/product.asp?productid=473, MicroCenter computer outlets in the United States, and elsewhere. Indeed, the northern Japanese city of Murakami

Figure 14.1 Commercially available covert vehicle tracker using GPS.

asked [1] two security companies to provide such a service for some 2,700 elementary and junior high school students after a 15-year-old girl was abducted in September 2003. These devices will have button to push if help is needed. Unfortunately, related experience in Brazil, where abductions for ransom are a constant threat, shows that an abductor's first action is to disable any such tracking device.

14.2   RF ID devices

These are devices that work in conjunction with an illuminating RF signal by retransmitting that signal back to a collocated sensor, often after imbedding the RF ID device's unique ID number.

There are two classes of devices:

1. Passive RF ID tags, such as those placed on merchandise for inventory control, theft detection, and, as of recent, tracking. An example of the latter application is the planned U.S. legislation that RF ID tags shall be implanted in all automobile tires sold in the United States.[1]

2. Active RF ID devices, such as those placed by motorists on their own windshields to automate and expedite the process of paying toll at toll gates. The signals from devices can readily be used to track vehicles' passage not only through toll gates but also on any road where the illuminating RF interrogator is placed. The motorist has no way of knowing this as these devices give no indication that they are being accessed and identifying themselves. If a motorist does not want his or her automatic toll-gate device to be used for tracking, that motorist can simply wrap it in aluminum foil and put it in the trunk (assuming the car body is made of metal and not fiberglass), or take it out altogether. These signals can also be used to mail speeding

Figure 14.2 Personal tracker based on GPS.

1. The three major U.S. tire manufacturers plan to place such ID tags in all tires sold in the United States. The tags could be read from 15 feet away even if the car is moving at 100 miles per hour. See http://www.technologyreview.com/articles/farmer0403.asp?p=2.

citations to motorists who took less time to go from point *A* to point *B* than would have been needed if their vehicle had been operated at or below the posted speed limit.

An example of an RF ID tag on a DVD player is shown in Figure 14.3.

Early in mid-2003, the largest U.S. retailer, Wal-Mart, announced [2] that by January 1, 2005, it would require RF ID tags from its suppliers to do business.

RF ID tags consist of a rudimentary antenna connected to a miniature and inexpensive microelectronic device ("chip") that simply inserts a unique digital code to the illuminating RF signal before reflecting a portion of that signal back. Texas Instruments, among others, has recently created an ID tag small and inexpensive enough to insert into clothing with padded sections [3]. The TI "laundry transporter" device works at 13.56 MHz, is ultra thin, 22-mm circular, and intended to be sewn into clothing, and designed and tested to withstand "the harsh industrial cleaning process." It has a 64-bit factory ID and 2,000 bits of memory that can be written to. The privacy problem with such applications is that if such devices are not disabled at the point of sale, a customer can be tracked indefinitely thereafter upon passage through any "choke point" with a interrogator/sensor capable of interfacing with that device. U.S. legislation is proceeding along the lines of mandating that all such devices be disabled at the point of sale. An individual has no way of determining if an RF ID tag has or has not been disabled at the point of sale. Most of us have been embarrassed at some time when a fully paid-for item's RF ID device caused the retail vendor's theft alarm to ring, then been waved off by the cashier who knew that the item was paid for.

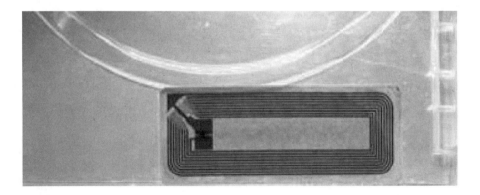

Figure 14.3   RF ID tag on a DVD player. (Courtesy of Mead Westvaco Company.)

Indeed, there has been some discussion that Euro bank notes (cash) may end up with RF ID tags embedded in them. [4] Japan's Hitachi has reportedly signed an agreement to embed sand-grain-sized RF ID tags into Euro notes [4]. This is yet another step in the constant war against counterfeit currency.

RF ID devices can be temporarily defeated by wrapping them in any conductive material, such as aluminum foil. A more permanent countermeasure would be to place the unit (e.g., the garment with an RF ID tag) in a microwave oven for a few seconds; enough microwave energy (~2 GHz) will couple through onto the device to burn the chip or melt the thin antenna wire. There is the possibility of damage to the item itself; the inner layers of CDs and DVDs, for example, usually get permanently damaged in a microwave oven that is turned on.

RF ID tags are big business, and their use is about to become massively more commonplace in all of the following scenarios:

1. RF ID tags could take the place of the ubiquitous optical UPC barcodes on merchandise. Merchandise can then be scanned without the need for an optical path. The holy grail is for supermarkets to be able to scan a cart full of groceries without one having to remove the groceries from it. There are numerous technical problems with this, such as the fact that all RF ID devices tend to respond at the same time to the illuminating interrogating radio signal, thereby making it very hard to separate one's response from that of another. Expensive three-dimensional scanning is a promising fix to this problem.

2. Automobile manufacturers could abuse this technology by configuring their cars to refuse to run unless one uses tires, windshield wipers, and other items imbedded with RF ID devices made by that same manufacturer. This would kill off competing vendors' products for such historically competitive items as tires.

3. RF ID tags could be placed on domestic animals and livestock to prove ownership. The U.S. Food and Drug Administration has approved injectable microchips for animals in 1996. The devices are so small they have already been injected in salmon.

14.3 Modern vehicles' black boxes

The mandatory use of crash-surviving, multitrack recording devices, or black boxes, in commercial aircraft is well known; these devices are actually bright orange despite their name. Not as well known is the fact that a watered-down version of these black boxes is inside most every car sold today.

As anyone who has tried to service his or her own car these days knows, it is nearly impossible any more to do the time-honored tune up (adjusting timing and dwell angle, adjusting vacuum advance, etc.) because these tasks are now automatically performed by the computer in each car. These same vehicular computers record one's vehicle's last few seconds (or minutes) of speed, breaking action, and so forth, as well as the maximum speed attained during the past x hours or days. They often also record whether the headlights and windshield wipers were turned on and numerous other settings. This information is readily retrievable and is often used in court proceedings to show driver negligence. Indeed, upscale cars in the United States are sold with On Star, a service whereby a stranded vehicle's engine and mechanical condition can be remotely diagnosed and relayed to the stranded motorist. The On Star device in such cars has a built-in GPS receiver which can be interrogated by On Star to reveal the vehicle's precise position at any instant in time. This can be handy if one is lost and is seeking assistance, or if one's vehicle has been stolen and the police need to find it; it is also a potential threat if the same capability is used to track a driver's precise whereabouts without that driver's knowledge or consent. Figure 14.4 from On Star's own Web site (www.onstar.com) shows this feature, which, depending on one's situation, can be viewed as a blessing or a curse. On Star, by the way, has nothing to do with stars; all communications are handled through terrestrial cellular channels.

The U.K. Department of Transportation is examining a plan to fit all vehicles with a different computing device that will charge drivers according to which road they use when.[6] The same underlying technology can readily be used for numerous other surveillance-related purposes, for issuing electronic speeding citations, and if integrated with the car's electronics, for ensuring that the car cannot exceed the posted speed limit no matter how hard one pushes on the gas pedal. This last feature could expose the

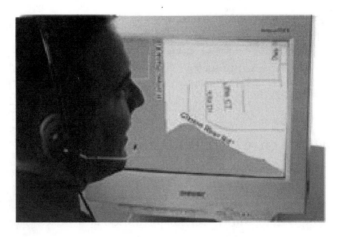

Figure 14.4   OnStar remote geolocation of On Star–equipped vehicles.

government to considerable liability if a motorist had to accelerate to avoid a fatal accident and could not.

14.4   Cell phones

A cell phone is not a passive device like some (though not all) pagers or beepers. A cell phone is in regular communication with the cellular network, which, in turn, learns the cell phone's whereabouts with a precision that depends on the following:

1. Whether or not the cell phone is GPS-equipped. Most cell phones sold in the United States these days are quietly equipped with GPS receivers as this shifts the technical burden of determining the cell phone's location (for compliance with the U.S. Communications Assistance to Law Enforcement [CALEA]) to each cell phone rather than to the cellular service provider.

2. The capabilities of the cellular service provider and the number of cellular sites in the geographical area of the cell phone in question. Geolocating a cell phone without GPS amounts to old-fashioned direction finding using some variant of triangulation, such as time difference of arrival (TDOA), phase interferometry, and the like.

But even without any of this technology, a cellular service provider and the security services it cooperates with can readily determine if a given GSM cell phone registered in, say, Switzerland is now switched on in the United States or in Greece, the Philippines, Bora Bora, or anywhere else where there is GSM service. Even if the SIM card is changed in favor of a locally purchased card, the GSM cell phone's international mobile equipment identifier (IMEI), a permanent serial number placed in that phone by its manufacturer, can readily be tracked. As such, the often peddled anonymous GSM cards [6] are not anonymous at all if used on a cell phone that was previously associated with a user through its IMEI identifier.

Cell phones store a lot of data. SIM cards in GSM phones often store up to 64 KB of data; CDMA, TDMA, and other technologies that do not use SIM cards store comparable amounts in the phone's own memory. This is particularly so in connection with the new fad of making every cell phone a camera and a display.

The data stored includes one's list of frequently and not-so-frequently called numbers, the last few numbers called or called from, photos with atrocious resolution, and sound files.

Cell phones that incorporate a PDA store everything a PDA does, too, which is usually sensitive personal and/or business information.

Given the small size of these devices and the ease and sickening regularity with which they are lost or stolen, one would think that they would be protected with strong encryption. Alas, they are not. The inconvenience of using widely available encryption for PDAs ends up causing large holes in security and privacy. As for the misconception that SIM card data is securely protected with one's PIN number (which is rarely used anyway), one need only recall that in early 1998, David Wagner and Ian Goldberg of the University of California, Berkeley, broke SIM security and published the results.

The countermeasures to cell phone privacy threats are to do the following:

1. Store nothing in a cell phone. Periodically delete the data stored in the cell phone's own memory regarding numbers dialed or dialed from, keeping in mind that this will only protect from a thief, not from local security services, getting that information.

2. When traveling, purchase (with cash, not with a credit card) both a new cell phone and, if in a GSM country, a new SIM card wherever one does not wish to have his or her cell phone become the beacon that would allow unwanted third parties to home in to. Of course, any calls placed with that new, clean cell phone should not be to telephone numbers that would have been routinely called by one's regular cell phone as so doing would disclose the new cell phone's number to unwanted third parties and negate its benefits.

14.5   Prepaid calling cards

While a prepaid calling card sold in many countries is impersonal, it is serial-numbered nonetheless and becomes very personal the moment one uses it. These cards are serial-numbered so that if, say, a box full of them falls off the delivery truck or is otherwise stolen, the telephone company can readily deny service to the serial numbers associated with the stolen cards. In the case of smart prepaid telephone cards, when the user does not need to enter anything on a telephone's keypad to communicate the card's serial number to the service provider, the card's serial number is still sent out automatically to the telephone company; this is why the telephone company can deny service to such cards beyond the expiration date printed on them. A collection of various nations' prepaid calling cards is shown in Figure 14.5.

Consider the scenario of a businessman on personal travel calling a competitor's office with a calling card, only to have that calling card company's records subpoenaed at a later time in an investigation of industrial espionage or impropriety.

The obvious procedure to maintain privacy while using such a card is to purchase it with cash at the location where it will be used (and not at the

Figure 14.5 Prepaid telephone calling cards.

location where one is traveling from) and to make calls to a single number only and never to more than a single number.

14.6 Credit cards

In their understandable effort to reduce their exposure to fraudulent charges, credit card companies have become quite adept at instantly identifying the precise location of any credit card's usage.[2]

Significant computing horsepower is constantly dedicated to identifying any credit card usage that suggests something out of the ordinary, such as the following:

1. Out-of-town charges;

2. Uncommon cash advances;

3. A pattern of very small charges (e.g. $5 gasoline purchases), which is the pattern often used by credit card thieves to determine if the card is still valid so as to proceed with a large purchase;

4. Concurrent usage of a credit card in two different locations (not uncommon when one of two spouses who have the same credit card number is on travel);

---

2. The reason given by credit card companies—that all this policing is to protect the credit card holder—is self-serving nonsense in any country, such as the United States, where credit card holders are legally liable for only the first $50 of fraudulent charges. The credit card companies are simply trying to minimize their own exposure to fraudulent charges.

5. Out-of-character charges (such as adult-shop purchases, jewelry purchases).

One must balance the benefits of credit card usage (such as the ability to contest charges for faulty merchandise or for breech of contract) with the fact that a credit card's record shows precisely who bought what, where, and when. Cash-advance ATM machines in particular tend to photograph the user during each transaction.

Smart cards (the ones with a built-in microchip, such as the American Express Blue card) offer no privacy advantage. The same applies to credit cards with one's photograph on them, which can actually be a nuisance if one wants one's spouse or offspring to fetch medicine from the pharmacy and the pharmacy refuses to accept cards from anyone other than the person shown in the photograph.

14.7 Intelligent mail

In the aftermath of the still-unresolved mailings of anthrax-laced mail in the United States shortly after the September 11 tragedy, the President's Commission on the U.S. Postal Service stated [7] the obvious, namely, that sender-identification technologies would enhance the security of the mail system.

While the motivation and concern are laudable, the solution proposed is naïve because it ignores the obvious fact that mail is international and any in-country legislation cannot impact what out-of-country senders of mail do. Besides, most commercial mail is already sender-identifiable because most commercial senders use postage machines that always identify the sender anyway. A number of commercial efforts to allow individual computer users to print postage stamps at home was a predictable commercial failure because no rational person would want to have to fire up a computer and printer to print a single stamp or to have to pay for the privilege of not doing the much simpler task of getting a booklet of stamps at the post office or at a convenience store.

14.8 Fax machines and telephone answering machines

When this author's home fax machine misbehaved a few years ago, its vendor proudly repaired it from afar by calling it and interfacing directly with its settings and memory. Indeed, anything stored in a fax machine's memory (such as the legend of all recent incoming and outgoing calls, entire faxes stored in memory, usually called phone numbers) can usually be readily retrieved from afar by anyone in possession of the know-how to interface with any one manufacturer's fax machine. Because fax machines are normally connected to the phone line at all times, one would only notice an incoming phone call that did not result in a fax, which one would most likely dismiss as a wrong number.

The fix to prevent the unauthorized remote retrieval of confidential or proprietary information in office fax machines is to select fax machines that do not store pages in memory and do not allow remote diagnostics; this usually means low-end fax machines.

Additionally, one should clear the machine's memory by regularly dumping the legend of stored traffic onto paper.

As with fax machines, so with digital telephone answering machines and every other piece of electronics connected to a phone line, to a network, or, soon, to a power line, as utility companies proceed with their plans to read the consumption meters remotely through the power line itself.

14.9   Office and home copiers

Most upscale photocopiers are no longer analog devices, but computers with a scanner and a printer. The scanned image is stored in the copier's hard disk before printing. As such it is every bit as amenable to data theft as the data in any computer. Unauthorized data removal be performed by an unscrupulous repair person, compromised employee, or anyone else. More insidiously, in the interest of minimizing downtime, some vendors have endowed their office copiers with telephone connections that call home whenever the machine comes close to needing service. While one can unplug the telephone cord going to the copier, an imbedded cell phone in the copier is much harder to identify or remove without incurring the wrath of the vendor or leasing company.

The fix is to ask prospective vendors some very probing questions as to just exactly how they know when their machines need servicing and to shun those peddling machines that call home.

14.10   Frequent-anything clubs

The whole idea behind frequent-flyer accounts, frequent-diner accounts, frequent-anything accounts is to motivate consumers to spend their money at the loyalty card account issuer's establishment. This is fine. What is not fine is the situation with the supermarket cards that charge inflated prices to those who do not surrender their shopping privacy at the door. Those who dismiss this intrusion (who cares if the supermarket knows if I prefer broccoli to zucchini?) will feel differently if their spouse's attorney subpoenas the supermarket data to show in court that they regularly purchased alcoholic beverages, select medications, or items of a personal nature.

The fix for this is to have a pocketful of such loyalty cards for the establishments one patronizes regularly issued to as many different made-up names and to use a different one every time one shops there. In the case of establishments, like airlines, where this scheme would not work, one has to make a conscious decision as to whether the benefits of having a frequent-flyer account outweigh the privacy penalties.

14.11 Consumer electronics

Most consumer electronics nowadays have memory, often lots of it. Digital cameras, in particular, use memory cards with hundreds of megabytes or even a few gigabytes of storage capacity; soon we will be seeing tapeless digital camcorders, although I wonder why a rational person would want to replace a $3 digital tape with a $1,000 digital memory card of comparable storage capacity.

Images erased in digital memories are no more erased than files are deleted in Windows; they stay very much intact until they happen to be partially overwritten by newer data. Digital memory cards use the standard FAT mode of storing data, which makes them vulnerable to the exact same techniques used in computer forensics to retrieve data that the user thought was long gone: the slack (digital memory space between the end-of-file and end-of-sector), the unallocated space (digital memory that was once used by a file that has since been marked as deleted), and so forth.

As with digital cameras, so with all consumer devices that use digital memories, such as MP4 music players, tapeless recorders, GPS navigation devices, tapeless telephone answering machines, paperless fax machines, and so forth.

The fix for the long memory of digital memories is basically the same as for all computer media: Overwrite the data numerous times. This is most easily done when the memory card is connected to the computer (e.g. after reading the digital photos into the computer for image enhancement prior to printing). If a computer is not available, take as many snapshots of the ceiling as can fit in the memory card, format the card, and then take another set of snapshots of the same ceiling until there is no room for more.

References

[1]   See http://www.usatoday.com/tech/news/2003-10-02-gps-kids-japan_x.htm.

[2]   http://news.com.com/2010-1071_3-5072343.html?tag=fd_nc_1.

[3]   http://www.ti.com/tiris/docs/news/news_releases/2003/rel8-11-03.shtml.

[4]   http://news.zdnet.co.uk/business/0,39020645.2135074.00.htm.

[5]   See http://observer.guardian.co.uk/uk_news/story/0,6903,1011463,00.html.

[6]   http://www.ptclub.com/Secretcommunications.html.

[7]   Veron, D., "Postal Service Pursues Intelligent Mail Despite Privacy Concerns," *Computerworld*, August 11, 2003, http://www.computerworld.com/security topics/security/privacy/story/0,10801,83866,00.html.

CHAPTER

15

Contents

Biometrics: Privacy Versus Nonrepudiation

A biometric is any observable, or, better yet, measurable parameter of a person. It can be a physical characteristic, such as one's iris, fingerprint, footprint, or retinal pattern, or one's face, hand, or foot geometry, the precise location of scars and moles on one's body, dental records (used in the identification of charred remains), DNA, and so forth. It can also be a behavioral characteristic, such as one voice, gait, or mannerisms, one's signature dynamics, one's keystrokes dynamics, or any other act or expression, such as one's proclivity for this or for that. During World War II, for example, Morse code telegraph operators were often identified by their timing in the transmission of dots and dashes. Because behavioral characteristics tend not to be unique, one may use a number of different behavioral characteristics (e.g., voice and gait and proclivities) in order to enhance the likelihood of a positive identification of an individual.

15.1 Are they effective? It depends

A biometric's effectiveness as a security measure depends on which of the different classes of functions the biometric is used for, namely, the following:

1. Authentication, or are you who you say you are? This is the concept behind passports, driver's licenses, and the use of fingerprints in laptops in place of user-entered passwords.

2. Identification, or are you in our database? This is the concept behind checking a suspect's fingerprints against a police organization's database or airport visitors' faces against a database of suspected terrorists.

3. Negative authentication, or are you not someone else? This admittedly odd-sounding name refers to inferring that an individual is not the one he or she appears to be. For example, it is plausible to try to infer from the pattern of one's usage of a computer keyboard, such as the time spacing between striking different keys, whether or not the person typing on John Doe's computer is John Doe.

The extent to which any of the above classes of functions can succeed depends largely on just how large the database is and on whether there is any effort underway to defeat the authentication or the identification. Comparing any biometric against a database of a handful of entries is clearly much simpler than comparing a biometric against a database of a few hundred million entries. The likelihood of error increases quite rapidly with the size of the database. Also, the success of a biometric identification or authentication is affected quite adversely if there is any effort to subvert it.

As such, the often-heard, simplistic generalizations that biometrics do or don't work are meaningless in the absence of specific qualifications that spell out the context. Using a biometric to authenticate a cooperative-authorized entrant into a controlled facility where only a couple of dozen individuals are allowed is technically trivial. Trying to identify suspected terrorists by scanning faces at a busy airport or suspected criminals by scanning faces at a football game are exercises in futility—not to mention the Orwellian overtones of such endeavors.

As with most new technological advances that leave the lab, biometrics as a means of enhancing security has been plagued with exaggerated promises to its own long-term detriment.[1] Marketers and entrepreneurs seeking to turn biometrics into a profitable venture are largely, but not exclusively, to blame for this. A lot of the blame rests with nontechnical politicians and law enforcers who assumed (incorrectly, because biometrics can be spoofed, as is shown in the next section) that biometrics would provide the long-sought irrefutable smoking gun.

Biometrics is big business these days, and it is getting bigger ever day. IBIA, the international organization of biometric devices and programs suppliers, estimates that the worldwide turnover of biometric devices and programs suppliers exceeded $500 million in 2002. As the next section shows, the faith in biometrics implied in this apparent commercial success may be misplaced.

---

1. In a U.S. Army Research Lab pilot effort involving 270 individuals, the Pentagon tested an iris-recognition technology from Iridian which claimed a 99.5% success. In reality, according to the Defense Department's Dr. Steven King (http://www.wired.com/news/politics/0,1283,50470,00.htm), the Visionics system recognized individuals only 51% of the time and identified an individual to within a range of 10 participants only 81% of the time.

15.2   **Biometrics can be easily spoofed**

Biometrics, as a science, is not new, contrary to popular belief. A conventional photograph in a passport or in a driver's license is a potent biometric, and so is the time-honored fingerprint. The problem with the former is that it can be defeated with a facial disguise or even with a grimace.[2] The problem with the latter is that it can be forged in numerous ways. Tsutomu Matsumoto, a Japanese cryptographer, used gelatin and plastic mold to create a fake finger having his own fingerprint; he showed that this fake finger dependably fooled 11 commercially available fingerprint-detection devices all the time [1]. This technique, commonly known as "gummy fingers," is not new. Some 10 years ago it was developed by Tom van der Putte, who presented it with Jeroen Keuning of Atos Origin Business Solutions in Bristol at the IFIP TC8/WG8 Fourth Working Conference on Smart Card Research and Advanced Applications (pp. 289–303), Kluwer Academic Publishers, 2000 [2]. Independently, the most common fingerprint scanner in Germany, Siemens's ID Mouse, was outwitted with simple tricks [3].

Numerous other fingerprint-based implementations for identifying authorized fingerprints were fooled during a German study and are discussed at length in the open literature [4, 5]. The devices fooled included the following:

1. Eutron's fingerprint reader Magic Secure 3100 manufactured in Korea using a CMOS TouchChip by STMicroelectronics;

2. PDA solutions BioHub and BioSentry by Biocentric Solutions, which were reported to have had extensive problems even with identifying authorized fingerprints;

3. Identix optical fingerprint scanner (used in the G81-12000 keyboard by Cherry);

4. IdentAlink's Sweeping Fingerprint Scanner FPS100U that uses Atmel's CMOS-Finger-Chip-Sensor FCD4B14;

5. Veridicom's 5th Sense Combo, which is highly resistant to being fooled by virtue of its use of an integrated smart card reader that reads reference data stored in the smart card.

The techniques used for fooling individual fingerprint sensors were many and included, for example, using openly available graphite powder to dust the fatty residue of the fingerprint already in the sensor from the

2. This writer recently attended a major yearly biometrics conference near Bethesda, Maryland, where a major U.S. company was demonstrating its facial-recognition technology, and volunteered to have his face entered into that company computer's database, which during that conference contained only a handful of faces. When this writer appeared in front of that same face-scanning machine a little later with just a facial grimace, that machine failed to identify him as being in its short database.

previous user, stretching an adhesive film over the surface of the sensor, and lifting that last user's fingerprint for use in creating a fake finger's fingerprint to fake that last user's identity.

Two relevant points are important here:

1. Roughly 2% of the general population lacks readable fingerprints.

2. A distinction must be made between individual fingerprint sensors, such as the above, which can be outfoxed, and conventional rolled fingerprints on paper, which are scanned and digitized and whose minutiae (the relative locations of the ridge endings and bifurcations of human fingerprints) are identified and compared with the minutiae of other fingerprints in the large databases of law enforcement organizations. The conventional law-enforcement paper-based rolled fingerprint systems are not amenable to spoofing, except, for instance, by the individual who has obliterated his or her fingerprints (by sandpapering or dipping the fingers in a strong acid or base—or even chlorine—prior to being fingerprinted), which is alerting in itself.

In addition to biometric-specific technical problems discussed later in this section, biometrics suffer from a number of fundamental problems that transcend the specific technologies used:

1. As with any detection concept, one has to deal with the false alarm and failure to identify probabilities that date back to the early days of radar. If the threshold for detection is set low enough to minimize the probability of false rejection, then one inescapably ends up with many false alarms (such as flocks of birds rather than airplanes, false fingerprint matches). If one sets the detection threshold high enough to minimize the probability of false alarms, then one inescapably ends up with many false rejections.

2. Biometric detectors are now being peddled in computers as replacements for manually entered passwords, with the implication that this advance is somehow more secure. It is not, for many reasons:

   a. A data thief is not going to bother with either the biometric or the password to gain access to one's hard disk. The thief will simply do what any computer forensics examiner does: disconnect the hard disk from the computer altogether, copy it magnetically, and view it at leisure track for track and sector by sector. The only protection against this threat is full-disk encryption of all tracks and sectors of the disk using any one of the numerous openly available and readily affordable commercial products that do this, such as Wingate (http://www.wingate.com) in the United States or Safeboot from Control-Break International in the United Kingdom.

b. Unlike a password, which is (or at least should be) only in the mind of the authorized user of a computer, one's fingerprint is all over: on one's credit card handed to numerous vendors and clerks, on one's toothbrush, door handle, steering wheel, drinking cup, fork, and so forth. It can be easily lifted using commercially available techniques, as well as home-brewed techniques such as the "gummy fingers" technique described above. Worse yet, unlike a password that can be changed at will, one cannot change one's fingerprint (or any other biometric) at will.

3. In addition to the vulnerabilities of the biometric sensors themselves, discussed in more detail below, the biometric system can be subjected to, for example, a classic man-in-the-middle attack. The data stream between the sensor and the computer (which may be far away in the case of access control or banking ATM terminals) can be intercepted, and fake data can be entered into the system to contaminate the database, for example, to accept otherwise unauthorized biometrics in the future.

4. The database itself can be compromised. This can be done by an insider or through hacking that gives the hacker administrator rights.

Although exuberant law enforcers embraced recent biometrics technologies (such as face recognition) with great expectations that such techniques would reduce the law enforcers' workload in identifying wanted persons, the results of field tests have been unmitigated disasters.

In a November 2002 publication [6], Thalheim, Krissler, and Ziegler showed that Cognitec's FaceVACS-Logon was outfoxed with photographs of authorized persons and, in the case of implementations that attempt to thwart deception with still images, with a short video clip of a registered person.

According to a Gartner report[7], *USA Today* printed on September 2, 2003, that face-recognition implementation from Identix and Visage "fared poorly in a pilot project at Boston's Logan Airport in 2002." Using 40 volunteers who played the role of terrorists for the purpose of that test and who attempted to trespass through two different security checkpoints using this technology, the systems failed 39% of the time.

The same Gartner report as well as numerous others [8], state that a two-year facial recognition trial by the Tampa, Florida, police department in Ybor City resulted in no arrests (but in numerous false identifications) and was stopped by Tampa mayor Pan Iorio. This followed the well-publicized 2002 Super Bowl event (dubbed "Snooper Bowl"), when the use of a facial biometrics system to detect known criminals resulted in not a single arrest but in numerous false matches. A report on face-recognition technology by the National Institute of Standards and Technology in 2000 stated that a mere 15 difference in position between the comparison photos "adversely affect[s] performance" (not to mention disguises using facial hair, sunglasses).

Similarly, a face-recognition trial at Palm Beach International Airport in Florida was terminated after the airport decided it was not worth the cost [9]. That system "failed to correctly identify airport employees 53% of the time according to data obtained by the American Civil Liberties Union under Florida's open records law." Visionics spokensman Meir Haahtan stated that the poor results were due to "incorrect lighting." [10]

Iris scanning systems, which look for the unique patterns of one's iris, fared somewhat better in the earlier mentioned tests by Thalheim, Krissler, and Ziegler. Although it presented an initial challenge to defeat, an implementation by Panasonic's Authenticam using PrivateID software by Iridian, was defeated using a digital image of a human eye sprayed onto mat inkjet paper at 2,400 × 1,200 dpi into which a miniature hole had been cut. According to the report by the above authors, Panasonic countered that the system used by these authors was a prototype and that the weaknesses identified would be fixed prior to that product's introduction to the market. Indeed, realistically, it is unlikely that one can obtain accurate photographs of the irises of authorized persons to fool the system.

There are numerous other biometrics, of course: palm prints, voice prints, retinal scans, and, ultimately, DNA. Retinal scan are the least commonly understood; the scan maps the precise pattern of veins in the retina as shown in Figure 15.1.

A palm scan, depicted in Figure 15.2, has already been in use for some time now in place of a passport for frequent-traveling U.S. citizens entering the United States from Europe.

With the notable exception of DNA, the issue is not if the various biometrics can be fooled, but how much effort and cunning is required to do so.

If one rejects the marketing hype that biometrics cannot be fooled, the use of biometrics in security has its place as an aid to, rather than as a replacement for, positive identification by a human based on personal recognition. As such, it is best viewed as a technology that enhances convenience rather than security.

Furthermore, the security afforded by biometrics should not be viewed depending entirely on the biometric sensor, be it a retinal scan, fingerprint, or whatever. Because the biometric system can be attacked in numerous other ways, such as through man-in-the-middle attacks, compromised insiders, compromised software updates, and so forth, a biometric system's security can only be assessed as follows:

1. By assessing the entire system, including the sensors, communications lines, databases, computers, and the power backup in the case of loss of electrical power;

2. By assessing the security procedures and policies in use (e.g., authentication of repairmen, administrators, software updates);

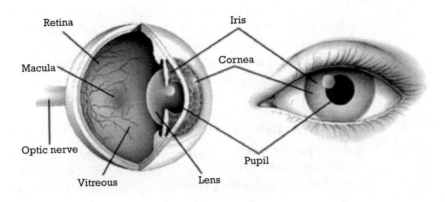

Figure 15.1 The retina, whose blood vessels are scanned as a biometric identifier.

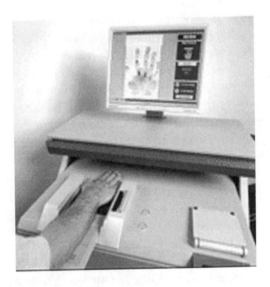

Figure 15.2 Palm-based biometric reader.

3. By accessing the system in the specific context of just exactly what it purports to protect and under what operational assumptions.

In the limited situation of using a biometric, usually a fingerprint, in place of a password to access a computer, there is no increase in security; quite the contrary, there is a decrease in security because the nontechnical user is likely to be less careful by mistakenly assuming that a biometric sensor will deter a data thief or a computer forensics examiner.

The ease with which biometrics can be—and have been—spoofed should also be a concern in judicial circles. Most judges and juries are not particularly well versed in technology. Defense attorneys are often equally technology challenged and do not know what questions to ask to cast doubt on the validity of fingerprint (or any other biometric) evidence that appears to place their client at the scene of a crime. Hardly ever is the question asked whether the fingerprint found could have been placed at the scene in order to incriminate a third party and to terminate any further investigation of other suspects.

15.3 Identification is not synonymous with security

Analytical thinking is the stock-in-trade of every engineer and scientist. It is arguably more valuable than knowledge; advances in the understanding of science and engineering often prove scientific beliefs of the past wrong, and analytical thinking is the ultimate human tool for seeing through fog.

Pseudoanalytical arguments, on the other hand, exploit impressionable individuals and bestow legitimacy on perhaps spurious beliefs and parochial hidden agendas. Such arguments have always been the stock-in-trade of every proselytizer, propagandist, and spin doctor, as well as of many politicians, advertisers, and others. Listening to pseudoanalytical arguments articulated by doctrinaire proponents of this or that is like watching a ritualistic performance of kabuki; it is definitely not an intellectual activity.

A currently relevant example of pseudoanalytical reasoning obfuscates the relationship between security and identification and tries to make these two concepts synonymous when, in fact, they are not. Indeed, it is obviously true that biometrics-based (or any other form of) identification of individuals seeking entry into, say, a nuclear weapons launching site or any other restricted facility is essential to that site's security. It is not true at all, however, that identification of all individuals walking down every Main Street in the world promotes security; if anything, it smells odiously of the "your papers please" regimes of yesteryear.

The false reasoning that tries to equate security with identification goes even further and exploits every civilized person's strong aversion to terrorism. The often-repeated argument is, If we could identify every person entering an airport or even merely driving by a building, then we could prevent future airplane-related terrorist attacks and future vengeful bombings of government buildings. This argument is logically false for a very simple reason: Any disciplined clandestine organization planning to perpetrate a terrorist attack selects as perpetrators individuals who are unknown to the security services of the targeted nations. As a result, one cannot identify individuals who are not on any watch list or in any other database.

Even in the case of routine criminality, first-time offenders are by definition not in anybody's database of wanted persons because they are first-time offenders. Unless the world degenerates to the point depicted in the movie *Minority Report* (where innocent individuals are arrested for a crime they have not yet committed but which it is predicted they will commit if not arrested) or to the point where citizens are arrested "for good measure" by oppressive regimes that fear any lack of overt subservience, today's information technology has no means of detecting malicious intent in otherwise law-abiding citizens.

Common sense would dictate that terrorist, spy, and other organizations with reasons to keep their operatives from being identified and apprehended will use operatives who are neither known to nor suspected by the targeted countries. In short, no identification of individuals who are not identifiable as a threat can enhance security; worse yet, relying on such identification actually reduces security because it lulls us into a false sense of security that reduces or eliminates the implementation of real, substantive security measures. This simple logic alone invalidates the fundamental premise of the pseudologic behind the identification-equals-security mantra when it is extended beyond the obvious authentication-for-access-to-controlled-sites scenario.

15.4 Societal issues

Unlike, say, differential equations or insulating materials, which are topics with no implications for societal conscience, the topic of biometrics is inescapably connected to a multitude of issues that society has a justifiably strong interest in, such as privacy, prevention of false accusation fostered by biometrics, confidentiality, repudiation, Orwellianism, freedom, and so on. Technologists can shrug such issues off, but the fact remains that tools developed for one purpose always get used for other purposes by governments and the private sector in subsequent years.

Engineers and scientists tend to prefer to focus on the strictly technical aspects of their fields, biometrics in this case, and to leave the societal aspects to others. This may be both unwise and inadvisable: Those unnamed others will likely have their own agendas, and we (and our children) will end up having to live with the consequences of far-reaching decisions by such unnamed others that get enshrined into law and, hence, into the reality of the future. Sooner or later we will be dust, but our children and their children deserve a livable society and not an Orwellian one.

Law and order is all well and good and essential, if we think of it in terms of preventing fraud, arson, murder, and mayhem. But we are all humans, not automatons. Lives there a child who has never lied, never stricken someone in anger, or never stolen another child's toy? Lives there an adult who has never done a single thing that would have landed him or her in jail if caught (e.g., exceeding the posted speed limit by more than 20 mph, a felony in the United States and in other countries for which one can be jailed)? Do we really want to empower immature 20-year-old policemen with the authority and the means to identify, arrest, and incarcerate any person in their country, based on a know-all law enforcement apparatus that embodies the Panopticon concept and is made possible with biometric identification? Recall *Atlas Shrugged* where Ayn Rand shows how a government that can criminalize everything or, equivalently, that knows everyone's every transgression since birth and can identify everyone is omnipotent because it can selectively and legally jail anyone it feels like, technically in the name of law and order.

This was not a diatribe in support of freedom, but a reasoned argument in support of being forthright about the many identified shortcomings of biometrics, which is evolving as the premier science of identifying—and misidentifying—individuals.

The world is now full of evangelists for this or that biometric technology or device; every vendor of such products is one. Responsible biometrics engineers and scientists should be the impartial assessors of these technologies, and the educators of the legal establishment that has embraced these technologies with unwarranted acceptance.

References

[1] http://www.vnunet.com/Features/1133650.

[2] http://cryptome.org/gummy.htm.

[3] http://extremetech.com/article2/0,3973,95158,00.asp page 2.

[4] http://extremetech.com/article2/0,3973,95887,00.asp,

[5] http://extremetech.com/article2/0,3973,85212, 00.asp.

[6] http://www.extremetech.com/print_article/0,3998, a= 27687,00.asp.

[7] http://www3.gartner.com/DisplayDocument?/doc_cd=117139.

[8] http://www.sptimes.com/2003/08/23/Opinion/About_face.shtml.

[9] http://www.businessweek.comtechnology/content/jul2993/tc20030722_2846_tc125.htm.

[10] Scheeres, J. "Airport Face Scanner Failed," May 16, 2002, http://www.wired.com/news/print/0,1294, 52563,00.htm.

Legal Issues

Disclaimer: Laws obviously vary widely from one country to another, and even within one country from one day to another. Nothing in this section should be construed as legal advice. The reader needing legal advice should consult a local attorney who is specifically knowledgeable about the legal issues surrounding electronic evidence.

Because the use of computers in general and the Internet in particular involve the full spectrum of human activities, it is understandable that a vast body of law and legal precedent is evolving in connection with the use and abuse of computers and of the Internet.

This chapter deals with two separate classes of legal issues:

1. Legal issues of interest to the user of computers with or without the Internet;

2. Legal issues pertaining to computer crime and legal evidence.

16.1 Software agreements that shift the legal liability to the user

The exfiltration of data from a user's computer to a vendor or his surrogate without that user's knowledge or permission used to be the essence of adware and spyware. A very similar practice has now become mainstream as part of the steadily increasing practice of online registration that even formerly reputable vendors use in an attempt to reduce the proliferation of unauthorized copies of their software.

Increasingly software providers have devised an interesting scheme to protect themselves from legal liability for the transmission of data from a typical user's computer to themselves or to their surrogates: They wordsmith end-user licensing agreements (EULA)—the small print that hardly anyone reads—that state that, by using the software, the user accepts such exfiltration of data!

A typical example is the GetRight EULA at http://www.getright.com that states,

> PRIVACY: By installing this software you consent to the automatic electronic transmission of personal identification information to Voelker Software for the purpose of verifying your purchase and compliance with this license agreement. This information may include but is not limited to your name, e-mail address, hard disk serial number, IP address, computer name and network ID.

While in many cases the software will simply not allow itself to be installed if an incorrect serial number or other vendor-provided enabling sequence of symbols is entered by the user, there have been cases [1] where the software took it upon itself to contact the vendor through the user's Internet connection and inform that vendor of a presumed attempt to install an unpaid-for copy of such software. But what if the accused user has done nothing wrong; for example:

1. The user merely mistyped the wrong enabling sequence when installing some software.

2. The user exercised his legal right (in the United States) to make an archival copy.

What if the vendor took it upon himself to report this noncrime as a crime to a user's employer, ISP, or law enforcers?

Similarly, in an attempt to shift the legal liability to the user, some in the online banking sector have devised terms and conditions that not only absolve the bank from any responsibility, but pass the blame to the individual user for most of everything that could go wrong. For example, the international bank HSBC's terms and conditions [2] state:

> You must not access the Internet Banking Service from any computer connected to a local area network (LAN) or any public Internet access device or access point without first making sure that no one else will be able to observe or copy your access or get access to the Internet Banking Service pretending to be you.

The document further states that the customer will actually be liable for any losses that occur as a result of gross negligence, defined as noncompliance with the above terms and conditions.

16.2 Cyber–SLAPP suits

There is a new form of a lawsuit in the United States, and possibly elsewhere as well, which is the Internet version of an abusive legal process that existed before. A powerful corporation or public figure who does not like what some individual is saying anonymously on the Internet files a lawsuit against an unnamed "John Doe" and obtains civil subpoenas that are served to ISPs to provide all information about suspected users so as to strip away their anonymity and identify them. What is abusive about such lawsuits is that the punishment of stripping a user's anonymity is doled out by the subpoena and not by a court of law.

In the United States, anyone can file a lawsuit and request subpoenas to be issued and served on anyone who the litigant states has information that could be useful. The issuing of such civil subpoenas is not monitored by the court unless the target of the subpoena files a motion to have a judge block the subpoena. But if that subpoena is served to an individual's ISP with a short time to comply, the individual concerned will not know about the subpoena in the first place until it is too late to file a motion in court to block it. ISPs are not required to inform the individual concerned, anyway, although many do if there is time to do so.

Not surprisingly, this scheme is quite effective in silencing and intimidating individuals who may post anonymous criticism about a powerful entity or person, hence its name "Strategic Lawsuit Against Public Participation" (SLAPP).

The legal mechanism abused in cyber–SLAPP suits was intended as a legal discovery method in connection with alleged libel, defamation, breach of contract, or copyright infringement.

16.3 E-mail

E-mail is used by practically 100% of U.S. businesses and 90% of Australian businesses [3]. Even though e-mail does not represent the official position of an organization, it can be every bit as damaging; witness the unofficial Microsoft e-mail that allegedly stated it would cut the air supply of (rival) Netscape and the trials and tribulations of Ollie North during the Iran Contra hearings as a result of e-mail.[1]

Contrary to popular belief, employee e-mail enjoys zero privacy.[2] An employer has every right (in the United States, anyway) to read employee e-mail, and many do.

Unlike an official organizational document that can have numerous ghost authors and editors before it is finalized, e-mail has an identifiable

1. See *Bourke v. Nissan Motor Corporation,* No. B068705 (California Court of Appeals, July 26, 1993). The court asserted that there is no inherent right to privacy for e-mail.

2. For instance, in the *Smyth v. Pillsbury Company,* 1996 W.L. 32892 (E.D. Pennsylvania 1996), the court stated clearly that employers' reading of employee e-mail does not constitute an invasion of privacy.

single author who, more often than not, mistakenly believes that it is private (it most emphatically is not) and may use language that betrays biases and other illegalities that can be used against the document's author.

Until recently, most organizations tended to proudly preserve such electronic skeletons in the closet for many many years through the routine process of making archival backups of the entire organization's databases. As some organizations' legal liabilities were proved with the help of such archived e-mail, many reputable organizations sought a way to clean up those closets for good measure. To minimize the plausibility of accusations that they do this for illegal purposes, these organizations have usually declared that storage costs for obsolete e-mail are high (which is quite amusing in these days of rock-bottom prices for archival magnetic storage) and therefore e-mail will be purged from records after rather short periods (often as little as one month). This can work only as long as an organization cannot be shown to have known that its purged records would have been subpoenaed (e.g., in the course of the discovery phase of a law suit already filed or as part of an ongoing investigation that the organization has been made aware of).

If e-mail is sent out of an organization, the problem is compounded because the organization loses all control of such e-mail and has no way of making it disappear.

It is also not at all clear if the attorney–client privilege that protects the confidentiality of all verbal communication between an attorney and his or her client extends to e-mail as well or not. A third party that obtains a copy of such communication (e.g., an ISP that routinely keeps backups of all e-mails going through its circuits) may well have to turn over such ostensibly privileged communication if subpoenaed or be found in contempt of court. Laws are not too clear on this; nor have they been tested enough.

Also legally unclear is the status of e-mail sent or received by people from their personal (rather than office-provided) computers that pertains to their official duties as government employees or even corporate employees (e.g., ones working from home or otherwise telecommuting): Can they remove such official e-mail from their personal computers or is that e-mail an official record whose preservation is covered by applicable laws? And what if the personal computer that these official e-mail records were legitimately kept on crashes or is sold or disposed of?

It is quite evident that laws have not kept up with the rapidly advancing popularization of the Internet and even of internal organizational networks. Perhaps an organization would be well advised to protect itself by creating and enforcing clear-cut policies with regard to the use of computers and especially e-mail, particularly e-mail that may leave the organization's perimeter (either electronically or physically), just as there have always been established procedures before an official letter on the organization's letterhead could be sent out.

Such policies should state the following clearly:

1. What is not allowed in the organization's e-mail (e.g., illegal acts such as harassment or discriminatory or defamatory prose);

2. Procedures for originating and handling what would be proprietary or otherwise confidential e-mail content;

3. The time after which all e-mail that has not been specifically marked for retention will be purged and the procedures and approvals needed for marking some e-mail for retention;

4. Procedures for allowing e-mail to be released outside an organization and the means for detecting and handling transgressions.

16.4 Copyright

The purpose of copyright law has always been to encourage creative works by giving a short-term monopoly to the author. These rights are limited to the following:

1. The right of reproduction;

2. The right to distribution;

3. The right to display;

4. The right to performance;

5. The right to create derivative works;

6. The right to digital transmission of performance.

The real issue comes down to money; a third party is not allowed to profit from the original author's copyrighted work. Copyright infringement (also referred to by copyright holders as "piracy" in a self-serving effort to invoke the evocative imagery of savages looting the neighborhood), is the illegal copying of some work for profit.

16.4.1 U.S. Digital Millennium Copyright Act of 1998

The use of computers has made it very easy to circumvent rightful copyright claims in text, imagery, speech, video, music, and everything else. In the spirit of stemming this frontal assault on the notion of copyright, the DMCA of 1998 was conceived in the United States; similar copyright-protection acts have been passed in numerous other nations as well.

In their haste to protect rightful copyright owners, technology-challenged legislators in most countries enacted laws with unintended consequences that have turned out to be worse than the problem they set out to correct.

In the United States, the DMCA makes it illegal to try to circumvent "technical self-help protection measures."[3] The problem with this is that

3. See Section 1201 of the Copyright Act.

enterprising vendors, individuals, and even law enforcement organizations have abused this in the following ways to ban perfectly legal activities so as to further their own equities and agendas:

1. To stifle scientific research and free expression. When Princeton University professor Edward Felten and a team of researchers at Princeton, Rice University, and Xerox Corporation tried to publish the results of a study performed in response to a public challenge by the Secure Digital Music Initiative to identify security flaws, they were threatened with a lawsuit by that same group for allegedly violating the DMCA. Additionally, many ISPs and bulletin-board operators are now censoring discussions of encryption and copying technologies. Indeed, some technology conferences were moved to non-U.S. locations so as not to run afoul of the DMCA.

    The highly respected IEEE, which publishes roughly a third of all computer science journals worldwide, now requires all authors to indemnify IEEE for any liabilities if a submission happens to violate the DMCA.

2. To stifle innovation. Vendors, such as DVD makers, use regionalization encryption to prevent a legally purchased DVD in one country from be played in one's own DVD player purchased in another country. Similarly, vendors who want to make products that are interoperable with existing products have been threatened with legal action for violating the DMCA. Sony reportedly sued makers of software that allowed owners of legally purchased PlayStation games to be played on a PC.

    Reverse engineering (taking something apart to see how it works), a technical practice that has historically been legally protected, is now largely illegal under DMCA and its non-U.S. versions. Similarly, a well-known vendor of computer printers invoked the DMCA in order to prevent a competitor from selling compatible ink cartridges for that vendor's printers.

3. To make a mockery of the fair use doctrine and law. This law, theoretically, allows any purchaser of copyrighted media to make and retain an archival copy of such legally purchased media. A user is now unable to do so without violating the DMCA. The DMCA makes circumvention illegal regardless of whether the underlying copying is legal! For example, it is legal to time-shift a copyrighted TV program to watch it at a more convenient time, but it is illegal to do the necessary interim step of defeating the encryption scheme used.

4. To weaken security. Ineffective or substandard security that ostensibly protects some copyrighted media cannot be exposed for the purpose of improving it; exposing it is a direct violation of the DMCA. These laws make it illegal for legitimate users of software to

identify and publicize security flaws of such software for the purpose of having such flaws corrected. Given the sickening litany of security-related bug fixes in practically all software of any consequence today (e.g., Microsoft operating systems, Microsoft Office, and practically all software by all vendors), these laws increase the vulnerability of every nation to cybercrime.

In summary, the DMCA gave copyright owners rights that they never had before it, including the ability to override public copyright policy, and has weakened national security in all nations with similar laws.

The problem with DMCA and DMCA-like legislation is the extent of its abuse by vendors: Imagine, for example, a Ford, Mercedes, or other vehicle refusing to move unless it has tires with a built-in RF ID tag that these cars approve. Car owners will be precluded from installing Firestone, Bridgestone, Michelin, and other tire brands that do not have this RF ID tag, and these tire vendors will be precluded from coming up with compatible RF ID tags because this would violate DMCA-like legislation. This is precisely what happened when an independent manufacturer of inkjet cartridges sold cartridges compatible with Lexmark printers by cloning the electronic handshake between the Lexmark printer Lexmark-made ink cartridges.

The DMCA has been roundly criticized by the American Association of Law Libraries [4].

The act also has had two unintended amusing effects:

1. Some U.S. proencryption individuals precede their encrypted files with a legal warning that quotes this act and reminds anyone inclined to break the encryption that doing so would be a federal offense. For example:

LEGAL WARNING NOTICE: The encrypted file below contains copyrighted material. In accordance with the Copyright Act, 17 U.S.C. 108(a)(3), as amended by the Digital Millennium Copyright Act (P.L. 105-304) and the Copyright Term Extension Act (P.L. 105-278), any attempt by anyone other than the intended recipient to circumvent the encryption protection on this copyrighted material is a crime that is punishable severely by law. END OF WARNING NOTICE.

It is unknown what the legal implications of this would be in the United States for, say, local law enforcement trying to circumvent someone's encryption under some conditions.

2. One can conceive of situations where a company can lightly encrypt information that it wants to protect, so as to be able to claim a violation of this federal law if a whistle-blower disclosed that information to the public.

As if the DMCA were not bad enough, a number of states are spawning their own versions of DMCA-like laws (dubbed super-DMCAs), supported by the MPAA, that have even more unintended consequences. A bill in the state of Colorado, for example, restricts distributing software or hardware "capable of defeating or circumventing" copy protection technology, even if their primary function is totally unrelated! By the same reasoning, a kitchen fork, which is capable of causing death, should be outlawed. A similarly naive bill in the state of Texas states that a user may not "conceal from a communications service provider . . . the existence or place of origin or destination of any communication [5]." This makes it illegal to use encrypted communications to send e-mail, firewalls, or even NAT because NAT operates by translating the "From" and "To" fields in Internet packets, which conceals the source and destination addresses. (Amusingly, NAT is the stopgap technology that has made it possible for today's Internet to survive despite the acute shortage of IP addresses). The Texas bill also makes anonymous speech over the Internet illegal.

Germany has pursued a novel approach to copyright protection by attempting to levy a copyright fee on every computer and CD writer sold, similar to royalty fees. This idea stems from the fact that the European Union leaves open the possibility of any member state compensating copyright holders through such a broad levy.

16.4.2 The Uniform Computer Information Transactions Act

The Uniform Computer Information Transactions Act (UCITA) is a draft law (already adopted in the states of Maryland and Virginia for purely selfish economic reasons, namely, to entice software makers to move to Maryland and Virginia so that these states can reap the obvious tax benefits). Sent in July 2000 to all U.S. states and territories for consideration, it has been plagued by controversy for good reason.

This act is good for a single sector of society, software makers, and would be more aptly named "The Software Industry Protection Act." For example:

1. UCITA allows software companies to avoid liability for damage caused by defective software, even if the problems were not disclosed to the customer at the time of purchase.

2. In its original draft, which UCITA has since backed off from as a result of massive opposition, UCITA allowed the manufacturer of software to shut down a buyer's software remotely if it deemed that the buyer had not upheld the software licensing agreements.

3. UCITA prohibits the transfer of software between companies, even in mergers and acquisitions.

4. UCITA obligates buyers to abide by terms that were not disclosed prior to the purchase of the software. This is what is colloquially known in the United States as buying a pig in a poke.

5. The notion that UCITA is intended to create uniform rules across all states (to favor software makers) has already been killed by the fact that the legislatures of two states, Hawaii and Illinois, have considered UCITA and have decided not to move ahead with it.

6. UCITA obligates a buyer of software not to use reverse engineering on the purchased software in an attempt to identify and correct security-related or other software flaws. The software buyer is therefore prevented from having any control over what software is running on his or her computer.

7. UCITA prohibits a software user who discovers flaws in purchased software from disclosing them. This flies in the face of the United States's (and every other nation's) need to enhance information security and protect its critical information infrastructure. One is therefore witnessing the spectacle whereby software manufacturers, through UCITA, are actually undermining U.S. Presidential Directive 63 about the protection of the U.S. critical infrastructure. Besides, this, as well as all other, UCITA provisions are toothless monsters in that any U.S. company can send software that it has purchased in the United States overseas for reverse engineering there. For example, under the European Union's fair use laws, software can be reverse engineered in Europe.

Luckily, most states in the United States have enacted legislation intended to prevent UCITA from taking effect in their respective territories.

Also, the American Bar Association committee that examined UCITA called it "extremely difficult to understand" and by, implication, unworkable, as stated by Bruce Barnes, formerly top technology official at National Insurance Companies in Columbus, Ohio, and now a consultant at Bold Vision LLC in Dublin, Ohio [6]. For example, UCITA is unclear as to whether or not it applies to goods that contain built-in software code.

Without the support of the American Bar Association, UCITA is highly unlikely to pass in any other state.

16.5   Can one be forced to reveal a decryption key?

It depends on the country and on the circumstances. The RIP law enacted in October 2000 in the United Kingdom empowers some within the British law enforcement community to demand that an individual either decrypt an encrypted file or provide law enforcement with the key for decrypting it;

refusal to do so is reportedly punished by a 2-year jail sentence. Astonishingly, disclosure to almost any third party that this demand has been made by law enforcement carries a 5-year jail sentence.

And what if one really did forget a decryption key? Unless the situation is unique and this claim can be substantiated, chances are that one will be in a lot of trouble.

An interesting situation comes about if the encryption used is involves the increasingly popular public-key-encryption cryptosystem, such as that used in the popular PGP software (see Section 11.3) freely available worldwide. If properly configured, the sender who encrypts a message for an intended recipient is physically unable to decrypt that same message; only the intended recipient can do so. It follows that one can only provide authorities with the decryption key for incoming encrypted messages and not for outgoing encrypted messages; it is hard to see how one can be held liable for the content of messages that others have sent unless they are particularly explicit with regard to that recipient's involvement or culpability.

In the United States, a regular subpoena can demand the production of documents and can even require one to submit to questioning. However, it is believed that the Fifth Amendment to the U.S. Constitution, which commands that no person "shall be compelled in any judicial case to be a witness against himself" empowers one to refuse legally to incriminate oneself, and, one would think, to refuse to provide the decryption key upon demand by any authority if that decryption key resides (or can be credibly claimed to reside) solely within that person's mind. The Fifth Amendment provides no protection for existing documents, and the government can compel the production of such documents, notably including cryptographic keys documented someplace.

Accordingly, if the decryption key is recorded in some media such as paper or magnetic storage media, then such media have to be surrendered upon demand under possible penalty for contempt of court or obstruction of justice. A number of court cases documented by Greg Sergienko in 1996 attest to the above interpretation [7].

This is legally treacherous territory as a defendant has to match the legal and financial resources of a government. Battling wits with pros who do prosecution 50 hours per week is an unwise course of action.

It appears, for example, that derivative immunity does *not* apply to documents decrypted with the aid of a key whose disclosure was forced on a defendant ("compelled production" in legalese). Some judges may view computer data as being analogous to personal papers, which are not protected from forced disclosure. Also, the applicability of the Fifth Amendment to a civil, rather than criminal, case, is doubtful; in *People v. Price* in Yolo County, California, the California Superior Court compelled production of a PGP encryption key in a civil case as long as the forced disclosure of the decryption key did not tie the revealer to the data. Also, Fifth Amendment disclosure applies only to persons and not to corporations.

Finally, there is considerable debate as to whether Fifth Amendment protection is enhanced if the decryption password itself is incriminating;

what if a judge grants immunity from prosecution for whatever the pass-word itself reveals (but not from what the decrypted documents reveal) and that password is "I committed the murder and the bloody knife is under the tree" and that is the essence of what the decrypted documents substantiate? Of course, if a password (e.g., "I am a vampire") is clearly irrelevant, then it is neither a statement nor a confession.

In early 2003, the conservative U.S. Supreme Court ruled that the related right of one to remain silent and not incriminate oneself (also known as the Miranda ruling) does not apply when authorities "aggressively" or even coercively interrogate someone who is not being prosecuted. The Bush administration had sided with the police viewpoint. A police-man who questioned a man who had been shot five times in the face, legs, and back, and who, believing he was dying, begged a policemen to stop questioning him as he waited for medical treatment was found by the Supreme Court not to have violated that man's Fifth Amendment rights because that man was not charged with a crime. Mercifully, the Court found that the man's Fourteenth Amendment rights to due process may have been violated as his questioning under such circumstances amounted to torture [8, 9]. (The man, blind and paralyzed, survived and subsequently sued the police.)

As interesting situation exists in the case of public-key encryption (see Section 10.2.3), where keys are notoriously long, are usually created by a machine, and being very random are nearly impossible to remember. In public-key encryption, however, the mere possession (or confiscation) of a decryption key (known as one's private key, versus the public key used to encrypt) is not enough to decrypt a document; one needs to activate the private key with a pass phrase that is supposed to reside solely in one's mind.

It appears, therefore, that one will have to surrender the private key even in the United States, but should be able to invoke one's Fifth Amendment rights to refuse to provide the pass phrase needed to activate that key.

In other countries, laws vary widely. The privilege against self-incrimination is also defined in the International Covenant of Civil and Political Rights (ICCPR) in article 14(3)(g) and applies to criminal prosecution, as distinct from administrative proceedings, although the European court may view certain administrative proceeding as tantamount to criminal ones.

In the Netherlands, the Dutch Code of Criminal Procedure (DCCP) does not mention any privilege against self-incrimination explicitly, but it does contain a number of provisions that amount to the same; for example, article 107 and article 125(m)(1) state that "a command to provide access to a protected computer cannot be given to a suspect"; similarly, the DCCP states that "it would not be in keeping with the spirit of the DCCP if the suspect would be compelled to contribute to his own conviction under threat of punishment."

For a detailed reference on European perspectives on this issue, see http://rechten.kub.nl/koops/casi-faq.htm.

In the worst case, authorities have been known to resort to "rubber hose cryptanalysis" (beating one with a rubber hose until he or she reveals the decryption key). Contrary to popular belief, coerced confessions are not invalid in many countries, including the United States. Misrepresentation of facts or outright lying by the police to a suspect during questioning or interrogation is insufficient to render an otherwise voluntary confession inadmissible in a U.S. court [10].

A detailed country-by-country list of the local laws about encryption can be found at the following Web sites:

- http://www.kub.nl/~frw/people/koops/lawsurvey.html;
- http://www.kub.nl/frw/people/koops/cls2.htm;
- http://strategis.ic.gc.ca/SSG/mi06318e.html.

Lists can be found elsewhere if one searches for the keywords "Crypto Law Survey." See also Chapters 10 through 12 on encryption. Basically, an individual or organization must adopt defensive strategies before becoming embroiled in any investigation or litigation.

16.6 Why is electronic evidence better than paper evidence?

1. It is far easier to search and catalog. For example, one can use software like MIMEsweeeper by Content Technologies (www.mimesweeper.com) to scan all corporate e-mail for evidence. Once the desired data has been collected, it is much less labor intensive to present it in a court than having to do so manually with paper and pencil.

2. Documents are individually stamped with the date and time of creation or last modification. In some cases one can even see the entire sequence of modifications.

3. It may well be that there is no paper evidence. Many documents are only in electronic form these days.

4. E-mail tends to be casual and include gossip, conspiracies, and so forth. It is also permanent.

5. Whereas it is often hard to identify the author of a typed paper document, it is almost always possible to identify the author of a document entered on a computer.

6. Some information that exists in the electronic version of a document does not show up on the printed version. Examples include the author's name, the date it was last updated, the actual formulas used in the computation of entries in a spreadsheet, and sticky note–like comments on the document.

It follows that even a staunch traditionalist lawyer would be well advised to opt for an electronic record rather than a printout of, ostensibly, that same record. At the same time, both prosecutors and defense attorneys and especially judges must realize that electronics records can easily be altered. If the person doing the altering is an expert, such alteration will never be discovered; if it is done by an amateur, it will add to his or her woes.

Electronic evidence does not reside only in personal computers. It also resides in personal electronic organizers such as the increasingly popular Palm line of devices and its imitators, ISPs' records and archives, corporate and other organizational databases, and, in those cases when organizations have elected to outsource their data storage, with third parties.

Additionally, given the increasing popularity of IP telephony (i.e., telephone conversations handled through one's computer), digital telephone answering machines (often implemented as part of one's PC, or more often, as a stand-alone device), and digital fax storage-and-forward machines, the evidence may also include records of telephone conversations and complete faxes as well.

In view of all of the above, let alone of the rest of the material in this book, today's lawyer absolutely has to be (or must become) current in these technologies in depth, or he or she will be doing a disservice to the client. Such reeducation cannot be perfunctory; it has to be in depth precisely because cases are won or lost on technical details, such as whether the electronic date of a document could have been altered, exactly how the chain of custody of a confiscated hard disk was handled, who else might have kept an electronic copy of a document that the opposition claims it is unable to locate, and so on. Without a thorough schooling in such matters, a lawyer will have no idea what to ask for, what is inconsistent, how to make sure that the electronic evidence being sought is not purged (thereby depriving the lawyer's client of possibly the only proof), or what is false and why. A law school that graduates lawyers who are not savvy about such matters is graduating unqualified lawyers for today's reality.

Because practically everything is committed to computer memory nowadays, there is hardly anything that cannot benefit from computer forensic evidence. Classic examples include the following:

1. Product-liability cases. Subpoenaed electronic records can show if the manufacturer was aware of any flaws in the product and failed to correct them, if there was any conspiracy to defraud or to misrepresent, and so forth.

2. Discrimination cases. Internal corporate computer records can show if there was awareness that decisions about an employee were influenced by that employee's religion, race, creed, color, sexual orientation, or ancestry (in the case of the United States) or whatever other criteria exist in other countries.

3. Sexual-harassment cases. Computer forensics can show if an employee sent inappropriate or suggestive e-mails to others, if he or she patronized adult Web sites at work, and so forth.

4. Divorce cases. Although the laws depend highly on where one lives, one recalls the case where allegations of a spouse's infidelity were supported by the subpoenaed records that showed that she was having a "cyberaffair" with someone else.

5. Criminal cases. There have been cases in which an individual's guilt or innocence was proved with the help of detailed forensic examination of computer hard disks (e.g., a claimed suicide note whose electronic date was after the victim died).

But even the most qualified attorney in the world cannot be expected to know the particular setup that the opposition has in terms of procedures, hardware, software, policies, and administration. The first step would be to discover those by taking a deposition from the system administrator ("Sysadmin") or whoever functions in that mode.

Perhaps even more difficult than collecting and presenting the electronic evidence is the task of convincing a nontechnical jury or judge of the validity of the evidence. It is understandable why such juries and judges hate listening to highly technical conflicting testimony about the validity of electronic evidence in a case: They simply cannot form an opinion because they don't have the background to do so. It is the lawyer's job to present such testimony and evidence in plain language that anyone can understand; to do so, requires a thorough understanding of these technologies as anyone who has tried to explain complex scientific or technical concepts to nonspecialist audiences will attest to.

Judges asked to approve subpoenas for producing electronic records have to be convinced themselves that what is sought is truly relevant and needed and not unduly burdensome. The advisory committee note to the amendment to Federal Rule 34 states succinctly that courts should ensure that discoveries are not abusive.

In the United States, the trend for courts has been increasingly in favor of interpreting the term *document* (even *written document*) to include computer files.[4] This is so even though the discovery rules have minimal explicit reference to computer files. The Federal Rules of Civil Procedure and Superior Court Civil Rule 34 merely state that "documents . . . [include] other data compilations from which information can be obtained, translated, if necessary, by the respondent through detection devices into reasonably usable form." In other words, a defendant providing a plaintiff with

---

4. Even as early as 1973, in *Union Electric Company v. Mansion House Center N. Redevelopment Company*, 494 S.W. 2d 309, 315 (MO), the court stated that "computerized record keeping is rapidly becoming a normal procedure in the business world."

Also, in *Crown Life Insurance Company v. Kerry Craig*, U.S. Court of Appeals, 7th Circuit 92-3180, the court rejected the assertion that written documents excluded magnetic media.

undecipherable machine language code in response to a request for production is not in compliance, and courts have so decreed.

In Canada, a recent review by the Canadian Department of Justice found that roughly half of the most relevant 600 federal statutes seemed to apply to paper as the means for exchanging information; proposed legislation is updating those statutes to include electronic means of so doing, as well. Even so, in at least one case [11] in 1988, an Ontario High Court found that a computer disk fell within the definition of a document.

16.7 Civil legal discovery issues

Knowing what to look for and where is not a simple matter with regard to computer evidence. While paper medical documents can reasonably be expected to be in the folder marked "medical" in one's home file cabinet, computer evidence about an alleged crime by an organization can be spread over numerous physical locations, not to mention numerous magnetic storage devices within any one location.

There is an entire professional field within information technology (complete with its own journals, professional societies, and the like) known as knowledge management (KM). It is an acknowledgement of the fact that information about any one issue is spread all over and it takes computer-assisted help to pull it all together from disparate places. Today's standard Web searches by any individual wanting to learn about, say, "Lymphoma" reach across the world; one uses a good search engine (such as http://www.google.com or http://www.metacrawler.com) to do the search and provide the locations for any documents retrieved (which usually number in the thousands or more). Most large organizations have an analogous situation when handling their own records. But these search techniques are not enough for an attorney who during a discovery process needs to find information often stored in unadvertised locations, such as on individual users' hard disks and in intentionally mislabeled electronic folders.

The attorney who is conducting the discovery must know (or learn) the opposition's hardware and software well enough that the correct electronic media can be subpoenaed; hardly any reasonable judge will bless a request to subpoena all of an organization's computer software and hardware in a fishing expedition.[5]

Some software store data in a readily readable form (known as ASCII text); others store it in a form that is not readable by humans, but requires the right software to translate it (the lawyer must know what that software is); still others store it in a password-protected form.

---

5. CIBA-Geigy requested that court restrict the plaintiff's request for electronic documents as it was "overly broad." (Case 94-C-987, M.D.L. 997 (N.D. Ill 1995).

Also, see the appellate court decision in *Strausser v. Yalamachi*, 669 So. 2d 1142, 1144-45 (Florida Appellate Court 1988).

For example, Netscape used to have an electronic forum where Netscape employees used to vent their true feelings, presumably without repercussions. Yet, it was precisely that forum's records that Microsoft subpoenaed to show that many Netscape employees privately felt that Microsoft had a better Web browser. This underscores the importance of a lawyer's knowing what to look for and where.

Subpoenaing electronic documents is an art based on solid science that the lawyer must have a good command of. If one requests subpoenas for entire databases due to a lack of knowledge of which portions to subpoena instead, chances are that the request will be denied or fought as either too onerous and disruptive or as containing mostly material that is irrelevant to the case pending. Conversely, if one's subpoena is too specific, chances are that it will miss a lot of relevant electronic evidence; for example, a request for an electronic document may not result in getting the electronic attachment that was appended to that document or the e-mail that precipitated it.

Electronic discovery of groupware (software that is supposed to help numerous individuals in a group organize and coordinate their activities), such as Meeting Maker and Lotus Notes with about 40 million installations worldwide, pose yet a different problem because the data sought is spread over many sites, databases, and magnetic media; because by its nature it contains information about many individuals' activities, subpoenas can be legitimately objected to on the basis of covering mostly data about matters that have nothing to do with the case in hand.

A gold mine of data usually exists in organizations' backup archives, which all organizations and individuals must keep to protect themselves and be able to recover from a catastrophic crash of the computing system. Most backups do not go back all that far. Individuals typically keep only one or at most two sets of backups. Organizations may keep up to 5 or 10 of them. All recycle them, meaning that the oldest one is used as the new medium for the next backup. Typically, backups go back for about a month. It follows that, from any savvy lawyer's perspective, time is of the essence; at a minimum, a lawyer must take steps to inform the opposition that no record should henceforth be purged until a formal subpoena is issued.

Even in the worst case, however, there may still be hope. As any individual computer user who has to go through the drudgery of backup-making will attest, backups on tape take many hours to complete; because if this, most individuals (and many organizations) back up only the changes since the previous backup. As such, records that are very very old may well still exist for the benefit of forensics evidence. (Hint to the individual or organization that does not want that to be the case: Use full backups every time, preceded by a full wiping of the previous backup.)

The reader is also referred to Chapter 2, which details other places where data is stored in one's computer.

Finally, the so-called anonymous free e-mail offered by assorted commercial organizations is emphatically not anonymous. It is not free either: One pays by providing these companies with a pair of eyeballs that will read assorted advertisements, which will pop-up on the screen every time the site is accessed. Unless a user of such services has taken knowledge-based extensive steps to shield him- or herself from disclosing his or her identity, most of those organizations have a fairly precise idea who the anonymous user is and can disclose his or her identity in response to a subpoena. If they don't know who a given anonymous user is, they can find out in response to a court order using any combination of the following techniques:

1. Retrieving through the user's Web browser the true e-mail address of the user (e.g., in the configuration of the Netscape setup or of the corresponding setup for Microsoft Explorer);

2. Readily observing the user's ISP at each connection and asking that ISP (with the force of a legal subpoena) to show who was accessing the free e-mail server at a particular instant in recent time;

3. Tracking caller ID information, if a direct call is placed.

A savvy attorney can subpoena any such commercial organization's records, and many have been doing so in rapidly increasing numbers. (AOL, even though it is not free, has had its share of individuals logging in with fake or stolen credit cards, and has been served and had to comply with numerous subpoenas. It can safely be assumed that other ISPs are facing subpoenas as well.)

Many individuals often disclose a lot of information about themselves and their personal preferences online, for instance, in chat rooms (digital one-on-one communications through the Internet, which are also archived and monitored),[6] in profiles they complete about themselves, and in Usenet forums. Such information can be of use to the attorney during a discovery phase.

Other sources of digital information in civil discovery are openly available to the well-informed attorney and require no subpoena whatever. There are, for example, some 40,000 or more digital bulletin boards known as Usenet forums on an equal number of different topics, and anyone can post his or her opinion on them. They range from the very useful (e.g., suicide prevention, cancer information) to the absurd.

Many individuals post their opinions under an assumed name (which may or may not be discovered through computer forensics of the individual's hard disk, depending on just exactly how such individuals anonymized their postings).

Luckily for the investigator, numerous organizations store all such postings (a vast amount), and anyone can access such organizations to find, for example, everything posted under a given username (true or assumed) over the years. One such organization is http://www.deja.com (it used to be dejanews.com).

---

6. In *United States v. Charbonneau*, No. CR-2-97-83, 1997 W.L. 627044, S.D. Ohio, September 30, 1997, the Court stated that there is no Fourteenth Amendment protection of privacy in AOL chat rooms.

Most proxy servers (see Section 9.6) are not as tight-lipped about their clientele as their users assume. Unless the client is knowledgeable enough to have taken all the necessary steps to launder his or her identity before it reaches the proxy server and to prevent the proxy server from finding it while that user is connected, proxy servers collect and store the information of who connected through them and to what eventual Web site. Subpoenas served upon them can produce these records, but only if the attorney involved moves fast enough.

At a minimum, a savvy plaintiff's attorney should send the opposition a written demand not to delete or otherwise tamper with evidence that is likely to be subpoenaed shortly thereafter. Better yet (in the United States), he or she could serve a detailed and specific request for production of documents and things (which must spell out what information is to be found where, including archiving media, backups, etc.); this should be augmented with a formal request to abstain from any routine procedures (such as routine deletions, defragmenting of hard disks) that could affect the data sought, followed by a Rule 30(b)(6) deposition of whoever knows most about the computers of the party being sued.

In the extreme, a plaintiff's lawyer can go as far as obtaining and serving upon the defendant a restraining order to prevent the destruction of any data of interest as well as calling a hearing to get an even more formal injunction by the court.

16.8   International policy on computer-related crime

The fact is that the Internet is an inherently transnational communications network. One can cause a denial-of-service attack on an Internet host from across the street just as well as from across the world.

Laws about computer evidence, computer crime, degree of legality of encryption, and so forth vary widely from country to country and change very rapidly. Because of the transnational nature of the Internet and of computer crime involving the Internet, there is a strong push lead by the United States to make uniform most countries' laws that pertain to computer crime. One may recall the spectacle of the individual who was arrested in the Philippines in mid-1999 for having allegedly been responsible for the infamous I Love You virus, only to be released shortly thereafter because he had broken no law in the Philippines at the time much to the annoyance of the FBI, which helped track and identify him.

The Organization for Economic Cooperation and Development (OECD) and the Council of Europe, as well as numerous other organizations around the world, have created a plethora of guidelines intended to harmonize criminal laws on computer crime around the world. Typically the United Nations also got involved with "Proposals for Concerted International Action Against Forms of Crime Identified in the Milar Plan of Action" (E/AC.57/1988/16), of which paragraphs 42 to 44 deal with computer crime.

Not surprisingly, the problems associated with making these laws uniform have been formidable because different societies have different laws and different perception of what crime is, let alone different procedures for such related issues as appeals. For example, some countries value privacy more than others and criminalize compromises of privacy whereas others don't. The ongoing dispute between the United States and Europe on this issue is a case in point (see Section 16.14). Then there is the jurisdiction issue, and each nation jealously guards its prerogatives.

Numerous excellent references on these issues, such as the "International Review of Criminal Policy. United Nations Manual in the Prevention and Control of Computer-Related Crime," are available online at www.ifs.univie.ac.at.

16.9 What is computer crime?

Computer crime, like any crime, is time and location dependent. A crime in one location is not a crime in another; a crime in one location may not have been a crime in that same location in the past and may not be a crime in the future. Computer crime is basically any act that is illegal in some location at a particular time that involves a computer in some manner.

The term *computer crime* can be subdivided into two broad categories:

1. Crime that only involves a computer in a tangential or peripheral manner, such as composing a libelous message.

2. Crime whose commission requires the use of a computer. Examples of this class of crimes include but are not limited to:

    a. Stock market manipulation by posting knowingly false messages on Usenet, with the intent of driving the price of a stock up or down for personal gain or revenge.

    b. Wholesale theft of credit card numbers stored with the Web host of an online retailer and fraudulent use of these stolen numbers for personal gain.

    c. Attacks on a targeted computer through such means as remote hacks, denial of service, and so forth.

    d. Identity theft made possible by the ease with which one can use the Internet to obtain vast amounts of ostensibly confidential information about anyone, especially in the United States.

    e. Use of computers to negate means for protecting copyrighted work and distributing it on a large scale for personal profit or simply as a sociopolitical statement.

Contrary to popular belief, computer crime is not hard to catch as long as law enforcement has the tools, budget, and equipment to pursue computer forensics. The ancillary societal problem associated with giving law enforcement a carte blanche to monitor computers and networks is that it would give law enforcement unprecedented powers to access individual data that in most cases has nothing to do with any suspected crime; this is so because it is the nature of computers and networks to store and relay massive amounts of data, only an infinitesimally small percentage of which has any relevance to crime.

16.10   What can a business do to protect itself?

A very good reference publication for providing guidance to businesses to minimize their legal exposure to liability is "E-Policy—How to Develop Computer, E-Mail, and Internet Guidance to Protect Your Company and its Assets," by M. R. Overly, American Management Association, at http://www.amanet.org.

If served with any variant of a legal demand that a company produce documents for the opposition's discovery, a defense attorney may consider the following options (if applicable):

1.   The qualifications and precise methods to be used by the plaintiff in handling the defendant's data;

2.   Identifying data residing on the hard disks identified by the plaintiff that are confidential, proprietary, or otherwise privileged or protected from the plaintiff's viewing;

3.   Obtaining comparable access for discovery of data in the plaintiff's possession.

16.11   Criminal evidence collection issues

16.11.1   Collection

The investigator meeting a suspect for the first time establishes upfront in a nonthreatening manner and before a suspect becomes defensive that the suspect is the sole user of the computer in question. This is to eliminate any subsequent claim to the contrary as the suspect's defense.

Even so, a savvy defense attorney can legitimately point out that it is eminently possible for files in one's computer to have been placed there without the defendant's knowledge in the following ways:

1.   In the case of a computer connected to the Internet or any other network, by a remote hacker or hostile Web site. There is ample factual evidence of software and malicious mobile code (meaning, in this case, software sent by a remote Web site to a user's computer) doing exactly that.

2.   In the case of a computer that is never connected to either the Internet or any other network (and this is becoming a smaller and smaller

percentage of computers), by software of suspicious origin (such as assorted shareware and freeware files). There is ample evidence of cases in which such software modified a computer without the computer owner's knowledge or permission.

Additionally, the collection of the computer evidence should be done in a manner that can be shown to have precluded the possibility that the collection process itself may have contaminated what was being collected. For example, there may be software that can do just about anything a user wants it to if the computer is turned on by an unauthorized user. Also, every time Windows is turned on, it actually writes new information on a disk and overwrites some older information.

About the only way to achieve this requirement of noncontamination is for the targeted magnetic media to be electrically disconnected from the computer and connected to another computer that will not boot that disk or run any software in it, but will merely make a magnetic duplicate of the targeted disk.

That magnetic duplicate should then be retained as the new uncontaminated master copy and should not be analyzed as such analysis may contaminate it. Instead, additional copies must be made from that uncontaminated master copy, and those additional copies can be analyzed forensically.

16.11.2 Handling

The key issues associated with the handling of any forensic evidence, including computer forensic evidence, are that the procedures used be able to withstand any challenge by the defense as to their legitimacy and admissibility as evidence.

This means that the handling of the evidence should adhere to the following criteria:

1. There is a clear and fully documented chain of custody of the evidence with no gaps whatever.

2. Each custodian of the evidence is in a position to preclude any possibility that the evidence could have been modified in any way, either intentionally or unintentionally.

3. That which is presented in court can only be that which was collected.

16.12 Federal guidelines for searching and seizing computers

As any new technology becomes popular enough to be adopted by a significant percentage of the population, it is inevitable that it will also be used in ways that violate some existing laws in any locality.

Automobiles, normally intended to take one to work or to a vacation spot, can also be used for illegal purposes (to escape from the scene of a crime, in the furtherance of kidnapping, to store contraband, to run someone over), and they have been.

Kitchen knives, normally intended to carve turkey and peel oranges, can also be used to maim and to kill, and they have been.

Electricity, normally intended to convey energy, can also be used to kill or to torture, and it has been.

Potassium tablets, normally intended to sustain life by replacing potassium lost as a result of severe dehydration, can also be lethal if administered in high doses, and they have been.

Telephones, normally intended to exchange social and personal pleasantries and to conduct legitimate business, can also be used for every conceivable nefarious purpose, and they have been.

Computers, normally intended to increase the efficiency of a variety of human tasks, can also be used to store evidence of a crime or as instruments of a crime (e.g., stealing others' credit card numbers or identity), and they have been.

All rational societies in the world have decided that, on balance, the beneficial uses of practically all technological and other advances of mankind outweigh the disadvantages of their occasional abuse. As a result, automobiles are legal everywhere, and so are kitchen knives and electricity and medicines and telephones.

Computers, however, seem to rub governments the wrong way by virtue of the fact that, in conjunction with the Internet and encryption, they allow individuals to create, store, and communicate ideas that individual governments find threatening. This is hardly surprising from a historical perspective. The totalitarian regimes of yesteryear also required the individual licensing of typewriters and of photocopying machines. Some regimes (e.g., Pol Pot's Communist regime in Cambodia) even banned doors, of all things, so that the regime could look into each house at any time it pleased. Today, even in the country most protective of individual rights, the United States, applicable laws allow federal agents to break the door down in a house—even when a judge has refused to give a warrant for a no-knock entry—and burst in; they only need to be of the opinion that breaking the door down is essential to preventing the destruction of evidence [12].

As with any technology, computers can be used to store evidence of what a regime may consider to violate existing laws or preferences, or as an "instrumentality" of a violation of such laws or preferences. Given that computers, small and big, are now used by nearly every organization and individual, it is hardly surprising that the absolute number of ways in which they have also been used for something a regime does not like is correspondingly higher than when there were fewer computers around.

The ways that a computer (or an automobile or a kitchen knife) can be used either to violate existing laws or simply to go contrary to the parochial preferences[7] of groups with financial and political clout are limited only by one's imagination. It would be pointless to list such obvious analogs to conventional crime as keeping double books (for tax evasion), or creating and sending ransom notes, writing or sending prose or imagery that is libelous or politically or otherwise offensive to some subculture(s) or to the regime itself.

Then there is the related capability of most modern computers to allow communications between individuals and groups that many governments take justifiable offense to, such as terrorists,[8] drug dealers, and spies.[9] Amusingly, the very same Internet and computer use that law enforcers vilify is in fact a gift from the gods to law enforcers anywhere in the world; computers and the Internet are the most effective media for wholesale surveillance ever popularized. Whereas in the past, security services had to think creatively, use physical surveillance, and engage in many of the tricks we have all enjoyed watching in the movies, today they only have to monitor—and they do—as much of the worldwide Internet traffic as possible and do computer forensics on all computers suspected of involvement in what a state may not like. Given that most terrorists, spies, drug dealers, and other criminals are not technologically savvy and will eventually and inevitably slip, law enforcers should actually be the most vocal supporters of everyone using computers and the Internet for everything.

Just as there are countless colorful stories of how a particular suspect was apprehended and convicted in the precomputer days—J. Arthur Conan Doyle's Sherlock Holmes and Agatha Christie's Hercule Poirot detail some particularly challenging fictitious ones—a plethora of stories involve computer-related crime as well. For what it is worth, here is a sampling of some, taken from authoritative sources; the reader has to filter out some of the understandable self-congratulatory air that permeates them:

7. Is the thorough assessment of a purchased piece of security-related software for the purpose of identifying its security weaknesses so that the buyer will know whether to depend on it or not illegal?

   Amazingly, in the United States it is illegal if it includes the—essential—step of defeating means inserted by that software maker to prevent such assessment, according to the DMCA, which was railroaded through Congress and signed into law just a few years ago. It is a sad commentary on today's reality that copyright laws are least based on the legitimate needs of authors, academicians, and scientists who have always been the prime creators of new concepts and ideas; instead, copyright laws today are controlled by the proverbial "800 pound gorilla," namely, the Hollywood studios and their desire to maximize their profits. Amusingly, a recent article in *Wired* magazine showed Hollywood's duplicity: Hollywood owes its existence to the fact that it knowingly stepped all over Thomas Edison's patents and moved to California to be far away from the reach of federal marshals.

8. This can be a big intellectual discussion in itself. Certainly the maiming or killing of innocent civilians is a reprehensible and cowardly act that nobody should condone. But the term *terrorism* is also used by repressive totalitarian regimes to apply to what most of us would consider freedom fighters.

9. Spying, the world's second oldest profession, has existed since the dawn of recorded history. Spies were able to communicate long before the advent of computers or before electricity was ever discovered. As such, the often-heard assertion by law enforcement groups that the control or elimination of the Internet will prevent spies' communications is laughable and is intended for consumption by the gullible in order to pressure legislative bodies to inch (or gallop) closer to an Orwellian society.

According to the U.S. Department of Justice's "Computer Crime and Intellectual Property Section" document, which has been made publicly available by that government organization at http://www.cybercrime.gov/searchmanual.htm#lc,

> In *United States v. Roberts*, 86 F. Supp.2d 678 (S.D. Tex. 2000), United States Customs Agents learned that William Roberts, a suspect believed to be carrying computerized images of child pornography, was scheduled to fly from Houston, Texas to Paris, France on a particular day. On the day of the flight, the agents set up an inspection area in the jetway at the Houston airport with the sole purpose of searching Roberts. Roberts arrived at the inspection area and was told by the agents that they were searching for "currency" and "high technology or other data" that could not be exported legally. After the agents searched Roberts's property and found a laptop computer and six Zip diskettes, Roberts agreed to sign a consent form permitting the agents to search his property. A subsequent search revealed several thousand images of child pornography. When charges were brought, Roberts moved for suppression of the computer files, but the district court ruled that the search had not violated the Fourth Amendment. According to the court, the search of Roberts's luggage had been a "routine search" for which no suspicion was required, even though the justification for the search offered by the agents merely had been a pretext. See *Whren v. United States*, 517 U.S. 806 (1996). The court also concluded that Roberts's consent justified the search of the laptop and diskettes, and indicated that even if Roberts had not consented to the search, [the] search of the defendant's computer and diskettes would have been a routine export search, valid under the Fourth Amendment.

According to the same official document identified above, despite the Fourth Amendment's protection against unreasonable search, agents may search a place or object without a warrant or even probable cause in a number of cases:

1. "If a person with authority has voluntarily consented to the search."

2. "It is common for several people to use or own the same computer equipment. If any one of those people gives permission to search for data, agents may generally rely on that consent, so long as the person has authority over the computer. In such cases, all users have assumed the risk that a co-user might discover everything in the computer, and might also permit law enforcement to search this 'common area" as well'." As such "Most spousal consent searches are valid."

3. "Parents can consent to searches of their children's rooms when the children are under 18 years old. If the children are 18 or older, the parents may or may not be able to consent, depending on the facts."

4. If a person has given implied consent.

For example, in *United States v. Ellis*, 547 F.2d 863 (5th Cir. 1977), a civilian visiting a naval air station agreed to post a visitor's pass on the windshield of his car as a condition of bringing the car on the base. The pass stated that 'acceptance of this pass gives your consent to search this vehicle while entering, aboard, or leaving this station.' During the visitor's stay on the base, a station investigator who suspected that the visitor had stored marijuana in the car approached the visitor and asked him if he had read the pass. After the visitor admitted that he had, the investigator searched the car and found 20 plastic bags containing marijuana. The Fifth Circuit ruled that the warrantless search of the car was permissible, because the visitor had impliedly consented to the search when he knowingly and voluntarily entered the base with full knowledge of the terms of the visitor's pass.

5.   If evidence is in plain view. "Evidence of a crime may be seized without a warrant under the plain view exception to the warrant requirement."

6.   If evidence is discovered during a search incident to a lawful arrest.

Pursuant to a lawful arrest, agents may conduct a 'full search' of the arrested person, and a more limited search of his surrounding area, without a warrant. See *United States v. Robinson*, 414 U.S. 218, 235 (1973); *Chimel v. California*, 395 U.S. 752, 762–63 (1969). For example, in *Robinson*, a police officer conducting a pat down search incident to an arrest for a traffic offense discovered a crumpled cigarette package in the suspect's left breast pocket. Not knowing what the package contained, the officer opened the package and discovered fourteen capsules of heroin. The Supreme Court held that the search of the package was permissible, even though the officer had no articulatable reason to open the package. See id. at 234–35. In light of the general need to preserve evidence and prevent harm to the arresting officer, the Court reasoned, it was per se reasonable for an officer to conduct a 'full search of the person pursuant to a lawful arrest'. If agents can examine the contents of wallets, address books, and briefcases without a warrant, it could be argued that they should be able to search their electronic counterparts (such as electronic organizers, floppy disks, and Palm Pilots) as well. Cf. *United v. Tank*, 200 F.3d 627, 632 (9th Cir. 2000) (holding that agents searching a car incident to a valid arrest properly seized a Zip disk found in the car, but failing to discuss whether the agents obtained a warrant before searching the disk for images of child pornography).

7.   If evidence is discovered after law enforcement enters by breaking down the door (when executing no-knock warrants).

As a general matter, agents must announce their presence and authority prior to executing a search warrant. See *Wilson v. Arkansas*, 514 U.S. 927, 934 (1995); 18 U.S.C. § 3109. This so-called "knock and announce" rule reduces the risk of violence and destruction of property when agents execute a search. The rule is not absolute, however. In *Richards v. Wisconsin,* 520 U.S. 385 (1997), the Supreme Court held that agents can dispense with the knock-and-announce requirement if they have a reasonable suspicion that knocking and announcing their presence, under the particular circumstances, would be dangerous or futile, or that it would inhibit the effective investigation of the crime by, for example, allowing the destruction of evidence.

When agents have reason to believe that knocking and announcing their presence would allow the destruction of evidence, would be dangerous, or would be futile, agents should request that the magistrate judge issue a no-knock warrant. The failure to obtain judicial authorization to dispense with the knock-and-announce rule does not preclude the agents from conducting a no-knock search, however.

In some cases, agents may neglect to request a no-knock warrant, or may not have reasonable suspicion that evidence will be destroyed until they execute the search. In *Richards,* the Supreme Court made clear that "the reasonableness of the officers' decision [to dispense with the knock-and-announce rule] . . . must be evaluated as of the time they entered" the area to be searched. *Richards,* 510 U.S. at 395. Accordingly, agents may "exercise independent judgment" and decide to conduct a no-knock search when they execute the search, even if they did not request such authority or the magistrate judge specifically refused to authorize a no-knock search. The question in all such cases is whether the agents had "a reasonable suspicion that knocking and announcing their presence, under the particular circumstances, would be dangerous or futile, or that it would inhibit the effective investigation of the crime by, for example, allowing the destruction of evidence."

Things must be appreciated in context. The point of the foregoing is that, even in a country known for its respect for individual rights and with a constitution that protects those individual rights, courts and law enforcement have carved elaborate paths whereby they can essentially get around what average citizens may consider to be their constitutional rights from governmental intrusion. In countries where there are no written constitutions or where the legal protection for individual rights is minimal or nonexistent, the individual can only depend on his or her own resources for protection from unwelcome intrusion by an oppressive regime.

16.13 Destruction of electronic evidence

Clearly, if a defendant can be shown to have destroyed data that has been subpoenaed or even after having been informed not to destroy any data in anticipation of a forthcoming subpoena, then such a defendant is likely to face additional penalties for having destroyed the data.

Even if a defendant can be shown to have known or reasonably expected that some data would be sought by a litigant or a prosecutor in connection with an ongoing civil or criminal case, and to have destroyed it, then it is also possible that such a defendant will face additional penalties [13–15].[11]

16.14 U.S.–European data-privacy disputes

European privacy regulations (the European Union's Omnibus Data Protection Directive, which has been in effect since October 1998) are far more stringent than U.S. ones (see Sections 1.4.1, 5.1, and 15.4). This has become a major point of contention between commercial entities on both sides of the Atlantic trying to access each other's databases through the Internet.

As of July 6, 2000, the European Parliament, representing the European Union's 15 member nations, had rejected a data-privacy deal made between the European Commission and the United States that would shield U.S. companies from European regulations on privacy. In particular, the European Parliament wanted new provisions that would allow Europeans to appeal any perceived violations of their privacy to some independent body and that would allow Europeans the right to sue U.S. companies for damages resulting from privacy violations.

Even so, it appears that this rejection by the European Parliament will have no impact because the Parliament's role was only to determine if the European Commission had acted within the scope of its authority in coming up with the above deal with the United States. The Parliament did not state that this authority had been exceeded, and the Parliament has no statutory authority to veto this deal.

16.15 New international computer crime treaty

In its zeal to attack computer crime, known as the "Draft Convention on Cybercrime," which is transnational in nature, a new international computer crime treaty goes beyond attacking computer crime and gives law enforcement unprecedented powers to attack privacy and possibly violate the Fifth Amendment to the U.S. Constitution.

It is a treaty involving the 41 Nation Council of Europe and the United States. It went through 19 drafts before its existence was revealed to the public.

This treaty is viewed by some (e.g., Libertarian Party U.S. presidential candidate Harry Brown for the November 2000 elections) as an end-run attempt by U.S. law enforcement to pressure the U.S. Senate into approving measures that it was unlikely to have approved otherwise by asserting that

10. Also in [3], when a defendant destroyed some evidence, the court stated, "Destroying the best evidence related to core issue in the case inflicts the ultimate prejudice upon the opposing party."

the United States would need to conform to international standards (on cybersnooping). Typically:

1. The treaty would enable U.S. law enforcement to order U.S. persons to reveal passwords and decryption keys, something which appears to be in violation of the U.S. Fifth Amendment against self-incrimination.

2. The treaty would do away with anonymous remailers (something already treated as illegal in some countries, such as France) and would require ISPs to surveil customers' Internet usage and store at least 40 days' worth of customer data.

3. The treaty would also make illegal some common and legitimate software, such as software used by practically every large commercial organization to test its own systems for security; the rationale given is that such software, which it calls "hacker tools," can also be used by criminals. As a result, corporate and commercial cybersecurity will suffer a serious and lasting blow (see November 1, 2000, editorial by Weld Pond in www.zdnet.com/zdnn/stories/news/0,4586,2647940,00.html).

16.16   The post–September 11 reality

"Good intentions will always be pleaded for every assumption of authority. It is hardly too strong to say that the Constitution was made to guard the people against the dangers of good intentions."

—Daniel Webster

The legal landscape changed precipitously after the tragedy of September 11, 2001, not only in the United States but around most of the world as governments scrambled to implement means for hopefully preventing major terrorist attacks in the future.

Constitutions, where they existed, were reinterpreted, and legal niceties were placed on the back burner[11] with regard to technical means for detecting early warnings of future terrorist attacks.

In the United States, the National Strategy to Secure Cyberspace included a proposed provision requiring ISPs to construct a centralized system for Internet monitoring [16]; this strategy became part of the new

---

11. Even before September 11, 2001, U.S. Courts repeatedly ignored the commonsense dictum that the punishment should fit the crime and went overboard with grotesque sentences: An Oklahoma man got a life sentence in 2003 for spitting on an arresting policeman's face (http://www.cnn.com/2003/US/Southwest/07/02/crime.spit.reut/ index/html); in 2002, the House of Representatives overwhelmingly approved a bill that would allow life sentences for malicious computer hackers (http://news.com.com/2100-1001-944057.html); even a 13-year-old boy was sentenced to several years in jail for changing his grade on the teacher's computer, just as Mathew Broderick's character did in the popular movie *War Games* to the amusement of movie goers for decades.

Department of Homeland Security's marching orders. This proposal, well intentioned as it may have been, was naïve for the following reasons:

1. U.S. ISPs number in the thousands. Many are unwilling or unable to assume the cost of implementing such a scheme.

2. It is unclear what should be logged and what not. If the criterion is to log traffic on ports 80 and 25 (used for Web browsing and e-mailing, respectively), savvy users could use thousands of other ports to do their Web browsing and e-mail.

3. The proposal [17] was very thin in specifying how this could be implemented.

4. The thin line between monitoring for counterterrorism purposes and broad-scale wiretapping for domestic police state control could easily be crossed.

5. Easily implemented anonymizing of Internet traffic (e.g., by posting an anonymous message in one of some 100,000 Usenet newsgroup forums from a wireless Wi-Fi hot spot that is open to everyone) fully defeat all Internet monitoring.

6. From a legal perspective, it is uncertain if such wholesale monitoring would survive a constitutional challenge for the following reasons:

    a. It makes an end run around constitutional directives that prohibit the government from wholesale storing of citizens' information by forcing commercial surrogates do that for the government.

    b. ISPs have "common carrier" status of which one of the central legal tenets is that it has to be "traffic blind"; this applies not only to the common carrier, but also to the organization forcing the common carrier to become "traffic aware."

As of March 2004, the U.S. Department of Justice, along with the FBI and Drug Enforcement Administration (DEA), had filed an urgent request with the U.S. Federal Communications Commission to expand the interpretation of CALEA to include monitoring the Internet as if it were the national telephone network, to have ISPs provide the technical means for making this easy, and to pass the costs of so doing to the Internet users.

While one can see the logic behind this as being to allow law enforcement the same access to packet network communications channels as it managed to get to wireline and wireless channels, it is as likely to succeed in catching terrorists, narcotraffickers, and spies as a voodoo doctor is in curing pimples. Such undesirables as terrorists, narcotraffickers, and spies have been served enough notice of the risks of using the Internet in an open manner that they are highly unlikely to do so. Furthermore, they can easily avail themselves of numerous means for securing anonymity and undetectability to defeat any such simple-minded interception.

In the meantime, the number of subpoenas served on ISPs for customer records has roughly doubled every month [18]. ISPs have been caught in the middle between their customers' expectations of privacy and governmental demands for information, especially when law enforcement officials have moved quickly and short-circuited legal reviews of such demands for information.[12]

Even though, according to the Administrative Office of the U.S. Courts, no federal wiretaps were constrained by the use of encryption in 2001, draconian laws have also been proposed to criminalize encryption by extending prison sentences for encryption used in the commission of a crime. This has been severely criticized: "Why should the fact that you use encryption have anything to do with how guilty you are and what the punishment should be? Should we have enhanced penalties if someone wore an overcoat?" asked Stanton McCandish of the CryptoRights Foundation [19].

In Europe, the European Union enacted a Directive on Privacy and Electronic Communications (Directive 20002/58/EC), which left the 15 EU member states free to adopt laws authorizing data retention for an unspecified length of time, but no less than one year. Critics from the legal profession have argued that the directive does not make a distinction between a terrorist, a hacker, and an online protester.

In Canada, the government has been debating the creation of a database of every Canadian with an Internet account. This would be of questionable use because any one can access the Internet without any account whatever by merely availing oneself of multiple means of anonymous access, such as open Wi-Fi wireless hot spots, long-distance phone calls to foreign ISPs, and so forth. Indeed, Gus Hosein, a visiting fellow at the London School of Economics, called this database "a dumb idea."

Even before September 11, the following was happening:

1. Japan was developing a "Temporary Mail Box" device for intercepting and storing e-mail traffic, with a budget of 140 million yen (US$1.4 million) for fiscal year 2001 [20].

2. Poland's Ministry for Internal Affairs and Administration (MSWiA) was drafting a new wiretapping law [27] similar to the British RIP Act and to the Russian SORM-2 (Russian for "System Operational Research Actions on the Documentary Telecommunications Networks").

3. In the United Kingdom, the RIP Act became law.

Concerns that laws such as the above conflict with Article 8 of the EU Human Rights Act, which asserts that "everyone has the right to his private

---

12. Whereas in the past a judge's order could be dispensed with to get the records of a suspected terrorist, the post–September 11 rules allow government agents to obtain the anyone's records if they claim it is "in connection with" a terrorism investigation.

and family life, his home and his correspondence," have been soft-pedaled since September 11.

16.17   The sky is the limit—or is it the courts?

The laws are not clear in most countries as to whether or not "passive interception" requires a warrant by law enforcement or is even legally performed by any citizen.

Along those lines, a U.S. Supreme Court decision at the turn of the twenty-first century stated that wiretapping is legal without a warrant because it does not involve physical trespass onto anyone's property; this has subsequently been reversed. Until very recently, however, this thinking seems to have persisted because it had been ruled that interception of the radio signals of cordless phones did not require a warrant in the United States.

The laws as to exactly which forms of surveillance require a warrant become very nebulous at this stage everywhere in the world.

› Can law enforcement (without a warrant) or even a regular citizen set up shop across the street and use a voyeur's telescope (a.k.a. stargazer's telescope) to watch a targeted room that happens not to have curtains? Can commercially available light-amplification night-imaging devices be used? Can these images be videotaped? Can they be used as legally obtained evidence in a court of law?

› Can law enforcement (without a warrant) or even a regular citizen go through someone else's trash placed by the curbside for collection by the trash collector? U.S. laws seem to make the subtle distinction that this is okay if the trash is at the curbside, but not if the trash is right next to one's house (on one's property).

› Can law enforcement (without a warrant) or even a regular citizen monitor someone else's electricity or water meter and make inferences about the usage patterns of the targeted premises?

› Can law enforcement (without a warrant) or even a regular citizen use commercially available thermal-imaging devices to make educated inferences about the activities going on inside a targeted house? Recently law enforcement in the United States did exactly that and detected an unusually high amount of heat inside the house. A subsequent raid showed that the owners were cultivating plants for illegal drugs.

› Can law enforcement (without a warrant) or even a regular citizen use commercially available laboratory equipment (e.g., gas chromatography) to make chemical analyses of what comes out of a neighbor's chimney or vents to detect, for example, chemicals used in the production of illegal materials?

The laws are constantly evolving as they try to catch up with rapidly evolving commercialized technologies. Some have argued that the framers of the U.S. Constitution never dreamed that one's house could be monitored without physical trespass, or they would have prohibited all such non-physical trespasses in the U.S. Constitution. We will never know.

References

[1] http://www.cotse.com/helpdesk/documents/editorialsinvasion.html.

[2] http://www.theregister.co.uk/content/archive/12741.html and www.counterpane.com/crypto-gram-0010.html.

[3] David Gillespie, "E-Mail—The Clayton Deletion," at www.lawnet.com.au.

[4] http://news.com.com/2100-1028-994667.html.

[5] http://www.theregister.co.uk/content/6/30003.html.

[6] http://.www.computerworld.com/storyba/0,4125,NAV47_STO68009,00.htm.

[7] Sergeinko, G. S., "Self Incrimination and Cryptographic Keys," http://www.rubberhose.org/current/doc/ sergienko.html.

[8] http://www.realcities.com/mid/mld/krwashington/5954763.htm.

[9] http://fresnobee.com/local/story/6862175 p-7799407c.html.

[10] *Frazier v. Cupp*, 394 U.S. 731, 739, 89, S.Ct. 1420, 1424-25, 22 L/Ed.2d 684 (1969).

[11] *Reichmann v. Toronto Life Publications Company*, 66 O.R. 2d 65, 1988 O.J. No. 1727, 30 C.P.C. ed 280.

[12] "Computer Crime and Intellectual Property Section (CCIPS), Searching and Seizing Computers and Obtaining Electronic Evidence in Criminal Investigations," http://www.cybercrime.gov/searchmanual.htm#lc.

[13] *Carlucci v. Piper Aircraft Corporation*, 102 F.R.D. 472 (S.D. Florida 1984).

[14] *ABC Home Health Services Inc. v. IBM Corporation*, 185 F.R.D. 180 (S.D. Georgia, 1994).

[15] *Computer Associates International v. American Fundware* (133 F.R.D. 166 D. Cob. 1990).

[16] http://www.nytimes.com/2002/12/20/technology/20MONI.html.

[17] http://news.com.com/2100-1023-955595.html.

[18] http://www.newhouse.com/archive/story1a041002.htm.

[19] http://www.usatoday.com/tech/news/techpolicy/2003-03-31-crypto-rights_x.htm.

[20] http://www.cryptome.org/carnivore-jp.html.

[21] http://www.cryptome.org/pl-sorm-rip.htm.

About the Author

Michael A. Caloyannides earned his Ph.D. at Caltech in electrical engineering, applied mathematics, and philosophy. He worked for 13 years in the aerospace industry as a senior technical staff member in a broad spectrum of technologies, including missile guidance, automated fingerprint recognition, design of a complete SIGINT system, covert communications over various radiofrequency channels, satellite communications, and digital modem design, for which he was awarded a U.S. patent.

He then worked in a comparably broad spectrum of areas for 14 years for the U.S. federal government, where he was awarded the prestigious Scientist of the Year award and the Meritorious Officer award, as well as five separate Certificates of Exceptional Accomplishment.

He is now a senior fellow for information technologies at Mitretek Systems, a Washington area think tank where he works on information security issues. In his spare time he consults for NASA on deep space exploration.

He has published numerous technical documents, as well as a book, *Desktop Witness* (John Wiley & Sons, 2002). He has given numerous invited seminars and technical presentations worldwide. He is an associate editor and regular columnist for the IEEE's magazine *Security and Privacy*.

He is married with two young children and was recently diagnosed with cancer from which he is in remission. For diversion, he flies airplanes as a commercial-licensed multiengine pilot and scuba dives with his wife. Dr. Caloyannides can be reached at micky@IEEE.org.

Index

For further information on these and other Artech House titles,
including previously considered out-of-print books now available through our
In-Print-Forever® (IPF®) program, contact:

Artech House
685 Canton Street
Norwood, MA 02062
Phone: 781-769-9750
Fax: 781-769-6334
e-mail: artech@artechhouse.com

Artech House
46 Gillingham Street
London SW1V 1AH UK
Phone: +44 (0)20 7596-8750
Fax: +44 (0)20 7630-0166
e-mail: artech-uk@artechhouse.com

Find us on the World Wide Web at:
www.artechhouse.com